A DoD CCRP/NDU Collaboration

This collaborative effort is a continuation of the series of publications produced by the Center for Advanced Concepts and Technology (ACT), which was created as a "skunk works" with funding provided by the Assistant Secretary of Defense (C3I). The early success of ACT led to the creation of ACTIS when the president of the National Defense University (NDU) merged the experimental School of Information Warfare and Strategy with ACT and ASD (C3I) made the Director of ACTIS the executive agent for the DoD Command and Control Research Program (CCRP). ACTIS has demonstrated the importance of having a research program focused on the national security implications of the Information Age and in providing the theoretical foundations for providing DoD with information superiority, as well as the importance of an educational program designed to acquaint senior military personnel and civilians with these emerging issues. As a result, ACTIS's educational programs are being merged with the Colleges of NDU and ACTIS's research programs are being transitioned to OSD under the direction of ASD (C3I).

DoD Command and Control Research Program

Assistant Secretary of Defense (C3I)
  Mr. Anthony Valletta (Acting)
Deputy Assistant Secretary of Defense (C3I) Acquisition
  Dr. Margaret Myers (Acting)
Executive Agent for CCRP
  Dr. David S. Alberts
  Mr. Larry Wentz* (Acting)

Opinions, conclusions, and recommendations expressed or implied within are solely those of the authors. They do not necessarily represent the views of the National Defense University, the Department of Defense, or any other U.S. Government agency. Cleared for public release; distribution unlimited.

Portions of this publication may be quoted or reprinted without further permission, with credit to the Institute for National Strategic Studies, Washington, D.C. Courtesy copies of reviews would be appreciated.

Library of Congress Cataloging in Publication Data

Lessons from Bosnia / edited by Larry K. Wentz.
    p. cm.
Includes bibliographical references.
ISBN 1-57906-004-8
  1. Yugoslav War, 1991- --Participation, American. 2. Yugoslav War, 1991- --Bosnia and Hercegovina. 3. IFOR (Organization)--History. 4. National security--Bosnia and Hercegovina. 5. United States--History, Military. 6. Bosnia and Hercegovina--History, Military. I. Wentz, Larry K.
DR1313.7.F672U656 1997
949.703--dc21   97-38128
                                                                                    CIP

*as of January 1998

The National Defense University

The Institute for National Strategic Studies (INSS) is a major component of the National Defense University (NDU) that operates under the supervision of the President of NDU. It conducts strategic studies for the Secretary of Defense, Chairman of the Joint Chiefs of Staff, and unified commanders in chief; supports national strategic components of NDU academic programs; and provides outreach to other governmental agencies and the broader national security community.

The Publication Directorate of INSS publishes books, monographs, reports, and occasional papers on national security strategy, defense policy, and national military strategy through NDU Press that reflect the output of NDU research and academic programs. In addition, it produces the INSS Strategic Assessment and other work approved by the President of NDU as well as *Joint Force Quarterly*, a professional military journal published for the Chairman, Joint Chiefs of Staff.

 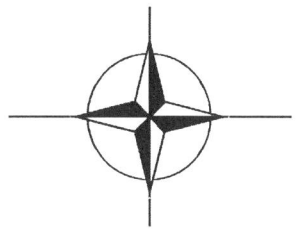

Lessons From Bosnia:
The IFOR Experience

Contributing Editor
Larry Wentz

Contents

Foreword xi

Acknowledgments xv

Preface xix

I. Introduction 1

II. Bosnia—Setting the Stage 9

III. Command and Control Structure 35

IV. Intelligence Operations 53

V. Civil-Military Cooperation 119

VI. The International Police Task Force 139

VII. Information Activities 167

VIII. Tactical PSYOP Support to Task Force Eagle 189

IX. Counterintelligence and HUMINT 225

X. Information Operations in Bosnia: A Soldier's Perspective 255

XI. C4ISR Systems and Services 273

XII. NDU/CCRP Bosnia Study 379

XIII. Lessons Learned About Lessons Learned 397

XIV. Summary 409

End Notes 445

Appendix A: The Dayton Peace Agreement Summary 467

Appendix B: Chronology of IFOR Events 475

Appendix C: References 481

Appendix D: Acronyms 489

About the Contributing Editor 501

About the Authors 503

Foreword

Knowledge is power, and today's age of the "information revolution" calls for new ways of attaining and controlling knowledge. Joint Vision 2010 is built on the premise that modern and emerging technology—particularly information-specific advances—should make possible a new level of joint operations capability. Sun Tzu reminds us, "Know the enemy and know yourself; in a hundred battles you will never be in peril." His timeless vision is about information superiority—the capability to collect, process, and disseminate an uninterrupted flow of information while exploiting or denying an adversary's ability to do the same. This is the central precept of JV 2010.

Information is a critical element of mission accomplishment for peace operations such as *Joint Endeavor*. First, a successful information campaign contributes to building and preserving public support for the operation. Second, the successful use of information can help the commander achieve operational goals by influencing parties, resolving crises, defusing misunderstandings, and correcting misperceptions. Such use of the information "weapon" will be more critical in peace operations where the traditional military tools (weapons) have a less central role in military activities. For *Joint Endeavor*, achieving "information dominance" through the employment of advanced information technology became a powerful tool in shaping the operational environment and helping the NATO-led Implementation Force (IFOR) successfully monitor the Former Warring Factions and enforce compliance with the Dayton Peace Accords. In a recent *Foreign Affairs* article, Major

General William Nash, the first commander of Task Force Eagle and Multinational Division North, observed that in Bosnia, "We don't have arguments. We hand them pictures, and they move their tanks."

The "CNN effect," coupled with the information revolution, creates formidable challenges for the military. Peace operations, in particular, require a more sophisticated understanding on the part of the military and civilian officials of news media behaviors and a more intricate melding of military, political, and public affairs objectives. In Bosnia, there was media presence throughout the country when IFOR arrived. The modern information networks serving the media, IFOR, and its coalition member nations (and as a matter of fact, the rest of the free world) provided an ability to share information at a speed and efficiency never before experienced. The problem soon became one of finding the useful details among the wealth of information available rather than a lack of information.

The U.S. Department of Defense has been successfully exploiting rapidly developing advances in information technology for military gain and Bosnia provided a unique opportunity to collect experiences in and insights into the use of advanced information technology in a multifaceted, first-time-ever NATO-led coalition peace support operation. Lessons were learned as NATO, the United States, and its allies and the other coalition members of IFOR took on the challenge of transforming, in real time, a go-to-war designed military capability into one to support the needs of a complex peace operation. This transformation included the integration of disparate military C4ISR systems and services and commercial services into the largest "federated" military information system ever built. E-mail, PowerPoint briefings, and video teleconferencing became the instruments of command and control.

Public Affairs, Civil Affairs, PSYOP, Counterintelligence, Human Intelligence, and the IFOR Information Campaign emerged as key players and initiatives in *Joint Endeavor*. Dealing with nongovernmental, private volunteer, and international organizations was new for NATO and many of its coalition partners and real-time adjustments were made to accommodate the humanitarian, economic, and civil reconstruction support aspects. Bosnia was a technology test bed as well, and served to further the U.S. DoD vision to apply advanced military information technology to support peace operations and to help achieve the JV 2010 vision of information superiority for joint operations.

This book tells the story of the challenges faced and innovative actions taken by NATO and U.S. personnel to ensure that IFOR and *Operation Joint Endeavor* were military successes. A coherent C4ISR lessons learned story has been pieced together from firsthand experiences, interviews of key personnel, focused research, and analysis of lessons learned reports provided to the National Defense University team. The book provides numerous examples that support the observation that DoD's vision is working for the Bosnia operation. However, much work remains to be done to achieve information superiority and the realization of JV 2010. The success of the IFOR operation was a major step forward, but this step was not due to technology alone. It was due mainly to the efforts of the dedicated, professional, and innovative men and women of the military, government, and contractors who were there and those who supported them.

Anthony M. Valletta
(Acting) Assistant Secretary of Defense C3I

Acknowledgments

The Honorable Emmett Paige, Jr., Assistant Secretary of Defense for Command, Control, Communications, and Intelligence (ASD/C3I), had the foresight to seize upon a unique opportunity to collect one-of-a-kind C3I insights into the deployment of NATO and U.S. forces in support of NATO's first-ever out-of-area operation in Bosnia. His tasking of the Command and Control Research Program (CCRP) at the National Defense University (NDU) to unify the C3I community activities and put together a coherent lessons learned story for the coalition command, control, communications, computers, intelligence, surveillance, and reconnaissance (C4ISR) aspects of *Operation Joint Endeavor* was unique in itself. As the NDU/CCRP Bosnia Study Director and Contributing Editor, I am in debt to him; the Deputy ASD (C3I), Tony Valletta; and the Directors J6, the Joint Staff, Admiral Walt Cebrowski, USN, and LTG Doug Buchholz, USA, for their continued interest and support of the study over the duration of the Implementation Force (IFOR) activities. I am also in debt to Dr. David Alberts, Director of the CCRP at NDU, for his support and the opportunity to lead a most challenging and interesting undertaking—a unique and unforgettable personal experience.

There were of course many people who have contributed to this effort and certainly more than can be mentioned here. A special thanks goes to those men and women who were there and those who supported them—in particular, those who took the time out of a demanding and intensive work environment to share their experiences and lessons with myself and members of the NDU/CCRP study team. The following organization elements and their staff provided numerous professional experiences, insights, and lessons to the study effort: Joint Staff (J2, J3, and J6), CISA, DISA, Air Mobility Command, Army War College Peacekeeping Institute, Center for Army Lessons Learned, CIA/DIA/NSA, LIWA, SOCOM, Air Force Historian, JITC, JIMC, ESC (CUBE), Army Materiel Command (BTIC), EUCOM (J2, J3, and J6), Joint Analysis Center, UCIRF/66th MI, USAREUR/5th Signal Command, USAFE, NATO, SHAPE (CISD/NACOSA), NC3A, AFSOUTH (CISD/RSSG), IFOR, CJCCC, ARRC, MND(N), MND(SW), MND(SE), C-SUPPORT, NAMSA, COMMZ (FWD), LANDCENT, IFOR/SFOR Joint Analysis Team, and the UK and French lessons learned teams to name a few. The Federally Funded Research Centers, in particular, IDA, CNA, and MITRE, provided valuable assessment insights as well. Our technical support contractor, Evidence Based Research, Inc. (EBR), and in particular, Dr. Richard Hayes, Rick Layton, James Landon, and Ms. Pascale Siegel, were active participants in conducting the study, collecting insights, assessing and presenting findings, and contributing to the preparation of this book.

A special thanks goes to the Director, the IFOR Joint Analysis Team (JAT), CAPT Peter Feist, GEN, his second in command, Wg Cdr Nigel Read, UKAFRO, and his multinational team. CAPT Feist's cooperation and willingness to collaborate with the NDU/CCRP study and share experiences and insights of mutual interest, including participation as JAT observers in country, provided an opportunity for the NDU/CCRP team members to view the operation through not only the eyes of U.S. personnel but NATO, the other framework nations (the United Kingdom and France), and members of other supporting nations as well. BG Bob Nabors, USAREUR/5th Signal Command, and his staff deserve special recognition for providing unique insights into the evolution of the communications and information systems as well as devoting critical resources to review our findings and story regarding the communications and information system lessons and experiences. USAREUR, Col Fred Stein, USA, provided helpful guidance in the communications and information systems areas as well. AFSOUTH (CISD)/IFOR CJ6, CDRE Peter Swan, RN, AFSOUTH (CSG), Col Bob Hillmer, USAF, and CJCCC, Col Scott Rodakowski, USA, Col Jack Dempsey, USA, and LtCol Stan Howard, USAF, provided unique IFOR insights to help focus the network management and communications and information systems piece of the study. On the SHAPE side, Group CAPT Derek Ainge, RAF, provided valuable insights from a SHAPE/NATO perspective to the study team and reviewed the C4ISR piece of the story for us. The authors in their chapters of this book also recognize many of the other individual contributors.

Special thanks are also due to Ms. Lois Burke of the NDU Graphics Department for the design of the cover and Mr. James Landon, Ms. Margarita Rushing, and Ms. Lydia Candland of EBR for their untiring help in editing and pulling the book together.

Finally, a special note of appreciation to my wife, Karen, for her support and for putting up with my seemingly endless weeks of travel, hours in front of the computer, and the inconveniences and lost weekends.

Preface

Peacekeeping is a soldier-intensive business in which the quality of the troops matters as much as the quantity. It is not just soldiering under a different color helmet; it differs in kind from anything else soldiers do. There are medals and rewards (mainly, the satisfaction of saving lives), but there are also casualties. And no victories. It is not a risk-free enterprise. In Bosnia, mines, snipers, mountainous terrain, extreme weather conditions, and possible civil disturbances were major threats that had to be dealt with from the outset of the operation. Dag Hammarskjold once remarked, "Peacekeeping is a job not suited to soldiers, but a job only soldiers can do."

Humanitarianism conflicts with peacekeeping and still more with peace enforcement. The threat of force, if it is to be effective, will sooner or later involve the use of force. For example, the same UN soldiers in Bosnia under a different command and mandate essentially turned belligerence into compliance over night, demonstrating that a credible threat of force can yield results. Unlike UNPROFOR, the NATO-led Implementation Force was a military success and helped to bring stability to the region and to provide an "environment for hope" in which a nation can be reborn. It is now up to a complex array of international civil agencies to assist in putting in place lasting structures for a democratic government and the will of the international community to ensure a lasting peace. The international community, after more than a year of NATO involvement, is just coming to grips with this realization.

Bosnia is a beautiful and fascinating country with rugged mountains and romantic medieval villages and cities. It's hard to understand why someone would want to destroy such beauty, or why the Serbs, Croats, and Muslims would perform inhumane acts of cruelty and atrocities against one another in the name of "ethnic cleansing." Although the media refers to "ethnic rivalries" in Bosnia, the truth of the matter is that all of the combatants were of the same ethnic group—Slavic. Bosnia's Muslims are Slavic, not Arab. However, in the words of Ivo Andric, himself a native Bosnian, "Bosnia is a country of hatred and fear. It is hatred, but not limited just to a moment in the course of social change, or an inevitable part of the historical process: rather it is hatred acting as an independent force, as an end in itself." Hence, with the breakup of the former Yugoslavia, Bosnia, with its richly mixed population of Serbs, Croats, and Muslims, became the principal battleground, the place where ancient and modern passions combined to fuel unspeakable cruelty.

In the early afternoon of April 6, 1992, gunmen holed up in the upper-floor rooms (the unofficial headquarters of Radovan Karadzic's Serbian Democratic Party) of the Holiday Inn in downtown Sarajevo opened fire on a "peace and unity" demonstration across the street in front of the Parliament Building, killing several of the demonstrators. For Sarajevo, these shots marked the start of the war. From then on it was all downhill.

The devastation that swept Bosnia and parts of Croatia was noticeable as soon as one stepped off the aircraft at Sarajevo airport. The control tower had obviously served as an irresistible target for Serb gunners and the airport terminal had been destroyed as well—baggage claim was a pallet at the edge of the tarmac. As one drove from the airport toward downtown Sarajevo, the devastation was even more severe, with homes, gas stations, apartment buildings, and office buildings savagely destroyed. The office building housing the Sarajevo daily newspaper, the *Oslobodjenje*, was severely damaged, its twin towers burned and collapsed as a result of heavy shelling. However, in spite of constant artillery, tank, and sniper fire, the paper was published every day during the war.

One of the saddest city sites was the destruction of the Austro-Hungarian masterpiece, the Sarajevo Library. A place of intellectual curiosity where many influential people passed through to contribute the best of their culture and intellectual gifts, it was not a player in the war but was ravaged by it. An estimated 1.5 million books were burned as a result of Serb artillery targeted against the facility and its symbol of intellectual curiosity.

Every available open space became a cemetery during the siege of Sarajevo. For example, there was a small cemetery in the park across the street from a large department store (which had a large shell hole in the 2nd floor from a direct hit) in downtown Sarajevo. As one stood on the hill overlooking the Olympic Stadium, one could see a sea of white, which upon closer inspection was actually hundreds of white crosses in a cemetery for those killed as a result of the siege of Sarajevo.

The 1984 Olympic Stadium and Ice Rink too had been severely damaged. The Olympic torch too had become a target for the gunners and was riddled with bullet holes. Standing at center rink, one could see the dust-covered 1984 Olympic clock and scoreboard still hanging in the less damaged portion of the rink—more than half of the rink structure was now a mass of twisted iron beams and girders. The rink was also home for some of the IFOR forces, including a UK military mess hall.

Destruction was not limited to Sarajevo and other large cities. As one flew over the countryside in a helicopter, signs of destruction were visible everywhere, from bridges to factories to single homes to entire villages.

Mostar, a wonderful, romantic medieval Turkish town of winding streets, little squares, and small shops, boasts one of the most famous confrontation lines in the world—the Bulevar, a street of once magnificent buildings shot to pieces by 10 million rounds of small arms fire. The city sits on the banks of the steep-sided Neretva River, which divides East from West. The beautiful Stari Most bridge, which linked the East with the West, was blown away in a fit of senseless Croat aggression in November 1993. Up to that point in time, the bridge had survived the fall of the Ottoman Empire and two World Wars. Banja Luka was also a beautiful city with tree-lined streets, cafes, parks, and the Vrbas River, where children would swim in the summer. It did not see the destruction of other large cities. The destruction was mainly limited to Muslim mosques, the Ferhad Pasha and Arnaudiya, which had been destroyed by either Serb soldiers or thugs who detonated several thousand pounds of dynamite under the mosques. After four centuries, all that remained of them was rubble. Other mosques had been destroyed throughout the country as well—the intent was apparently to destroy history and all traces that the Muslims had ever lived in Bosnia.

Even in the large city of Zagreb, Croatia, there was visible evidence of the war, e.g., roped off areas of land mines at the international airport. There was also a waist-high brick wall that surrounded the UN compound in Zagreb. Each brick in the wall carried the name of a loved one lost in the war—a monument to Croatian suffering.

There were moments of friendliness in spite of the devastation. During a jeep ride from Mostar to Sarajevo, children lined the streets and ran up to the road to wave at us as we passed through the towns—much as children have done in other wars. Almost everyone experienced a memorable encounter with the elderly, who were most appreciative of the NATO-led intervention and showed their gratitude by stopping you in the street and saying "Thank you. Thank you!" This happened to me in the Old Turkish Quarter in Sarajevo.

This book is not, however, about the devastation and suffering in Bosnia and Croatia. Instead, it's about NATO and the participating nations' first-ever effort to put in place a credible NATO-led coalition peacekeeping force to meet the intent of the military annex of the Dayton Accord and establish a stable peace environment. Included are insights into the multinational force experiences, challenges, successes (in particular, human ingenuity in addition to technology and perseverance), and lessons learned in putting in place a one-of-a-kind C2 structure and federated C4ISR system to support the peace operation.

The peace operation was a first in many different respects. The NATO-led operation in Bosnia-Herzegovina, *Joint Endeavor*, was NATO's first-ever ground force operation, its first-ever deployment "out of area," and its first-ever joint operation with NATO's Partnership for Peace partners and other non-NATO countries, including the Russians. It was a first deployment of USAREUR in support of a ground operation. This was a first-ever for the French in support of a NATO-led operation. It demonstrated that the alliance could adapt its forces and policies to the requirements of the post-Cold War world, while continuing to provide collective security and defense for all allies. It was also tangible proof that, in addition to carrying out the core functions of defense of the alliance, its military forces had the flexibility to be used outside of the NATO area, for operations under the authority of the UN Security

Council and with clear political objectives defining the military tasks. NATO's own military capabilities and its adaptability to include forces of non-NATO countries were decisive factors in the alliance's role in implementing the military annex of the Peace Agreement. The operation showed that the alliance remains vital, relevant, and prepared to deal with the new, multifaceted security risks facing Europe with the end of the Cold War.

Peace operations such as *Joint Endeavor* place different, and at times conflicting, demands on the supporting coalition military operation, civil-military cooperation, its C4ISR infrastructure, and associated information collection, use, and sharing. There are doctrine, culture, and language differences that need to be coordinated and merged to achieve unity of effort. Unintended consequences accompany the use of commercial and advanced information technologies and services and need to be accommodated. Information operations drive policy and doctrine. For Bosnia, the operation differed considerably from what NATO, the U.S., and other militaries had organized, equipped, and trained for during the Cold War. Lessons from Bosnia provide a window to the future and an opportunity to improve the military support to future peace operations.

Finally, the book tells the story of adapting a "go-to-war" equipped and trained military force to meet the challenges of a major peace operation. In peacekeeping, no operation will be quite like any other; each will have its own complexities, missions, and mandates. But some lessons have been learned the hard way through experience, and are still being learned in Bosnia, which could usefully be applied elsewhere. An attempt has been made to share with the reader the IFOR Bosnia experiences, both good and bad, and to highlight those lessons learned as a result of these experiences.

I. Introduction
Larry K. Wentz

Background

More than 4 years of war turned the once-beautiful Yugoslavia into a living nightmare, and into one of the bloodiest battlefields in Europe's recent history. The realities of the situation were seen daily on the television and in newsprint. There were images of homes, villages, and parts of cities destroyed, refugees carrying children and suitcases, war-wearied elderly women, and crying soldiers.

Like Rome, the Balkan crisis wasn't built in a day and it's difficult to understand. Although the conflicts have deep roots, the recent war can be immediately traced to the events of 1991, when Slovenia and Croatia declared independence from the former Yugoslavia. The Serb-dominated Yugoslav government allowed Slovenia to leave, but the Serb minority in Croatia rejected secession and fought to keep its homelands in that country. In 1992, similar Serb rebellions erupted in Bosnia. The Serb revolts were fortified with arms and forces from the Yugoslav government.[1]

The United Nations attempted to mediate between the warring parties, and over time placed more than 45,000 peacekeepers in the former Yugoslavia. Dozens of cease-fires were worked out by international mediators but broke down. The Bosnia civil war culminated in the Dayton Peace Agreement (see summary in Appendix A) and the subsequent deployment of a NATO-led multina-

2   *Lessons from Bosnia*

City Damage (Sarajevo)

Country Damage (Mostar)

tional military force into Bosnia and Croatia. The NATO-led force was called the Implementation Force—or "IFOR"—and the operation, which began on 16 December 1995, was code-named *Joint Endeavor*.

IFOR was a 60,000-person, 36-nation coalition force. Many of the national forces earmarked for IFOR, largely the French and British, were already in Bosnia as part of the United Nations Protection Force (UNPROFOR). The United States, which had no ground units in Bosnia before December 1995, began to deploy its initial units (e.g., reception units, advance headquarters) on 6 December, although the bulk of the 28,000 troops, mostly Army personnel stationed in Germany, deployed after D-Day. The U.S. deployment involved the movement of approximately 18,000 personnel, primarily from the 1st Armored Division, into Bosnia to form the core of the framework Multinational Division (North)—MND(N). Another 10,000 U.S. personnel were deployed into Bosnia, Hungary, and Croatia as part of various NATO organization elements and as the U.S. National Support Element (NSE) for the U.S. forces in Bosnia.

Operation Joint Endeavor provided a unique opportunity to capture experiences and lessons from NATO's first-ever ground force operation, its first-ever deployment "out of area," and its first-ever joint operation with NATO's Partnership for Peace partners and other non-NATO countries, especially the Russians. The book brings together a broad range of experiences to tell the IFOR story and to share some of the lessons learned by NATO and the U.S. and other military forces that supported the operation.

National Defense University Role

The operational deployment of complex command, control, communications, computers, intelligence, surveillance, and reconnaissance (C4ISR) systems in support of the NATO-led peace operation in Bosnia provided a unique opportunity to collect coalition C4ISR experiences and lessons learned. It also provided an opportunity to perform an analysis of the effectiveness of such complex command arrangements and supporting C4ISR systems. In recognition of this unique opportunity, Mr. Emmett Paige, Jr., Assistant Secretary of Defense for Command, Control, Communications, and Intelligence (ASD(C3I)), tasked the Command and Control Research Program (CCRP, formerly the Center for Advanced Concepts and Technology (ACT)) at the National Defense University (NDU) to perform such a study. On February 15, 1996, the director of CCRP was tasked to undertake this project in his role as the ASD(C3I)'s executive agent for the CCRP.

The CCRP charge was broad and covered both the effectiveness of command arrangements and the effectiveness of the supporting C4ISR systems. The study addressed all of the classic issues of C4ISR, including structures, functions, capacities, doctrine, and training. Furthermore, an attempt was made to pull together the related ongoing C4ISR community activities and build a coherent C4ISR story, including lessons learned. The Joint Staff endorsed the effort and the J-3 was designated as their point of contact for the study.

CCRP was sensitive to the need to be unobtrusive and to minimize demands on military organizations in the theater of operations. In-theater travel and visits, while necessary for some aspects of the study, were limited to those required to support a quality product. Research activities were initiated in February 1996, and it was expected that they would continue for at least 6 months after the exit of major U.S. forces from Bosnia. With the transition of IFOR to the Stabilization Force (SFOR) on 20 December 1996, the NDU effort was adjusted to focus on putting the IFOR story together as a first priority. The collection of SFOR experiences and lessons learned continued but at a much lower level of effort.

Operation Joint Endeavor was well underway before the NDU study effort was initiated and it was quickly determined that a number of other organizations had initiated efforts that would provide important information that the NDU effort did not need to duplicate. Therefore, CCRP made identifying all related efforts its first priority. These included lessons learned activities, research efforts, and assessments of C4ISR performance in Bosnia.

The roundup of all relevant efforts was a key element of CCRP's four-part, highly leveraged plan for accomplishing the mission of assessing C4ISR effectiveness and collecting lessons learned. CCRP employed a strategy based upon attention to four principles: coordination, collaboration, integration, and focused research. Key findings of the study will be provided to the doctrine developers in the joint community and the services. In addition, study insights and results will be used to develop professional military education (PME) materials, such as this book, for use at all levels of professional schooling.

About the Book

This book summarizes the NDU study findings, insights, and lessons from the Bosnia experience. It is based upon NDU study team members' experiences and analysis derived from visits to the theater of operation, from interviews of key personnel who participated and supported the operation, and from research of the vast material developed on the Bosnia experience. Several participants[2] in the IFOR operation, including some members[3] of the NDU team, made chapter contributions based on personal experiences, insights, and lessons learned. The book is structured to tell the story of the NATO and U.S. involvement in a way that shares both the successes as well as those things one would do differently the next time around. Where lessons learned have been clearly observed, they are so identified.

Chapter II sets the stage for *Operation Joint Endeavor* with a brief overview of the Balkan environment and the players. This discussion is then followed by a summary of the UN and NATO actions leading up to the deployment of the NATO-led Implementation Force (IFOR).

Peace operations (operations other than war) tend to be ad hoc coalitions of the willing with politically driven command structures. IFOR was no different. The Dayton Accord established three structures for implementation (with no one in charge of the overall operation): an Implementation Force for the military aspects, a High Representative to coordinate civil tasks, and Donors Conferences to stimulate reconstruction. Chapter III introduces the unusual and somewhat complicated C2 structure put together to implement the military aspects of the Dayton Accord.

Intelligence operations in a coalition environment are difficult. Intelligence is also one of the hardest things to share, since each partner has a natural tendency to mask his/her intelligence capabilities and to retain control of product dissemination. An attempt to unravel the mystique of coalition intelligence operations in the *Operation Joint Endeavor* environment is presented in Chapter IV.

For NATO, civil-military cooperation was a new experience, and represented one of the more interesting challenges faced by the military. Chapter V is devoted to this unique aspect of the IFOR operation. Differences in NATO and national approaches are covered, as well as the associated dealings with the international organizations (IO), non-governmental organization (NGO), private voluntary organizations (PVO), and other civil organizations.

Annex 11 of the Dayton Accord requested that the UN establish an International Police Task Force (IPTF) to assist the parties in discharging their public security obligations. Chapter VI addresses the establishment of the IPTF and its relationships with the military.

Many military officers are now convinced that victory is determined not just on the ground but also in the media reporting and the use of information to achieve public support for the military operation and to influence the behavior of the warring factions. Chapters VII (Information Activities) and VIII (Tactical PSYOPS) address various aspects of the IFOR media operations and the IFOR Information Campaign (IIC). Given the high level of importance placed on force protection and the key role that human intelligence plays in peace operations, Chapter IX focuses on the Counterintelligence and Human Intelligence support to the ground force commanders. Chapters VIII and IX reflect the firsthand experiences of military personnel who were there on the ground in Bosnia accomplishing the mission in the Task Force Eagle area of responsibility (MND(N)).

While no outside observer can acquire the in-depth knowledge possessed by the soldiers who lived the IFOR operation, one can get some interesting perspectives from observing and interviewing soldiers in action at many levels during selected field and aviation operations. Chapter X provides some firsthand, on-the-ground observations of a U.S. military officer who participated as a senior NATO observer in the Task Force Eagle area of responsibility from May 1996 to July 1996. His snapshots from the division to the foxhole provide interesting insights into the command and control problems experienced at the tactical level, with a particular emphasis on the impact of information technology.

The extension of NATO C4I systems and national C4ISR systems into the Croatia and Bosnia areas was a real challenge for NATO and the IFOR framework nations (the United States, United Kingdom, and France). NATO had an extremely limited ability to deploy forward and the warring faction fighting and NATO air strikes had destroyed a large portion of the Bosnia telecommunications infrastructure. The IFOR CJ6 goal (strongly supported by United States Army Europe (USAREUR's) 5th Signal Command, the major provider of tactical communications infrastructure for the operation) was to provide a single, integrated multinational network for IFOR. The "federated" NATO-national C4ISR network realized was the most complex and extensive ever put together by a military force. The challenges of implementation, integration, interoperability, and operation and management are covered in Chapter XI.

Chapter XII addresses the NDU study approach and shares its experiences in attempting to leverage the community lessons learned activities through the use of coordination, collaboration, integration, and focused research. Particular emphasis is given to the unique collaborative arrangement established between the Supreme Headquarters Allied Power Europe (SHAPE) sponsored IFOR Joint Analysis Team (JAT) and the NDU team to share findings and lessons learned. The use of a "Bosnia C4ISR Roundtable" to encourage the U.S. community to share and cooperate and the use of NDU as a clearinghouse for lessons learned activities are also emphasized. A by-product of the NDU study was "lessons learned about lessons learned." Chapter XIII addresses this subject and concludes that the U.S. process is broken. The IFOR JAT came to a similar conclusion for the NATO process and an initiative it proposed to fix the NATO system is addressed as well.

According to the Center for Army Lessons Learned, "A lesson is learned when behavior changes." Chapter XIV summarizes the findings and observations of the NDU study and presents a number of IFOR-related experiences that have the potential for becoming lessons learned.

II. Bosnia—Setting the Stage
Larry K. Wentz

Disraeli, at a time (1878) when yet another result of Balkan instability was being worked through at the Congress of Berlin, stood at the Dispatch Box in the British House of Commons, and said:

> No language can describe adequately the condition of that large part of the Balkan peninsula—Serbia, Bosnia, Herzegovina—political intrigues, constant rivalries, a total absence of all public spirit...hatred of all races, animosities of rival religions, and absence of any controlling power...nothing short of an army of 50,000 of the best troops would produce anything like order in these parts.[4]

History has a way of repeating itself. The message makes a sober but telling conclusion.

The Environment

The most important physical feature of Bosnia as a scene of military operations is its wild terrain. The brushy mountain country, craggy peaks, and roadless forest areas offer troops numerous places to hide, opportunity to shift forces unseen even from the air, and locations for ambush. Deep gorges make transverse movement difficult, and there are few secondary roads and rail lines until the central uplands east of the mountains are reached. Here the fertile land supports large population centers and industry, farming, and lines of communication are better. The major transportation routes are by road, rail, and inland waterways.

With the exception of its coastal areas, the Balkan Peninsula has a central European climate, characterized by warm and rainy summers and cold winters. The coastal areas enjoy variations of the Mediterranean type of climate, with warm, dry summers and mild, rainy winter seasons.

Bosnia-Herzegovina covers a land mass of roughly 51,197 sq km (see figure 2-1). It is slightly larger than the state of Tennessee. The CIA estimated the demographic distribution of Bosnia's pre-war population as consisting of 44 percent Muslim, 33 percent Serb, and 17 percent Croat. Four years later, the CIA statistics indicated a Serb plurality of 40 percent, followed by 38 percent Muslims and 22 percent Croats.[5]

A large part of the in-country infrastructure, such as power, water, and telecommunications, was destroyed by the war. Consequently, IFOR forces had to bring with them most, if not all, of what they needed to execute the peace operation. In addition, minefields were numerous and added a certain risk factor to all deployed personnel.

There are a number of players involved in the Bosnian tragedy. First, there are the ethnic groups, which consist of the Serbs (Orthodox Christians), the Muslims (of similar Slavic origin to the Serbs and Croats), and the Croats (of the Roman Catholic faith). The Serbs want to create a "Greater Serbia," establishing territorial ties with Serbia and Croatian Serb areas. The Muslims tend to favor an ethnically mixed state for Bosnia and the Croats hope to stake out their own areas of Bosnia.

Figure 2-1

Second, there are the factions, which consist of the Bosnian Army (primarily Muslim forces), the Bosnian Croats (united in a federation with Bosnian government forces), the Croatian government, the Bosnian Serbs (rebels supported by Yugoslavia), and the Croatian Serbs.

Capacity for Self-Governance[6]

Bosnia's most crucial deficiency is not incapacity for self-governance. The fundamental source of dysfunction is the absence of a formula for governance acceptable to each of its ethnic constituencies. Until this core issue is resolved, no amount of international largesse, infrastructure repair, or specialized training will suffice to put Bosnia back together again. Thus political will, not governmental capacity, is the key ingredient missing from the recipe for peace.

If a workable political formula ultimately emerges, there are numerous secondary factors relevant to governing capacity (e.g., economic resources; reintegration of refugees, displaced persons, and former combatants into productive society; and linkages between governing elite and organized crime) that will also play a vital role in shaping Bosnia's ultimate destiny.

The Economy[7]

Bosnia's economic challenges would have been daunting even without the convulsions of civil war. The shock of exposing their centrally planned economy to the discipline of global competition would have been harsh enough, owing to Bosnia's relatively primitive level of development, even by East European standards. By 1989, when the framework of state-centric economics collapsed along with the Berlin Wall, the Bosnian economy was in a deplorable condition. Inflation stood at almost 2,000 percent, and per capita debt for all Yugoslavia was the highest in Europe. Compounding the task of economic adjustment, nearly half of the 1990 federal budget for Yugoslavia was consumed by the military establishment. Lacking the means to continue propping up uncompetitive state-run enterprises, the government slashed subsidies and unemployment skyrocketed.

Social Disruption[8]

A further consequence of this war, which was waged largely against civilian targets, was massive emigration. Over a million Bosnians, 20 to 25 percent of the pre-war population, fled the country. These refugees came disproportionately from the ranks of professionals and skilled laborers, causing a "brain drain," but also creating a potential source of remittances useful for recovery after the conclusion of the conflict. In addition, in excess of a million inhabitants were dislodged from their homes and remain internally displaced within the country.

Status of the Public Security Apparatus[9]

Throughout most of its recent history, including the Tito regime, the public security apparatus (i.e., the judiciary, police force, and penal system) served as a fundamental instrument of state control. Yugoslavia's disintegration into ethnically defined entities during the first half of the 1990s had the further effect of converting many local police organizations into agents of intimidation and brutality against those of different ethnic origins. Without a fundamental reorientation in the functions performed by police and other institutions of public security, especially regarding minority rights, a multiethnic political community cannot be expected to endure. Police and judicial training programs alone will not suffice because the critical deficiency is not one of capabilities, but rather how political authorities employ those capabilities. As long as nationalistic political leaders continue to dominate the political process, the public security apparatus will be exploitable as an instrument of persecution of ethnic minorities.

The relationship between the constabulary and the armed forces in Bosnia was quite fluid during the war, in large part because of the nature of the conflict. Indeed, much "ethnic cleansing" was actually perpetrated by police elements. Shifting from the police to a military unit was no more complicated than a change of uniform. As military demobilization took place pursuant to the Dayton accord, the process was reversed, and many ex-soldiers were absorbed into police units. As a result, police strength, in proportion to the civilian population, was several times higher than the European standard of one for every 330 citizens. Apparently this also flooded police ranks with individuals possessing little or no background in law enforcement. One recent study indicated that over 80 percent of current Federation police officers have less than 6 years experience, and in many cases this experience is of a paramilitary nature. In sum, there is no shortage of police manpower, but the pool from which the various Bosnian police forces have been drawn was not confined to personnel with bona fide expertise in law enforcement.

UN Operations in the Former Yugoslavia[10]

After the death of Marshal Tito and the disintegration of the Soviet empire in the late 1980s, the forces that had held Yugoslavia's fractious peoples together were no longer present. When Serbian leaders sought to unify their nation into a greater Serbia, the Republics of Slovenia and Croatia began moving toward independence. The Yugoslav People's Army (JNA) reacted by putting pressure on both Croatia and Slovenia to disarm their "illegal paramilitary groups."

In June 1991, the crisis in Yugoslavia deteriorated into open conflict when Croatia and Slovenia unilaterally declared their independence from the Republic of Yugoslavia. The Yugoslavian

(Serbian-dominated) government promptly started a military campaign to seize the Serb-populated area of Croatia, the Krajina region. About 30 percent of Croatian territory was seized by the JNA. The JNA, after losing a series of sharp skirmishes with Slovenia, elected not to become heavily involved in a conflict with them and negotiated a withdrawal of forces.[11]

Efforts to stop the fighting and resolve the conflict led to the UN Security Council Resolution (UNSCR) 713 in September 1991, which called for a complete and general arms embargo on the former Yugoslavia. This was followed by UNSCR 749 in April 1992, which authorized the deployment of the UN Protection Force (UNPROFOR). This was the beginning of more than 4 years of military activities by the UN in the former Yugoslavia to bring about a cessation of the fighting and to assist in the delivery of humanitarian relief to the beleaguered population. These activities included the UNPROFOR, *Operation Provide Promise* (airlift of humanitarian aid), the UN Preventive Deployment (UNPREDEP) force in Macedonia, the UN Transitional Administration for Eastern Slavonia (UNTAES), and the UN Confidence Restoration Organization (UNCRO) in Croatia.

UN Protection Force (UNPROFOR)

The initial UNPROFOR deployed to Croatia in 1992 to monitor the cease-fire arrangements between the Croatian and Yugoslavian (Serb) forces. Authorized for a period of 1 year (via UNSCRs 743 and 749), the UNPROFOR was subsequently extended several times over the next few years until it eventually transferred its peacekeeping authority to NATO on 20 December 1995. During this time, it grew in size and area of responsibility. The UNPROFOR deployed into Bosnia after that state declared its independence and degenerated into civil war. The UNPROFOR also expanded into Macedonia in December 1992 to prevent that state from being drawn into the conflict. When the conflict spread to Bosnia-Herzegovina, the headquarters of the UNPROFOR, initially located in Sarajevo, was relocated to Zagreb.

The UNPROFOR developed into the largest, most expensive, and most complex peacekeeping operation in the history of the UN. By March 1994, it had expanded to more than 38,000 troops from 37 countries, the largest contributions coming from the United Kingdom, France, and Pakistan. No U.S. ground forces were committed to the operation; the U.S. role in the UNPROFOR was limited to logistical and other support, including a medical hospital provided by the Joint Task Force (JTF) Provide Promise. Some 15,000 UNPROFOR troops were deployed to Croatia and another 1,000 to Macedonia. The rest were stationed in Bosnia to monitor the fragile peace and to assist in the delivery of humanitarian aid to beleaguered populations. The annual cost of the UNPROFOR was estimated at approximately $1.6 billion.

In addition to its military forces, the UNPROFOR had a civil department that dealt with political, legal, and humanitarian issues. Chief among these were economic issues, arranging for prisoner care and transfer, securing passage of supply convoys, and most importantly, mediating between the warring parties. The UN High Commissioner for Refugees (UNHCR) representative was designated as the Secretary General's Special Representative for operations in the former Yugoslavia and remained in this capacity after the termination of the UNPROFOR.

Operation Provide Promise

Pursuant to the UNSCR 725 passed in June 1992 and under the auspices of the UNHCR, the U.S.-led coalition airlift operation, called *Operation Provide Promise*, commenced deliveries in July of critical humanitarian aid to cities in Bosnia, principally Sarajevo. The policies governing the multinational airlift operation were coordinated by a high-level working group (HLWG) of one-star generals from the participating nations: the United States, United Kingdom, France, Canada, and Germany. The HLWG also provided a single point of contact for dealing with the UNHCR, specifically the Airlift Operations Coordination Group (AOCG) at the UNHCR in Geneva, which coordinated all airlift and airdrop missions going into Bosnia and Croatia.

The U.S. Joint Task Force-Provide Promise (JTF-PP) was subsequently formed on 1 February 1993 to consolidate oversight of all of the U.S. activities in support of the UN mission in the former Republic of Yugoslavia. These activities included the conduct of U.S. airlift operations, including airdrops, force extraction, and peace operations. The JTF-PP, commanded by CINCUSNAVEUR, had its headquarters at Kelley Barracks, Germany. There was also a small headquarters nucleus in Naples, Italy, as well as a JTF-PP Forward situated in Zagreb. Eventually, the JTF-PP comprised more than 1,200 people, mostly on temporary duty. Reserves were used extensively.

More than 176,000 STONs of food, medicine, and supplies were delivered by *Provide Promise* from February 1993 to January 1996, the longest lasting humanitarian airlift in history. The operation involved 14,660 equivalent C-130 leads or about 13.8 (equivalent) C-130 sorties per day. The U.S. portion of this airlift consisted of two C-130s operating from the Italian air base at Falconara, Italy, and an indeterminate number of C-141s from Rhein Main Air Base in Germany. Other nations contributing airlifters included Germany (two C-160s) and Canada, France, and the United Kingdom (two C-130s each). The U.S. Air Force flew approximately 45 percent of the airlift sorties.

Operation Provide Promise also conducted emergency airdrops of food and medicine to regions isolated by the Bosnian Serbs. More than 19,800 STONs were dropped, primarily by U.S. C-130s, in the 19-month period starting in February 1993 (equivalent to 2.8 C-130 sorties per day).

Other activities performed by JTF *Provide Promise* included the operation of a U.S. 60-bed emergency medical treatment center at Camp Pleso in Zagreb, Croatia, for a UN military population of more than 47,000. In December 1995, this center was replaced with a smaller Czech medical battalion facility. JTF *Provide Promise* also supplied imagery to the UN and NATO from July 1995 to early November during the period of *Operation Deliberate Force*.

On 1 January 1996, nearly 3 years after its formation, the JTF *Provide Promise* began deactivation. It turned over its residual missions and organizations to the U.S. Army, the largest one being Task Force Able Sentry in Skopje, Macedonia. The U.S. Army TF Able Sentry monitors and reports troop movements along the Serbia/Macedonia border as part of the UN Preventive Deployment Force (UNPREDEP).

UNPREDEP—UN Preventive Deployment Force

In 1992, UN Secretary General Boutrous Boutrous-Ghali recommended an expansion of the UNPROFOR mandate into Macedonia to deter the spread of conflict into that region. Subsequently, the Security Council authorized the establishment of a UNPROFOR in the former Yugoslav Republic of Macedonia (FYROM) via Resolution 795 of 11 December 1992. In February 1993, the UN deployed the first troops (the Nordic battalion) into Macedonia. In June 1993, the first American troops, Task Force Able Sentry, were sent into the country. The UNPREDEP was established as a distinct operating entity in the FYROM by UNSCR 983 of 31 March 1995.

In June 1996, the UNPREDEP military troop component consisted of two mechanized infantry battalions: a Nordic composite battalion and a U.S. Army task force, supported by a heavy engineering platoon from Indonesia. The total strength of the military component was 1,000 troops, including approximately 500 U.S. troops. In addition, there were 35 UN military observers operating in country under the operational control of the UN commander and 26 UN civilian police monitors were deployed under the control of the Chief of Mission. The authorized strength of the civilian component was 168.

The UNPREDEP operated 24 permanent observation posts along the 420 kilometers of the Macedonian side of the border with Serbia and Albania. It also operated 33 temporary observation posts. Nearly 40 border and community patrols were conducted daily. An Interim Accord was signed between Greece and the FYROM on 13 September 1995 that paved the way for the admission of the FYROM to a number of European organizations.

After the termination of the UNPROFOR, the Secretary General recommended that the UNPREDEP be continued and that it become an independent mission, reporting directly to the UN HQ.

UNTAES—UN Transitional Administration for Eastern Slavonia

The Government of Croatia and the local Serb authorities signed the Basic Agreement on the Region of Eastern Slavonia, Baranja, and Western Sirmium on 12 November 1995. Under the agreement, the Security Council was requested to establish a Transitional Administration for an initial period of 12 months. Not later than 30 days before the end of the transitional period, elections for all government bodies would be organized by the Transitional Administration.

On 15 January 1996, the Security Council passed a resolution (UNSCR 1037) to set up a UN presence in Eastern Slavonia to oversee its eventual transfer back to Croatia. It thus established the UNTAES with a military component of up to 5,000 troops. On 31 January 1996, the Security Council authorized the deployment of 100 military observers.

NATO responsibilities to the UNTAES operation were twofold. First, NATO agreed to provide air support to the forces of UNTAES in case of attack by either the Croatians or the Serbs. Second, NATO agreed to extract the UNTAES forces should the situation warrant such an action.

UNCRO—UN Confidence Restoration Organization

In March 1995, Croatia ended the presence of the UNPROFOR in Croatia. At the same time, it approved a UN troop presence under a revised arrangement, called the UN Confidence Restoration Organization (UNCRO), as established by the UNSCR 981 of 31 March 1995. Upon termination of UNCRO on 15 January 1996, most of the UN forces in Croatia were transferred to the Commander, Implementation Force (COMIFOR).

NATO/WEU Operations in the Former Yugoslavia[12]

The political basis for NATO's role in the former Yugoslavia was established in June 1992 when the NATO Foreign Ministers announced their readiness to support peacekeeping activities under the aegis of the Conference on Security and Cooperation in Europe (CSCE)—subsequently renamed the Organization for Security and Cooperation in Europe (OSCE). In December 1992, the NATO foreign ministers stated their readiness to support the UNPROFOR peacekeeping operations under the authority of the United Nations. This marked the start of several NATO operations conducted in support of the UN over the next 4 years. The Alliance initiated maritime operations by NATO naval forces, in conjunction with the Western European Union (WEU), to monitor and subsequently enforce the UN embargo in the Adriatic (*Operation Sharp Guard*). NATO air forces were deployed to monitor and, subsequently, to enforce the UN no-fly zone over Bosnia-Herzegovina (*Operation Deny Flight*). NATO also provided close air support to the UNPROFOR during its deployment to Croatia and Bosnia, and in response to Serb mortar attacks in Sarajevo, NATO launched a series of air strikes against the Bosnian Serbs (*Operation Deliberate Force*).

Operation Sharp Guard

In July 1992, NATO ships of the Standing Naval Force Mediterranean, assisted by NATO Maritime Patrol Aircraft (MPA), began monitoring operations in the Adriatic (*Operation Maritime Guard*), joining the WEU ships also monitoring Adriatic ship traffic under *Operation Sharp Guard*. In November 1992, NATO and WEU forces in the Adriatic began enforcement operation in support of UN economic sanctions and the arms embargo of the countries of former Yugoslavia. Subsequently, at a joint session of the North Atlantic Council and the Council of WEU on 8 June 1993, the combined NATO/WEU *Operation Sharp Guard* was approved. Operational control of the NATO/WEU Task Force, designated Combined Task Force 440 (CTF 440), was delegated through SACEUR to the Commander, Allied Naval Forces Southern Europe (COMNAVSOUTH) to carry out the functions of CTF 440. The COMNAVSOUTH staff has been augmented by a WEU staff element. The commander and deputy commander of CTF 440 were both from the Italian navy.

In the 2-year period between January 1993 and December 1994, *Operation Sharp Guard* amassed 12,500 ship-days of operations (an average of 17 ships at sea at any given time) and flew 3,800 MPA sorties (averaging 5 per day). The operation challenged 31,400 ships, boarding a total of 2,575 ships (3.5 per day) and diverting 643 ships to Italian ports for additional inspection.

There were three Operational Task Groups (OTGs) under CTF 400, made up of ships from many nations. The OTGs were supported by land- and carrier-based fighter aircraft operating in the area and by MPA assets from eight nations. The NATO Airborne Early Warning Force (NAEWF), which employed eight E-3As and two E-3Ds, also supported *Operation Sharp Guard*.

Following the Dayton Accord in November 1995, *Operation Sharp Guard* stopped enforcing the economic sanctions imposed by the UN. The arms embargo was lifted gradually, beginning on 14 March 1996 (90 days after signature of the Peace Agreement) when the import of all but heavy arms was permitted. *Operation Sharp Guard* ceased operations on 18 June 1996.

Operation Deny Flight

In October 1992, the UN established a no-fly zone over Bosnia-Herzegovina. NATO AWACS aircraft began monitoring operations of this no-fly zone in October 1992. On 31 March 1993, the UN Security Council authorized enforcement of the no-fly zone via UNSCR 816. The resulting NATO enforcement operation, called *Operation Deny Flight*, began on 12 April 1993 under the Allied Forces Southern Command (AFSOUTH) OPLAN 40101. *Deny Flight* was a joint/combined airborne reconnaissance (RECCE) and combat air patrol (CAP) operation designed both to enforce the no-fly zone and to conduct strike operations in support of the UN peacekeeping forces.

In June 1993, the NATO foreign ministers offered protective airpower for the UNPROFOR, and in January 1994, the Alliance leaders reaffirmed their readiness to carry out air strikes to prevent the strangulation of Sarajevo by the Bosnian Serbs. This commitment was underscored when, on 28 February 1994, the first military engagement ever undertaken by NATO occurred: four Bosnian Serb warplanes, originating out of Banja Luka, violated the no-fly zone and were shot down by NATO aircraft.

Subsequently, limited NATO air strikes were conducted in support of UNPROFOR in August, September, and November 1994.

In May 1995, additional NATO air strikes were carried out on Bosnian Serb positions, after which hostages were taken by the Serbs but subsequently released on 18 June. On 11 July additional air strikes were conducted to defend the UN Protected Zone in the Srebrenica area.

During the 33-month duration of *Operation Deny Flight*, almost 80,000 sorties were flown (30 percent CAP, 28 percent strike, 25 percent surveillance and RECCE, and 17 percent "other"). About 47 percent of the sorties were flown by the U.S. military, 30 percent by the USAF alone. Fighter and bomber sorties originated from bases in Italy and from carriers operating in the Adriatic. The tanker and surveillance sorties originated from bases in France and Germany.

These flights, along with those of *Operations Provide Promise*, *Sharp Guard*, and *Deliberate Force*, were coordinated by the Combined Air Operations Center (CAOC) of COMAIRSOUTH located in Vicenza, Italy. Run by the U.S. Air Force, the CAOC coordinated the air operation over Bosnia of the other NATO countries as well. The CAOC began operations in the spring of 1993 on a temporary basis with about 78 people assigned. By December 1995, it had become a permanent facility with more than 400 personnel assigned.

Following the conclusion of *Operation Deliberate Force*, NATO conducted two additional air operations under *Operation Deny Flight* on 4 October and 9 October. The *Deny Flight* mandate was terminated on 20 December 1995 with the transfer of authority from UNPROFOR to NATO IFOR.

Operation Deliberate Force/Dead Eye

On 30 August 1995, in response to a Bosnian Serb mortar attack on Sarajevo, NATO commenced a series of air attacks on Bosnian Serb military targets in an operation known as *Operation Deliberate Force*. These attacks continued until 20 September 1995 when CINCAFSOUTH and the UNPROFOR commander concluded that the Bosnian Serbs had complied with the conditions set down by the UNPROFOR commander. During *Operation Deliberate Force*, there were 3,515 sorties flown by 8 countries and NATO. The United States conducted two-thirds of the sorties (2,318) with the United Kingdom (326), France (284), Netherlands (198), and Spain (121) making up the bulk of the rest. Again, Italian air bases and carriers in the Adriatic were used to launch these strikes. This NATO air campaign has been given much of the credit for bringing the warring parties to the negotiating table in Dayton, Ohio, in November 1995.

In support of *Operation Deliberate Force*, NATO conducted suppression of enemy air defense (SEAD) operations against the Bosnian Serb integrated air defense system from 9 September to 14 September 1995. This operation was called *Dead Eye*.

The WEU and the Yugoslav Conflict[13]

In addition to its participation in *Operation Sharp Guard*, the Western European Union (WEU) conducted two additional operations in the former Yugoslavia, one on the Danube and the second in Mostar Bosnia.

Danube Operation

The WEU operation on the Danube provided logistic support of the UN embargo against the former Yugoslavia. Overall, more than 300 police and customs officers and 11 patrol boats were active in embargo activities on the Danube. Close coordination was maintained with the riparian states of Bulgaria, Romania, and Hungary (associate partners of the WEU). The Coordination and Support Center was situated in Calafat, Romania.

Mostar Operation

Since July 23, 1994, the WEU also assisted the European Union in administering the City of Mostar through the establishment of a Unified Police Force. This Unified Police Force was manned jointly by the Croats and Muslims of Bosnia-Herzegovina, and by police officers deployed by the WEU countries.

NATO Ground Operations in the Former Yugoslavia[14]

Deployment of NATO-led forces into the former Yugoslavia was the culmination of years of international activity and negotiations to bring the warring parties in the former Yugoslavia to the negotiating table and to start the rebuilding process in the region. Following the signing of the Bosnian Peace Agreement in Paris on 14 December 1995, NATO was given a mandate by the UN, on the basis of UNSCR 1031, to implement the military aspects of the Peace Agreement. The NATO-led multinational force was called the Implementation Force—or "IFOR"—and the operation, code-named *Joint Endeavor*, began on 16 December.

The role of the IFOR was to help the parties implement a peace accord to which they had freely agreed in an even-handed way. IFOR was not in Bosnia to fight a war or to impose a settlement on any of the parties. In addition to its principal task, it was also helping to create a secure environment for civil and economic reconstruction. Its mission was limited to 12 months. However, the North Atlantic Council issued a statement on 10 December 1996 that announced that NATO was prepared to extend its participation and on 12 December 1996, the UN Security Council adopted Resolution 1088 authorizing continued participation by NATO. On 20 December 1996, IFOR was replaced by a NATO-led Stabilization Force (SFOR), code-named operation *Joint Guard*, whose mission was to continue to secure the environment for an additional 18 months.

Operation Joint Endeavor

The NATO-led IFOR was the largest military operation ever undertaken by the Alliance. It demonstrated that the Alliance could successfully adapt its forces and policies to the requirements of the post-Cold War world, while continuing to provide collective security and defense for all Allies. It was tangible proof that, in addition to carrying out the core functions of defense of the Alliance, its military forces had the flexibility to be used outside the NATO area, for operations under the authority of the UN Security Council and with clear political objectives defining the military tasks. NATO's own military capabilities and its adaptability to include forces of non-NATO countries were decisive factors in the Alliance's role in implementing the Peace Agreement.

Under the authority of UNSCR 1031 of 15 December 1995, NATO was responsible for the implementation of the military aspects of the Bosnian Peace Agreement, signed by all parties to the conflict. There were also civilian aspects of the Peace Agreement, which were the responsibilities of other international and non-governmental organizations. One of the goals of the military mission, however, was to create secure conditions for others to carry out non-military tasks associated with the Peace Agreement.

In accordance with the Peace Agreement, IFOR had the following primary military tasks:

- ensure continued compliance with the cease-fire;

- ensure the withdrawal of forces from the agreed cease-fire zone of separation back to their respective territories, and ensure the separation of forces;

- ensure the collection of heavy weapons into cantonment sites and barracks and the demobilization of remaining forces;

- create conditions for the safe, orderly, and speedy withdrawal of UN forces that have not transferred to the NATO-led IFOR; and

- maintain control of the airspace over Bosnia-Herzegovina.

The IFOR had a unified command and was NATO-led, under the political direction and control of the Alliance's North Atlantic Council, as stipulated by the Peace Agreement (annex 1A). Overall military authority was in the hands of NATO's Supreme Allied Commander, Europe (SACEUR), General George Joulwan. General Joulwan designated Admiral Leighton Smith (NATO's Commander in Chief Southern Command (CINCSOUTH)) as the first commander in theater of IFOR (COMIFOR). With the retirement of Admiral Smith in July 1996, Admiral Joseph Lopez was appointed as CINCSOUTH and also replaced Admiral Smith as COMIFOR. For the duration of the IFOR operation, the COMIFOR headquarters was split-based between Sarajevo and Naples.

The IFOR operated under Chapter VII of the UN Charter (peace enforcement). Its rules of engagement provided for the robust use of force, if necessary, to accomplish its mission and to protect itself. If force needed to be used to ensure compliance with the terms of the Peace Agreement, IFOR would observe the international legal principles of proportionality, minimum use of force, and the requirement to minimize the potential for collateral damage.

The IFOR consisted of elements sent to the theater by participating nations and of elements of UN peace forces already in place and transferred to NATO command and control. Every NATO nation with armed forces committed troops to the operation. Iceland, the only NATO country without armed forces, provided medical support. But IFOR was more than just a NATO operation. In addition to troop contributions from NATO nations, a significant number of other nations were participating in the IFOR. As of September 1996, non-NATO participating nations included Albania, Austria, Czech Republic, Estonia, Finland, Hungary, Latvia, Lithuania, Poland, Romania, Russia, Sweden and Ukraine—all of which are Partners for Peace countries—plus Egypt, Jordan, Malaysia, and Morocco.

The non-NATO forces were incorporated into the operation on the same basis as forces from NATO member countries. They took their orders from the IFOR commander through the multinational divisional commanders, and had liaison officers at SHAPE and the IFOR Headquarters in Sarajevo. In addition, arrangements were in place at NATO Headquarters in Brussels for political consultations with non-NATO IFOR troop-contributing nations. Participation by non-NATO Partnership for Peace nations in IFOR not only contributed to the accomplishment of IFOR's mission but also provided all the participating forces with practical experience of operating with each other.

The participation of Russia was very important for the success of IFOR's mission. It was also a crucial step in the evolving NATO-Russia cooperative relationship. Russian forces joined the IFOR in January 1996. Russia's participation was subject to special arrangements between NATO and Russia. The Russian contingent was directly subordinate to Colonel General Leontiy Shevtsov, as General Joulwan's Russian deputy. In theater, the Russian brigade was under the tactical control of the U.S.-led MND(N).

An advanced Enabling Force of 2,600 troops began deploying to Bosnia and Croatia on 2 December 1995. Their task was to facilitate the smooth flow of the deployment by establishing the headquarters, communications, and logistics necessary to receive the main body of 60,000 IFOR troops to be deployed into the area. Elements of the Enabling Force were from Allied Forces Southern Europe Headquarters in Naples, Italy, and the Allied Command Europe Rapid Reaction Corps (ARRC) in Moenchengladbach, Germany. The rest were provided by other NATO commands as well as by NATO nations. The deployment of the main body of troops was activated on 16 December, after final approval by the North Atlantic Council of the Operational Plan (OPLAN 10405), and the UNSCR 1031 of 15 December, authorizing the IFOR's mission.

The transfer of authority from the commander of UN Peace Forces to the commander of IFOR took place on 20 December 1995, 96 hours after the NATO Council's approval of the main deployment. On that day, all NATO and non-NATO forces participating in the operation came under the command and/or control of the IFOR commander. IFOR secured conditions for the safe, orderly, and timely withdrawal of the remaining UN forces not coming under NATO command and control.

By 19 January 1996, 30 days after the transfer of authority from UNPROFOR to IFOR (D+30), the parties to the Agreement had withdrawn their forces from the zone of separation on either side of the agreed cease-fire line. As of 3 February 1996 (D+45), all forces had been withdrawn from the areas to be transferred. The transfer of territory between Bosnian entities was completed by 19 March 1996 (D+90), and a new zone of separation was established along the inter-entity boundary line (IEBL).

In assessing the situation in Bosnia and Herzegovina 4 months after the beginning of the IFOR deployment, the North Atlantic Council concluded that the IFOR had been successful in bringing about a more secure environment. The parties continued to respect the cessation of hostilities and had generally complied with the major milestones in the Peace Agreement.

All heavy weapons and forces were to be in cantonments or demobilized by 18 April 1996 (D+120), which represented the last milestone in the military annex to the Peace Agreement. Due to technical problems, the parties to the Peace Agreement were not able to complete the withdrawal and demobilization or cantonment of heavy weapons and forces by the deadline, although the revised deadline set by SACEUR of 27 June 1996 (D+180) for the cantonment of heavy weapons was met.

In some areas, compliance had fallen short of requirements under the Peace Agreement. The parties had released most prisoners of war but not all. Minefield clearance from the zones of separation and areas being transferred fell behind schedule. However, IFOR continued its efforts to monitor de-mining operations and to lend assistance to the parties in other areas. IFOR also continued its efforts to remove impediments to freedom of movement and to project a sense of security throughout the country. It played a key role in creating the conditions for peace, but ultimately peace depended on the parties themselves.

The international community responded to the positive achievements in the implementation of the Peace Agreement by suspending sanctions against the parties. After the Agreement was initialed, the UN Security Council suspended economic sanctions against the Federal Republic of Yugoslavia (Serbia and Montenegro) and began phasing out the arms embargo. The UN terminated the arms embargo on the former Yugoslavia on 18 June 1996, but indicated that sanctions against the Federal Republic of Yugoslavia or the Bosnian Serb authorities could be reimposed if they fail significantly to meet their obligations under the Peace Agreement.

NATO and NATO member nations assumed primary funding responsibility for IFOR. In accordance with NATO practice, this was based on a mix of common and national funding. Common-funded costs were borne by the NATO Military Budget and the NATO Security Investment Program (formerly, Infrastructure funding). Non-NATO countries were responsible for their own national contributions to IFOR, with the exception of the common-funded costs that were met by NATO.

For lasting peace in Bosnia-Herzegovina, full implementation of the civilian aspects of the Peace Agreement was crucial as well. By implementing the military aspects of the Agreement, NATO helped to ensure a secure environment conducive to civil and political reconstruction. A timely conclusion of an arms control regime and of confidence- and security-building measures were also of fundamental importance to the peace process. The civilian aspects of the Agreement were carried out by appropriate international and non-governmental organizations. The London Peace Implementation Conference of 8-9 December 1995 set up the framework for these efforts. The High Representative named at the London Conference, Carl Bildt, was charged with monitoring the implementation of the Peace Agreement and coordinating the activities of the organizations and agencies involved in civilian implementation.

In view of the importance of the civilian aspects of the Peace Agreement, IFOR provided increased support for civilian tasks within the limits of its existing mandate and available resources. IFOR worked closely with the Office of the High Representative (OHR), IPTF, the International Committee of the Red Cross (ICRC), and the UNHCR. The OSCE, the International Criminal Tribunal for the former Yugoslavia (ICTY), and many others, including more than 400 non-governmental organizations (NGOs), were also worked with closely. IFOR offered a range of support facilities to these organizations, such as emergency accommodation, medical treatment and evacuation, vehicle repair and recovery, transport assistance, security information and advice, and other logistical support.

IFOR continued to assist the efforts of these organizations in tasks that were essential to the long-term consolidation of peace in Bosnia and Herzegovina. IFOR units worked with the OSCE on election preparations and human rights monitoring in OSCE field offices. Logistic and other support were provided to the ICTY in the investigation of war crimes and assistance was provided to the UNHCR in the return of refugees and displaced persons. Help in the maintenance of law and order was provided to the IPTF and air and ground transport assistance was made available to the OHR and others. IFOR units provided mine awareness training and education to local schools and community groups. Substantial support was also provided to all agencies by the IFOR Information Campaign, in the form of both printed material and electronic media.

IFOR military engineers repaired and opened more than 50 percent of the roads in Bosnia and Herzegovina, and rebuilt or repaired over 60 bridges including those linking the country with Croatia. They were also involved in de-mining and repairing railroads; opening up airports to civilian traffic; restoring gas, water, and electricity supplies; rebuilding schools and hospitals; and restoring key telecommunication assets.

Finally, IFOR included a specialized group of about 350 personnel such as lawyers, educators, public transportation specialists, engineers, agricultural experts, economists, public health officials, veterinarians, communications experts, and many others. These were part of a civil-military team, referred to as CIMIC (Civil-Military Cooperation), which provided technical advice and assistance to various commissions and working groups, civilian organizations, NGOs, and IFOR units, as well as to the parties to the Agreement and to local authorities.

Operation Joint Guard

The mandate for the NATO-led IFOR expired on 20 December 1996. On 10 December 1996, the North Atlantic Council, meeting in Ministerial Session, issued a statement on Bosnia and Herzegovina. The statement announced that NATO was prepared to organize and lead a Stabilization Force (SFOR) to take the place of IFOR, authorized by a UNSCR under Chapter VII of the UN Charter. On 12 December 1996, the UN Security Council adopted Resolution 1088 authorizing the establishment of SFOR as the legal successor to IFOR. SFOR was activated on 20 December 1996.

The role of IFOR (*Operation Joint Endeavor*) was to implement the peace. The role of SFOR (*Operation Joint Guard*) was to stabilize the peace. The difference between the tasks of IFOR and SFOR is reflected in the names of their missions. SFOR had the same rules of engagement as IFOR for the robust use of force, if it should be necessary to accomplish its mission and to protect itself. Its specific tasks were to—

- deter or prevent a resumption of hostilities or new threats to peace;

- consolidate IFOR's achievements;

- promote a climate in which the peace process could continue to move forward; and

- provide selective support to civilian organizations within its capabilities.

SFOR also stood ready to provide emergency support to UN forces in Eastern Slavonia.

SFOR's size, with around 31,000 troops in Bosnia, was about half that of IFOR. Building on the general compliance with the terms of the Dayton Agreement ensured during the IFOR mission allowed the smaller-sized SFOR to concentrate on the implementation of all the provisions of annex 1A of the Peace Agreement, i.e., to stabilize the secure environment in which local and national authorities and other international organizations could work; and provide support to other agencies (on a selective and targeted basis, in view of the reduced size of the forces available).

NATO envisaged an 18-month mission for SFOR. The North Atlantic Council planned to review SFOR's force levels after 6 and 12 months with a view to shifting the focus from stabilization to deterrence and completing the mission by June 1998.

The SFOR was also a NATO-led unified command under the political direction and control of the Alliance's North Atlantic Council, as stipulated by the Peace Agreement (annex 1A). Overall military authority was again in the hands of NATO's SACEUR, General George Joulwan, who designated General William Crouch (NATO's Commander of Land Forces Central Europe (LANDCENT)) as the commander of SFOR (COMSFOR). COMSFOR's headquarters was in Ilidza.

The NATO and 18 non-NATO nations that participated in IFOR also participated in SFOR. In addition, Egypt, Jordan, and Morocco participated in the Alliance's Mediterranean dialogue. Slovenia and Ireland also joined SFOR, bringing the total of non-NATO participating nations to 20.

In view of the importance of the civilian aspects of the Peace Agreement, SFOR planned to continue to provide support for civilian tasks. However, with fewer forces at its disposal, SFOR would need to prioritize its efforts and carefully select where they could be applied. To be effective, SFOR and the other organizations would also need to continue to plan together and identify mutual objectives to ensure that the limited SFOR support could be applied where and when needed.

III. Command and Control Structure
Richard L. Layton

The purpose of this chapter is to give the reader an overview of the command and control (C2) structure that was in place when the Implementation Force (IFOR) entered Bosnia in December 1995, and how that structure evolved throughout the course of the operation. *Operation Joint Endeavor* is a unique case in the history of peace operations. It is the first operation NATO has conducted out-of-area, or out of its normal area of protection. Also, a number of countries who have worked together for a long time in NATO and a large number of countries who had never been together formed *Operation Joint Endeavor.* Overall the operation was successful, in part because of the personal relationships of the commanders and staff involved. The Rules of Engagement (ROE) for the operation were not defined before the troops were deployed and therefore had to be pushed down from NATO Headquarters during and after the deployment of forces. Although the mission could have failed in the early stages due to the lack of a unified political direction by NATO and the weak interaction between the civil and military authorities in Bosnia, the "people on the ground" found ways to make the mission a success.

The IFOR Command Arrangements

The three framework nations (the United States, United Kingdom, and France) formed the basis for the multinational divisions (North, South West, and South East, respectively). OPCON (operational control) and OPCOM (operational command) of the divisions were also assigned to the ARRC. HQs IFOR was split between Naples and Sarajevo and the HQs ARRC was located at Ilidza near Sarajevo. The U.S.-led MND(N), with its HQs in Tuzla, was the largest division and included brigades from Turkey, Russia, and a third non-U.S. brigade referred to as the NordPol brigade (made up of troops from Finland, Sweden, Norway, and Poland). The British-led MND(SW), with its HQs located in Banja Luka, was built around a British brigade along with troops from Canada, the Netherlands, and Denmark. Finally, the French-led MND(SE), with its HQs in Mostar, was the smallest division and was comprised of troops from France, Italy, and Portugal. Both the British and French already had a large number of troops in Bosnia in support of UNPROFOR and the Rapid Reaction Force. Hence, the bulk of the deployment activities for IFOR were the NATO command unit forces, the U.S. forces, and the forces of the other participating nations.

The Allied Forces Southern Command (AFSOUTH) Headquarters served as the operational-level headquarters for this operation, due in part to the recent success of *Operation Sharp Guard* (maritime control) and the need to use air bases on Italy's territory. AFSOUTH, located in Naples, Italy, is a 45-year-old peacetime NATO headquarters, which had the mission to watch over naval deployments in the Mediterranean Sea. AFSOUTH was neither staffed nor equipped to lead a land force into combat. Had IFOR encountered more combat in this operation, the headquarters structure probably would have failed without much additional U.S./NATO staff support and equipment. There is a belief, in some minds, that Headquarters IFOR and the Allied Rapid Reaction Corps (ARRC) constituted a Joint Task Force. This was not the case in Bosnia.

NATO's ability to influence events during early preparation for IFOR helped to avoid problems encountered by UNPROFOR and to ensure a clear definition of military tasks under a unified chain of command. This is largely attributable to close involvement of NATO military planners with Contact Group negotiators prior to and during Dayton to ensure that security tasks that could be accomplished realistically were incorporated into the agreement. Consequently, there is clear language hammered into the General Framework Agreement stating that IFOR "will operate under the authority of and subject to the direction and political control of the North Atlantic Council (NAC) through the NATO chain of command." UNSCR 1031 provides NATO with the mandate and the necessary political authority to direct NATO and non-NATO forces under IFOR. However, NATO's robust military terms of reference highlight the paucity of authority for the civil activities of the High Representative—the weak link in the implementation of the Dayton Accord. In any future operation that depends on the success of both military and civil tasks, NATO will want to ensure that its civil counterpart also enjoys a commensurate amount of authority to fulfill its responsibilities.

Shortfalls in C2 Arrangements

The lack of unified political direction for the overall peace implementation process was a risk to the success of IFOR. The General Framework Agreement establishes three structures for implementation—an Implementation Force for the military aspects, a High Representative to coordinate civil tasks, and Donors Conferences to stimulate reconstruction. (Figure 3-1 illustrates the C2 structure for civil and military tasks.) NATO's robust terms of reference in the General Framework Agreement highlight the paucity of authority for the High Representative. The High Representative is not a UN Special Representative with UN authority and his political guidance comes from a Steering Board of the Peace Implementation Council, which is not a standing internationally recognized political

38 Lessons from Bosnia

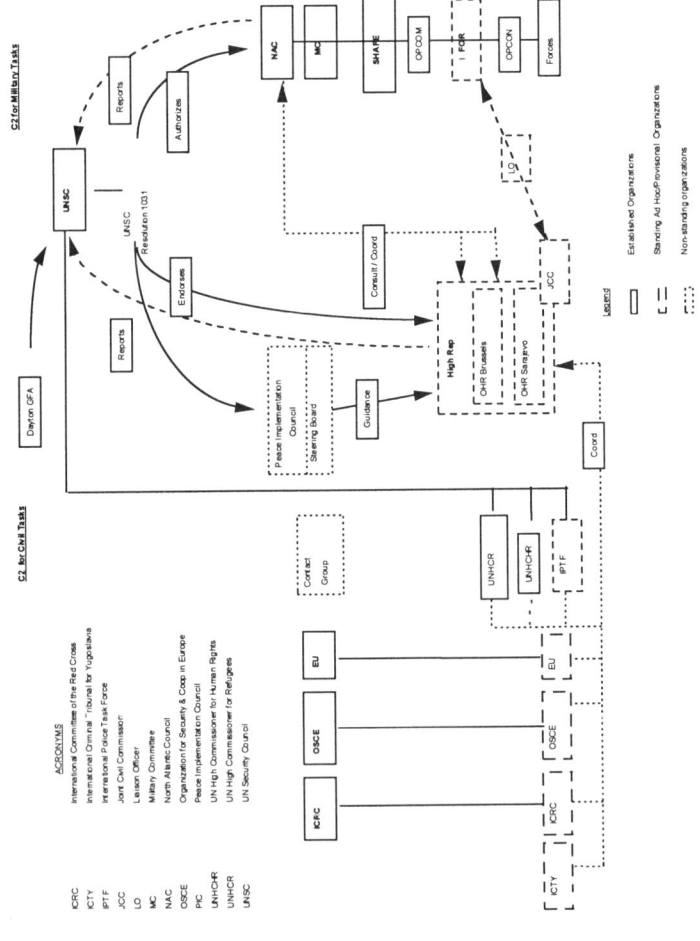

Figure 3-1. Unity of Direction at Higher Levels

organization. Given the UN's reluctance to play a lead role, there is no internationally recognized political organization providing overall political direction. Consequently, the three structures remain virtually autonomous, operating within a loose framework of cooperation and without a formal structure for developing unified policy. The absence of a standing political organization with which the NAC can coordinate policy exacerbates synchronization of civil/military implementation at the strategic level and NATO's role in implementing the Peace Agreement. In any future operation that depends on the success of both military and civil tasks, NATO will want to ensure that its civil counterpart will also enjoy a commensurate amount of authority to fulfill its responsibilities.

At SHAPE, the Partnership Coordination Cell, with resident liaison teams from PfP nations, provided secure facilities for IFOR Liaison Officers and for SHAPE's IFOR Coordination Center (ICC) (see figure 3-2). The ICC has been the key link in arranging initial contacts with non-NATO nations, coordinating plans, and resolving national issues with SHAPE. Plans to deploy National Liaison Teams to a National Coalition Cell (NCC) in theater did not materialize and an alternative location at Naples satisfied neither the desire of nations to be represented in theater nor to maintain contact with their contingents.

COMIFOR and COMARRC have been given OPCON over their main combat troops (see figure 3-3). Early impressions from IFOR operations suggest that this amount of command authority does not suffice, and that OPCOM should have been granted. OPCON does not permit (1) assignment of a separate employment to force components, (2) does not allow the redress of imbalances and shortfalls within the forces assigned, and (3) does not allow the reassignment of forces. The above three activities are important for the fulfillment of the mission, are in the interest of economy of effort, and would be authorized with delegation of OPCOM. A study conducted by a NATO's Central Region Chiefs of Army Staff Working Group addressed this very subject. The study results were published in September 1995. It was concluded that Conflict Prevention, Peacemaking, and Peacekeeping would require OPCON. Peace

40 Lessons from Bosnia

Figure 3-2. NATO C3 Support to Non-NATO Contributors to IFOR

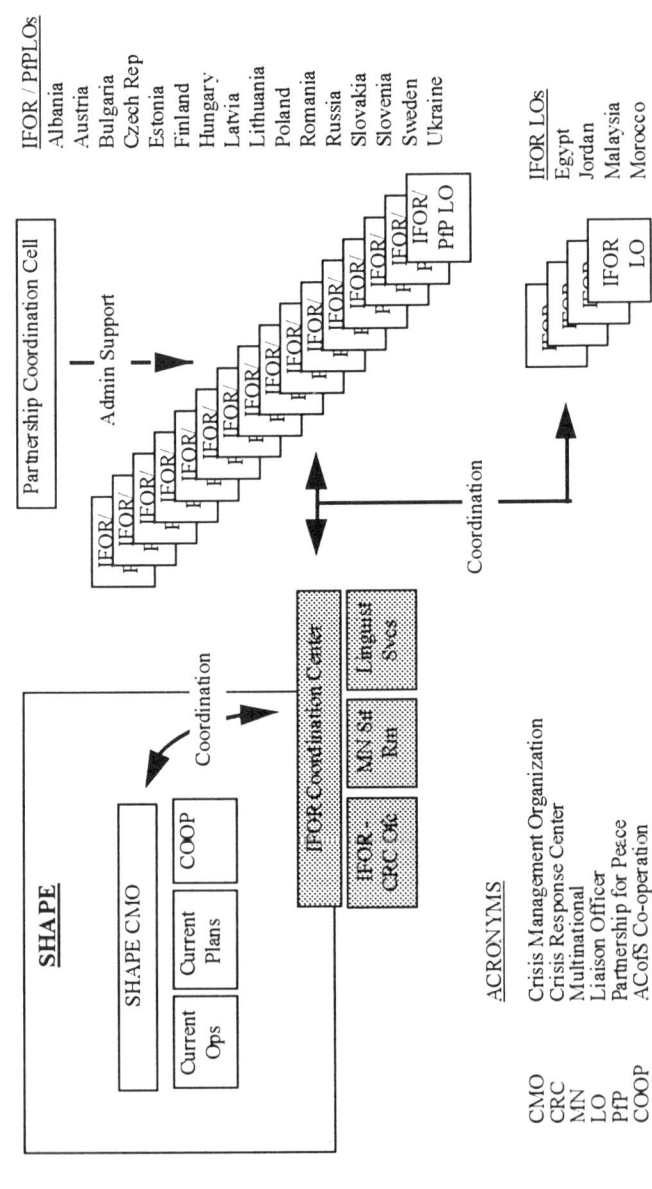

Command and Control Structure 41

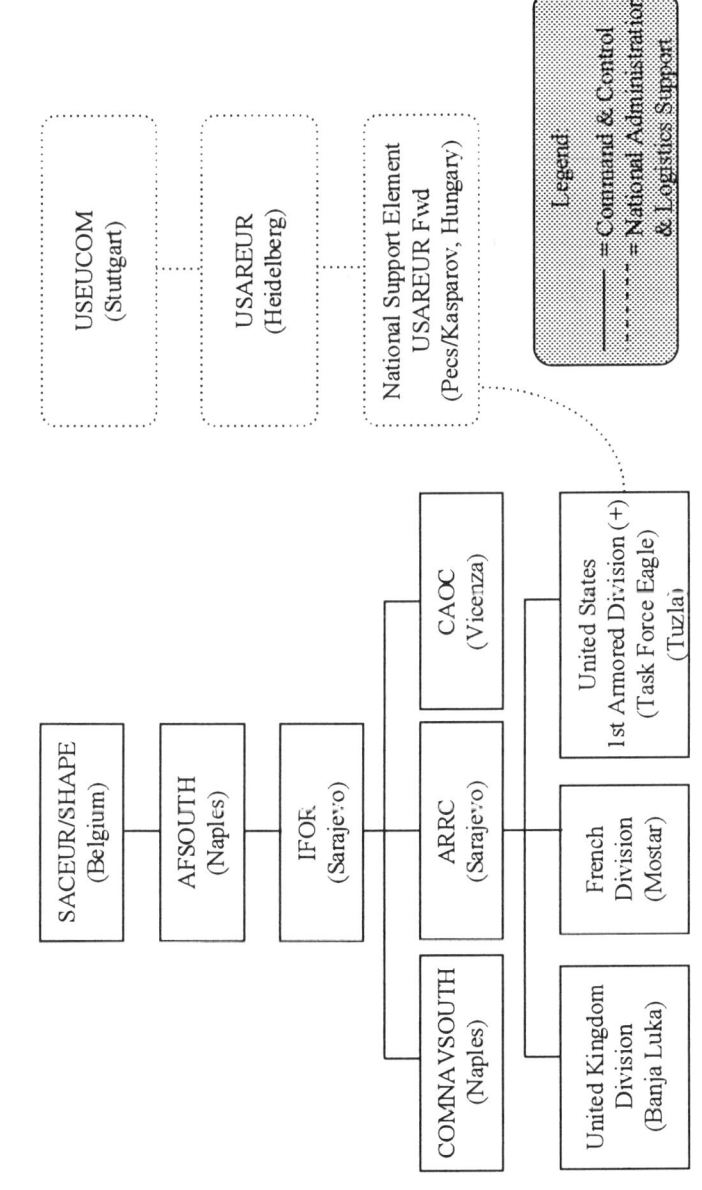

Figure 3-3. NATO Task Force Organization

Enforcement, however, being the most demanding non-Article V mission and entailing the possibility of combat, would require OPCOM. IFOR's mission under Chapter VII of the UN Charter is Peace Enforcement. Furthermore, it is anticipated that the current definitions of NATO command levels such as OPCOM, OPCON, TACOM (tactical command), and TACON (tactical control) may be part of the problem and will have to be investigated and discussed in this context.

Although COMIFOR exercised OPCON over assigned forces, it is estimated that there may have been as many as 10,000 other forces in theater area under national C2, including national support elements in Croatia and Hungary, naval forces operating in the Adriatic under national OPCON, UN Forces in Croatia and Macedonia, and forces pending TOA. Without TACON as a minimum, COMIFOR had no control over these forces and could only coordinate their activities. Although these conditions caused no serious incidents, an operational emergency could have created problems with ROE and force protection. In addition, COMIFOR needed at least TACON to manage any redeployment of forces until they are out of theater. It is also a fact that there was no operational reserve force available for the IFOR phase of the operation. U.S. Marines were stationed afloat and occasionally in the region, however if needed it would have taken days to have them in place to respond in an operational crisis.

There were also some shortfalls in the U.S.-related command arrangements. Most significant was that the command relationships between NATO authorities, USCINCEUR, and USAREUR were not well defined, which led to inefficiencies and confusion. At the center of this issue was how the Army (Component) fulfills its Title 10 responsibilities. The root cause of the problem was the absence of a U.S. JTF command equivalent that had the authority, expertise, and staffing to properly provide U.S. C2 and coordinated logistics for out-of-sector U.S. service members. In accordance with National Security Decision Directive 130, the U.S. PSYOP forces were not placed under IFOR C2. These forces remained under USEUCOM control. This caused some problems in the product coordination and approval process and inhibited flexible use of PSYOP elements at the tactical level. Another significant C2 shortfall was inadequate early coordination with humanitarian organizations, particularly non-governmental organizations (NGOs).

Special Arrangements

Because of the unique nature of this operation, some of the IFOR C2 relationships required special arrangements. For example, a special agreement was established between the U.S. Secretary of Defense, William Perry, and the Russian Minister of Defense, Pavel Grachev, for the employment of Russian forces in IFOR. Coordination that began in October 1995 between SACEUR and General Grachev produced an agreed option for the employment of Russian forces in IFOR, whereby SACEUR has overall control of the Russian brigade through the Deputy Commander for Russian forces, Colonel General Shevtsov. COMARRC exercised TACON of the brigade through the Commander MND(N), in whose area the brigade operates. OPCON remained with the Russian chain of command, with MG Nash having tactical control over the forces. Figure 3-4 depicts the current command arrangement between the SACEUR and Russian forces assigned to MND(N). As with the other politically dominated C2 structures, this one would be problematic under stress, particularly if new missions were required. Operationally, U.S. and Russian forces had to go through an interpretive process to get orders from the MND(N) to the Russian brigade and the same coming back to MND(N). The arrangements did, however, initiate military cooperation between Russian and NATO forces.

Figure 3-4. IFOR C2 for Russian Forces

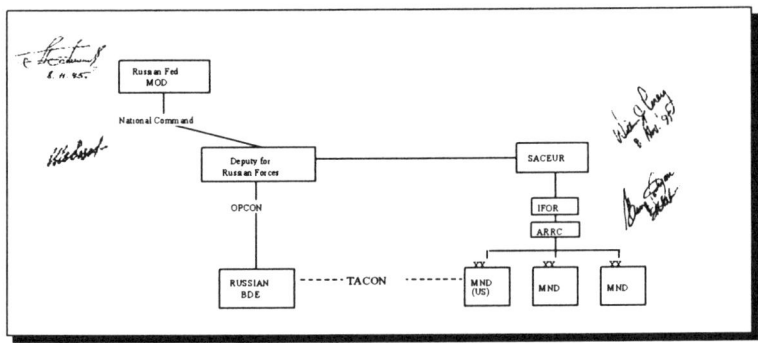

Putting the IFOR C2 Structure Together

The integration of 14 PfP nations and 4 other non-NATO nations under NATO C2 has been a major success due to experience from the PfP Program and innovative C2 arrangements at several levels (see figure 3-5). For example, national offices were brought into multinational HQs and senior national officers were "dual hatted" as deputy commanders as practiced in the Nordic-Polish brigade. At the political level, non-NATO nations have been acquainted with NATO's consultation process in NAC(+), expanding NATO process, and the Senior Political Committee (Reinforced) meetings. The Ad Hoc Planning and Coordination Group at NATO HQ has facilitated military planning and coordination, especially during force planning.

IFOR established a Joint Military Commission (JMC) as the central body for commanders of military factions to coordinate and resolve problems. Two or more FWF military representatives (usually commanders) attended meetings under IFOR supervision

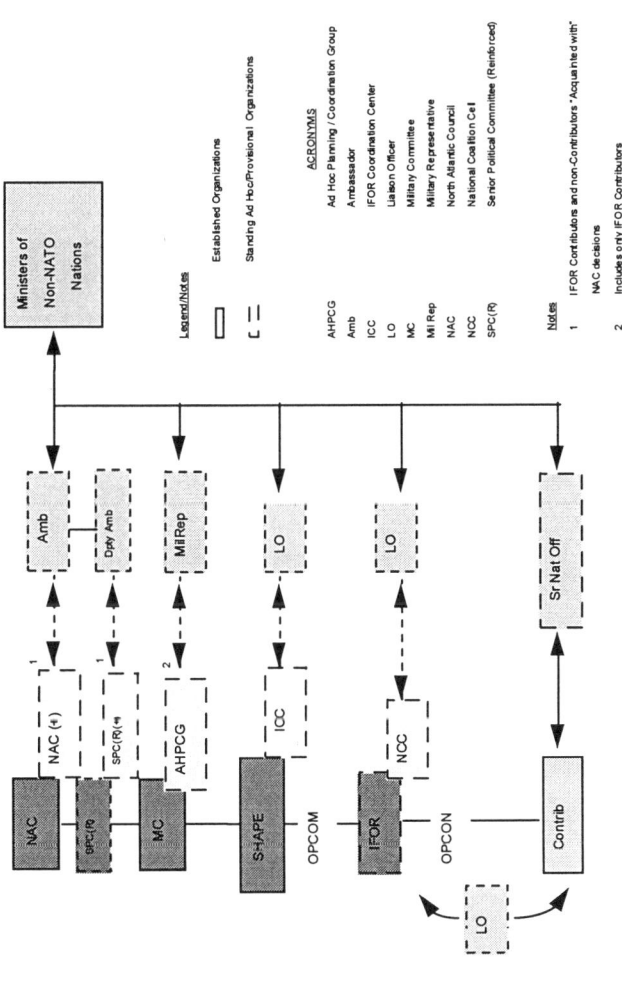

Figure 3-5. Integration of Non-NATO Contributors to IFOR

to coordinate joint activities, disseminate intent and instructions, and resolve differences. COMIFOR delegated routine JMC chairmanship to COMARRC who issued instructions to ensure the parties' compliance with the military aspects of the GFAP. Below the COMARRC level, the MNDs, their subordinate brigades, and battalions established subordinate military commissions. At these lower levels, the JMC activities included disseminating policy, issuing instructions to factions on policies and procedures, coordinating GFAP-required actions, resolving military complaints or questions, coordinating civil-military actions where appropriate, and developing confidence-building measures between the parties.

The command arrangements at the outset of IFOR operations for the Public Information Office (PIO), PSYOPS and CIMIC operations, and some aspects of the Intelligence operations (e.g., counter intelligence) also required innovative adjustments to effectively integrate them into the overall IFOR command structure and operation. OPLAN 40105 called for PIO and coalition press and information centers with each of the major IFOR headquarters. In Sarajevo, IFOR and the ARRC decided to share a single press center located in the Holiday Inn, but this caused confusion in the chain of command—dual command relationship and sometimes conflicting guidance. At the multinational divisions, the commanders preferred to bring their own national PI assets to run the PI program and this too introduced some confusion into the IFOR PI operation—conflicting IFOR and national doctrine, procedures, and guidance on the nature and amount of information to be released to the media.

The CIMIC and PSYOPS operations also suffered command and control problems. The activities of the units deployed to the multinational divisions were managed and controlled from the headquarters operations in Sarajevo, which caused operational problems for the local tactical commanders to which the units were attached. Finally, it was important that the activities of the PIO, CIMIC, and PSYOPS be carefully coordinated, while at the same time preserving the objectivity of the PI and CIMIC activities. A number of different coordinating mechanisms were used by IFOR, the ARRC, and the MNDs to accomplish this both internally and externally.

The ARRC's basic structure of MNDs, brigades, battalions, and corps troops has proved effective for the integration of national forces into multinational formations. While these structures are basic in the UK and U.S. framework divisions, the French Division (MND(SE)) normally operates with regiments. In recognition of its integration requirements, the French re-organized into brigades and battalions to facilitate the incorporation of battalions and brigades from other nations. To date this has been effective.

The U.S. SOF established a Special Forces operating base in San Vito, Italy, and a forward operating base in Sarajevo under IFOR. Liaison control elements were assigned to coalition and NATO units to integrate intelligence, operations, communications, close air support, and medical evacuation. SOF also helped survey and monitor the zone of separation, supported civil-military activities, and provided liaisons with the FWF. Commander, Special Operations Command Europe (also Commander, Special Operations Forces, IFOR) assumed OPCON of all SOF elements in support of *Operation Joint Endeavor* except for SOF afloat, PSYOP, and CA forces. U.S. PSYOP forces remained under USEUCOM command and control and CA forces under USAREUR command. As noted earlier, the command relationships of the U.S. PSYOP and CA forces were not clearly defined at the outset of the operation and this caused problems for the deployed forces. There was a Combined Joint Special Forces Operations Task Force located in Sarajevo which the U.S., UK, and France SOF elements supported. The United Kingdom and France also had their own national SOF units supporting MND(SW) and MND(SE) respectively.

The maritime and air operations were run through COMNAVSOUTH, COMSTRIKFORSOUTH, and COMAIRSOUTH (see figures 3-6 and 3-7). Maritime forces operating in the Adriatic are subject to political constraints that were in conflict with the principle of unity of command. The peacetime command structure of AFSOUTH with two maritime PSCs pro-

48 Lessons from Bosnia

Figure 3-6. Maritime Component Commands

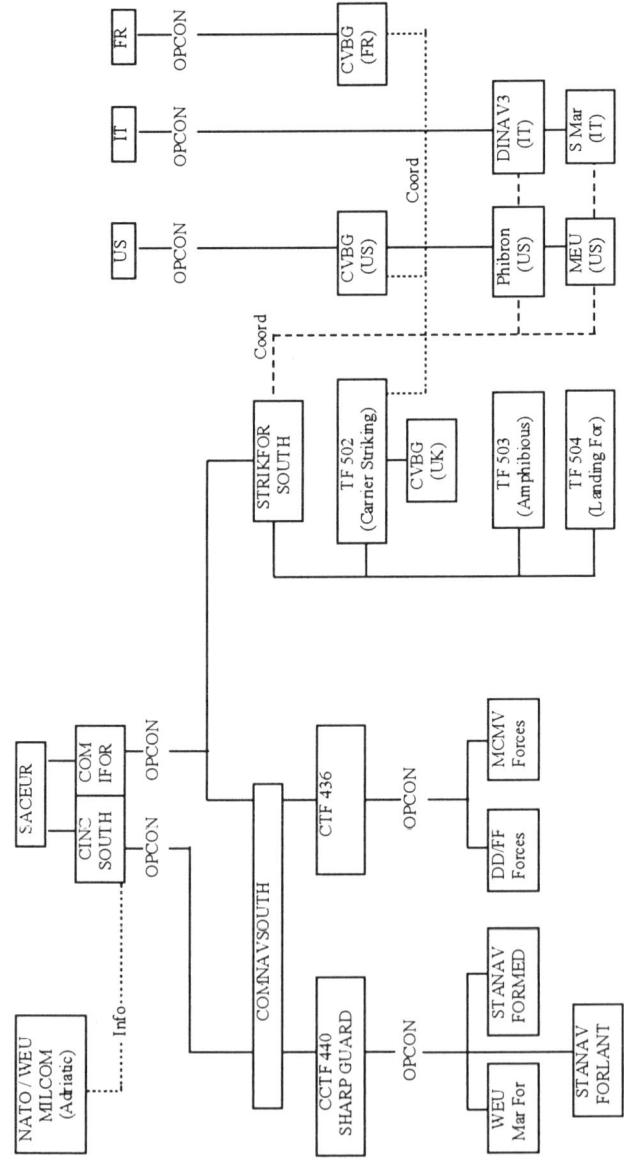

Figure 3-7. IFOR Air Component C2 Structure

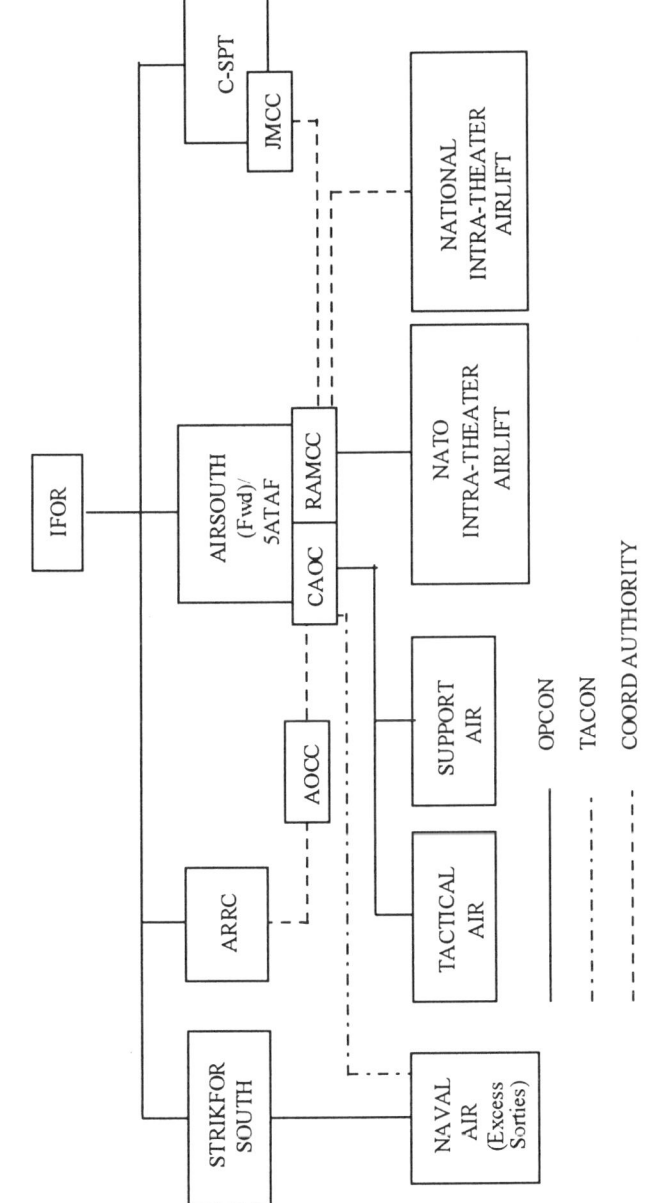

vides flexibility in accomplishing a wide range of maritime tasks in a large maritime region. However, under IFOR conditions and limited to the Adriatic only, it was assessed by AFSOUTH that current maritime tasks could be accomplished by a single NATO Task Force/ NATO Expanded Task Force in accordance with NATO's concept of Multinational Maritime Forces (MNMFs). Despite the limited degree of integration, however, effective coordination between the parties involved as provided unity of effort in this low-threat maritime environment and has supported IFOR operations well. Naval forces currently operating in the Adriatic under NATO and national OPCON have achieved interoperability through common NATO tactical and procedural standards.

Command of air operations has been achieved by designating the IFOR Air Component Commander as the Joint Force Air Component Commander (JFACC). A single layer C2 structure was established at the Combined Air Operations Center (CAOC) in Vicenza, and was responsible for the entire air effort, simplifying the C2 for air operations. The air tasking process draws together all the different tasking requirements and unifies them in a single order, the Air Tasking Message. The IFOR Air Component Commander and JFACC, with comprehensive authority from COMIFOR, exercises command, control, and coordination authority for airspace, air operations, and air forces operating throughout the Air Tactical Area of Operations.

An IFOR Commander for Support (C-SPT) was established in Zagreb, Croatia. His responsibilities included coordinating the sustainment, movements, medical, engineering, and contracting operations of the national logistic elements; and commanding selected IFOR units in support of the deployment, execution of peace implementation, and redeployment of IFOR. C-SPT was also designated as the single point of contact for all IFOR matters pertaining to relations with the Croatian government. The NATO Maintenance and Supply Agency (NAMSA) established a field office in Split, Croatia. They were responsible for all NATO common-funded contracting and contracting for all scarce resources in theater. They provided liaisons with C-SPT and the framework division headquarters. NAMSA headquarters in Luxembourg held all contracts for the theater. The ARRC COSCOM commander was designated the COMMZ Forward Commander and was located in Split, Croatia, as well. He was responsible for reporting movement into theater to C-SPT. Finally, three National Support Elements were established to support the framework nations' movement activities: the United States in Kaposvar, Hungary, the British in Split, Croatia, and the French in Ploce, Croatia.

All troop-contributing nations used the national logistics stove-pipes to support their forces in Bosnia. The lead nations, also known as framework divisions, were assigned the responsibility for coordinating support for the various multinational brigades and battalions assigned to work in their sector. C-SPT was also assigned the responsibility to serve as CINCIFOR's logistics commander. C-SPT set up the roles of the Engineer Coordination Center (ENGCC), the Joint Logistics Operations Center (JLOC), the Joint Movement Control Center (JMCC), the Medical Coordination Center (MEDCC), and the Theater Contracting Coordination Center (KCC). C-SPT is a positive way in which to address multinational logistics.

Some Future Considerations

There are some lessons to be learned from the deployment to Bosnia from a command and control structure viewpoint:

- NATO should have defined the operation from the beginning in both civilian and military contexts.

- ROE should have been set at the NATO level, not just at the national level, for the operation.

- The designation of a contingency reserve forces should have been set in the initial planning stages.

- The ARRC should have had OPCOM and OPCON for the operation.

- NATO needs to redefine its command and control arrangements (OPCOM, OPCON, and TACOM).

- Potential confusion and conflict between missions may result when national forces (U.S. Title 10) requirements conflict with NATO OPCON direction (force protection for an example).

IFOR Headquarters (Sarajevo)

IV. Intelligence Operations[15]
Larry K. Wentz

Introduction[16]

Intelligence is one of the hardest things to share in a coalition environment. Each partner, no matter how dedicated to the general cause, has a natural tendency to mask his intelligence capabilities and to retain control of what tasks he performs and how his products are disseminated. Furthermore, there are differences in national doctrine and disclosure rules. For IFOR, there was some confusion as to roles and responsibilities and duplication of effort. In spite of this, the coalition members were willing to cooperate and share information. The nations shared intelligence to a remarkable degree and certainly beyond most expectations.

The intelligence setting for *Operation Joint Endeavor* was Bosnia-Herzegovina, Hungary, Croatia, Serbia, and parts of the Central European Region. IFOR and the nations had one eye on the military activity of the former warring factions (FWF) and the other on potential disruptions to civil order. Intelligence had to cast a wide net, far beyond the theater of operation, to grasp the influences in the area. For the United States, as a global power with vital interests outside of the NATO area, this was an operation of worldwide proportion and implications.

Operation Joint Endeavor, probably more clearly than any other recent operation, showcased the strategic, theater (operational), and tactical levels of intelligence operating in joint and combined roles. Additionally for the United States, the interagency (DIA (Defense Intelligence Agency), CIA (Central Intelligence Agency), NSA (National Security Agency), DOS (Department of State), and others) role was highlighted as well.

The nature of the operation muddled any clear division among the strategic, theater, and tactical levels. At the tactical level, the deployed functional units contributed to the reconnaissance and surveillance plans, to the intelligence reporting process, and to the synthesis of information that painted the picture for the commanders. Tactical commanders at the brigade and battalion levels needed access to political intelligence and so-called "strategic intelligence" in order to make some sense of the big picture to meet their locally focused peace operations responsibilities. As a result, "total mission awareness" had to be pushed to much lower levels than for conventional operations. The United States as a global power needed flexibility to deal with a broader set of strategic intelligence requirements and implications. The theater and tactical commanders needed help to reduce battlefield uncertainty related to peace operations and to adapt warfighting-oriented capabilities to meet some of the unexpected peace operation requirements. The national (strategic) and theater levels of the intelligence community gave priority attention to the intelligence gaps, stepped into the area of operation with specially equipped forward support teams, and designed and fitted "purpose-built" collection systems to exploit the non-lethal environment.

The core requirement of IFOR was to monitor the military situation and the Dayton Accord compliance-related activities. In the coalition peace operation environment of *Operation Joint Endeavor*, this also included extensive interaction with indigenous populations and non-military organizations, such as the NGOs, PVOs, and IOs. These organizations have representatives in country before the military arrive, while the military are present, and after the military leave. They are important players that the military needs to be prepared to deal with in peace operations.

Exploiting intelligence capabilities across service and agency boundaries and enhanced sharing of information among echelons of command, NATO and the participating coalition partners also became essential to meet mission needs. Yet, missing from most off-the-shelf intelligence doctrines, plans, tactics, techniques, and procedures were the multi-service/agency and multinational dimensions for operating in a coalition peace support environment.

During the Cold War, NATO and national intelligence capabilities were designed and deployed to collect against known Warsaw Pact military capabilities; soldiers were trained to predict enemy maneuver, objectives, and courses of action. The national intelligence systems were organized, staffed, and equipped for sensor-to-shooter targeting with go-to-war, mobile tactical assets.

The end of the Cold War brought a change in the types of operations the national military forces of NATO were planning for, training for, and being asked to support. There was much more emphasis on support to peace operations and this was forcing a concurrent change in intelligence support activities.

Warfighting and peace operations require different skill sets. Equipped to function in a tactical fight, NATO and the national tactical forces were less prepared to function in a peace support role. The *Operation Joint Endeavor* challenge was to transform an intelligence structure that could monitor tactical military capabilities into one that provided current and predictive intelligence of intentions in a non-lethal, coalition peace operation environment.

The Mission

The theater intelligence mission was to—

- develop and coordinate plans, policy, procedures, and organizations for collecting, producing, and issuing military intelligence, and for conducting counterintelligence activities required for the security of the command;

- develop and provide intelligence to counter the threat to IFOR personnel and activities from subversion, espionage, sabotage, and terrorism;

- warn the COMIFOR and subordinate commanders of imminent hostilities;

- develop and monitor intelligence of military-political events affecting the IFOR area of responsibility; and

- provide guidance and oversight for liaison between IFOR and other intelligence and security agencies and operations.

The first challenge facing IFOR was to understand the intentions of the FWF and determine their resolve to use military force. A second challenge was integrating the NATO and national intelligence doctrines, capabilities, and procedures into the *Operation Joint Endeavor* environment and the IFOR structure.

Making a Difference

Bosnia was more peaceful than expected. There were few overt physical attacks on IFOR facilities and personnel. The FWF were generally in compliance (but continuously testing IFOR resolve) with the General Framework Agreement for Peace (GFAP). One must be reminded, however, that the situation could have changed for the worse at a moment's notice.

Upon arrival in country, IFOR made it very clear to the FWF at the outset that they were different than UNPROFOR and were there to enforce compliance with the Dayton Accord, using force if necessary. Checkpoints were bulldozed, roadblocks were shut down, and the FWF equipment and forces placed in cantonment areas and barracks. On 19 February 1996, COMIFOR held a meeting of the Joint Military Commission on board the USS *George Washington* aircraft carrier. COMIFOR stated that the reason for having the meeting on board the "Spirit of Freedom" was to give the leaders of the FWF a display of the firepower the United States was prepared to use in the enforcement of the Dayton Peace Accord. IFOR's tremendous military firepower was certainly a major deterrent but the military also put a lot of faith in the deterrent power of "information dominance." IFOR, through its intelligence operation (supported by significant national contributions, especially from the United States), was able to make it clear to the FWF that they could monitor them any time of the day or night and under all weather conditions. The ability to see, understand the situation, and strike with precision no doubt had its effect in deterring aggressive actions on the part of the FWF and maintaining the peace during the IFOR operation.

Violations were experienced from time to time: weapons discovered in unauthorized locations, soldiers and tanks in the Zone of Separation, and unauthorized police checkpoints. Such violations were detected by the IFOR intelligence operation, and swift actions were taken when the FWF tested IFOR's resolve. The intelligence operation was an IFOR success story. In spite of remarkable challenges, it was a powerful tool that helped IFOR successfully monitor FWF activities and get the message to the FWF and the local population that IFOR was there to make a difference.

Threat Environment

Although Bosnia was more peaceful than expected, the threats were real. The three FWF not only possessed combat power but also had a robust intelligence collection capability. In the case of the Serbs, there was an active information campaign targeted against NATO, member NATO nations, and IFOR. The Karadzic regime was extremely well organized and had a seamless military-political-media continuum. They were the home team, spoke the home language to the home culture, and had an internal security system that could apply thuggery to keep people in line if all else failed.

There were land mines everywhere, snipers, and the possibilities of civil disturbances. Terrorists, organized crime, and petty criminals were also considered in the threat picture. Local civilians were hired as linguists, cooks, maids, handymen, electricians, and carpenters and their activities needed to be monitored.

The local, national, and ethnic media were well established and generally trusted. The population of Bosnia was to a large extent literate and relatively well educated and used to all forms of media that characterizes an "information society." There were of course exceptions such as Gorazde, an isolated Muslim-dominated enclave where the population had little access to the news media and the outside world. The international, national, and local television, radio, and print journalists were everywhere questioning soldiers and reporting on events as they occurred. Finally, some of the toughest terrain in the world and formidable weather conditions posed a significant challenge to mobility and everyday survival of the intelligence operations and collection efforts.

Intelligence Operating Environment

The Bosnia operating environment was marked by large areas of operation and interest and difficult terrain and weather conditions. There were multiple belligerent factions and a "front line" that was 360 degrees. There were a large number of consumers and a wide spectrum of threats and intelligence requirements to accommodate. The operation had to adapt to differences in NATO and national methodologies and procedures. Force protection measures and the constant threat of land mines forced an adaptation of normal operating procedures. The operation had to monitor a wide spectrum of threats including the FWF, criminal activities, extremists, civil disturbances, and terrorism. FWF equipment storage sites and barracks, the Zone of Separation, mass gravesites, and potential "hot spots" caused by freedom of movement, resettlement, and inter-ethnic conflicts had to be monitored as well.

Intelligence planning dovetailed with operations planning. Yet, several uncontrollable factors shaped the intelligence planning effort: troop end strength (force caps), pre-deployment reconnaissance constraints, IFOR and national command structures, simultaneously developed plans, and the intelligence capabilities peculiar to participating nations. These factors established the conditions within which intelligence plans and relationships were developed.

Forces were tailored to ensure that factional hostilities could be predicted and force protection measures could be implemented. The troop end strength of 20,000 U.S. soldiers affected the augmentation of intelligence units and cells from outside the command. Any time new units or personnel were added to the force, an equal number of personnel had to be removed. With the United States planning to deploy a division MI battalion, a corps MI brigade, half of an echelons above corps (EAC) intelligence group, and one-third of the DCSINT staff, augmentation would be necessarily limited.

Before deployment, only one military reconnaissance of Bosnia was authorized. This drove intelligence planning in directed ways. Requirements increased, and became urgent, for overhead imagery of base camp locations, routes, bridges, and staging areas. When the reconnaissance ban was lifted and hasty reconnaissance commenced, it was clear that overhead imagery did not tell the whole story.

The near-simultaneous publishing of the SACEUR OPLAN, AFSOUTH campaign plan, and ARRC OPLAN only broadly addressed intelligence reporting procedures, information-sharing techniques, and national intelligence responsibilities required to understand and operate in the multinational environment.

National intelligence support plans were closely held and therefore it was not clear to IFOR and others what nations would bring what capabilities in terms of intelligence systems to support IFOR requirements. USAREUR planning had to take into consideration the known intelligence strengths and weaknesses of the *Operation Joint Endeavor* partners to plan its support arrangements. For instance the U.S. technical prowess in satellite imagery, intelligence electronic warfare adaptability, and rapid processing capabilities needed to be balanced with the HUMINT (human intelligence) expertise of the United Kingdom and France. There was a planning concern of several of the nations that the U.S. technical capabilities, with its downlinks, high-speed processors, specialized communications, and specialized manning, would overshadow the allies and their intelligence methods. The extent to which nations would be willing to share information with NATO and coalition partners was also unclear.

Peace Operations Requirements Differ

Intelligence requirements in Bosnia varied depending upon the phase of the operation but consistently required expertise in military, political, cultural, and economic issue areas. The information environment was complex and consisted of numerous, nontraditional sources. The major challenge was leveraging information from these sources, which were as varied as public affairs, civil affairs, PSYOP, military police, political advisors, UN organizations, the IPTF (International Police Task Force), IOs, NGOs, PVOs, joint commissions, government agencies, intelligence organizations, and even the commercial Internet. Interestingly enough, these sources were also consumers of information and intelligence. Hence, the cumulative information and intelligence requirements were tremendous and difficult to anticipate. In addition to traditional databases, non-traditional databases needed to be developed to address the varied needs such as police checkpoints, storage sites, license plates, personalities, treaty compliance, site declarations, mass gravesites, ethnicity, and others. The databases therefore had to be flexible enough to quickly respond to requirements from the commanders as well as a wide range of other consumers.

Analytical efforts differed as well. It was difficult to collect and exploit the full range of information, identify indicators, and provide predictive analysis. The analysts were trained for hard targeting-based analysis supporting military courses of action; they were not as well prepared for "softer" analysis of political issues, treaty compliance, civil unrest, vigilante activities, election support, refugee movements, and faction and population intentions. Since soft analysis was more challenging and difficult, there was a tendency to be more reactive and analyze what happened rather than predict what might happen. In retrospect, indicators of events were often there—the challenge was developing the expertise to recognize them and then using these insights to influence outcomes. This placed high demands on intellectual and analytical flexibility.

During *Operation Joint Endeavor*, military interaction with civilian organizations was more than civil-military cooperation. Civilian agencies (i.e., NGOs, PVOs, and IOs) had developed a network of influential contacts, compiled historical and specialty archives, and established relationships with local leaders and business people. They understood the infrastructure of the region, and the political and economic influences. Identification of the civilian organization strengths, limitations, and vulnerabilities were intelligence requirements. These same civilian agencies and centers of operation were sources of intelligence information as well. Intelligence requirements for civilian organizations were stated in collection plans. The IFOR system of civil affairs liaison officers (LNO) proved particularly well suited to interact with these organizations. The UNIPTF, which had some 1,600 members throughout Bosnia, provided its daily situation reports to COMIFOR through the IPTF LNO. These reports covered freedom of movement violations, human rights violations, and other incidents.

Some Early and Interesting Challenges

The U.S. Joint Pub 2-0, *Joint Doctrine for Intelligence Support to Operations*, states, "There is no single intelligence doctrine for multinational operations. Each coalition or alliance must develop its own doctrine." NATO intelligence doctrine states, "In peacetime, NATO commanders have to rely largely on Member Nations for the intelligence they need. In wartime, the majority of NATO commanders' intelligence may still come from the member nations; however, they will also acquire intelligence from many different sources and agencies such as assigned combat units, reconnaissance units, and aircraft." The U.S. Army FM 100-23 states, "Peace operations take place in environments less well-defined than war....the traditional elements of combat power may not apply....the political and cultural dimensions become more critical....the needs of the commander involved in peace operations are in some ways more complex than those of the commander conducting combat operations."

At the outset of *Operation Joint Endeavor*, the first task was to separate the FWF by no later than D+30 (19 January 1996) and create a "Zone of Separation" (ZOS). The ZOS was 4 km wide, 2 km on either side of the Agreed Cease-Fire Line (ACFL). The ACFL was the line where the fighting stopped. The aggressive timeline to get the FWF personnel and equipment out of the ZOS created a number of challenges. For example, the required U.S. ground forces to reconnoiter the ZOS in MND(N) would not be fully deployed until early February 1996. The mine hazards made ground reconnaissance difficult and the weather in late December 1995 and early January 1996 limited use of ground reconnaissance and airborne theater imagery platforms. Because of these factors, organic U.S. helicopter assets (the AH-64s) were used to reconnoiter the ZOS in MND(N).

The second most important mission was ensuring that the FWF placed all units and equipment (based on D+90 FWF declarations) in designated barracks and cantonment areas by D+120 (17 April 1996). This too presented some interesting intelligence challenges related to approving/disapproving FWF declarations, especially when the ARRC, which was dissatisfied with the D+90 declarations, levied a requirement for the FWF to re-declare barracks and cantonment sites at D+120. In addition to initial problems associated with translating the original FWF data and removing inconsistencies, it became necessary to scrub databases to eliminate duplicate records as well. There were often multiple declarations at a single site, e.g., three separate declarations for three separate warehouses all on the same compound. The divisions also had some problems interpreting the ARRC guidance, regarding FWF unit and artillery consolidation, so the ARRC's envisioned end-state was unclear and frustrated Division Intelligence Preparation of the Battlefield (IPB) development. The U.S. approach to verification in MND(N) was to assume that what was declared by the FWF was there and to go look for equipment that was not there. The British and French approach in MND(SW) and MND(SE) respectively was to go verify that what the FWF said was there was in fact there. As a result, the U.S. verification efforts were much more intensive and demanding.

Although the ACFL was where the fighting stopped, it was not the final division of territory between the entities established under the GFAP. Rather, the IEBL was the line that the parties in Dayton agreed to as the boundary between them. The IEBL came into effect at D+45, replacing the ACFL ZOS. In many cases, the IEBL and the ACFL were one in the same but there were also those cases where they were not. An area of transfer (AOT) from one FWF to another occurred in these cases. This created additional challenges since some villages now fell either in an AOT or on the IEBL creating potential "hot spots." It was necessary to determine the ethnic majority of these villages. In some cases the villages fell on the wrong side of the IEBL (e.g., Muslims in Serb territory). Although HUMINT was the ideal way to verify, the shear number of villages precluded doing this.

Another challenge arose in late January 1996 when de-mobilized soldiers began entering the local police forces in large numbers. Not surprisingly, IFOR began to notice an increase in the number of police checkpoints, particularly along sensitive areas of the ZOS. The police restricted civilian freedom of movement in many areas and often carried weapons. In short, they were "skirting" the provisions of the GFAP by transferring soldiers to local police forces. In response to this action, the ARRC issued specific guidance to the FWF regarding "legitimate" police forces and activities. The ARRC also provided guidance to the MNDs to close unauthorized police checkpoints. In response to the ARRC guidance, the divisions established police checkpoint databases and initiated monitoring and reporting activities.

The diverse languages in the Balkans region (see figure 4-1) proved to be a real challenge for IFOR and the participating nations. For example, the U.S. military did not have enough trained linguists for the theater. USAREUR had to fill a large number of linguist requirements to provide translators for the battalions and brigades of the U.S.-led MND(N) and for the intelligence positions in U.S. military intelligence (MI) units. As in *Operation Desert Storm*, the United States relied on contracting local nationals for a majority of its linguist support. Military linguists were primarily saved for those positions requiring access to classified or otherwise sensitive information. The relationships among the FWF complicated the hire of local nationals in Bosnia. A native speaking Muslim was not necessarily able to function effectively in a Serb or Croat enclave. In addition, most native linguists had little or no background in the military and therefore had difficulties in translating military "lingo."

A contract for linguist support was awarded to BDM Corporation on 10 December 1995. BDM provided linguist contractor support for operations in Haiti, Somalia, and southwest Asia. BDM hired U.S. linguists and native linguists. The contract eventually supplied a sufficient number of native speakers with English capability to allow U.S. units to conduct operations. However, no distinctions were made as to the level of English proficiency required. Native speaking linguists were hired though less qualified speakers would have been sufficient and considerably cheaper for many positions. BDM contracted a total of 57 U.S. linguists and 439 native linguists for a cost of $13 million. Costs included billeting, transportation, and management.

In some areas, such as those occupied by the Serbs, an information campaign targeted against NATO was already in full operation when the IFOR troops arrived. Hence, the IFOR Information Campaign (IIC) was at a disadvantage at the outset because it had to compete immediately with an already established and effective campaign that could get inside of the IFOR decision loop and outmaneuver some of the initial IFOR efforts. IFOR also had some problems adapting to the local population's media consumption habits. While IFOR relied primarily on printed material (*The*

Figure 4-1. Languages in the Balkans Region

Herald of Peace, posters, and handbills) and AM radio to start with, the Bosnians' preferred medium was television. Also, IFOR radio transmitted on AM and the Bosnians listened mostly to FM radios. Adjustments were made to accommodate other media forms such as FM radio and television and mechanisms were also put in place to achieve IIC integrated product development. The PSYOP capability Commando Solo (an EC-130 aircraft configured for radio and television broadcasting) was not, however, deployed during the IFOR portion of the operation. It was deployed in the September 1997 time frame to support SFOR activities related to the Bosnia elections. A Combined Joint IFOR Information Campaign Task Force was established to coordinate the activities of Public Affairs, Civil Affairs, PSYOP, International Organizations (e.g., UN-IPTF, UNHCR, OSCE, OHR, and others), and IFOR command elements. They also orchestrated the IIC for IFOR.

The IIC proved to be a difficult task and the jury is still out on its overall success for the IFOR operation. It was certainly a success during the first 9 months of the operation in support of force protection and military compliance activities (transfer of AOTs and placing heavy weapons in cantonment areas). LTG Mike Walker, UKA, Commander ARRC, said, "the IIC was an unqualified success during military compliance activities (D+3 through D+120) and in support of the September 1996 National elections." There were also some successes against the Serbs, e.g., the use of war criminal awareness posters and the destruction of 252 tons of Bosnian Serb munitions (*Operation Volcano*). Information was used effectively by the IFOR commanders as a non-lethal weapon to communicate intentions, might, and resolve to the local population and FWF.

The use of maps was another unanticipated issue area. The Yugoslav maps used a local grid coordinate system and there was no system for converting them into UTM coordinates. Interpolating grid coordinates caused compliance verification problems when exchanging information with the factions, so in the end the FWF were provided WGS-84 UTM maps, taught how to use them, and then required to use them for compliance discussions.

Operational Security (OPSEC) was particularly challenging for the IFOR operation. The operational environment was reasonably stable for Bosnia. However, the lack of an obvious threat bred a sense of complacency, which is a threat in and of itself. Other types of OPSEC risks had to be managed as well. There were numerous television and print journalists questioning soldiers, and the soldiers had to be briefed to ensure they did not release classified information to the media. Every day, hundreds of local national workers entered IFOR areas of operation. It was a challenge to keep a close eye on these daily visitors. OPSEC is an operations function, not a security function per se. Therefore, there must be a proponent for OPSEC functions and the functions must be integrated into the planning and execution of the operation.

COMSEC and INFOSEC issues had to be dealt with as well. Although the military communications and information systems operated SECRET system-high, other systems were not secure. The UN VSAT network, the Internet, INMARSAT, cellular, and commercial PTT telephone systems were not protected and were used frequently for command and control purposes. Configuration management and information protection measures (e.g., virus protection and intrusion detection and protection) were slow in implementation. Diskettes were shared between classified and unclassified systems and there was a lack of discipline and standard operating procedures to effectively control the situation. There was a lack of security devices such as secure telephones, safes, and shredders. Security was an ongoing responsibility for which improvements were continuously made over the duration of the operation.

Making it Happen

The U.S. intelligence effort in support of *Operation Joint Endeavor* was massive. The national, theater, and tactical intelligence, surveillance, and reconnaissance assets included aerial systems (manned and unmanned), surface systems, and satellite systems. The most responsive manned aerial systems were the U-2, P-3s,

JSTARS, RIVET JOINT, and the NATO E-3s (and to a lesser extent the U.S. E-2Cs). These systems could respond to changing conditions by modifying their mission while in flight. These systems had one disadvantage in that they put personnel at risk so the standoff requirements tended to limit the depth of the sensor capabilities. The unmanned aerial vehicles (UAVs) did not put personnel at risk, provided reduced detection (smaller cross-section), and supplied a broad range of collection capabilities (SIGINT, ELINT, EO, IR, and live video). Their greatest limitation was their lack of flexibility; they either needed to be pre-programmed or controlled by personnel within line of sight. Both the manned and unmanned systems were susceptible to reduced capability due to adverse weather.

The land-based assets ranged from CI/HUMINT teams to dedicated SIGINT and electronic warfare (EW) units to Special Operations Forces (SOF). CI/HUMINT and SOF were also a valuable complement to the national and theater assets in that they could verify and obtain information. The national satellite systems provided worldwide, quick-reaction coverage of areas of interest, especially remote or potentially hostile areas. Limitations include degraded imagery due to atmospheric and weather disturbances. U.S. national systems were controlled by the U.S. intelligence community and provided direct support to the National Command Authorities. Information from national systems was provided through service component Tactical Exploitation of National Capabilities Program (TENCAP) systems. The deployed National Intelligence Cells (NICs) and National Intelligence Support Teams (NIST) facilitated U.S. and IFOR command access to U.S. national information.

Two U.S. theater-level analysis centers supported the U.S. and IFOR requests for information. The USAREUR Combat Intelligence Readiness Facility (UCIRF) in Augsburg, Germany, provided multi-spectral SIGINT support and all-source intelligence access to deployed U.S. forces; maintained an IFOR threat database; and installed and maintained U.S. collection, processing, and analysis systems deployed in country. The USEUCOM Joint Analysis Center (JAC) in Molesworth, England, integrated imagery and other intelligence and inserted IFOR-releasable information into the LOCE system for broader access by authorized IFOR consumers. There was a close working relationship between the JAC and the U.S. NIC at the ARRC and with Task Force Eagle in support of MND(N). The JAC committed about 70 percent if its intelligence collection and analysis efforts to the IFOR operation. The U.S. Navy Fleet Ocean Surveillance Information Facility (FOSIF) provided maritime information to the NATO Combined Air Operations Center in Vicenza, Italy, as well.

Joint Endeavor was clearly a CI (counterintelligence) and HUMINT intensive environment. The establishment of the G2X staff officer dedicated to CI/HUMINT asset management for the MND(N) (Task Force Eagle) was an effective means to manage HUMINT collection, management, processing, and dissemination. CI/HUMINT provided invaluable support to force protection and insights into intentions and the general "pulse" of the operational environment. The force protection measures in the U.S.-controlled areas were strict and had some impact on the ability to carry out CI/HUMINT activities. Measures such as the four-vehicle convoy rule, the wearing of full battle dress, and restrictions on leaving the immediate area of operation did not permit the teams to operate to their fullest potential. An exception was ultimately granted for the CI/HUMINT teams allowing them to operate in two-vehicle convoys during the daylight hours. In spite of the freedom of movement restrictions, CI/HUMINT was one of the success stories of the operation.

The other intelligence disciplines proved important as well. SIGINT provided warning and a hedge against conventional threats. On 30 August 1996, the NATO AWACS flew its 50,000th flying hour in support of operations in the former Yugoslavia. IMINT used the full spectrum of traditional assets from hand-held to national capabilities to monitor verification sites and for the surveillance of "hot spots" and FWF compliance activities. There were also some non-traditional IMINT sources such as the Combat Camera Crew products, the AH-64 gun camera tapes, and the OH-58 cockpit tapes that proved invaluable. In addition, downlinked UAV imagery provided near real-time surveillance support. Areas such as the ZOS were mined and other areas were denied easy access from the ground; hence, the use of the advanced surveillance and reconnaissance capabilities avoided the need to put soldiers in harm's way. OSINT (open source intelligence) provided indications and warning of increased tensions in local areas, supported predictive analysis efforts, and helped focus and queue other collection efforts. The "Night Owl," which was produced by the U.S. at Camp Lukavac in MND(N), provided a daily summary of news and media commentary—a Bosnia version of the Pentagon's "Early Bird." Through its publication and use, commanders and staff were able to gain a better appreciation for the political, economic, and cultural environment. MASINT (Measurement and Signature Intelligence) was used to support treaty compliance, early warning, and force protection. The cumulative effect of the intelligence operation sent a clear signal to the FWF that IFOR was capable of knowing all and seeing all—information dominance.

Under UNPROFOR, Joint Commission Officers (JCOs) were employed to deal with the FWF and in that capacity, they formed a close working relationship with the factions. At the outset of the IFOR operation, the JCOs served as the IFOR "direct telescope" regarding FWF activities. In fact, IFOR division commanders used them in this role throughout the operation because they were the most credible source of information on the capabilities and intentions of the FWF.

U.S. Special Forces conducted operations employing a wide range of capabilities and were among the earliest to deploy into the area. Special Forces established an operating base in San Vito, Italy, and a forward operating base in Sarajevo under IFOR control. Special Forces assisted UNPROFOR, NATO, and non-NATO forces and provided liaison with non-NATO forces and the FWF. They also assisted with surveying and monitoring the demarcation line and ZOS and supported civil-military activities. The Special Forces liaison control elements assigned to NATO and coalition units supported integration of intelligence, operations, communications, close air support, and medical evacuations. The interface with NATO and non-NATO forces proved to be of great value to the IFOR operation.

For peace operations, co-opting factions' C2 may be a better strategy than destroying it. During *Operation Joint Endeavor*, it became clear that the FWF needed the ability to command and control their forces in order to be able to comply with the Dayton Accord. Therefore, actions such as jamming, electronic deception, and physical destruction were not used by IFOR.

Commanders found themselves spending a lot of time conducting diplomacy and mediation to resolve disputes and conflicts. They were able to deter violence and diffuse potential conflicts by developing a positive relationship with key FWF leaders and local community leaders. Regular visits and meetings with all parties concerned developed mutual trust and respect that became invaluable in resolving conflicts through means other than force. Insights and understandings derived from these relationships were invaluable to the overall success of the IFOR information operation.

A New Venture for All

Preparation for *Operation Joint Endeavor* engaged the intelligence community up front. An intensive U.S. IPB process made products on weather, terrain, and force protection available to the deploying forces. Other IPB products for treaty compliance, cantonment sites, weapons storage sites, and personalities were developed after initial deployment. The IPB was different in later phases of the operation as the focus changed to peace support requirements.

Tools for analyzing and exploiting the conventional combat environment were adapted for the peace environment. Intelligence forces were formed and trained. USEUCOM and the ARRC led an effort to assign responsibilities for intelligence production. The U.S. and NATO structures did not always work in harmony to de-conflict and align production efforts. The importance of identifying the right products, accomplished by designated experts, and delivered to the right customer in a timely manner is the hallmark of good IPB. However, for NATO and IFOR this became a challenge due to the unknowns associated with the first-ever peace operation and the need to establish an IFOR peace-oriented IPB process and meld it with national approaches as the operation unfolded. The mix of uneven intelligence experiences and capabilities of the participating nations was a factor as well.

USAREUR, in support of Task Force Eagle and the ARRC, developed IPBs for treaty compliance. Cantonment areas, weapons storage sites, refugees, the politics of freedom of movement, and the right to inspect sites were compliance issues that needed to be addressed. Task Force Eagle tracked ZOS violations using aggressive reconnaissance and surveillance (R&S) operations based on a thorough IPB analysis and an extensive database capability. Databases were also established and used for minefield tracking, critical event tracking, and other GFAP-related monitoring activities. As the process for putting in place democratic institutions in Bosnia took hold, the intelligence effort shifted to supporting federal and planned municipal elections. Election monitoring requirements included watching cross-border refugee migration and potential voting corruption.

The fast-paced IFOR and national planning efforts had some negative impacts on the orchestration of theater intelligence production. Several organizations, in their enthusiasm to provide useful products, ended up duplicating efforts. For instance, for the United States both the Task Force Eagle and the UCIRF produced assessments on the links between NGOs and foreign forces; and both the JAC and the USAREUR Forward Deployable Intelligence Support Element (DISE) produced pieces on political-military analysis. Likewise, while some efforts were duplicated, other critical areas fell short. For *Operation Joint Endeavor*, the roles of all the intelligence producers could have been more clearly defined. A better division of effort could have been assigned among the IFOR, ARRC, and MND players.

Link analysis, sometimes called pattern analysis, was a practical tool for supporting USAREUR Forward and Task Force Eagle. The analyses associated indicators, personalities, and contact networks, and then related activities that could point to probable future events or actions. They also helped determine force protection vulnerabilities and threats. The downside to the initial IFOR link analysis activity was that it took months to develop the field intelligence and contact network that led to the first results. Collection and analysis operations that began in January 1996 received their first products in March 1996.

During the separation of the FWFs, Task Force Eagle Analysis and Control Element used some locally developed tools to manage the sites that were approved for FWF relocation. These tools were passed to the Joint Military Commission (JMC) so that FWF could be notified which sites were approved and which were not. An example of one such tool was the method developed by Task Force Eagle for downloading information from its intelligence processing system to diskette, then uploading it into a Microsoft Office Excel spreadsheet. Because the JMC did not have direct access to the Task Force Eagle database, the ability to place selected fields of a database into a spreadsheet proved invaluable in the intelligence production activities. Everyone, including the non-NATO allies, seemed to have the Microsoft Office suite of software, so the Excel spreadsheets became a useful and effective tool for sharing information. The only drawback was that the Excel spreadsheet data could not be plotted onto a computer-generated map or graphic.

Prior to deployment, USAREUR created an all source correlation database on the U.S. All Source Analysis System (ASAS). The JAC-provided ground order of battle and equipment baseline information was not in a format that would easily auto-parse into the Army system. Hence, most of the data had to be entered manually. As a result, the analysts that deployed probably knew a lot about entering data into ASAS and less about the target environment itself since they did not have time to study it in detail. Task Force Eagle deployed with its Balkans-based military database filled with military order of battle and designed for war not peace operations. In the early phase of the operation it was fortuitous that such a database had been developed since without it, Task Force Eagle would not have had a baseline from which to direct its early reconnaissance and surveillance activities.

Relying on a Military Integrated Data System/Intelligence Database (MIDS/IDB) dump was viewed by USAREUR/Task Force Eagle intelligence staff as problematic (earlier attempts in garrison were unsuccessful) at the time and certainly not the optimal solution during deployment—ASAS databases need to be developed before deployment. The MIDS/IDB was apparently a larger issue than the IFOR operation. The general military intelligence databases maintained by the theater and national intelligence production elements (DIA, JICs, and JAC) have used an IDB data scheme for almost 10 years. The Army evidently has not yet adopted this scheme in ASAS or WARLORD.

USAREUR (Task Force Eagle elements) had planned, rehearsed, and conducted conventional operations in pre-deployment training (Mountain Shield exercises) to the point that the commanders' information requirements could be predicted. In actuality, however, information requirements for *Operation Joint Endeavor* were not so easy to predict, and information sources came from diverse elements and unanticipated sources. Pre-deployment military databases provided a snapshot of what to expect militarily, but multiple new databases became the "bread and butter" of Task Force Eagle and IFOR operations. They had license plate databases, key personality databases, environmental databases, mass grave databases, imagery target deck databases, Named Areas of Interest databases, Request for Information databases, and more. Without them, predictive analysis, mission management, and technical control would have been virtually impossible. Database management knowledge and the automation skills to manipulate information required new levels of dexterity in *Operation Joint Endeavor*. On-the-job training, discovery training (i.e., trial and error method), and contractor support became the norm for building the necessary expertise for analysis and information system operation.

The JAC maintained the U.S. theater database, a fusion of air, ground, and maritime intelligence, which was culled and disseminated to U.S. elements through the Joint Deployable Intelligence Support System (JDISS). This all-source, U.S.-only processing system was available at all U.S. intelligence nodes. The JDISS provided the primary link to the rest of the U.S. intelligence world and intelligence operations could not function without it.

The ARRC too maintained similar databases for authorized use by and appropriate distribution to IFOR, the MNDs and participating nations. The United States placed IFOR-releasable information on the LOCE server for use by the ARRC and other authorized IFOR users. The U.S. National Intelligence Cell at the ARRC also responded directly to COMARRC needs.

Several other automated systems were key to storing information and delivering timely intelligence, especially during the deployment phase. The UCIRF created and maintained the theater force protection database, called Blackbird. Force protection teams interviewed the local populace and passed information, to include digitized images, to the Blackbird database with their Theater Rapid Response Intelligence Package (TRRIP) systems. New information was passed through the Secret Internet Protocol Router Network (SIPRNET) to the INTELINK national level database. In this way, the collateral database could be shared immediately from U.S. national to tactical levels.

The ARRC inherited the UNPROFOR databases during the transfer of mission in December 1995. UNPROFOR provided some mine data but the information was not organized. Mine location data was vital for the security of the military and the population. The ARRC assigned responsibility for mine data development and archiving to the divisions. Native language speakers proved crucial for translating mine information delivered by the FWF and interpreting poorly drawn schematics. The U.S. intelligence and engineering communities coordinated responsibilities for mine and terrain databases from the start of *Operation Joint Endeavor* and were able to add to the NATO effort.

The ARRC provided GFAP compliance monitoring and reporting guidance to the divisions, monitored the overall compliance activities, and maintained a number of databases covering ground order of battle, cantonment weapons status, personalities, and other areas of interest to the ARRCs mission. They used the UK-provided THISTLE information system and NATO-provided systems such as CRONOS (with intelligence applications) for this purpose as well. The ARRC also had other capabilities such as geographic information support systems that provided maps and boundary databases. The Allied Military Intelligence Battalion (AMIB) provided human intelligence support to the ARRC as well.

The NATO CRONOS system provided several intelligence applications for use by IFOR, the ARRC, and others. Applications such as the Prototype ACE Intelligence System (PAIS), Crisis Response Prototype (CRESP), and Recognized Air Picture (RAP) were used for displaying and distributing intelligence information. These applications used information from a number of different sources.

PAIS, originally designed for use at the strategic level, was used at the theater (operational) level to view and analyze order of battle (ORBAT) information, personalities database, weapons cantonment database, and other related databases for monitoring the warring factions and related IFOR activities. The ORBAT and other monitored information were imported from LOCE, the ARRC, and other sources. Using PAIS subroutines, ORBAT information could be overlaid on a map with military symbols indicating the position of units, events, and facilities.

CRESP was used for situation monitoring and reporting and received its inputs mainly from the ARRC's THISTLE system. With the TOA to the SFOR, the CRESP evolved to be "the Operations Support System" and was used to monitor incidents, SFOR deployments, the IEBL, locations of minefields, and other areas of interest to the commander of SFOR.

The IFOR live, real-time air picture was produced at the CAOC and distributed over CRONOS to key command centers using server and workstation software developed by the SHAPE Technical Center (now the NATO C3 Agency—the Hague). A software package (ARKONA) developed by the German Air Defense Programming Center was modified to allow the RAP to be displayed on PCs as well as high-end workstations.

An Operational Analysis Branch (OAB) was an integral part of the ARRC staff. This branch had been a part of the ARRC for years and had worked and trained with the military staff. The mission of the small five-man cell was "to give independent analytical and scientific advice to the commander to aid his decision-making over the spectrum of ARRC activities." Throughout its year-long deployment, the OAB provided this type of support to the commander and his supporting staff in such diverse areas as military compliance with the GFAP, traffic surveys, transition and redeployment planning, elections support, information management, and software tool development.

The initial emphasis of the OAB analysis was on GFAP compliance issues. Compliance went better than expected so in February 1996, the OAB shifted its assessment activities to issues related to return to normality, freedom of movement, and redeployment. A major task undertaken by the OAB at this time was to develop normality indicators to provide a measure of operational success in terms of changes in the social and economic situation in Bosnia—"to assess the beneficial impact of the security framework provided by IFOR." The ARRC used soldiers (mainly U.S. Civil Affairs teams in MND(N) and in MND(SW) and regular unit patrols in MND(SE)) to collect the raw data. Data were collected on food and other staple goods, fuel stock and traffic on main roads, use of community buildings and private housing, social activities related to schools and churches/mosques, sports events, and farming activities. The data were collected twice a month on 109 towns spread throughout Bosnia and sent to the ARRC to be analyzed. Two control towns were selected to represent the worst case (Bosansko Grahovo, a ghost town) and best case (Tomislavgrad, a normal town) situations. A monthly assessment of the sampled towns against the control towns using a simple red (poorest), amber, yellow, and green (best) relative-rating scheme was employed to quickly judge and display the status of towns and Opstinas. The monthly data was then used to forecast trends. In October after 8 months of collection and analysis, the ARRC came to the following conclusions:

- The general recovery was continuing. Some towns (such as Bosnia Grahovo) showed signs of more rapid recovery while others (such as Han Pijesak, Gorazde, Rogatica, and Odzak) showed signs of slower recovery.
- In general terms, the conditions in the Republika Srpska and the Federation were more or less equivalent, with signs of improvement in both.
- Basic needs were being met throughout Bosnia.

Weather operations and support to IFOR forces during *Operation Joint Endeavor* were a success. The Staff Weather Office (SWO) provided numerous briefings and products that included satellite weather imagery of the central region and the area of responsibility (AOR), 24- and 48-hour forecasts, and weather impacts on operations. Thanks to the use of a German satellite communications weather broadcast system, the amount of real-time useful weather data to the troops in the field was, in USAREUR's view, the best in the history of the U.S. military. From either a logistics or reconnaissance point of view, the commander needed weather information far away from the physical confines of the AOR. Weather forecasts were routinely briefed (by forecasters within the AOR) on locations such as Dover, Delaware (CONUS logistics point of debarkation), and Istres, France (U-2 aircraft base). The valid requirement for this type of information expanded the need for trained personnel at remote locations, stretching the capabilities of the United States, in particular, and created some shortfalls in weather support later in the operation.

The MNDs produced daily intelligence summaries (INTSUM) for the ARRC. The document went out every evening at 2300 hours. Its format was dictated by the ARRC and was driven by treaty-compliance deadlines. As there was no real "doctrinal format" for a peace operations INTSUM, the compliance aspects provided an easy and logical way to organize the potential peace enforcement issues for the commanders. The divisions had other reporting requirements as well. For MND(N), two other products were developed daily. The intelligence input for the morning battle update briefing (BUB) went out at 0730 hours and covered any significant reporting that came in after 1600 hours the previous afternoon. The JAC Balkan INTSUM was published daily at 2300 hours so inputs from it were used for the morning briefing as well as inputs from the brigade daily INTSUM (due at 2000 hours) or periodic intelligence reports (INTREP) due at 0300 hours. The other product was the intelligence input for the evening BUB that occurred nightly at 1800 hours. This input covered all of the day's major events and issues. Operational reports, press releases, and ground reporting from the brigade INTREPs at 1500 hours were used to create the briefing. The INTEL products and BUB were disseminated to all subordinate brigades and other appropriate command elements. The Task Force Eagle INTSUMs were also posted daily to the INTELINK for broader intelligence community consumption and they relied on U.S. V CORPS in Heidelberg to do this for them. There was a lot of intelligence information at Task Force Eagle that was not available elsewhere and needed to be posted to the INTELINK so that the intelligence community could use it for long-term analysis. There was a problem in finding time at the Task Force Eagle level to get the information on INTELINK.

The BUB occurred twice daily in the MND(N) headquarters "Battle Star" command center. The G2 and G3 briefed jointly. Once the briefing slides were loaded into the PowerPoint presentation, they were displayed on a big-screen television monitor in the command center. Following the morning briefing to the Commanding General, the presentation was put on continuous "auto-pilot" throughout the day with slides rotating once every 15 seconds. The idea was that one could walk into the command center and get a complete update on the Task Force Eagle operation in about 15 minutes—a sort of "Task Force Eagle Headline News."

Intelligence Doctrine, Concepts, and Capabilities in Transition

Since the end of the Cold War, NATO and national intelligence needs have expanded into areas not of concern in the confrontation with the former Warsaw Pact. As a result, NATO and national doctrines had either changed or were in the process of changing when *Operation Joint Endeavor* was launched. The NATO intelligence doctrine, which was based on Cold War scenarios, was under review to consider adjustments to accommodate the needs other types of operations such as peace support where the intelligence activities differ from the traditional combat operations.

The IFOR intelligence community faced the unique collection challenges of coalition peace operations at the outset of *Operation Joint Endeavor*. Traditionally, intelligence tended to focus on the enemy. However, it was not always clear who and what was an enemy in the IFOR operation. Instead, there were collection needs to support monitoring human rights and freedom of movement and verification of cantonment inventories. These activities and others required new and different databases and collection approaches. In peace operations as well as combat, the side with the best situation awareness has the greatest advantage. In the multi-faction and multiethnic setting of Bosnia, there were, by definition, many sides. For IFOR, there were also releasability issues related to sharing information and capabilities among 36 nations. These nations included the Russians, Partnership for Peace (PfP) countries, and others with whom NATO had never shared or anticipated sharing intelligence information.

The synchronization of the IFOR information operations with the commander's intent and objectives was a recognized need and actions were taken early on to establish means to improve the ability to do this. However, since this was an evolving doctrine area for NATO and many of the nations, application and understanding of the components and critical activities varied greatly between individuals and units. It was recognized that information operations could give the commander options the same as maneuver and firepower. Most events had an informational aspect that could be exploited. Evaluating these in the context of information engagement and then exploiting them with a synchronized effort was a challenge. Difficulties included identifying sources and participants, establishing objectives, integrating into the battle staff and planning process, and establishing a process and methodology to manage exploitation and use the results. Over time, IFOR and the nations were able to both individually and collectively synchronize the intelligence assets not only among the intelligence collection assets but with operational reconnaissance assets as well. For the first time, CI/HUMINT was synchronized with other assets and the communications systems facilitated re-tasking. Dynamic re-tasking of CI/HUMINT strategic, theater, and tactical assets was possible. Furthermore, using different intelligence assets to queue others worked quite effectively.

There was no single doctrine for multinational intelligence operations or intelligence architecture. The nations developed their own approach to establish the foundation on which IFOR built its coalition intelligence operation. NATO did not implement its Cold War intelligence architecture, but tailored a multinational intelligence organization with shared responsibilities that included NICs at the ARRC and integrated positions within the IFOR command structure. A U.S. NIC was collocated with ARRC headquarters at Ilidza. The United Kingdom and France deployed NICs, and conducted intelligence operations under the direction of COMARRC. Other national contingents had intelligence representation at brigade level, with varying degrees of effectiveness. Each nation brought certain strengths and weaknesses to the table and its own national augmentation. For example, U.S. NIST formed from the JCS's National Military Joint Intelligence Center (NMJIC) capabilities supported the dual U.S. and NATO structure. They were able to provide rapid answers to the commander's priority intelligence requirements (PIR) and were valued additions to the overall intelligence operation. Procedures, responsibilities, and command relationships for integrating the U.S. NISTs were not fully developed and as a result, the NISTs operated and supported command elements differently. Some problems were experienced in passing U.S. military staff special access clearances to the NIC and obtaining access to NIC/NIST TS/SCI level elements and information. For example, it took the Deputy Commander Joint IFOR Information Campaign Task Force, a U.S. officer, until February 1996 to obtain access to certain U.S. NIC elements. The breadth and depth of U.S. intelligence support to IFOR and the framework nations operational elements are illustrated in figure 4-2.

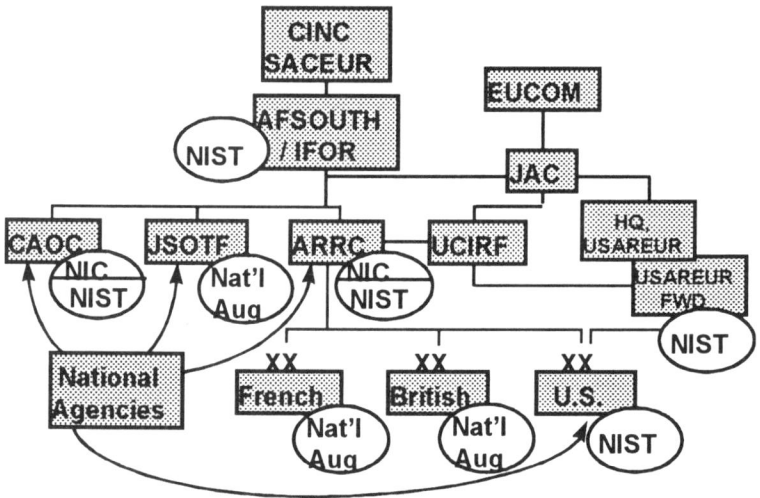

Figure 4-2. U.S. Intelligence Support for NATO

The basic intelligence principles remained appropriate guides for getting the operation started. The intelligence staffs had to provide the commanders and their staffs with intelligence estimates based on the commanders' PIRs. The intelligence cycle of direct, collect, process, and disseminate were employed to create inputs to the IPB. There was, however, little doctrine on how to conduct an IPB in preparation for or during peace operations, so this presented a significant challenge at the outset of the operation.

None of the manuals addressed how to verify specific treaty compliance issues such as those laid out in the Dayton Accord. Creative and innovative staffs came through and developed techniques and approaches to peace operations IPB and intelligence analysis.

USEUCOM, USAREUR, USAFE, NAVEUR/6th Fleet, and intelligence operators down the line employed existing doctrine and incorporated proven intelligence functions to plan for sanctuary and forward intelligence operations. Documents such as USEUCOM Directive 55-11, Joint Pubs 2-0 and 3-07, and service publications provided guidance for establishing joint U.S. intelligence support for coalition operations other than war. Where there was no doctrine, new architectures, tactics, techniques, and procedures were devised to provide support to U.S. elements, NATO, and especially non-NATO allies in the coalition environment. U.S. doctrine in FM 100-18 and FM 34-1 describes a split-based intelligence operational concept. The concept consists of broadcasting intelligence through a multilevel information system structure; providing for shared situational awareness among the different levels; tailoring assets tactically for efficient management of scarce resources; and synchronizing the intelligence system with the commander's operational concept across the operational spectrum. The principles of split-based, tactical tailoring and broadcast dissemination were the starting point for U.S. intelligence support planning for *Operation Joint Endeavor*. The Army doctrine of maneuver warfare dominated the intelligence architecture's implementation for Task Force Eagle (Bosnia was not, however, maneuver warfare).

Six intelligence functions, detailed in FM 34-1, were written into the USAREUR campaign plan: IPB, force protection, indications and warning, situational development, target development, and battle damage assessment (BDA). The de facto *Operation Joint Endeavor* intelligence architecture supported this doctrine and facilitated integration of these functions. However, the functions were designed to support conventional combat operations, and had to be adapted for use in a peace operation.

The split-based concept and the employment of sanctuary and forward elements are depicted in Figure 4-3. The intelligence operational terms for split-based parts are sanctuary and forward. A sanctuary can be located wherever it best supports the forward elements. There can be more than one sanctuary if there are various echelons of players. For *Operation Joint Endeavor*, one sanctuary was located at the UCIRF in Augsburg, Germany, the other at the JAC in Molesworth, England. The UCIRF and USEUCOM's JAC were separate theater sanctuary pieces.

USAREUR tactically tailored its intelligence forces and deployed them forward in the DISE. As the operation developed, so would the intelligence support provided. Broadcast dissemination meant that both EAC and echelons corps and below (ECB) information-processing systems received raw information and analyzed intelligence directly at their locations. Specific processing systems, some used only at certain levels, had to be deployed as part of the forward package to provide intelligence system connectivity to databases. For instance, the processing systems used at EAC did not "talk" to the ECB systems. To fix the problem, some EAC processing systems had to be deployed to ECB intelligence centers.

The JDISS, sponsored by DIA's General Defense Intelligence Program, was one of these systems. The JDISS is a computer workstation (including laptops) that compartmentalizes highly classified intelligence information by intelligence discipline. This EAC system was the primary connectivity to U.S. national databases during *Operation Joint Endeavor*. There were more than 750 JDISS workstations deployed in USEUCOM, with over half at the JAC. JDISS provided immediate access to nearly all of the theater- and national-level databases. NISTs equipped with JDISS gave COMIFOR, COMARRC, and COMEAGLE (Commander MND(N)) direct access to the latest U.S. national information. However, the JDISS, a strategic and operational tool, could not be electronically connected for data exchange to the processing systems at corps and division. Instead, a workstation was modified at corps and division to take advantage of the JDISS capability. All

Intelligence Operations 85

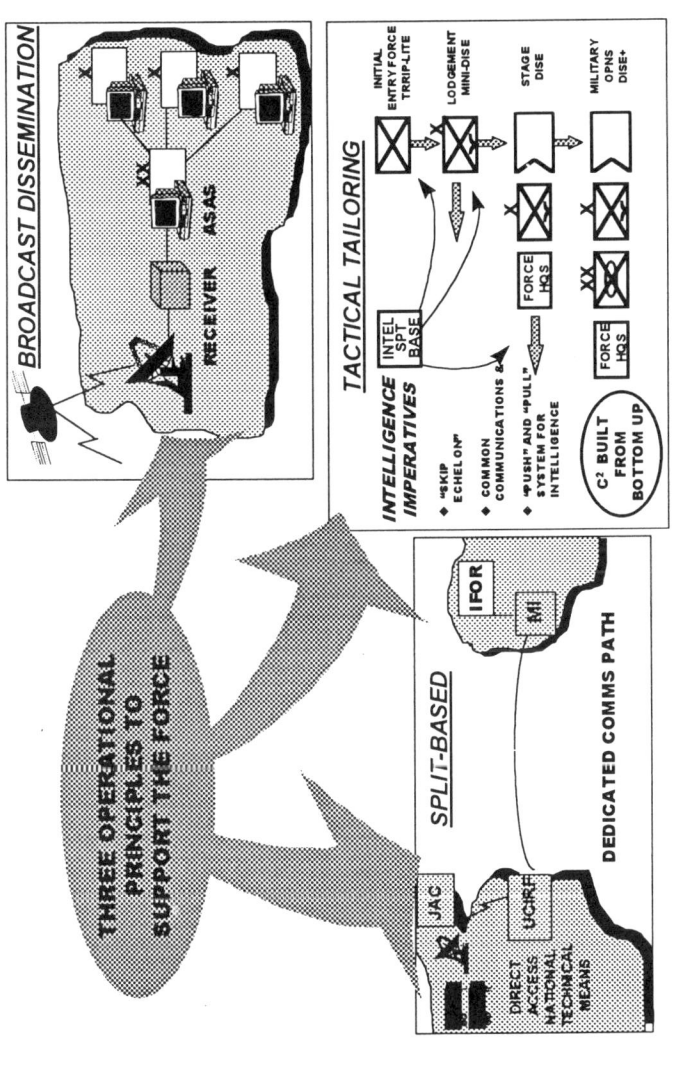

Figure 4-3. Split-based Intelligence Concept

the intelligence centers agreed that this system capability was vital to their operations. The lack of connectivity between EAC and ECB systems was caused by security restrictions on certain intelligence information being processed with other kinds of intelligence information. Another factor was that intelligence systems proliferate at ECB because technologies have not matured to allow for a single processor that can be networked from U.S. national to tactical levels. The lack of multilevel security created a complex IFOR information system environment and contributed to the duplication of fielded capabilities and excessive use of scarce bandwidth.

Operation Joint Endeavor pushed an early fielding by the United States of some systems such as an upgraded ASAS and the use of theater discretionary funds to purchase others such as the Theater Rapid Response Intelligence Package (TRRIP). There were no programmed funds during the operation to keep these systems maintained, so USAREUR obtained help from the Department of the Army to sustain these fielded capabilities. The ASAS, a corps and division processor, was the heart of Task Force Eagle ACE operations. This asset had limited storage, retrieval, and information parsing functionality, and was not user-friendly. The division and brigade intelligence processor, the WARLORD (ASAS-W), was a better tool. The most effective processing system deployed was the TRRIP. Used by force protection teams, the ACE, and USAREUR Forward DISE, the TRRIP could transmit digital imagery, pull still images from videotape, scan and transmit documents, and create and transmit written reports. It linked to U.S. national databases, pushing and pulling intelligence.

To push all this information around required large communications pipes. Trojan Spirit II, an intelligence-only communications pipeline, provided the throughput for the intelligence system in *Operation Joint Endeavor*. Intelligence providers could deliver voluminous information to user processing systems. Trojan Spirit II deployed with all the forward intelligence elements and was key to the success of the operation. It provided 128kb/s pipes to the brigade level. A prototype Joint Broadcast System (JBS), deployed as part of the BC2A advanced technology implementation, was made available to intelligence users for UAV (Predator) transmissions and imagery dissemination. It provided plenty of bandwidth, but technical and experimental restrictions on its use required the dedicated communications switches of Trojan Spirit II to be relied on for operational purposes.

Managing all of the information available to the commander and his staff became a serious problem. Users did not have adequate tools to search for available information. Likewise, there were inadequate tools for managing information collection, storage, and distribution. This was particularly true in the area of coordinating, integrating, and fusing intelligence, surveillance, and reconnaissance capabilities and making this information available to the user in a timely fashion. In reality, the intelligence process was not as smooth a cycle as one might have expected. There were numerous stove-piped processes that provided information directly to the commander or his intelligence staff on the ground. In the end, it was up to the commander and his staff to sort things out. As a result, the process placed too much of a burden on the commanders with data overload and not enough on imparting knowledge to them and their staff. The bigger the pipes got, the worse the problem got. Imagery was a good example. There were hundreds of images in the database, but getting to them and finding the one you needed was a nightmare and therefore limited their use in affecting decision making.

In the final analysis, it was the willingness of the nations to collaborate (up to a point), to go the extra mile to exploit existing and field advanced capabilities, and to share information beyond expectations that was the key contributor to the success of the IFOR intelligence operation. It also took creative and innovative staff to develop the techniques and approaches for the IPB and intelligence analysis to make it really happen. It demanded greater intellectual and analytical flexibility as well to produce predictive templates and analysis. The experiences gained by IFOR and SFOR will certainly serve to shape NATO and the member nations' future intelligence doctrine and architecture for peace support operations.

IFOR Experiences More Open Sharing—A Good Attempt at a Difficult Problem

Intelligence flowed neatly across channels, with U.S. support nearly transparent to NATO. The ARRC's use of NICs was actually its doctrine for the Cold War as well as what it did in Bosnia and therefore, it was able to make effective use of these capabilities. Figure 4-4 shows how requests for U.S.-provided information flowed. IFOR access to the JAC allowed the U.S. intelligence elements to provide selected technical information that otherwise was not readily available to NATO. Some of the allies employed their long-established HUMINT capabilities to great effect, the United Kingdom and France in particular. The United Kingdom had a great deal of background in these types of operations based on its experiences in northern Ireland and, was able to effectively apply this experience in Bosnia. For example, the ARRC (a UK-led operation) made very meaningful contributions to the IFOR CI/HUMINT activities.

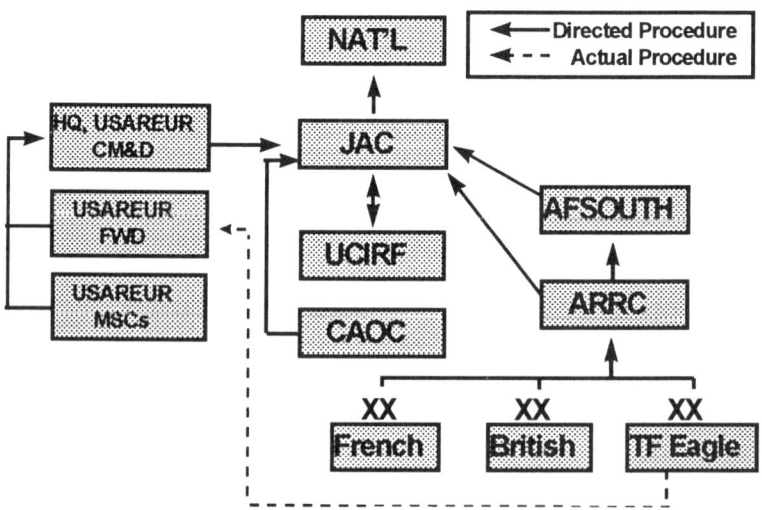

Figure 4-4. Requests for Information Flow

One area that varied across the IFOR operation was information sharing. Theater plans did not elaborate releasability and sanitization procedures of sensitive national information. U.S. intelligence elements enacted U.S. national procedures and were able to successfully release classified information to the partner nations. It was sometimes a one-way street. NATO and many of the NATO nations had not yet made the change that the U.S. intelligence community had made in terms of more open sharing. There were basic disconnects in how the United States and others viewed information sharing with coalition partners in warfare and security operations and how intelligence supports decision making. As a result, these differing philosophies affected responsive intelligence analysis and dissemination by NATO elements, such as the ARRC, to U.S. commanders (i.e., from the U.S. commander's perspective). For example, the ARRC G2, a UK officer, released information strictly on a "need to know" basis. This conflicted with U.S. doctrine of shared situational awareness and broadcast intelligence. UK and French reporting flowed directly into the ARRC, with little getting into U.S. hands.[17] As a result, the Commander MND(N) relied heavily on the U.S. intelligence structure that was more responsive to his needs and provided greater detail. This situation was symptomatic of U.S. commanders' frustrations with working in a coalition environment that controls the intelligence process.

USEUCOM created a parallel U.S. structure for managing collection requirements and requests for information to ensure that MND(N)—Task Force Eagle—benefited from U.S. ground-based to space-based intelligence systems. The U.S. intelligence structure ran from Task Force Eagle through USAREUR FWD to USAREUR Main to the EAC intelligence centers, the JAC, and UCIRF. Task Force Eagle nevertheless sent its requirements both to the ARRC as well as to USAREUR FWD (see Figure 4-4). Through its NIST, Task Force Eagle could also "backdoor" requirements to the national-level systems. USAREUR FWD supported Task Force Eagle with terrain and long-term analyses, and had the force protection lead. A USAREUR-FWD-led Force Protection

Working Group directed the *Operation Joint Endeavor* force protection intelligence efforts. Despite the complexity and redundancy, the system seemed to work reasonably well.

Over time, some common principles guided and national actions facilitated improved intelligence sharing and dissemination for IFOR. There was a multi-layer information (intelligence) sharing structure established which consisted of national-only, NATO-releasable, and IFOR-releasable categories. IFOR-releasable was a new category established and approved by NATO for this operation. In order to facilitate the sharing process, NICs, coordination cells, and liaisons were established and used by the nations and IFOR. IFOR dissemination was enhanced through the deployment and use of the U.S. Linked Operations-Intelligence Centers Europe (LOCE) network. The CRONOS data network was used to distribute the CAOC-generated RAP to all IFOR C2 nodes as well as other IFOR-releasable information, an example of NATO and national sharing.

USAREUR EAC units provided direct support to NATO. USAREUR intelligence units assigned to Task Force Eagle deployed their combat electronic warfare intelligence (CEWI) assets to conduct the early warning mission of detecting FWF military activity. The intelligence concept had to adapt capabilities to accomplish the mission. CI/HUMINT was the intelligence discipline that most accurately targeted the intentions of belligerents, so a large and pervasive CI/HUMINT capability had to be put in place to ensure reliable and timely returns. CEWI equipment enhancements had to be defined and created to broaden environmental capabilities. Civil action emerged as a paramount intelligence consideration in *Operation Joint Endeavor* because of the unknown temperament of the population. NGOs, PVOs, and IOs took on increased importance and needed to be included in collection plans. IPB tools like event, situation, and decision support templates had to be used differently for *Operation Joint Endeavor*, because their war preparation techniques did not always apply. For example, IPB for a combat operation might have an enemy command and control center labeled as a named area of interest (NAI), but for a peace support operation like *Operation Joint Endeavor*, a NAI might be something more abstract like the frequent meetings of local faction leaders.

While focused on *Operation Joint Endeavor*, USAREUR intelligence still stayed current on developing world situations. For example, missions supported by the USAREUR Deputy Chief of Staff, Intelligence (DCSINT) and the 66th MI Group during the same time frame as *Operation Joint Endeavor* included support to USASETAF operational deployments to the Great Lakes in Uganda and to Liberia, TF Able Sentry in Macedonia, the Khobar Towers bomb site in Saudi Arabia, and other worldwide indications and warning events.

In the end, the NATO-led IFOR shared intelligence to an unprecedented degree in order to accomplish its mission. Achieving a coalition-shared intelligence picture required a major shift in the intelligence-sharing paradigm for coalition operations. In previous coalitions, the U.S. national level provided intelligence support to the operations by sending primarily NOFORN products and reporting via U.S.-only intelligence channels. Since U.S. intelligence personnel in the theater often needed operational intelligence in a releasable format in order to conduct coalition operational planning and force protection, intelligence officers in theater continually had to contact the originating intelligence producers for permission to disclose or release intelligence to the coalition. As a result, in past operations U.S. intelligence sharing in theater would often be time-consuming and unresponsive. This changed for *Operation Joint Endeavor*.

There were a number of factors that contributed to the U.S. change. For example, the Director of Central Intelligence (DCI) commissioned a task force in early 1996 to examine the release and dissemination of U.S. intelligence in support of IFOR. Recommendations from this task force led to the enactment of a new DCI directive and concept of operation titled "Guidelines and CONOPS for U.S. Intelligence Sharing with IFOR." The intelligence dissemination principles in the 1996 revision of DCI Directive 1/7 placed greater U.S. emphasis on the direct dissemination of IFOR-releasable intelligence products and reporting from the U.S. national level. The intent of the directive was to ensure that the majority of U.S. theater-level operational and situational intelligence for force protection and threat warning was produced not only at the U.S. system high level but also at the REL NATO and REL IFOR level. Production at these levels would allow coalition-tailored products to be provided directly to the theater coalition command staffs at the ARRC and IFOR. Alternatively, products could be placed directly on the LOCE network or air-gapped to the Task Force Eagle IFOR independent LAN. As a result, the dissemination of releasable operational intelligence could be made directly to IFOR members without obtaining permission from Washington. Coalition intelligence support and threat warning could be near real-time, as the majority of initial sanitation and tailoring work was done at the U.S. national level prior to transmission.

Another influencing factor was the findings and actions taken on the recommendations of a U.S. Defense Science Board Bosnia Task Force. The task force visited the theater in 1995 and found numerous systemic barriers to achieving information dominance. Their recommendations focused on policy, organizational, equipment, and technology changes needed to make a dramatic improvement in force effectiveness and protection. Many of the recommendations were approved as part of an expedited implementation of the Bosnia Command and Control Augmentation (BC2A) initiative and the JBS. Less than a year later, the Task Force re-visited the theater, including visits to U.S. and IFOR command centers in Bosnia. The Task Force found impressive changes that dramatically improved force effectiveness and increased protection.

Although BC2A/JBS made a real contribution to improving the flow of information, more remained to be done to field high bandwidth connectivity to additional sites. Furthermore, improved information management tools and techniques were highlighted as being needed as well. Three broad tasks were cited for urgent consideration: (1) continue the process of getting information and tools down to the battalion level; (2) execute a paradigm shift where higher level intelligence centers become more proactive and push tailored products to lower level users via improved techniques for smart pull; and (3) organize collection management teams to integrate information from national, theater, and organic intelligence, surveillance, and reconnaissance assets and provide the warfighter with needed information. In the longer term, it was noted that information management deserved greater attention.

U.S. actions taken in response to these activities and other initiatives to improve intelligence sharing and dissemination had a significant impact on the coalition community. NATO, IFOR, and even U.S. units and officials in theater reported that they saw a fundamental shift at the U.S. national level to support intelligence sharing with IFOR and NATO. The United States was seen as disclosing unprecedented amounts of operational intelligence from the U.S. national to the theater level. U.S. and IFOR members noticed the change and were impressed not only by the revised U.S. intelligence disclosure policies regarding operational intelligence, but by the rapid implementation of these policies. In fact, U.S. intelligence sharing with IFOR was implemented on many levels. At the national level, sanitized tailored intelligence products and reporting were being placed on the EUCOM/NATO intelligence dissemination system, LOCE, directly from the National Security Agency (NSA), Defense Intelligence Agency (DIA), and the JAC, Molesworth, England. Tailored hard copy IFOR-releasable intelligence products were forwarded from the national intelligence producers and the JAC and were sent directly to EUCOM for further person-to-person dissemination as required.

The U.S. DCI CONOPS for IFOR was implemented across the theater. The U.S. "National Intelligence Pipe" was turned on at the IFOR-releasable level and produced a high volume of operational intelligence for the United States, NATO, and IFOR consumers. According to both IFOR operators and intelligence officers, the problem became one of not quantity or timely dissemination but finding the right intelligence in short order—an observation also made by the U.S. DSB Task Force. The U.S. intelligence community now needs to focus on filtering and fine tuning what U.S. intelligence is provided, in what format, and via what means.

Improved intelligence sharing and dissemination was one of the successes of *Operation Joint Endeavor*. The use of NICs was a major factor in achieving this success. At the ARRC in Ilidza, the United States, United Kingdom, Canada, France, Germany, Belgium, Italy, Greece, Denmark, Norway, and Sweden established national cells.

The United States was a major NIC contributor. The mission of the U.S. NIC at the ARRC was to provide U.S. theater and national intelligence to the ARRC commander and unique Intelligence support to U.S. senior leadership in Sarajevo. It also provided NATO I&W support, assisted the ARRC with collection management tasking of U.S. theater and national collection resources, and kept the U.S. theater and national intelligence agencies informed of the situation in Bosnia. In addition to the U.S. NIC at the ARRC, one also existed at the NATO CAOC in Vicenza, Italy. U.S. NIST were also deployed. These teams were composed of DIA, NSA, CIA, and other intelligence resources that were used to provide the supported commander's access to the entire DoD intelligence infrastructure. NISTs supported AFSOUTH (FWD) in Sarajevo, MND(N) headquarters in Tuzla, USAREUR (FWD) in Hungary, and the U.S. NICs at the ARRC and CAOC.

An IFOR Intelligence Coordination Cell (ICC) was established at the JAC and consisted of representatives from several NATO nations—participation was on a voluntary basis. The purpose of the ICC was to answer special theater requests for information (RFIs). If a command element down range could not find what they needed locally or on the LOCE network, they could send an RFI to the ICC for assistance via the LOCE network. Members of the ICC would then search for the required information using both NATO and there own national sources. ICC members were connected to their respective national intelligence organizations and could use this access to obtain additional IFOR-releasable information to answer an RFI. The national representatives were also used to clarify requests from members of their own armed forces down range (language differences). An intelligence product was developed in response to the RFIs and sent back to the requester via the LOCE network. The ICC was in a sense an "IFOR INTEL Help Desk." Other national IFOR-releasable products were also placed on the LOCE servers for broader IFOR-authorized user consumption.

Because the U.S. LOCE system was an accredited NATO system, there was means for disseminating, storing, and retrieving IFOR intelligence and information. The LOCE network was extended to IFOR, the ARRC, and the multinational division headquarters. A correlation center was established at RAF Molesworth where imagery, order of battle, and other intelligence information were placed on servers for access by and distribution to authorized users. The system also provided secure voice, e-mail, and bulletin board services. Multiple reporting of the same information was found on the LOCE system. This made it difficult at times to find and retrieve new, value-added intelligence products. National level, such as U.S. intelligence producers, needed to be made more aware of what was already available in theater before placing new products on LOCE. They were not always aware of whether information or reporting was being provided via other products, or if critical value added was being provided by the new products, or if time-critical information was being disseminated via LOCE e-mail.

Theater Collection Management

On 15 December 1995, the COMIFOR gave collection management authority for aerial platforms to the CAOC. The CAOC was established during JTF *Provide Promise* as a NATO air space management and targeting center. It was under the NATO air component command (COMAIRSOUTH) for *Operation Joint Endeavor* and exercised tactical command (TACOM) over all *Operation Joint Endeavor* air space. As a result, air force personnel from various NATO nations were used to resource the CAOC. The CAOC used NATO collection management procedures outlined in the Collection Coordination Intelligence Requirements Management (CCIRM) system. By U.S. Army intelligence standards, CCIRM was predominantly an RFI management system rather than a collection management system. Within NATO, requests for information flowed through the chain of command to the CCIRM manager. CCIRM was designed as a reactive vice proactive system. Figure 4-5 shows how requests for information collection tasking flowed.

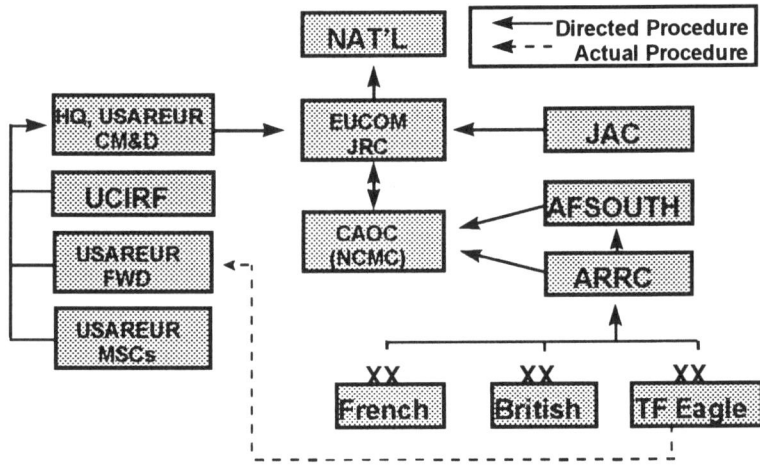

Figure 4-5. Requests for Information Collection Tasking Flow

The ARRC, a British-dominated headquarters, was multinational and deployed in Ilidza. Within the NATO structure, each MND transmitted requirements through the ARRC to the CCIRM manager at the CAOC. At the CAOC, the CCIRM manager determined the best platform to satisfy the requirement and either tasked a NATO TAC RECCE squadron or requested a national platform to satisfy the requirement. The CAOC controlled national TAC RECCE aircraft chopped to NATO. The CAOC also had TACON of the Predator and JSTARS (the United States actually controlled both of these platforms—the 16th Air Force Deputy Commander was dual hatted as CAOC director).

USEUCOM created the National Collection Management Cell (NCMC) to support the CAOC with collection management of U.S. aerial platforms. The NCMC was part of the U.S. NIC in Vicenza and acted as a forward element of USEUCOM J2's collection management division. However, the NCMC did not do collection management per se. Instead, it responded to requirements generated through the NATO structure or passed through U.S. channels via USEUCOM. When the CAOC determined that a requirement was best satisfied by a U.S. national platform, the CAOC requested that the NCMC task the appropriate organization. However, the NCMC had to clear all tasking with USEUCOM J3, Joint Reconnaissance Center (JRC).

In an attempt to better manage the airborne RECCE platforms, NATO created within the CAOC an Intelligence, Surveillance, and Reconnaissance Cell (ISARC) in January 1996. Initially, it was a single room in the CAOC where all sensor feeds available to do near real-time collection tasking were located. Later the ISARC terms of reference were expanded to include the CCIRM cell and process as well as the TAC RECCE platform managers. The NCMC was also made part of the ISARC. The NCMC members spent much of their time in the U.S. NIC coordinating U.S. theater RECCE platforms (U2, Rivet Joint, and P-3).

The CAOC had TACOM of airspace above 3,500 feet. All U.S. aerial reconnaissance, surveillance, and intelligence platforms (except the Pioneer and helicopters) flew above the 3,500-foot threshold. Therefore, flight tracks had to be coordinated with the CAOC. While the NCMC tasked an organization to perform the mission, air space management coordination with the CAOC was a unit responsibility. The establishment of recurring flight tracks took at least a week and sometimes as long as 3 weeks. Platforms could only fly in approved tracks and had to be in the Air Tasking Message (ATM). The ATM (sometimes referred to as the Air Tasking Order (ATO)) was the longstanding 48-hour planning and tasking vehicle to de-conflict air space. The ATM used in Bosnia differed from a standard U.S. ATO. It included in-theater friendly air movements (e.g., Red Cross and UN) but did not include army helicopter movement. Aerial platform organizations sent LNOs to the CAOC to assist in the education process and to enhance the air space management coordination process. The everyday interaction of the LNOs was crucial for developing an understanding between CCIRM, air space, and platform managers.

The ATM was formulated from a "target deck" developed by the CAOC based on requirements submitted by various organizations. There were some 1,500 targets in BiH that required periodic coverage (i.e., about every 3 days). In addition, there were approximately 200 one-time targets. The CAOC published a daily document that projected requirements out 7 days. This was the planning/forecasting mechanism used by the NATO reconnaissance squadrons and the NCMC. From this document, the collection managers built the 48-hour ATM.

Early in the deployment, an air defense threat threshold was established that impacted on the collection capabilities of some platforms, like the U.S. Air Reconnaissance Low (ARL)—a near real-time communications intelligence (COMINT) and imagery intelligence (IMINT) system—and UAVs. CAOC and NCMC representatives indicated that the threat established for the AOR by the JAC adversely affected the management of aerial platforms. The CAOC required ARL to fly above its optimal elevation specifications; thus, the product did not satisfy commander Task Force Eagle tactical needs. During the same time frame, NCMC and CAOC used Predator to look for threat air defense sites that were not Task Force Eagle or USAREUR (Forward) tactical requirements. The competition to have both theater and tactical requirements satisfied by scarce theater collection assets meant that the tactical commanders came to rely on those sources that responded to their needs.

Predator and other UAVs were surveillance platforms that could monitor a situation for a specified period of time. ARL was a reconnaissance platform that also flew surveillance missions and could downlink in real-time. Most real-time surveillance assets were downlinked to an operation and talked directly to an operator. UAVs were targeted against "spots on the ground." However, sensor packages on reconnaissance platforms, like the electro-optic U2, were on-line and accomplished some collection in route to or between the spots on the ground. Every Predator mission included a number of ad hoc tasking coordinated just prior to takeoff or while airborne that supplanted tasking in the ATM. The ability to do some dynamic re-tasking of these assets made them more flexible and responsive to the ground commander. The need to fly above 3,500 feet and incorporate tasking in the ATM limited the dynamic re-tasking options for the ground commander; it was not always clear 48 hours in advance where its use might be best applied.

Theater Intelligence Systems

The E-3A and to a lesser extent the E-2C were used continuously, both in prior operations such as *Deny Flight* and for *Joint Endeavor*. While the E-3 was primarily classified as a command and control platform, NATO used the E-3s employed in Bosnia as surveillance assets. No U.S. E-3s were employed in the Bosnia operation. Those used were supplied by NATO (the NATO Airborne Early Warning (NAEW)), the United Kingdom, and France. Two E-3 orbits were maintained. The aircraft were linked together and linked to the Airborne Command and Control (ABCCC) aircraft, the Navy fleet, a Control and Reporting Center (CRC) on the Italian coast, and the Italian (NATO) air defense radar. The CAOC was linked to this network through the CRC so that it had a continuous, real-time picture of all air activity over the Bosnia AOR.

While the geography (distances prevented direct UHF connectivity) and technical incompatibilities demanded some occasional ad hoc network architecture changes, the communications network (SATCOM, VHF/UHF, and HF radios; Tactical Data Links (TADIL-A and B), JTIDS, and LINK-1 data links) generally worked effectively. In addition, key U.S. intelligence platforms were directly linked into the tactical data links so that near real-time intelligence-derived tracks or track amplifications could be fed directly to the surveillance and C2 nodes. A less understood and usually ignored portion of the surveillance architecture was the simultaneous reporting by the intelligence platforms into the broadcast systems, i.e., Tactical Data Dissemination System (TDDS) and Tactical Information Broadcast System (TIBS). Both TDDS and TIBS were received in the CAOC and then fed into the RAP display that was maintained on a system called ADSI (Air Defense System Integrator). This caused some redundant reporting.

One interesting but somewhat frustrating aspect of the surveillance operation was the fact that the air situation picture or RAP was a NATO product coming primarily from NATO sensors (NAEW) and managed by the NATO CAOC. The NATO commanders consistently refused to provide the air picture to U.S. theater headquarters based on the logic that they would then have to provide it to all NATO capitals. This greatly frustrated some U.S. commanders and DISA engineers who wanted to implement a Common Operation Picture (COP) on the U.S. Global Command and Control System (GCCS) as part of the BC2A initiative.

U.S. EAC capabilities provided continuous coverage of Bosnia and Hungary throughout the deployment, sustainment, and redeployment phases of *Operation Joint Endeavor* as seen in Figure 4-6. A combination of air-breather platforms and unmanned aerial vehicles (UAVs) at theater level provided coverage in support of COMIFOR, COMARRC, and Commander Task Force Eagle requirements. (As noted earlier, the Commander, Task Force Eagle essentially had access to every conceivable national, theater, and tactical asset the United States could bring to bear to support the operation.) Also available to COMEAGLE were two organic airborne collectors: the Guardrail Common Sensor (GRCS) fixed-wing aircraft and the QUICKFIX helicopter. GRCS was modified for the environment and effectively collected in the Balkans.

Joint Surveillance Target Attack Radar System (JSTARS)

JSTARS is not just an aircraft. It's really two systems: the Air Force E-8 aircraft and the Army ground-station modules. JSTARSs first deployed to support *Operation Joint Endeavor* from

Intelligence Operations 101

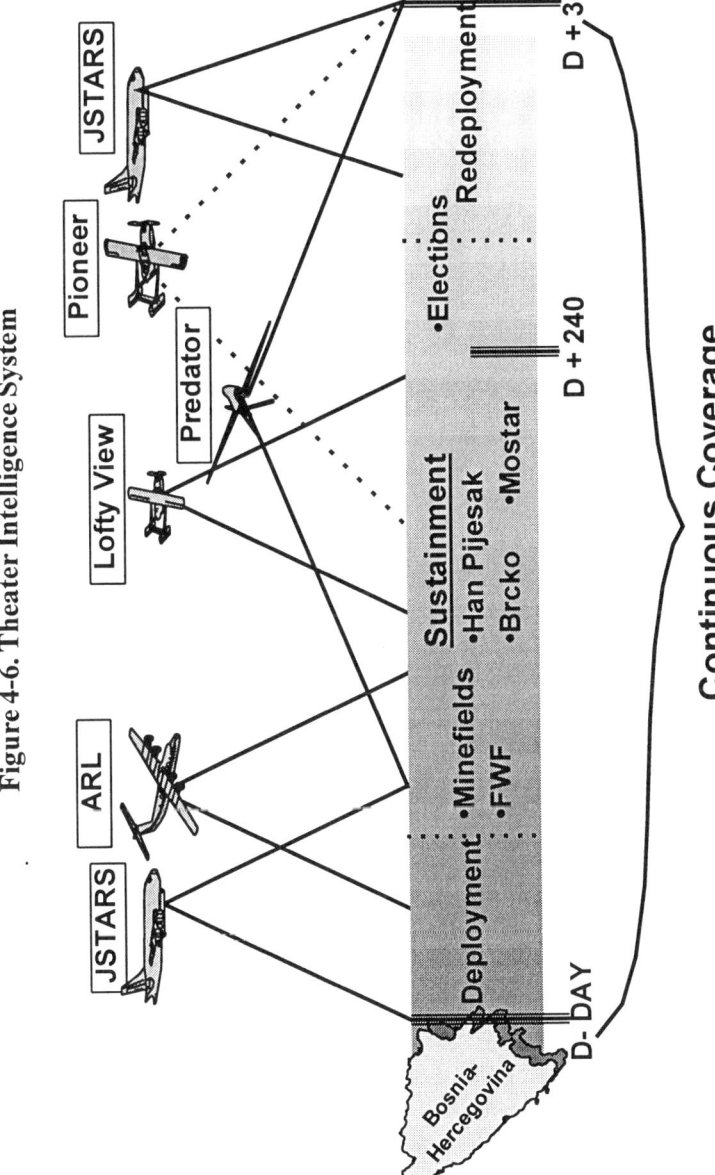

Figure 4-6. Theater Intelligence System

14 December 1995 to 27 March 1996. A second deployment began on 1 November 1996 with end-of-mission scheduled for 31 December 1996. Hence, JSTARSs operated during the IFOR deployment and redeployment phases only. For both of the missions, the JSTARS E-8 aircraft operated from and was supported by crews at the Rhein-Main AB, Germany. USAREUR provided the administrative and logistical support to the two ground-station modules (GSM) at the Intermediate Staging Base and the four within Bosnia-Herzegovina. There were high expectations for its use in Bosnia but heavy terrain masking in mountainous Bosnia precluded optimal orbit tracks. Friendly forces were intertwined and intermingled among the FWF, and JSTARS could not distinguish friend from foe. JSTARS, designed to meet wartime requirements of detecting opposing force movements, was less useful in *Operation Joint Endeavor*. The JSTARS's SAR did identify some convoys and trench-lines but could not provide the necessary resolution for required recognition. It was best used to queue other assets such as HUMINT and ground reconnaissance. A ferry site along the Sava River that was being used for moving military equipment in and out of Bosnia was identified as well as a railhead where armored vehicles were being loaded. Both of these success stories still required ground confirmation. Ironically, as IFOR's mission became more successful, the movement of civilian populations increased, and although this made JSTARS's task of tracking the military vehicles harder, it excelled at measuring this increased freedom of movement both quantitatively and geographically.

Unmanned Aerial Vehicles (UAVs)

UAVs proved their value too because they were flexible, accurate, and available. There were two theater-level UAVs—Lofty View, a short-range asset that supported ARRC requirements, and the Predator which provided the long-range and long duration capability. Developed in the last 2 years, the Predator was first used in Bosnia for JTF *Provide Promise*. The Predator operated out of Tazsar, and provided support throughout *Operation Joint Endeavor*.

It was a theater (not tactical) platform controlled by the ARRC and flown by the CAOC. There were a few cases where control was delegated to the division level for a period of time. The system was often used against point targets as a "mini-U2," even though it was best designed for active surveillance.

The Predator video was disseminated to all Bosnia C2 nodes over JBS once it became operational in May/June 1996. The Predator had both a line of site (LOS) and a SATCOM link back to its home base at Taszar, Hungary. From there it was forwarded to the JAC via a VSAT connection. The JAC sent it back to the JBS injection point in the United States over the DISN Leading Edge Service T-3 extension to CONUS. The CAOC then used the video display provided via JBS to direct the Predator operators to affect real-time tasking changes. JBS could not be used to disseminate P-3, ARL, or Lofty View video because these three platforms only had LOS downlinks. Furthermore, supporting multiple VSAT connections back to the JAC was prohibitively expensive, and a means to automatically hand off the data feed and route it to JBS as the platform moved in/out of view of the various downlink points was not available.

The Predator field experience of MND(N) suggested that the 10 hours "eyes on" for any given mission versus an advertised 16 to 20 hours did not meet the "sold as" expectations at the tactical level. The lack of pilots also limited its surge capability. In spite of this, the system was viewed as one of the most successful capabilities supporting intelligence efforts in MND(N). They used it successfully to provide coverage of lines of communications, rallies, demonstrations, and live operations in the Hans Pijesak area. For example, the Predator played a significant role in the Han Pijesak incident when an angry crowd of Bosnia Serbs confronted COL John R. S. Batiste, Commander of 2nd Brigade Combat Team (BCT), and some of his soldiers. The Serbs thought the United States was going to arrest General Ratko Mladic. Predator monitored the situation and its high-resolution video camera exposed events as they were happening, downlinking images immediately, revealing the faces and numbers of those opposing U.S. entry to the town. COMARRC later tasked Predator against Han Pijesak for 30 consecutive days. This was viewed by some as an inappropriate use of the capability given that other platforms were better suited for point targets of this nature. Predator maintenance was scheduled in conjunction with poor weather forecasts so little to no noticeable operational time was lost due to maintenance.

Task Force Eagle received UAVs in direct support when U.S. Marine Corps (USMC) VMU-1 was attached to the 165th MI Battalion in June 1996. The deployment of the Pioneer UAV IMINT platform provided operational data on Army use of a tactical UAV at division- and brigade-task force levels during peacekeeping operations. The ability to quickly satisfy information requirements and dynamically re-task at the tactical level was demonstrated. Nevertheless, Pioneer's performance was often disastrous—five crashes were caused by engine, generator, rocket-assisted launcher, or on-board computer failures. Precipitation or clouds, line-of-sight problems, and an outmoded imagery dissemination system also imposed constraints. The line-of-sight radius for the video downlink was 30 miles, and even less in the mountainous Bosnia terrain. Maintenance was also a problem with a field-level perception that it was down more than it was up. Of the seven birds deployed, six were operational and the remaining one was used for spare parts.

Intelligence Electronic Warfare (IEW) Operations

U.S. national and theater special intelligence collectors flying in support of NATO and U.S. requirements reported directly to Task Force Eagle ACE and other intelligence centers. Tactical IEW systems were adapted to collect in the primitive environment in BiH.

Eagle Focus was the name of a collection and reporting effort conducted from sanctuary that was created to directly support Task Force Eagle. *Eagle Focus* combined U.S. national, theater, and remotely fielded collection operations in order to streamline and focus the intelligence efforts on Task Force Eagle requirements.

Its successes provided valuable intelligence to the field commanders and demonstrated the simultaneous and synergistic possibilities of certain multiechelon intelligence operations.

ELINT and SIGINT were supplied by USAF RC-135s, the RAF Nimrod R2s, French C-160s, German Atlantiques, and U.S. RC-12 Guardrails based in Hungary. ELINT and SIGINT data were placed on the LOCE server for distribution to authorized IFOR consumers.

Task Force Eagle organic IEW assets were unable to fully exploit the environment. Part of the reason was that the go-to-war design of tactical intelligence units and capabilities were not tuned to the commercially oriented capabilities of the belligerents and other entities. The infusion of low-cost, state-of-the-art communications systems made predicting the threat very difficult. Guardrail could and did collect on the targets called for in the operation and was also a key source for direction finding. Ground-based assets were used to tip Guardrail and this worked very well. Since the ARRC only provided MND(N) limited visibility on NATO counterparts, Guardrail allowed some visibility on adjacent sectors.

QUICKFIX, used to locate and collect on tactical VHF communications, was of little value in the Bosnia environment since most of the critical targets were not in the VHF range. Some useful intercepts were produced but commercial radios placed on EH-60s would have provided a better capability. An AR8000 was placed in the QUICKFIX and this resulted in an immediate increase in performance. There were other possible contributing factors to the poor performance of QUICKFIX. It had no communications with a ground station and it was not well supported in country.

The AR8000, basically a fancy bearcat scanner, provided increased frequency spectrum over the MND(N) organic capabilities. Its portability allowed it to be used by convoys, inspection teams, force protection teams, and security patrols. In order to accommodate reporting requirements, there needed to be an accompanying secure radio to allow its use by convoys and force protection teams.

The Mobile Integrated Tactical Terminal (MITT) was a very good processor for ELINT data and had the FWF not complied with the requirement to shut down their radar, this would have been a critical division asset. Its "frame-grabber" capability provided an unanticipated, but essential, capability to exploit AH-64 gun camera, Combat Camera footage, and amateur video. Unclassified, annotated, exploited images could be produced within 12 hours and provided to allies or the FWF without the hassle of requesting a classification downgrade. The lesson from MND(N) was that divisions need an organic imagery exploitation and production capability.

NSA constructed systems and components tailored to the specific requirements of the environment. The systems were called "purpose-built" systems. With these new capabilities, Task Force Eagle performed ground-based and airborne collection more effectively. In this way, national intelligence systems enhanced and directly supported the operational commander. Technical reporting—exploiting and deriving elements of collected information to reconstruct the target structure—was not accomplished well; consequently, long-term analysis suffered. Task Force Eagle was not doctrinally prepared or resourced to do this. They did, however, reorganize their ACE to include a SIGINT analytic cell. Strategic and theater (operational) capabilities provided solutions that significantly improved the ability to effectively inform the commander.

Imagery Intelligence (IMINT) Operations

U-2R aircraft flying from Istres, France, provided imagery in support of IFOR. The U.S. Navy P-3C Orions based at Sigonella, Italy, with their Cast Glance/Cluster Ranger video-datalink systems monitored incidents in the Bosnia area.

Air Reconnaissance Low's (ARL) main operating base was Budapest, Hungary, for the first deployment and Taszar, Hungary, for the second. The ARL system consisted of one aircraft and 69 personnel. The ARL was a workhorse for Task Force Eagle, but it did manifest areas for improvement. The ARL downlink, called a remote vehicle terminal (RVT), did not always receive the video or selected images on the same day of the mission. Terrain masking limited the line-of-sight connection. It took two to three days to get the complete ARL video mailed or couriered to the Task Force Eagle ACE. COMEAGLE retained tasking authority over the IMINT assets assigned to Task Force Eagle. He directly controlled their use and their collection focus. These were the assets that provided the best IMINT returns to the commander. One of its successful uses occurred during the time frame that IFOR was trying to encourage the FWF to move into their barracks and cantonment areas before the D+120 deadline. In order to build confidence that all sides were complying, and to convince the FWF that IFOR was omnipotent, the ARL was flown during a Joint Military Commission meeting with all of the FWF in attendance and live video was downlinked to the site for viewing by them.

The USAF Eagle Vision system operating at Ramstein AB, Germany, provided access to a direct downlink from the French commercial satellite imagery system, SPOT. The SPOT provided lower resolution broad area coverage.

New sources of imagery appropriate for ground commanders emerged from *Operation Joint Endeavor*. Specifically, Combat Camera products, gun cameras, UAV video, hand-held digital cameras, and video cameras were highly productive. However, effective methods to exploit, catalogue, archive, and maintain registries of such images did not exist. An exploitation cell was deployed to Taszar, but they were not tasked to do these functions. Meanwhile, the JBS sites recorded Predator video on VHS tapes. Doctrine and CONOPS to guide and assign of responsibility for overall video collection management, archiving, and dissemination was lacking.

Some images found their way to the imagery servers at the JAC, but much of the imagery from TRRIP never found its way to a theater-level server. The Predator ground-station module did a good job of capturing still images from the motion sequences and images were loaded on the LOCE imagery server at the JAC. One problem associated with this was that imagery from the Predator had to be manually manipulated to move the image to the appropriate collateral server at the JAC. Automated capabilities were not networked. Improvements were underway to provide secure guard gateways at the JAC so that imagery could be moved between servers at all classification levels (SCI, U.S. Secret, and NATO Secret). Elements using and developing low-level imagery such as TRRIP and other hand-held sources did not establish adequate techniques and procedures for use, integration, and distribution of their products. Hence, it is understandable that collection management of video platforms was difficult.

An unintended consequence of exploiting visual sources such as gun camera video in the benign environment of the Bosnia peacekeeping operation was that fighter pilots could obtain video on all of their potential targets. These videos were put together into target folders that allowed the pilots to do target studies and see exactly how the target would appear on their cockpit display.

Finally, the U.S. IMINT tasking and processing cycle was a problem. A process developed to support maneuver warfare was not responsive enough to meet COMIFOR demands for the peace operation. Work-arounds were required to meet the response time expectations of COMIFOR requests. The adverse weather conditions in Bosnia also affected national-level IMINT operations. UAVs were somewhat helpful in filling the gap but they too had their limitation since they were designed for shoot-look-shoot not look-look-look.

Counterintelligence (CI) and Human Intelligence (HUMINT) Operations

The G2X was established at the Task Force Eagle to give the commander priority emphasis on his requirements. The G2X provided mission management and coordinated the CI and HUMINT effort within the Task Force Eagle area of operation. The Allied Counter Intelligence Unit and the Joint Forces Intelligence Teams were combined organizations assigned to the ARRC. The allied teams that operated in the Task Force Eagle area coordinated their missions with the G2X. The DHS (Defense HUMINT Service) and the CIA representatives on the G2X accepted HUMINT tasking directly. The NIST handled straight RFIs. When an operation in the Task Force Eagle area was required, it was first de-conflicted at the G2X. The USAF Office of Special Investigations also had teams in the area that coordinated with the G2X. Three or four-person operational control elements were formed at each brigade, plus one at Task Force Eagle headquarters to manage CI and HUMINT tasking, control the teams, and maintain quality control of the product. Quality control of the product was an area that needed improvement as tactics, techniques, and procedures, and feedback to the collectors were handled by teams in a decentralized manner. As with other intelligence operations, the JDISS was the EAC system that connected Task Force Eagle with DHS. Important imagery was sent to DHS and put on the DHS HUMINT imagery server with an IIR.

A significant number of intelligence capabilities were applied to force protection. Force protection teams were formed and displaced throughout the area of operation. These teams consisted of two counterintelligence agents, an interrogator, and a driver. They were required to operate in uniform and in four-vehicle convoys. In April 1996, COMEAGLE relaxed the convoy requirement to two vehicles for the force protection teams. A force protection information report (FPIR) was written at the team level and transmitted via TRRIP to the brigade operational control element. Because of its digital camera capability, the TRRIP allowed FPIRs to include still images of the people they were interviewing. The FPIR also fed the UCIRF's force protection database BLACKBIRD. The BLACKBIRD database was eventually modified to archive hand-held produced imagery. The allied partners at first did not trust the omnipresent force protection teams assigned to them. Later in the operation, they praised their value. The technology and the quality of the soldiers impressed them. The Army and USAREUR benefited greatly from the perceived goodwill and information sharing that was realized from the force protection team activities. The information these teams provided became the cornerstone for determining and recommending force protection actions.

Open Source Intelligence Operations

Open Source Intelligence (OSINT) was not widely practiced in intelligence circles prior to *Operation Joint Endeavor*. The 165th MI Battalion's document exploitation team at Camp Lukavac provided this unique service by producing a daily newsletter called the *Night Owl*. A U.S. military editor with eight contract linguists staffed the *Night Owl* and exploited and translated Muslim, Serbian, and Croatian television, radio, and newspaper reports of events in the area of operation. The newsletter was available on the Internet and hundreds of its articles were included in the Task Force Eagle databases. Of noteworthy mention were its incisive accounts of public reaction to IFOR's presence. Avid supporters and users of the newsletter included the U.S. embassy and the IFOR Information Campaign staff at IFOR headquarters in Sarajevo. An important and new contribution to the intelligence effort, the Lukavac team paved the way for future OSINT operations.

Measurement and Signature Intelligence (MASINT) Operations

Remotely Monitored Battlefield Sensor Systems (REMBASSs) provided a valuable collection asset for Task Force Eagle. The REMBASS provided early warning and treaty compliance data throughout *Operation Joint Endeavor*. The initial emplacement of these systems monitored the withdrawal of the FWF from the ZOS and confirmed FWF reports of departure. As the factions withdrew, the systems were moved to monitor critical areas of concentration of FWF equipment, suspected areas of treaty violations, and force protection around base camps. REMBASSs provided wide area coverage without the need to physically man a given area, had a 15 kilometer range, and were used for perimeter security.

However, some problems were encountered in logistics maintenance, minefields, and training areas that limited their potential use. Logistics shortfalls stemmed from the fact that REMBASS and I-REMBASS (Improved-REMBASS) were not organic to the 1st Armored Division, but were obtained on loan. Loan agreements did not include maintenance support, so resupply had to come from depot maintenance in the United States.

Because REMBASS was not organic, Task Force Eagle staffs initially were unaware of its capabilities, employment techniques, and requirements for a comprehensive reconnaissance and surveillance plan. Furthermore, emplacing REMBASS in a mine environment is not taught at the intelligence school nor is it included in REMBASS doctrine found in FM 34-10-1. All these factors combined to limit the potential use of REMBASS.

Ground surveillance radars (GSRs) were useful as surveillance devices in *Operation Joint Endeavor*, but their full utility was hampered by a poor logistical repair system and the age of equipment and technology. Ranging to 10 kilometers for people and 15 kilometers for vehicles, these radars detected day and night movement. Throughout the Task Force Eagle sector, the AN/PPS-5C GSRs were used to monitor named areas of interest, cantonment areas, and intersections, and to provide force protection to base camps. In some cases, radar teams positioned on top of high areas had excellent line of sight and early warning. However, terrain masking was a great limitation in Bosnia. In addition, radars broke down after extended use. The lack of timely transportation to evacuate and return the GSRs from Germany severely hampered their potential use at Task Force Eagle. More observation posts were required to monitor the same number of named areas of interest as these assets decreased.

Staff Weather Operations (SWO)

Historically, weather has had a significant impact on military operations; *Operation Joint Endeavor* was no exception. The mission of the USAF 7th Weather Squadron (WS) and USAREUR weather office was to provide accurate, timely, and relevant weather intelligence. Headquarters, 7th WS, began supporting *Operation Joint Endeavor* in April 1995 by gathering climatological data for the IPB and by conducting briefings on weather in the anticipated AOR. On 10 December 1995, 7th WS commenced daily briefings to both the USAREUR CAT and the DCSINT. Briefings included satellite weather imagery of the Central Region and the AOR, 24- and 48-hour forecasts, and potential weather impacts on operations. Also in December 1995, 7th WS deployed personnel to Taszar, Hungary, to provide staff support to USAREUR (Forward), the NSE, and the Intermediate Staging Base (ISB). Weather operations included integrating weather intelligence into the planning process, establishing and refining procedures for the dissemination of weather warnings and weather advisories, and overseeing USAF weather assets in Hungary. As part of the ARRC, a 7th WS officer deployed 20 January 1996 to Sarajevo to provide staff weather support. The Unified Weather Forecast (UWF), the official *Operation Joint Endeavor* forecast from which all other *Operation Joint Endeavor* weather products were based, was issued twice a day by the AFSOUTH SWO.

When Task Force Eagle deployed to Tuzla, an 11-person weather team from Detachment 2, 7th WS, deployed with the unit and established Task Force Eagle weather operations at Tuzla Main. The detachment provided staff weather support to the Task Force Eagle commander as well as weather support (flight weather briefings, warnings and advisories, observations, upper air soundings, etc.) to units in the MND(N). In order to increase weather coverage at areas near chokepoints, COMEAGLE tasked 7th WS to provide weather forecasters and observers at several base camps. The 7th

WS weather personnel deployed forward and established mobile weather operations at camps such as Doboj, Zenica, Uglivek, and others, depending upon seasonal and mission requirements.

Observations

Operation Joint Endeavor did not provide a rationale for ignoring the conventional combat and major theater of war role of the ground force component. It did reveal, however, some experiences that have intelligence operations implications. NATO and the nations need to consider these implications as they prepare for the future. Some general observations that may become lessons learned follow:

- Commanders need to gain a more complete understanding of the integrated operations/intelligence process and how to leverage intelligence in support of peace operations—the Information Age is forcing a paradigm shift.

- IFOR intelligence operation clearly demonstrated the ability and will of member NATO nations to cooperate and leverage their resources in support of a common NATO mission.

- Doctrine, CONOPS, TTP, and IPB need to be adjusted to accommodate peace operation requirements.

- Tactical intelligence capabilities designed to fight battles need to be adjusted to accommodate peace operation requirements.

- For peace operations, tasks need to be defined with a clear end-state for meaningful IPB to occur.

- Strategic to theater to tactical intelligence systems interoperability continues to be a problem as well as coalition interoperability. The proliferation of intelligence systems at all levels is also an issue. Multilevel security is a means to an end in solving many of the related issues.

- IFOR to a large extent and the United States in particular achieved information dominance.

- The IFOR Information Campaign had spotty success in adapting to the Bosnia consumer environment and countering the established Serb information campaign targeted against IFOR.

- PSYOP and the information campaign need to make adjustments to more effectively accommodate the capabilities offered by global television and the Internet.

- Military interaction with civil organizations (i.e., NGOs, PVOs, and IOs) was more than civil-military cooperation. These organizations were both providers and consumers of intelligence and needed to be incorporated into the intelligence planning.

- NATO and national intelligence architectures need to be adjusted to meet the peace operations requirements.

- Training continues to be an issue, especially as regards information systems operation and maintenance and intelligence analysis capabilities. Some functions—like collection management for peace operations in a coalition environment—required specialized knowledge and skills that were not adequately addressed in formal military training programs. The formal training system must re-emphasize basic intelligence skills while finding a methodology for dealing with an accelerating technology base and widely divergent areas of operations.

- IFOR experienced more open sharing of information in spite of differing national polices on release and dissemination of intelligence. The United States had a more open policy on sharing.

- There were too few military linguists to support the operation. It was necessary to use contracted linguist support.

- Low-tech as well as high-tech solutions had high payoff at the theater and tactical levels.

- Not all coalition partners use or can afford U.S. technology. The United States will not want to share all of its advanced technology with all elements of a coalition of the willing. This has interoperability, sharing, and operational effectiveness aspects that need to be dealt with.

- CAOC had 3 years of experience with theater platforms and was operational at the outset of *Operation Joint Endeavor*. Developing collection management approaches to exploit the video systems of the UAV and ARL was difficult. The CAOC could manage the RECCE platforms but had little experience with managing the video sensors. The CAOC control of the theater platforms frustrated the tactical commanders and in their view, limited their tactical flexibility.

- Doctrine and CONOPS to guide and assign responsibility for overall video collection management, archiving, and dissemination were lacking. There is a future use aspect that needs to be addressed as well.

- U.S. systems such as Trojan Spirit, JWICS, UAVs, DISE, ASAS WARLORD, TRRIP, and others (including the innovative exploitation of Apache Gun Camera video, Combat Camera video, and hand-held video cameras using the freeze frame capabilities of MITT and commercial devices such as the SNAPPY) were key to enhancing the effectiveness of the intelligence operation. The efforts of the JAC (including its ICC), Task Force Eagle ACE, NICs, and NISTs were valued contributors as well.

- Peace operation databases need to be more flexible than those used for conventional operations. Databases such as those for the U.S. ASAS need to be developed prior to deployment.

- CI/HUMINT became the source of choice for the tactical commanders.

- Extension of broadband communications pipes to lower echelons is still not adequate to meet tactical intelligence dissemination needs. Extension of Trojan Spirit II to the brigade level was a major step in the right direction.

- For the United States it was necessary to rely on national-level agencies to provide technology and systems to respond to the *Operation Joint Endeavor* peace operations aspects of the environment. National agencies were able to design, procure, and field systems that dealt with environment-specific shortfalls more rapidly than they could have been acquired and deployed by the military. USAREUR, as a deploying force, recognized that it must maintain dialogue with U.S. national intelligence agencies to identify systems for environment-specific problems for collection, exploitation, and dissemination.

- Sensor-to-shooter intelligence and maneuver warfare-oriented intelligence did not provide a foundation for long-range analysis and did not accurately target the intentions of low-tech belligerents.

- The proliferation of new and prototype advanced technology systems at the analytic nodes, without additional manning, sometimes detracted from mission accomplishment and often increased the load on available resources.

- The U.S. split-base support concept was not fully trusted at the tactical level, but trust is something that is earned over time. Brigades tended not to trust anything they did not produce themselves and there was a feeling that higher echelons did not understand how to package products for lower level use. Not as surprising was the fact that the coalition intelligence environment caused problems for U.S. forces when the United States was not in charge.

- The U.S. Army concluded that it needed to review doctrine in light of coalition control of the intelligence process in a non-U.S. pure environment.

- The division of tactical, theater (operational), and strategic has become less distinct and planning staffs and commanders at all levels will have to learn how to deal with this new environment.

- Tailored response packages may eventually demand that only the essential capabilities be deployed forward with a correspondingly higher reliance on split-based support from a sanctuary.

- The future operations and intelligence community will require leadership that is technology smart and flexible.

- Innovation and intellectual creativity were keys to success.

The majority of intelligence that the United States produced was tailored, timely, and releasable to IFOR. The U.S. intelligence community consistently disseminated actionable intelligence without divulging sensitive sources and methods. The challenge for the future is to continue community advances in this expanding arena of intelligence support to coalition operations, by continuing to fine-tune the process, procedures, and capabilities. When U.S. and NATO consumers can find and retrieve the operational and tactical intelligence they need when they need it, the policy advances made to date will be further advanced. Refining the NATO and national, and the

U.S. in particular, approaches with coalition partners will ensure that U.S. and NATO-led coalitions in the future will have a near real-time, easily accessible, common picture of the battlefield for all coalition partners.

V. CIMIC: Civil Military Cooperation
James J. Landon

In today's complex world, international and non-governmental civil organizations have become increasingly important in the formulation of political, social, or economic solutions to world crises. In most cases, these organizations are a crucial part of long-term solutions. More often than not, they must take over economic and political development after a peace operation or formal military involvement has ended. The traditional guarantors of global security—military forces—must now find ways to work more closely with these various organizations. The crisis in Bosnia-Herzegovina sharply demonstrated the new roles and responsibilities that these organizations have come to shoulder in the post-Cold War world, and the high hurdle that the challenge of coordinating activities with these civil organizations presented to the IFOR deployment.

This chapter addresses some of the most critical observations of IFOR Civil Military Cooperation (CIMIC) operations. While most observations were interrelated and crossed organizational lines, four main functional areas can be identified: Multiple CIMIC Doctrines; Deployment and Reserve Support; CIMIC Command Structure and Organization; and Civil Coordination.

Background

The General Framework Agreement for Peace (GFAP) in Bosnia and Herzegovina authorized the establishment of IFOR to ensure compliance with the provisions of the GFAP. The military aspects of the GFAP had the principal assigned tasks of:

- The establishment of a durable cessation of hostilities;
- The establishment of legal authorization for IFOR to take required actions to ensure compliance with the agreement and the force's own protection; and
- The establishment of lasting security and arms control measures which aimed to promote a permanent reconciliation and to facilitate the achievement of all political arrangements agreed to in the GFAP.[18]

While all provisions were broad in nature, the third provision—the promotion of a permanent reconciliation and the facilitation of political arrangements—presented the greatest amount of ambiguity. Given the inherently political and civil nature of the dispute, IFOR maintained a pivotal interest in the implementation of civil and political aspects of the GFAP. Successful accomplishment of IFOR military responsibilities would constitute only one leg of a three-legged stool which included political and civil responsibilities—all of which were required to create a stable, solid structure.

Recognizing this fact, the GFAP provided for supporting tasks that IFOR could undertake within the limits of the above identified principal tasks and available resources. These supporting tasks included—

- To help create secure conditions for the conduct by others of other tasks associated with the peace settlement;
- To assist the movement of organizations in the accomplishment of humanitarian missions; and

- To assist the UN agencies and other international organizations in their humanitarian missions.[19]

For the most part, the responsibility for coordinating the vast array of implied supporting tasks fell to a small, often unnoticed staff section—CIMIC/Civil Affairs. CIMIC, the NATO acronym for Civil Military Cooperation, was thus to play an unprecedented role in achieving the objectives of the GFAP. The implementation of the civil aspects of the GFAP was essential to IFOR's exit strategy and the return to normalcy for the people of Bosnia and Herzegovina. CIMIC was the vital link between military and civilian organizations operating in theater.

The primary and supporting military objectives outlined in the GFAP that had civil or political implications were translated into a comprehensive CIMIC Campaign Plan, which was to guide civil-military activities during the IFOR deployment. This CIMIC Campaign Plan envisioned

- Conducting civil military operations in support of the military implementation of the GFAP;
- Promoting cooperation with the civilian populace, various agencies, and national governments;
- Leveraging capabilities of NGOs, IOs, and national governments;
- Creating a parallel, unified civilian effort in support of the GFAP implementation; and
- Being prepared to assist governmental, international, and non-governmental humanitarian, public safety, and health contingencies.[20]

Translated into a comprehensive set of tasks, CIMIC operations were instrumental in facilitating a wide variety activities in support of the OHR and other organizations such as the OSCE, UNHCR, World Bank, European Union (EU), ICRC, and others who were responsible for implementing the majority of civil actions outlined in the GFAP. CIMIC personnel also participated in Joint Civil Commissions (JCCs) set up by the OHR at the regional level to facilitate civil actions throughout Bosnia Herzegovina. It also set up CIMIC Centers at the cantonal (local) level to implement civil reconstruction and improvement plans. These centers operated in each of the Multinational Divisions MNDs where there was a demonstrated need and available resources.

The wide range of specific CIMIC support to the coordination and implementation of civilian tasks demonstrates the pervasive nature of CIMIC operations. This support included—[21]

- **Electrical Power & Coal:** CIMIC personnel worked on a daily basis to facilitate cooperation between IFOR and the *Elektroprivreda*. CIMIC personnel coordinated with IFOR for increased security presence when cargo of a strategic nature such as electrical transformers and hydroelectric turbines and turbine shafts were being transported through contested territory.

- **Natural Gas:** CIMIC facilitated installation of a temporary power line and a pre-heating boiler allowing for the restoration of safer distribution pressure and gas odorization to over 50 percent of Sarajevo.

- **Roads and Bridges:** CIMIC personnel facilitated the repair or reconstruction of roads and bridges by coordinating between World Bank, IMG, IFOR/ARRC engineers, and local agencies. CIMIC personnel also performed numerous bridge, overpass, and road surveys.

- **Telecommunications:** In collaboration with the staff of IFOR CJ6 AFSOUTH, CIMIC personnel proposed an alternative short-term Global System Mobile (GSM) solution that could have provided limited cellular telephone communications for the period before and during the elections. The Telecommunication Infrastructure cell has monitored the development of telecommunications legislation, regulations, and plans for privatization that are being led by the European Bank for Reconstruction and Development (EBRD).

- **Water:** CIMIC performed periodic joint environmental inspections of the recharge aquifer at the Bacevo well field outside Sarajevo. This source provided 80 percent of the potable water for the Sarajevo area. Assistance was also provided to facilitate the shipment of laboratory materials for water analysis.

- **International Police Task Force (IPTF):** With the organization's strength just over 1,600 personnel, IPTF has been able to make major developmental strides. The CIMIC Police Working Group was instrumental in generating the plan and subsequent employment of the IPTF with Federation police throughout the country. CIMIC also developed the plans for the reorganization of Federation and *Republik Srbska* (RS) police forces.

- **Legal/Property Rights:** CIMIC personnel worked closely with the Commission on Human Rights and the Commission for Real Property Claims of Displaced Persons and Refugees, as well as the Human Rights Task Force Property Subcommittee, which operated as a watch-dog committee for the Dayton commission. CIMIC personnel also worked closely with Federation and RS committees appointed to review and revise property laws. This activity resulted in the drafting of changes to property law, and procedures for taking claims of displaced persons and refugees.

- **Refugees and Displaced Persons:** CJCIMIC (Combined Joint Civil Military Cooperation) provided a liaison officer to the OHR and the UNHCR to work on issues dealing with refugees and displaced persons. The staff also worked closely on freedom of movement and repatriation issues.

- **Non-governmental Organization Liaisons:** CIMIC NGO Liaisons coordinated transportation requests to move hundreds of tons of food and other goods throughout BH and the Federation to aid in feeding the civilian population. CIMIC personnel shared information of interest with the NGOs and provided them with an opportunity to obtain clarification of their questions from IFOR's perspective.

- **Office of the High Representative:** A CIMIC officer filled a critical role at OHR as the Special Assistant to the Chief of Staff. This position required liaison with senior officials from all international organizations. CIMIC personnel also augmented OHR staff located at the Regional Joint Civilian Commissions in Banja Luka and Tuzla. CIMIC teams provided administrative and logistic support to include performing infrastructure assessments and compiling information as part of a countrywide database. In addition, CIMIC personnel worked with local authorities to facilitate and coordinate civil-military and civil agency assistance.

- **World Bank:** CIMIC financial functional specialists provided valuable assistance to the World-Bank sponsored Emergency Recovery Program. This program funded working capitol and capitol improvement loans up to DM 300,000 to war-impacted businesses. The IFOR team analyzed and recommended for approval in excess of 20 loans worth DM 4,000,000 and trained local nationals to perpetuate the program. They also used experience gained in this involvement to provide direction to USAID (U.S. Agency for International Development) as they began a working capitol program that complements the World Bank's program for lending to Federation enterprises.

The above activities demonstrate that IFOR CIMIC operations played a critical role in the success of the IFOR deployment by using a flexible campaign plan, an adaptable force employed both tactically and operationally, and coordination efforts with civilian NGOs and IOs. The second half of this chapter focuses on the general observations and lessons learned as a result of these CIMIC activities.

Multiple CIMIC Doctrines

The concern that outbreaks of instability, combined with failing national societies and human suffering, could become unpredictably explosive and seriously threaten international peace and security has produced a modern interest in a form of international intervention that far transcends traditional global responses. A broader, more ambitious form of intervention, these "second generation" peacekeeping operations have led to an increase in global engagement in a wide range of intra-state conflicts, as well as involvement in the process of national political reconstruction, including the rehabilitation of collapsed state structures. During these operations, some of the tasks assigned to military peacekeeping forces were no longer clearly distinct from humanitarian action, as in the cases where the peacekeeping mission included ensuring the delivery of humanitarian relief supplies. In some cases, the blurring of responsibilities was compounded by the fact that the political objectives of peacekeeping were unclear and mandates were ill-defined. The IFOR deployment to Bosnia Herzegovina epitomizes the characteristics of second generation peacekeeping.

While the United States has gained considerable experience with second generation peace support operations in the last 10 years, NATO has not. Before the IFOR deployment, there was no common understanding within IFOR of the capabilities, limitations, roles, and missions of CIMIC units and personnel during these peace support operations. As a new type of operation, IFOR commanders and staff had to incorporate civil-military tasks into their overall operations based upon the varying perspectives of their personal knowledge and experience. This varying degree of experience can be observed in the IFOR deployment not only within individual commanders, but more importantly, through the various national approaches.

The search for a common NATO doctrine for the conduct of peacekeeping operations inevitably involves major problems, not the least of which is the difficulty reconciling different historic attitudes of contributing nations toward these non-traditional operations. Doctrinal development has been hampered by institutional factors. During the Cold War "traditional" peacekeeping period, military personnel from the superpowers were de facto excluded from participating in operations. Military forces from the superpowers were likely to be seen as interested parties rather than as honest brokers in whatever conflicts they became engaged.[22] The underpinnings of this concern are readily observable in the multinational approaches exhibited during the IFOR deployment. This divergence in national approaches is due in part to different nations being involved in different types of military commitments in the last 50 years, and in part to different perspectives of their own national interests. To place these doctrinal differences in the context of the IFOR deployment, some generalities are presented in the following text box and in figure 5-1.

Operationally, recognition of multinational approaches to peace support operations manifested itself through a decentralization of command and control. A March 1996 policy directive from COMARRC delegated the extent and method forces became involved in civil tasks to the judgment of the individual MND commanders.[23] The divergent CIMIC approaches and flexible interpretation of guidance had two effects. First, it underscored the need to reconcile the divergent tenets of national doctrine and develop a common NATO doctrine for CIMIC operations. Second, and more immediately, the various national approaches (such as force protection measures) had an effect on local perceptions, the building of support for IFOR's mission among the population, and the development of "unity of effort" within IFOR itself.

During the early IFOR deployment, many nations conducted individual stove-piped surveys and assessments of required tasks. There was no central planning or coordination of data collection, with the result that operations and activities were similarly stove-piped in national, functional staff or civilian agency channels. Cross-national coordination relied to a great extent on "swivel-chair" interfaces.

National Approaches - Illustrative Examples

Russian Federation: Like most nations, Russia's peacekeeping doctrine is a relatively recent development. The general concept of "Operations to Maintain Peace" encompasses a much broader range of activities that includes much of what the West would call peace enforcement or counterinsurgency. In support of the IFOR deployment, the basic tenet of Russian military doctrine that has been most apparent is its rigid command structure and adherence to written orders. Thus, while many NATO armies routinely perform implied tasks in any operation, this is not standard Russian practice. Russia considers the Dayton Peace Agreement its principal "written order," and has restricted itself to very limited support to the civil agencies. This limited support has been in practice directed only to certain ethnic (Slavic, orthodox) groups.

United States: The United States perspective on peacekeeping operations is one of the more "high intensity" approaches. U.S. doctrine stresses the need to achieve decisive "victory" and the quick resolution of conflicts through the securing of popular support. Criticism of American peacekeeping doctrine includes the comment that it lacks the subtly required for internal conflict, and has been associated with an inexact and counterproductive use of force. Translation of U.S. peacekeeping doctrine in Bosnia has resulted in the dominance of force protection measures, the undertaking of major infrastructure projects, and CIMIC activities centered on coordination and liaison.

France and the United Kingdom: France, and to a lesser extent the United Kingdom, politely refused the augmentation of their MND with U.S. Army Civil Affairs personnel. This was done not because they do not undertake CIMIC activities, but because either they have their own civil affairs personnel (France) or because of the integral part that civil affairs operations play in their conventional operations (United Kingdom). In each case, the French and UK MNDs have been much more active assisting civil organizations with direct support to local, "hearts and minds" projects.

NATO: NATO's draft doctrine for peace support operations has tried to be responsive to the various national approaches, and has therefore taken a very broad view of how to accomplish this new type of mission. NATO's approach acknowledges the changing security environment following the end of the Cold War, and sets the stage for a more expansive commitment beyond its former concentration on collective defense. NATO's approach is based on the principles of traditional peacekeeping, with missions of observation, interposition forces, and transition assistance.

128 Lessons from Bosnia

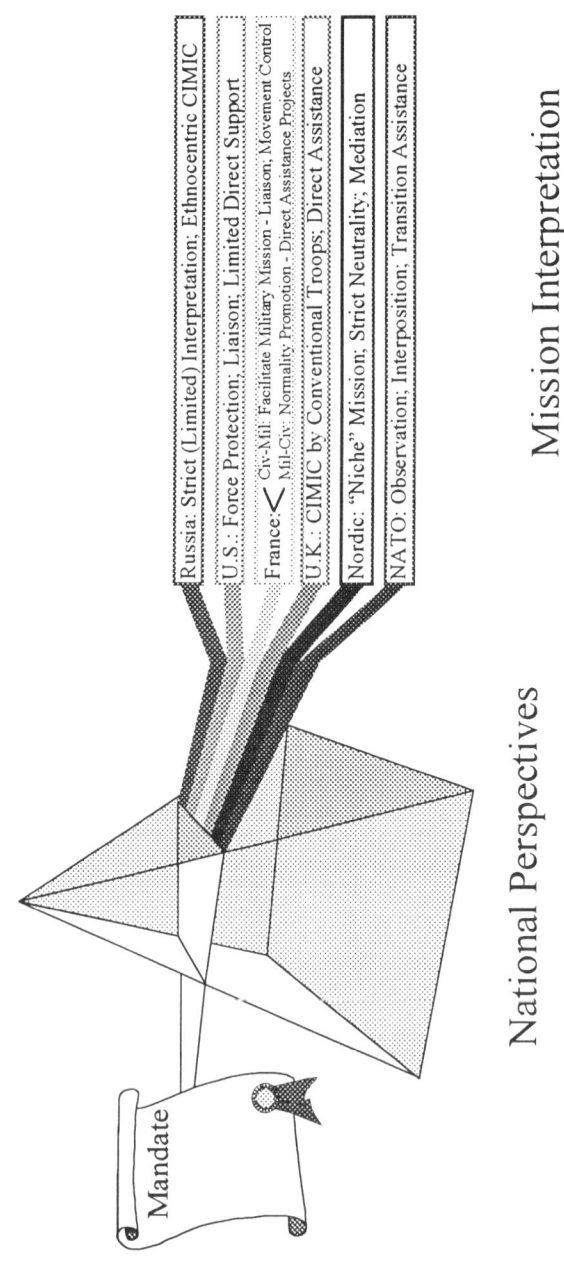

Figure 5-1. National Peacekeeping Perspectives Drive IFOR Mission Interpretation

Deployment and Reserve Support

The IFOR deployment has illuminated the fact that many traditional ground-combat commanders have little knowledge of civilian affairs or understanding of CIMIC activities. This lack of knowledge was demonstrated in many areas, but none more so than in the campaign planning stage. During the development of the OPLAN, it was reported that there was only one Civil Affairs officer assigned to assist AFSOUTH in the planning of the IFOR deployment. The campaign plan not only inadequately identified military tasks for CIMIC, but also negatively affected CIMIC deployment, manning, and logistics requirements.

Across the theater, high praise has been levied on the efforts of the U.S. Army Reserve Civil Affairs assets. A large part of their ability to interact effectively with the local population, NGOs, and representatives from other governmental and supra-governmental organizations is the very fact that they are reservists who bring to the operation their civilian perspective and transferable skills. In fact, 96 percent of the U.S. Civil Affairs structure is comprised of reservists. The late mobilization of these assets, and the resulting delay in their deployment into theater, placed the deploying lead ground elements at a disadvantage.[24] Lessons learned have shown that the early deployment of Civil Affairs personnel in the theater of operations can be a great force multiplier, setting the stage for the introduction of follow-on forces into an environment that has benefited from specialized interaction with the local population. The impact of this loss of strategic liaison would have been greater had the OHR not also been delayed in its deployment into theater. The lesson has been re-learned that in operations in which the civil implementation of the overall objectives plays such a key role, Civil Affairs assets have an important, timely role to play.

The final deployment and Reserve support observation builds upon the negative consequences of the above points. Once the Civil Affairs deployment began, it was learned that some nations (most significantly France) neither planned for, nor needed, U.S. Civil Affairs assets in their MND. Rather than revise the Civil

Affairs manning requirements now being implemented by the Presidential Select Reserve Call-Up, the excess U.S. Civil Affairs personnel were absorbed by the IFOR and ARRC headquarters, resulting in an increase in these HQ CIMIC structures by two to three times. While basic logistical support to this overflow was not provided, the main impact was that the excess staff began to get involved in functions normally assumed at lower levels of command. In all, 352 CIMIC personnel deployed to Bosnia from the United States, compared with 40 from France and a total of 50 from all other nations.

CIMIC Command Structure and Organization

A Combined Joint Civil Military Cooperation (CJCIMIC) staff element was implemented at IFOR headquarters to facilitate coordination of CIMIC activities with NGOs and IOs. The CIMIC organization was to focus on liaison with the civilian organizations from the governmental to local opstina level to regenerate national regulations and promote limited nation rebuilding. The structure was also to provide an avenue for the numerous aid agencies to interface with the military on support arrangements related to their projects in theater. CIMIC Centers were established at all levels of the IFOR command to provide a location for NGOs to meet and coordinate with the military. A Joint Civil Commission was established to facilitate interactions between the military and civil agencies on GFAP civil matters and humanitarian assistance activities. A Joint Military Commission rounded out the formal coordination structures, which was established to interact with the FWF on GFAP military matters.

Early on in the IFOR deployment, it became clear that there was a disconnect between the CJCIMIC and the ARRC CIMIC organizational structure. To highlight the point, it was observed that the CJCIMIC had been getting involved in infrastructure projects relating to Sarajevo, and the ARRC CIMIC assumed responsibility for political/military interface and the resolution of constitution development issues—a seeming reversal of roles. Two conditions created this situation. As previously mentioned, both CJCIMIC and ARRC CIMIC headquarters were overstaffed with the CIMIC assets refused by the United Kingdom and France. Second the decision that the city of Sarajevo occupied such a key position, specifically with regard to the world media, that a special CIMIC Center would have to be created just to deal with the implementation of civil projects in this city. CJCIMIC assumed this responsibility, but when the CJCIMIC commenced operations in Sarajevo, it did so in the backyard of the ARRC CIMIC. One hundred CIMIC personnel, or almost 30 percent of the total CIMIC personnel in Bosnia, support these two headquarters alone.

The problems inherent in having two headquarters responsible for the same area of operations are obvious. The decision was made to deviate from the OPLAN to adapt to unexpected situations on the ground. While addressing the needs of the immediate situation, the deviation from the OPLAN resulted in the loss of the traditional functions of the higher IFOR headquarters over the subordinate ARRC headquarters. In response to this situation, the Chiefs of Staff of IFOR and the ARRC published Terms of Reference for CIMIC operations and responsibilities in the IFOR Theater in order to help define and clarify the overall CIMIC command structure.

Closely related to the IFOR - ARRC CIMIC "turf battle," some coalition offices were dissatisfied with what they saw as an overall failure to put in place a command structure capable of synchronizing the efforts of both the military and civilian components in what should be a tightly integrated operation. As a military-military example, there were approximately 70 personnel at CJCIMIC; half of these were active with project management, and the other half involved in liaison. Despite this manpower, it was observed that there appeared to be no coordination/cooperation with CIMIC activities with the French-led division at MND(SE). From the civil-military aspect, the CIMIC mission was to help create a parallel, **unified** civilian effort in support of NATO Peace Plan implementation. However, the formidable civil-military obstacles standing in the way of this objective were many and varied. In one civil-military example, an exemplary **military** performance in the reconstruction area prompted a strongly worded criticism from one of the UN **civil** agencies (which may have been embarrassed by its own conspicuous lack of success).

To some U.S. CIMIC officers, one of the biggest challenges they faced was to not trivialize the multinational contribution. These officers felt that they had to convince other nations that despite its large deployment of Civil Affairs personnel, the United States was not trying to dominate the operation or force its doctrine on other nations or NATO, despite the fact that the United States had a clear lead in the development of CIMIC procedures tested in recent operational deployments.

Civil Coordination

The civil-military mission of the IFOR deployment had among its goals promoting cooperation with the civilian populace, various agencies, and national governments; leveraging the capabilities of NGOs, IOs, and national governments to achieve end state; creating a parallel, unified civilian effort in support of NATO Peace Plan initiatives. Implementation of the military aspects of the Dayton Peace Agreement provided the essential secure environment and freedom of movement for the commencement of the civil aspects of the Agreement. As such, delay in civil implementation was anticipated. What had not been anticipated, however, was the amount of lag time that the civil coordination structures required before they could become operational. In the absence of functioning civil implementation institutions, IFOR received public pressure to take a larger role in implementing GFAP civilian tasks.

Overall responsibility for the implementation of the civil and military tasks agreed to in the Dayton Peace Agreement was divided between the North Atlantic Council (NAC) through the NATO chain of command and the Peace Implementation Council (PIC) Steering Board through the OHR. Initially, no formal mechanism existed to develop the unified political direction necessary to synchronize civil and military policy between these two bodies. Given the importance of an integrated civil military effort in Bosnia Herzegovina, this was a significant shortfall that had ramifications across all issue areas.

Under the Dayton Peace Agreement, the OHR was tasked to coordinate the activities of the civilian organization in B-H to ensure the efficient implementation of the civilian aspects of the peace settlement, and to remain in close contact with the IFOR commander to facilitate the discharge of their respective responsibilities. But the civilian implementation institutions mandated by the Dayton Peace Agreement began the operation under considerable disadvantages. These organizations had to be created, funded and staffed on the ground after the military deployment. This delay resulted in public pressure for IFOR to take on a larger role in implementing civil tasks. This public pressure resulted in a limited self-fulfilling prophecy. Once the OHR established itself in theater, the impression created was that where the OHR should have been taking the lead on projects, such as providing gas, electricity, water, etc., it was expecting that IFOR would take the lead. As a result, "mission extension" was a natural occurrence because of the competence and ability of the CIMIC organization and a lack of visible activity in these areas by civil agencies.

Another problem with civil coordination centered on established structures. The High Representative was not a UN Special Representative with UN authority. His political guidance came from the Steering Board of the Peace Implementation Council (see Figure 5-2), which was not a standing internationally recognized political organization. As such, the absence of an organization with which the North Atlantic Council (NATO's standing political body) could coordinate policy hampered synchronization of civil military implementation of the GFAP. Given the UN's reluctance to play a lead role, there was effectively no internationally recognized political organization providing overall direction. As a consequence, actors operated autonomously within a loose framework of cooperation, but without a formal structure for developing unified policy.

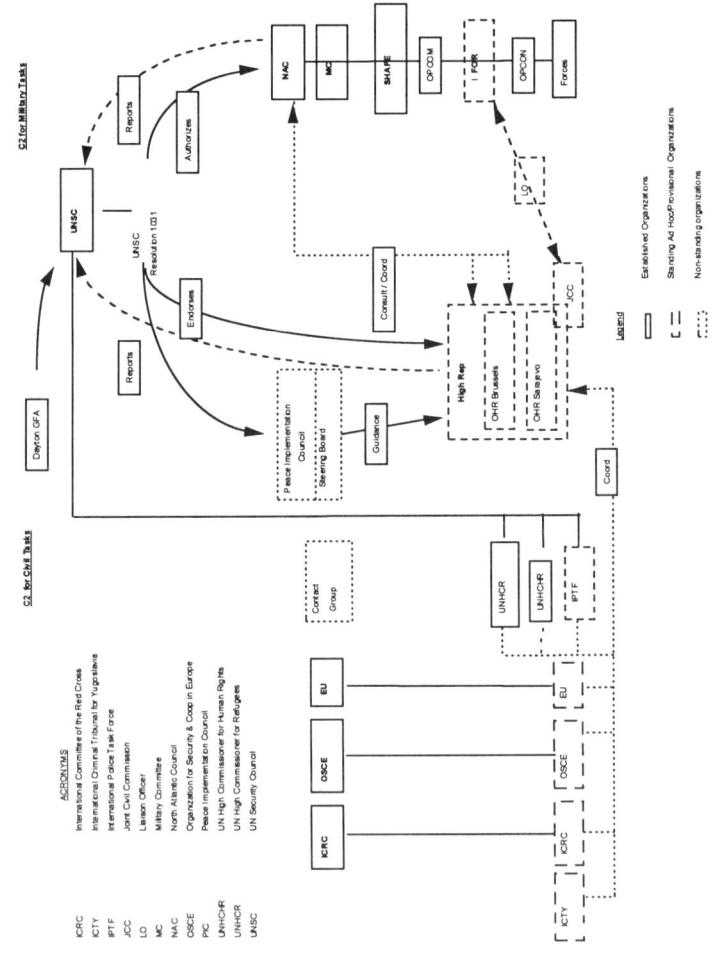

Figure 5-2. IFOR Civil Military Coordinating Structures

The civil cooperation situation in Bosnia was unique in that members of the non-governmental and supra-governmental relief and development organizations were already actively engaged when the IFOR deployment commenced. In fact, there were an estimated 530 NGOs in theater at D+1. But this situation created its own set of problems. First, as mentioned earlier, the CIMIC assets were delayed in their deployment. As UNPROFOR forces withdrew or transferred into IFOR, valuable CIMIC turnover opportunities were lost. Lacking any advanced information, the NGOs assumed that IFOR would continue, if not increase, the same type of support that UNPROFOR provided to them. The philosophy advanced by IFOR, however, was quite different than UNPROFOR's. IFOR refused to provide what it thought the NGO community could provide for themselves because of the fear of causing a dependency on IFOR for essential aspects of support. Paramount in this philosophy was the promotion of self-sustaining activities in preparation for IFOR's eventual withdrawal. The ARRC did send personnel in early to brief the NGOs on what to expect, educate them on what IFOR troops would be doing, but the briefing was only given in Sarajevo and not in the field where a majority of the NGOs were located.

CIMIC activities at MND(N) best epitomize the combined impact that doctrine, command structures and organizations, and mission interpretation had on the promotion or prevention of civil coordination. First, the CIMIC Center is doctrinally the central location for all NGOs to meet with the military. At MND(N), the CIMIC Center was located inside the gate at Tuzla Main, whereas most of the NGOs were 20 minutes away in downtown Tuzla. With access to the base by non-IFOR personnel strictly limited, the effectiveness of the CIMIC Center as a tool for coordinating NGO and military activity was greatly reduced. Second, force protection regulations hampered CIMIC personnel's ability to perform their CIMIC mission effectively. When CIMIC personnel were able to muster the needed four vehicles to leave the base, they arrived at an NGO site with a heavier military presence than some NGOs desired. As a related issue, the appearance of the need for great security when outside the protected confines of Tuzla Main worked counter to the efforts of CIMIC personnel to create an impression among the local population that the internal situation had improved. Finally, with the inaccessibility of the Tuzla CIMIC to the NGOs and the restrictive procedures limiting the CIMIC staff's ability to visit the NGOs, the requirement to communicate indirectly had increased. Despite this requirement, MND(N) had only one phone line of "dubious reliability," and had no fax or e-mail capability. Almost all communication between MND(N) and the NGOs had to be relayed through intermediaries, generally with a 24-hour turnaround time.

Despite these shortcomings, CIMIC personnel were able to coordinate effectively with the NGOs. Across the theater, CIMIC officers have had high praise for the efforts and working relationship with the NGOs at the tactical level. CIMIC forces were able to overcome obstacles and provide early support by placing liaison officers and functional specialists within responsible civilian agencies. CIMIC Centers and Elements, along with systematic CIMIC reporting structure, were established at command levels from SHAPE down to battalion level. CIMIC assets maintained liaison, coordination, and planning with key NGOs and IOs in theater, and collected critical and timely information. Key in this regard, and drawing on lessons learned from past peace support and complex emergency deployments, was the establishment of CIMIC Centers as the focal point for civil military coordination activities.

NATO civil-military activities prior to the IFOR deployment were very narrow in scope. Prior to the IFOR deployment, CIMIC operations were generally regarded as "rear area" activities associated with host-nation logistic support and alleviating displaced person interference with military operations. This combat-oriented approach had little relevance in the Bosnia context. The essence of the IFOR mission was to maintain a safe and secure environment so that reconciliation and reconstruction could take place. Since mission accomplishment depended upon effective civil-military cooperation, such cooperation, and the CIMIC organization designed to facilitate this cooperation, became a vital "front-line" asset.

Multinational peace operations are accompanied by doctrine, culture, and language differences that challenge the overall coordination of the mission and ability to achieve unity of effort. Traditions, concepts, customs, and attitudes are often not compatible, and require active efforts to find the "middle ground." In particular, there was no common understanding or approach to CIMIC operations at the outset of the IFOR deployment. Ground commanders generally lacked a basic understanding of the role and value of CIMIC. This lack of understanding led to misperceptions that CIMIC activities were contributing to mission creep, and resulted in unanticipated constraints being placed on CIMIC operations until the value became more apparent to commanders. Unofficial doctrine, tactics, and procedures were essentially developed as the operation progressed. With more than 30 nations participating, there was an added challenge to merge the cultural differences to achieve unity of effort and avoid clashes in these cultures. Liaison activities became a very important way of addressing many cross-cultural difficulties, and were used effectively to facilitate coordination.

Given the very broad range of approaches and policies present, only a few common principles emerge. However, there are several points of commonality which should perhaps be stressed in order to help the international community work together effectively. They include:

1. Recognition that different types of military roles and missions are appropriate in different kinds of crises. Limited military roles are appropriate for situations dominated by humanitarian disasters. When the rule of law has broken down and relief workers cannot do their work in safety, local security roles become appropriate. Peacekeeping, where the primary mission derives from a cease-fire or settlement agreement that needs international supervision, is another qualitative dimension.

2. Belief in the fundamentally political nature of peace support and humanitarian assistance missions. While military support may be necessary to ensure proper resolution, these are not primarily

military missions, but rather primarily situations where the conditions must be created in which the parties are able to manage their differences and take over the functioning of their own society.

3. Broad recognition of the roles and value of non-national actors. Both the international community and the NGO/PVO community have technical expertise and political postures that enable them to work toward longer term solutions in the countries where the crises occur. As this recognition grows, the desirability of finding new ways to work with these non-national actors is becoming more broadly understood.

4. Realization that appropriate linkages to the key civilian agencies of their governments (foreign ministries, disaster relief officials, and long-term development specialists) are crucial both to successful mission accomplishment and to development of successful transition strategies.

The IFOR deployment, in many regards, is a living prototype of a post-Cold War response to complex global instability. It was the kind of operation that has been foreshadowed for years, and the kind of operation we may expect to see more of in the near future. The international paradigm for global conflict resolution has shifted. A resultant paradigm shift in the development of civil-military coordination is looming over the horizon. If properly addressed, the lessons from the IFOR deployment can serve as a guide to lead new concepts of civil-military cooperation into the 21st century.

VI. The International Police Task Force[25]

Andy Bair and Michael J. Dziedzic

The Mandate and Resources

The Mandate

The approach adopted under the Dayton Peace Accords (DPA) differed fundamentally from UNPROFOR. The mandate for UNPROFOR was largely humanitarian, facilitating delivery of relief supplies and shielding Moslem enclaves in territories occupied by Serb forces. In discharging their numerous mandates, UNPROFOR commanders had to consult political authorities in both NATO and the UN before force could be used. This unwieldy "dual key" command and control arrangement rendered UNPROFOR powerless to respond to tactical developments. The Contact Group countries (i.e., the United States, United Kingdom, France, Germany, and Russia), especially the United States, insisted that IFOR would not suffer these debilitating vulnerabilities. To discharge its responsibilities under annex 1A of the DPA (i.e., to ensure the separation of forces, their confinement to cantons, and downsizing), therefore, IFOR would be endowed with a single chain of command (NATO), executive powers, robust rules of engagement, and overwhelming force.

UNSCR 1035 articulates the mandate for both IFOR and the IPTF (21 Dec 1995). As was the case with IFOR, however, the raison d'être for the IPTF originates in the DPA. Annex 11 of Dayton explicitly states that responsibility for maintaining a "safe and secure environment for all persons" rests with the signatories themselves;[26] however, to assist in discharging their public security obligations, the parties requested that the IPTF be created and that it perform the following functions:

- To monitor and inspect judicial and law enforcement activities, including conducting joint patrols with local police forces.
- To advise and train law enforcement personnel.
- To analyze the public security threat and offer advice to government authorities on how to organize their police forces most effectively.
- To facilitate law enforcement improvement and respond to the requests of the parties, to the extent possible.

The IPTF was not armed and was not empowered to enforce local laws. Since its purpose was to help already established law enforcement agencies maintain public order and assist them in adopting methods of policing consistent with international standards, the IPTF could only function effectively with the consent of the parties. In the absence of such collaboration, the IPTF possessed neither the mandate nor the resources to preserve public order independently. The dilemmas this would generate for IPTF officials do not appear to have been anticipated or well understood by drafters of this annex. The IPTF's first Deputy Commissioner, Robert Wasserman, offers the following insights into this situation:

> It appears the framers of Dayton perceived that the IPTF would somehow simply monitor local police to see they didn't get out of hand and then advise willing parties on how to professionalize the police with modern practices. There was no thought given to the fact that the ethnic rivalries meant there was no functioning police to protect minorities after Dayton. And Annex 11 used the term 'internationally

accepted standards of policing,' which are non-existent. There are internationally accepted human rights standards, but policing reform required something far more descriptive.[27]

In circumstances where implementation of Dayton ran counter to interests of one of the parties (e.g., the transfer of Serb-held suburbs of Sarajevo to the Federation or the resettlement of Moslems to strategic locations in the ZOS), local police either withdrew or became active protagonists. In such instances, IFOR was compelled to become involved. While IFOR could provide "area security" or reinforced patrolling to deter lawlessness, its forces were not trained or equipped for riot control or law enforcement tasks. Nor was it considered prudent to engage in activity that smacked of policing. Thus, when the police force of one of the parties refused to cooperate with the IPTF—because doing so would have damaged their vital interests—an "enforcement gap" arose. There were no effective sanctions available to the IPTF to punish noncompliance, and this gap was never satisfactorily bridged during the life of the IFOR mission.

Peace Mission Organization

By establishing IFOR under NATO auspices, the "dual key" problem suffered by UNPROFOR was resolved for purposes of implementing the military provisions of Dayton, but the consequence was to fragment implementation of civilian aspects. The two inter national actors concerned with maintaining a safe and secure environment, IFOR and the IPTF, were divided from each other organizationally with the IPTF falling under the UNMIBH. Yet a fourth actor, the OHR, was delegated a coordinating role by the GFAP, but without authority over either organization. The IPTF commissioner was simply directed to consult with the HR. Responsibility for organizing the pivotal national elections, moreover, was assigned to the OSCE, which itself regularly spoke with contradictory voices.[28] In addition, the UNHCR, the World Bank, numerous other international organizations, and several hundred NGOs had vital independent contributions to make to various aspects of the peace-building process.

During the first crucial months, the HR made no effort to promote coordination among the various civilian entities by convening regular meetings of the "principals" or heads of the other key international organizations operating in Bosnia. Only after the mission was well underway was the HR ultimately prodded into conducting weekly "Principal Meetings" to bring a measure of coherence to the peace operation.[29] Obtaining strategic unity of effort out of this fragmented structure, therefore, could only be achieved through considerable exertion and continuous attention. At the operational level, the national and municipal elections compelled the key institutional actors (IFOR/SFOR, OSCE, IPTF, OHR) to establish a Joint Elections Operations Center for more timely exchange of information and coordination of responses.

Size and Composition of Civ-Pol

In the wake of SCR 1026 (30 November 1995), a UN assessment team visited Bosnia in December 1995 to establish the requirements for this anticipated Civ-Pol mission. The principal factor used to determine the number of IPTF personnel was the combined strength of the Bosnian police forces. As the Secretary-General reported to the Security Council on 13 December 1995, the total was 44,750 (32,750 in the Federation and 12,000 in the Serb Republic).[30] Using a ratio of one monitor for every 30 local policemen, the IPTF was authorized 1,721 monitors.[31]

On December 24, 1995, the UN Secretary General issued a *note verbale* inviting UN member states to contribute to the newly established monitoring mission. Over 40 countries responded, and the first contingent of monitors began to deploy a month later. The original plan called for the IPTF to establish more than 100 field offices. When the UN deployed, it initially established a headquarters in Sarajevo; regional headquarters in Tuzla, Banja Luka, and Sarajevo; 14 district offices; and 54 field stations. *The IPTF did not approach full strength until August 1996.*

The only skills required to qualify for the IPTF were fluency in English, the ability to drive, and 8 years of experience in policing (as policing was defined in the donor country). During the initial stages of deployment, it was not uncommon for IPTF members to fall short of even these minimal standards. Of the three requirements, the most vital was competence in English. Without the ability to communicate, personnel were incapable of making any contribution to the mission. Another serious constraint was lack of credibility for those monitors who were not proficient as police officers. Local Bosnian police cadres tended to regard themselves as technically superior to IPTF personnel, particularly those from developing states. In addition, the long-range objective was to reorient Bosnia's various police agencies to function in accordance with principles of democratic policing. Police monitors from autocratic regimes could not be expected to grasp the nuances of democratic policing themselves, let alone imbue these ideals in their Bosnian counterparts.

The need to conduct screening in the donor country <u>before</u> deployment to Bosnia became apparent at an early stage, and an effort was made as early as March 1996 to do this in a few donor nations. Prior to recruiting the second rotation for duty after December 1996 (a normal tour in Bosnia being 1 year), the UN began routinely examining volunteers in source countries before deployment. To improve the English competence of incoming personnel, the IPTF Training Unit developed an English aptitude test (speaking, reading, and writing). To avoid compromise of the exam, the IPTF insisted that a member of their training staff accompany the teams administering the qualifying exams. This has significantly enhanced the quality of incoming IPTF personnel. The quality of the force was also greatly enhanced during recruitment of the second rotation by specifying to donors the spectrum of seniority and skills required to staff the organization (e.g., supervisors, forensics specialists, trainer/mentor, etc.). Once the UN demonstrated it was serious about getting qualified people, most countries responded positively and began producing personnel with appropriate capabilities.

Prior to deployment in the field, newly assigned police monitors underwent a 1-week screening and orientation course at the IPTF training facility outside Zagreb, Croatia. Personnel were tested for English language skills and driving ability. The primary function was to provide specific information and training required for the mission in Bosnia. Among the topics covered were the mandate, IPTF reporting forms, computer literacy, attributes of the mission area, mine awareness, and an orientation to IFOR/SFOR.

Logistic Support

When UNPROFOR transferred authority for the Bosnia operation to IFOR in December 1995, it also transferred the existing UN logistical and communication infrastructure to the NATO-led operation. NATO contingents already deployed in Bosnia and the more combat-capable non-NATO units also came under IFOR command. This made it possible for IFOR to begin operations immediately and to reach its full complement of over 60,000 troops expeditiously. No consideration was given to the needs of the IPTF, however, even though it was to be a UN-supported activity just like UNPROFOR had been.

The consequence of this for the IPTF was that it had to build its entire operation essentially from the ground up. Although UNPROFOR had included a Civ-Pol mission, the Dayton accord left them in limbo. The UNSCR authorizing the formation of the IPTF, and the United Nations Mission in Bosnia-Herzegovina (UNMIH) to manage it, was approved in late December 1995. Organizers then had to confront the ponderous task of procuring essential resources via the UN's logistic support system and recruiting some 1,700 qualified police monitors from around the world. Even the United States was delayed in fielding its contingent. The result was a considerable lag in bringing the IPTF up to operational status, and a serious gap in readiness when the Sarajevo suburbs were transferred to Moslem authority in February-March 1996.[32]

Since the IPTF was under UNMIBH auspices—as opposed to being part of an integrated mission with combined military and Civ-Pol components—logistical limitations became a chronic operational concern. In addition to the UN's inherent bureaucratic lethargy, the IPTF faced an uphill battle for resources because of its unfortunate parentage. Many in the United States had heaped condemnation on the UN for the demise of UNPROFOR. Yet when it came to finding a sponsor to sustain this creature of the U.S.-brokered Dayton Accord, the UN was the most attractive alternative. It took time for the IPTF to recover from the animus that had developed between the United States and the UN. While improvements were made with the passage of time, shortcomings in transportation, communications, and interpreters continued to plague the mission well into the SFOR phase.

Chronic deficiencies in UNMIBH logistics support were enumerated in a 10-page memorandum to the IPTF Commissioner from his Deputy Chief Logistician in late July 1996. The impact on operations was summarized as follows:

> Based upon the IPTF subordinate relationship to the UNMIBH, the IPTF has no organic assets. All logistical support is to be provided by UNMIBH. The general level of support by UNMIBH has been inadequate. As of 29 July, the required communications, vehicles, reasonable fuel supply, EDP [Electronic Data Processing], and medical support has [sic] not been completed...The current IPTF logistical status to support the mandate is unacceptable, and unless rectified prior to 15 August 1996, may cause the IPTF to fail in all or part of the critical mission requirements.[33]

Shortages of mission-essential items such as communications equipment, vehicles, and medical care plagued the IPTF from the earliest days of its deployment.[34] Many items that were ultimately transferred to the IPTF from UNPROFOR stocks (e.g., vehicles and office furniture) routinely arrived in damaged or unserviceable condition and had often been stripped of associated items such as jacks or tool kits.[35] The problem was exacerbated by the Chief Administrative Officer of UNMIBH, who refused to process IPTF requests for support prior to the arrival of each influx of personnel. Since deployments extended over a 6-month period (March-August), a persistent delay was built into the process of achieving operational status.[36] Summarizing the situation, a senior IPTF logistician asserted that, "During formal and informal discussions with IPTF Monitors, from the IPTF Stations, Districts, and Regions, almost without exception all have indicated that UNMIBH logistical support has been unresponsive, or totally inadequate."[37]

Aggregate data compiled by the IPTF headquarters staff substantiate these impressions. Communications equipment was chronically in short supply, with deficiencies of 25 percent for handheld radios, 29 percent for vehicle radios, and 65 percent for satellite links (at the end of July 1996).[38] Transportation was another major limitation. The IPTF had been issued 516 vehicles as of 30 July, yet only 454 were operational. This constituted a 21 percent shortfall from the 574 required to carry out mandated responsibilities.[39] UNMIBH made no provision to replace total losses in spite of regular attrition, a problem that was accentuated by the recurring failure of donor countries to ensure all their monitors could drive.[40] Even simple items, such as snow tires and chains, began to loom large in late September after the UNMIBH Administrative Officer refused repeated IPTF requisition requests. This was in spite of the fact that 75 percent of IPTF vehicles had bald tires, and November was one of the snowiest months in Bosnia.[41] This had serious operational implications since the municipal elections were slated at the time for 22 November, and this electoral process was likely to be contentious, involving efforts by tens of thousands of prospective voters to cross the IEBL.

It was perhaps inevitable that the IPTF would turn to IFOR to ameliorate certain shortcomings in mission support. As the operation was being established, the IPTF sought assistance with medical care, fuel, maps, security for its vehicle maintenance facility, and access for its personnel to military stores (e.g., PXs). With the exception of maps (which were readily available) and PXs (which were not), the support that IFOR sought was decentralized and available only by negotiating directly with one or more of IFOR's contributing countries.[42]

This scattershot approach proved to be particularly inappropriate for purposes of medical care. The UN's medical staff assumed that IPTF personnel would be able to "depend on the medical support system provided by IFOR medical facilities."[43] Consequently, in January 1996, they directed UNPROFOR's Medical Coordination Center (MEDCOC) in Zagreb to make the necessary arrangements before it had to terminate operations on 1 April 1996.[44] IFOR did agree to provide emergency medical evacuation. For other medical support, MEDCOC was directed to approach each national contingent possessing medical units to make arrangements. Given that the willingness and capacity of these national contingents to take on such additional burdens varied widely, this did not result in reliable and comprehensive medical coverage. As late as 30 July 1996, UNMIBH had not made any formal arrangements for medical support other than emergency evacuation. Even though nations such as Norway allowed IPTF personnel to use their medical services on an informal, space available basis, this still left many gaps. In the view of a senior IPTF official, this situation "jeopardizes the IPTF operationally, and more seriously, from a personal safety aspect."[45]

IFOR also provided other forms of support to the IPTF, including co-location of radio transmitters (for security) and fuel on a cash reimbursable basis. In the latter case, however, British forces later refused to refuel IPTF vehicles because UNMIBH had failed to provide reimbursement. In mid-July, IFOR agreed to formalize a "Logistics Support Package" involving co-location of communications antennas and diesel fuel storage sites, and, in emergency cases only, to provide fuel, medical care, water, rations, shower facilities, and maps.[46] This alleviated the most extreme potential implications of the IPTF's logistical shortcomings, but the chronic problems remained well into the SFOR phase of operations.

As the IPTF entered its second year, logistic support had improved considerably. Arrangements with SFOR were in place, UNMIBH itself became more responsive, and logistics pipelines began operating predictably with the simple passage of time. Nevertheless, its operational capacity continued to be impeded, in particular by inadequate transportation. The IPTF's aging vehicle fleet required excessive maintenance and had never been large enough to accommodate fully its multiple tasks in the first place.

The Mission

Phases of the Operation

The Dayton Peace Accord established the authority and purpose for both the IPTF (annex 11) and IFOR (annex 1A). The only reference to duration pertains to IFOR, stating that the parties "...welcome the willingness of the international community to send to the region, for a period of approximately 1 year, a force to assist in the implementation of the territorial and other militarily related provisions of the agreement as described herein."[47] Although annex 1A had largely been fulfilled after a year, the most crucial civilian aspects of the DPA (e.g., refugee returns, municipal elections, status of Brcko, war criminals) remained outstanding. Accordingly, a subsequent military force, SFOR, was authorized by NATO and the United Nations. SFOR's expected duration was 18 months, until June 1998. The IPTF mandate was also extended, but only for a year, until December 1997.

Owing to the crucial role performed by Amb. Richard Holbrooke in forging the Dayton agreement, the State Department was the lead agency for orchestrating the U.S. role in implementation. No pol-mil plan was developed to guide this effort.

During the IFOR phase of the operation, the IPTF focused on monitoring local police and judicial authorities for compliance with internationally accepted standards in their daily operations and treatment of minorities, and on facilitating the September 1996 national elections. During the SFOR phase greater attention was given to training and restructuring local police forces so their future conduct would conform to norms of democratic policing (See Guiding Philosophy of the IPTF Mission, below).

The Deployment Gap

The first real test for the IPTF came when neighborhoods surrounding Sarajevo were transferred from the Serbs to the Federation in early 1996. The Dayton Agreement directed that control of certain high ground and buffer zones around Sarajevo that had been fiercely contested during the war be transferred to the Federation so the city would not be as vulnerable to Serb artillery fire in the future. These suburbs were populated by over 100,000 ethnic Serbs. Many were not permanent residents but had themselves been displaced from other locations in Sarajevo by the fighting. The transfer of these seven municipalities (Vogosca, Centar, Novi Grad, Ilijas, Hadzici, Ilidza, and Grbavica) was scheduled to take place simultaneously on 4 February 1996, 45 days after implementation of the DPA had begun.

As the date approached, the IPTF was not yet functional. None of the senior leadership had yet arrived, fewer than 400 monitors were on hand, and very few field stations had yet been opened. Other crucial deficiencies were described by two IFOR public safety specialists assigned to assist the IPTF during this early period:

> In addition to manpower difficulties and almost no command and control structure, IPTF faced other critical deficiencies. Habitable office space was at a premium. Also scarce were phone links, for example, between IPTF headquarters and IFOR, the support base in Zagreb, and field stations. In addition, radios, base stations, vehicles, and petroleum products were in short supply.[48]

In addition to the unpreparedness of the IPTF, the OHR had not done any detailed planning for the transition. Consequently, on 4 February the High Representative and the IFOR commander announced that the transfer would be delayed. The concept would also be changed to a phased process occurring over a 6-week period ending in mid-March. This adjustment provided an opportunity for the IPTF to become partially operational and for IFOR to render crucial assistance with planning, logistics, and communications. Serb authorities in Pale took advantage of the delay, however, to prepare for a sweeping evacuation of the suburbs and to more thoroughly ransack fixed property so that incoming Federation citizens would inherit little more than a wasteland.

In mid-February, as the OHR, IPTF, and IFOR began to conduct the first transfer, Serb authorities implemented their own plan to relocate ethnic Serbs into the Serb Republic. They employed local Serb police and marshaled recently demobilized military vehicles and the VRS logistical infrastructure to facilitate movement of inhabitants and their belongings. From late January through mid-March 1996 some 100,000 Serbs fled Sarajevo for RS territory. At least some of the dwellings being evacuated belonged to their Serb occupants, who were clearly entitled to the electrical wiring, plumbing fixtures, and window frames they carted off. In the absence of an authoritative mechanism to establish ownership, the international presence was powerless to prevent homes and apartments from being gutted. In addition, various buildings and industrial facilities were either set ablaze or booby-trapped. This turmoil created an impression of lawlessness, especially when these images were captured, and to a certain extent magnified, by international news coverage.

The transfer of Sarajevo suburbs was a defining moment for the entire peace mission. Although the limited assets available to the IPTF were skillfully employed, the organization would clearly have been much better equipped to handle the exigencies of this crucial event if it had been fully operational. Indeed, experience made a significant difference, as each successive transfer was handled more smoothly than the previous ones, even though planners had specifically reserved the more troublesome locations until the end. In general, the IPTF was more successful at managing the behavior of local uniformed police forces than they were at controlling the conduct of vandals and provocateurs from both sides of the ethnic divide.

An evaluation of whether the peace mission met this defining moment successfully depends on the yardstick used. If measured against the number of persons killed (one) in this volatile operation, then the transfer must be considered a remarkable accomplishment. Much more was at stake, however, as this event set the tone for the entire operation. If Dayton was to work, Serbs and Moslems had to have confidence that they could live together in relative safety. The message derived from this experience was that even under the cognizance and apparent protection of international military and police forces, it was not safe for Serbs to remain in Moslem neighborhoods. The international community could not dissuade the Serbs from fleeing *en masse*. Nor could they prevent significant destruction of property and intimidation aimed at compelling others to flee when they otherwise might have remained. This event also revealed a serious enforcement gap that would persist throughout the operation. IFOR would not engage in law enforcement and the disruptions did not constitute an imminent threat to life, and, therefore, did not trigger an IFOR response. The IPTF, on the other hand, had neither the authority nor the resources to act.

As each suburb was transferred, Federation authorities (Muslims and Croats) took political and administrative control. This was an accomplishment for the Dayton Accords. Since IFOR had just established its presence in Bosnia, however, all parties were anxious to gauge what this would signify. While the outcome could clearly have been much worse, it was not reassuring either, and IFOR would not have another window of opportunity to create a stronger impression on the Bosnian Serb leadership.

IPTF Relations with Entity Police Forces

Annex 11 of DPA describes functions that the IPTF is to perform, which essentially amount to monitoring, restructuring, and mentoring the law enforcement and judicial apparatus in Bosnia.[49]

Although the parties theoretically requested such assistance, the Serb Republic did not participate in negotiating the Dayton Accords and did not freely consent to such intrusions. Thus, from the very start, the relationship between the IPTF and police forces of the Federation was generally more constructive than it was with the RS.

As of August 1997, the RS had persistently refused to submit to IPTF restructuring, and when not subject to IPTF monitoring, RS police continued to engage in conduct contrary to the DPA. Thus, the relationship with the RS was not one of collaboration, and at times, it became somewhat confrontational (e.g., when the IPTF encountered RS roadblocks, erected in violation of the principle of freedom of movement). In contrast, within most of the Federation IPTF monitors were normally able to establish a professional working relationship, and they served as a catalyst for combining Bosniac and Bosnian Croat police forces into amalgamated entities at the municipal, cantonal, and Federation level.

In performing its monitoring function, the IPTF suffered from an **enforcement gap** that plagued the entire peace operation. Abuse of ethnic minorities by police officers continued to take place in all three ethnic communities. Certain municipal police chiefs, moreover, were notoriously corrupt and enmeshed in networks of illicit activity along with their political mentors.[50] When circumstances allowed, the IPTF could call upon IFOR/SFOR to back them up to compel compliance with the DPA. This was a suitable mechanism for dealing with ongoing activities such as roadblocks, weapons caches, or illegal detention of ethnic minorities. After the fact, however, the IPTF was reduced to conducting investigations and imploring appropriate authorities to act in accordance with their own laws.[51] As the authors of a study of Bosnian jurisprudence have concluded, these entreaties have tended to have only superficial effect:

> IPTF monitors often become aware of human rights abuses or other misconduct by police officers of the Entities. Reports of these activities are usually generated and passed up the

chain of command...Generally, in the Entities, such conduct is condoned or overlooked and the officer is transferred, not dismissed.[52]

It remains to be seen whether efforts to restructure and reform the police will have a profound and lasting impact on police accountability and on their treatment of minorities.[53]

Vetting and Restructuring of Indigenous Police Forces

The initial challenge for the IPTF, in this regard, was to establish the actual size of police establishments in the Bosnian Federation and the Republic of Srpska (RS). These units had burgeoned during the war, and the distinction between the police and army (already blurry in the Yugoslav police state) was further clouded by use of certain police elements as paramilitary forces. Indeed, the origins of the Moslem army were in its police force. As a result of wartime expansion, both the Federation and the RS had a ratio of one policeman for every 60-100 citizens, as opposed to the European standard of 1:380. After establishing their size, the next task was to obtain an agreement from the two entities about the extent to which their mutual police forces would be reduced.

The agreement on restructuring Federation police forces is contained in the Petersberg Declaration on the Federation of Bosnia and Herzegovina, signed on 25 April 1996 in Bonn. This agreement obligated the Federation to reduce their police establishments to 11,500. Even though this left a ratio of one policeman for every 200 inhabitants (almost double the European standard), it nevertheless reduced their constabulary to a third of its previous size. This was agreeable because government expenses could be reduced, it would bring the parties a step closer to conformity with the European model of community policing, and would afford their public security forces access to international assistance. The RS refused to submit to a restructuring program for its police forces until September 1997 when the Plavsic-Karadzic schism made it possible to begin a partial effort.

The IPTF was a central player in the Federation's "downsizing" program.[54] They helped craft a 40-question, multiple choice exam designed to test comprehension of the new Bosnian Constitution, the new Code of Conduct, and the role of policing in a democratic society. In addition, each aspirant had to take a written psychological test to identify those requiring further evaluation. The latter was conducted by an IFOR psychologist seconded to the IPTF for this purpose. The multiple choice exam was printed by IFOR (to avoid compromising the exam) and administered by IPTF members, with assistance from members of the Ministry of Interior.

Screening was conducted by canton, with the first exams administered in August 1996. Instead of allowing all serving police officers to compete for positions in the reduced force, Federation authorities sent for testing only the number of applicants needed to fill the billets available. Thus instead of "vetting," which implies a process whereby those guilty of incompetence, corruption, or abuse (to include war crimes) are expunged, the process served to "downsize" these forces.[55] Out of the first batch of 1,350 taking the exam, only 29 failed the multiple choice portion, and only 10 were identified for further psychiatric evaluation (only 1 was ultimately found to be mentally imbalanced). After the exams were administered in the first several cantons, the entire process was suspended because the multiple choice test had been compromised.

The restructuring process regained momentum with the arrival of the second IPTF contingent in late 1996 and the designation of a Deputy IPTF Commissioner for Restructuring. Building on the testing that had already been completed, the IPTF set about to certify that all personnel allowed to remain in the Federation's police forces met the following requirements:

- Educational prerequisites and a background check showing no evidence of improper conduct.
- No evidence of psychological disorders and a passing score on the police knowledge examination.

- Completion of induction training involving an introduction to international standards for policing, human rights, and the structure of the Federation police force.

In late 1996 the IPTF recognized that the focus of its mission needed to evolve, with more emphasis given to training and the restructuring process and less to monitoring. Accordingly, they created a second Deputy Commissioner's position with specific responsibility for restructuring. In recruiting the second contingent of monitors, moreover, the IPTF sought personnel with skills relevant to the task of restructuring.

To train police officials at all levels in the Federation in the principles of democratic policing and human rights, the IPTF collaborated with bilateral programs from the United States (i.e., ICITAP), Germany, and Austria. This entailed leadership training seminars in these countries to familiarize Federation police officials with law enforcement principles such as community policing and to expose them to investigative and enforcement techniques for dealing with transnational challenges such as drug trafficking, organized crime, and smuggling. In addition, the United States and other interested countries collaborated with the United Nations to provide basic police equipment.

Until September 1997 the RS had only received training that served the broader purposes of the peace mission, such as election security and VIP protection. Other programs were confined to the Federation until Biljana Plavsic agreed to permit restructuring to begin among those RS police units that were loyal to her (about a quarter of the force).

The certification process for all Bosniac personnel in the Sarajevo Canton was completed in February 1997, and all 10 cantons comprising the Federation, along with the 1,000-member police force of the Federation itself, were scheduled to be completed by September 1997. Initially only Bosniac personnel could be certified because there were no Croat volunteers. As of August 1997, however, this barrier had been overcome in three cantons (Sarajevo, Gorazde, and Mostar), and joint Moslem-Croat police forces had been formed in almost all the municipalities of these three cantons. An Embassy assessment noted as of 5 August that "Since the integration of police in Sarajevo and Gorazde Cantons and in Mostar, we note that there have been few problems among the police themselves, and joint patrols are becoming the norm."[56] All 11,500 Federation police officers were slated to complete the 4 weeks of induction training by August 1998.[57] Assuming this process continues to progress as planned, the IPTF anticipates there could be a viable, integrated Federation police force in a couple of years.

Support for Elections

To monitor the 14 September 1996 national elections effectively while preserving the capacity to respond to potential disturbances, the IPTF developed a plan calling for a more flexible posture. Only 600 of its roughly 1,700 personnel were left to man static positions (i.e., at IPTF headquarters, the 3 Regional and 14 District headquarters, and 51 stations). This allowed for the creation of 400 2-person Mobile Patrol Teams (providing coverage of 19 voter routes and 4,000 polling places), with a reserve comprised of a dozen strategically located "Hot-Spot" teams, each having 25 personnel.[58] The IPTF collaborated with IFOR to identify the most likely trouble spots and then established coordinated patrolling patterns for these areas. A number of OSCE officials were also incorporated into IPTF patrols on 14 September.

The IPTF gave particular attention to IEBL-crossing points along voter routes. Their function was to monitor local police as they searched vehicles and occupants for weapons and contraband. During this electoral period, only wanted criminals could be detained by indigenous police forces. After the search was completed, drivers were given a certificate, signed by both the local police and IPTF, that exempted them from further searches that day. Prior to the elections, IFOR assigned communications personnel to IPTF headquarters, and on election day, senior IPTF officials were incorporated into IFOR's command post. The intent was to ensure connectivity with IFOR should IPTF patrols encounter a hostile situation requiring a response.[59]

In contrast to the controversy swirling around other aspects of the elections (e.g., intimidation of opposition candidates and restrictions on their access to the media, manipulation of the voter registry for municipal elections by the RS, and suspiciously high turnout of Moslem voters), the actual conduct of the elections on 14 September was remarkably placid. Several factors contributed to the absence of serious disruptions, but the *sine qua non* was the cooperation of governing elites in all three entities. Postponement of the municipal elections removed contention from the process, because elections were then reduced largely to a contest over who would govern within each of the ethnic communities. In all three cases, nationalist leaders, exploiting the advantage of incumbency to the fullest, expected to be victorious. Thus, elections conferred a mantle of legitimacy on them that was useful for furthering their aims. This prospect motivated interior ministers from each of the entities to instruct local police to cooperate, which they did. As one experienced observer noted: "The IEBL crossing plan developed by the interior ministers is an excellent example of strategic instructions issued to local police for the accomplishment of a sensitive mission and the local police executing the instructions in a calm and competent manner."[60] Without this, even the most detailed planning and harmonious cooperation by the international community would have served merely to limit damage caused by inevitable confrontations and protests.

Nevertheless, the tranquil atmosphere on election day was enhanced by the extensive planning and coordination undertaken by the IPTF and its counterparts, especially IFOR and the OSCE. The IPTF's advanced preparations were touted by a veteran U.S. military peacekeeper, as follows:

> The IPTF has a superb plan to assist the local police as it prepared for the 14 September elections. The IPTF prepared a comprehensive duties and responsibilities handbook for

the local police as well as established a national election planning cell to facilitate planning and coordination in support of the elections.[61]

It was also vitally important that members of the international community with electoral responsibilities (i.e., the OSCE, IFOR, and the IPTF) had made extensive efforts to coordinate their actions. IFOR, in particular, provided crucial support in the form of Civil Affairs planning specialists for the OSCE and the IPTF, as well as logistic support for distribution and post-election collection of ballots.

Coordination and Cooperation

Guiding Philosophy of the IPTF Mission

Perhaps the most enduring contribution the IPTF mission made to the conduct of future Civ-Pol operations was the articulation and operationalization of the concept of "democratic policing." A step beyond the "community policing" approach adopted in Haiti, this model explicitly links reform of the police with transformation of the political process. The essence of this innovative approach to policing is captured in the IPTF "Commissioner's Guidance Notes for the Implementation of Democratic Policing Standards":

> For Bosnia-Herzegovina, the police must realign their missions from the protection of the state to the protection of citizen's rights. Service to the public must become the police's calling...A democratic police force is not concerned with people's beliefs or associates, their movements or conformity to state ideology...Instead, the police force of a democracy is concerned strictly with the preservation of safe communities and the application of criminal law equally to all people, without fear or favor.[62]

The "democratic transition of the Federation" thus became more than a by-product of IPTF activities.[63] In the words of Commissioner Paul FitzGerald, "It is a mandate."[64] To execute this mandate, the Commissioner directed that action be taken in three essential areas:

1. Affirmative police activities by public security establishments, to demonstrate that their role is public service, not state control.
2. Acceptance of a democratic Standard for Policing by which each policeman's performance would be measured.
3. Demobilization of superfluous personnel and re-vetting of the force to ensure that those with backgrounds incompatible with democratic policing were discharged.[65]

While the detailed articulation of this concept in a 40-page document was a major advance, devising an effective scheme for implementation was an even more vital and challenging matter. As of the publication of this work, this remains a work in progress, but demonstrable progress has been made within the Federation.

Relationship Between the Military and Civ-Pol

International responsibility for security matters is divided, in the Dayton Peace Accords, between the IPTF and IFOR. Annex 11 relegates the tasks of monitoring, inspecting, training, and assisting Bosnia's law enforcement and judicial systems to the IPTF. Military aspects of DPA are treated separately in annex 1A.

Within the confines of their respective mandates, both IFOR/SFOR and the IPTF performed well. When called upon to support implementation of "civilian" aspects of Dayton, however, acute difficulties periodically arose. Some of the key provisions of Dayton (e.g., freedom of movement, refugee return, apprehension of war criminals, municipal governance, and the status of Brcko) regularly revealed an "enforcement gap" that remained largely unresolved well into the second year of the peace mission.

Military assistance, principally in the form of Civil Affairs police specialists, was invaluable in establishing an operational capability for the IPTF and reducing the initial deployment gap. Their role was especially crucial in planning for the pivotal transfer to Moslem control of half a dozen Sarajevo suburbs and in marshaling the IPTF's limited resources to address each successive transfer. Once the IPTF had become fully operational, Civil Affairs personnel provided liaison between the two organizations, ensuring that operational information was exchanged between the two entities on a daily basis. IFOR also provided certain forms of logistic assistance (See Logistic Support, above).

Given that the IPTF mandate had only been approved by the UN in late December 1995, and the transfer of Sarajevo suburbs took place scarcely 3 months later, the capacity of the mission to meet this critical initial challenge hinged on getting the IPTF functioning in a timely manner. Indeed, according to the Dayton Accords, the original transfer date was to be late February, at which point none of the senior IPTF leaders was even on station. To help the IPTF begin functioning as expeditiously as possible, IFOR detailed a half dozen Civil Affairs officers with backgrounds in planning, operations, training, and logistics. Among their vital contributions were the following:

- Establishment of the IPTF Command Center, including the overall design, operational procedures, and development of a communication net linking IPTF Headquarters with stations in the field and with IFOR.
- Secondment of a logistics specialist to serve as acting Chief of Logistics to manage the influx of personnel and procurement of radios, vehicles, and facilities so monitors could begin performing their duties.
- Secondment of a senior police administrator to serve as Special Assistant to the Chief of Staff, in particular to draft the plan for transfer of the Sarajevo suburbs and to coordinate IFOR support for the IPTF during this operation.

- Secondment of a training specialist to the training base at Camp Pleso, Croatia, to provide curriculum assistance and classroom instruction to meet the initial surge of 200 incoming police monitors per week.

Once the IPTF had become operational, the focus shifted to long-term tasks, such as the downsizing and restructuring of local police forces. IFOR Civil Affairs advisors contributed significantly to this phase of the operation. This included drafting the Agreement for Restructuring the Police and the Principles of Policing in a Democratic State, which were signed by the Federation at Bonn in April 1996, and serving as the staff for the Commission on Police Restructuring. Another crucial IFOR responsibility was to be prepared to evacuate IPTF personnel, if necessary. Evacuation procedures were drawn up by Civil Affairs liaison personnel. In addition to their daily function of exchanging operational information between the two organizations, they also provided the interface between IFOR and the IPTF in preparing for and supporting national and municipal elections and in dealing with the organized crime threat.

Observations

Success of the Mission

The police restructuring program that has been developed to imbue a new ethos of public service is still in its early stages. To have any lasting impact, many more years of consistent effort will be necessary. The status as of mid-1997 was as follows:

(1) *Screening and Vetting* - This component of the restructuring process was designed to ensure that local police forces meet minimum standards of experience, training, and suitability and that indicted war criminals or persons with substantial criminal records are prohibited from remaining on or joining the force. As of

May 1997, 3 of the 10 cantons in the Federation had been vetted and screened, with the remaining cantons scheduled for completion during 1997. To date, there has been very little progress in the Serb Republic because RS officials, including the Minister of Interior, have refused to cooperate with the IPTF.

(2) *Training and Equipping* - A comprehensive program has been developed to supply local police officials at all levels with training in the principles of democratic policing, respect for human rights, and internationally accepted standards. The United States, Germany, and Austria have conducted leadership training seminars to familiarize Federation police officials with Western law enforcement principles and to expose them to investigation and enforcement techniques associated with major crime problems such as drug trafficking, organized crime, and smuggling. In addition, the United States and other interested countries are cooperating with the United Nations to implement a program to provide local police with basic equipment. This program has been limited to the Federation, however, because RS officials have not cooperated with the IPTF.

Police restructuring and training programs, however, will not prevent a resumption of conflict in Bosnia. The critical deficiency is not one of police capabilities but rather how those capabilities are employed. As long as xenophobic political leaders command the allegiance of police forces, the public security apparatus will continue to be exploitable as an instrument of repression and genocidal policies.

Without consensus among the parties on the core issue of Bosnia's identity, many matters integral to the Dayton process, such as refugee returns, municipal governance, the status of Brcko, or the disposition of war criminals, will continue to be regarded as matters of national survival. The outcome of each will heavily influence Bosnia's ultimate destiny. The various police forces in Bosnia will be crucial players in the process that determines the outcome of each of these critical disputes. Only the most optimistic assessments would maintain that the central issue in dispute—integration vs. partition—will have been resolved by Jun 1998. The peace that prevailed under IFOR and SFOR has been deceptive, therefore, because it was a product of external intervention. There can be no confidence that peace will be self-sustaining because numerous core issues capable of precipitating conflict remain unresolved.

Respect for Human Rights During and After the Peace Operation

This issue is at the core of the quandary in Bosnia. Ethnic populations were the targets of violence during the war, more so than opposing armies. The outcome was "ethnic cleansing." The carnage was stopped just short of its ultimate goal of homogeneity. If Bosnia's three nations are now to live together in a single state, respect for minority rights must become integral to the political and judicial processes. Abuse of minorities has continued to be a chronic concern, however, and no ethnic group has an unblemished record in this regard.[66]

If Bosnians are to coexist peacefully, then impunity for actions against ethnic minorities must end, and institutions that dispense justice equitably must begin to flourish. The IPTF's pathbreaking initiative to transform Bosnia's police forces into agents of democratic policing is the linchpin for this transformation. It will not be sufficient, however, since judicial and penal systems are also subject to abuse. One aspect of the system that appears to merit particular scrutiny is pre-trial detention. This is a major concern given the preference of police for suspect interrogation, as opposed to the tedium of gathering physical evidence. There are numerous areas where safeguards are weak, disregarded, or totally lacking. These include manipulation and abuse of the supposed 3-day limit on police detention, the regular failure to notify detainees of their rights, and the lack of prohibitions against use of illegally obtained evidence.[67] These serious flaws in Bosnian jurisprudence were not resolved by the DPA, as authors of a major study of the Bosnian legal system conclude:

164 *Lessons from Bosnia*

> Although *GFAP (the General Framework Agreement for Peace or DPA)* contained provisions related to the Constitution, Human Rights and Policing, insufficient attention was, in our view, given to the administration of justice and the development of a system of laws which not only comply with Human Rights but also and more importantly ensure that they are protected. In this respect GFAP and the Constitutions of both entities seem to have created an unwieldy structure of Human Rights Courts and subsidiary organizations which sit on top of a system which is almost certainly fundamentally flawed. While breaches of Human Rights will almost certainly be identified by this system, they will be difficult to rectify unless a properly functioning, independent system of justice, at all levels is developed to protect them.[68]

The court system lacks autonomy because it has been subordinated, de facto, to the police. Municipal police chiefs and ministers of interior, in turn, have operated as agents of control for the leadership of the ruling party. As vestiges of a communist-era police state, minus the veneer of ideology to lend a whiff of legitimacy, the Federation and the RS currently are political regimes in transition. The only outcome compatible with a multiethnic state is a bona fide democracy that practices majority rule while guaranteeing minority rights.

Human rights monitoring organizations, such as the Commission on Human Rights created by annex 6 of the DPA (including the Ombudsman and Human Rights chamber), must be nurtured so they can perform a watchdog function over formal institutions of government. Bosnian human rights organizations, in turn, must develop robust linkages with counterparts internationally. All of this will require an arduous process of institutional development that will take many years to complete. This represents the peace-building phase of a peace operation. It is not yet certain, however, that Bosnia is solidly headed down this path.

Concluding Action Agenda

Some actions that could serve to improve the effectiveness of the IPTF are—

Objective Standards for Democratic Policing: Perhaps the most significant contribution the IPTF will make to the conduct of future peace operations is the articulation of specific, observable standards for democratic policing. A major stride forward will have been taken if these become recognized as "the international standards of policing."

Pre-Mission Assessments: In December 1995, the UN assessment team focused essentially on numerical factors such as the total number of personnel and police stations in the forces of each ethnic community. This was sufficient only to determine the numbers of monitors required, neglecting the other missions (e.g., training, advising, and restructuring Bosnian police forces). Future assessments should take into account the manning and resources needed to perform all CIVPOL missions, as well as the extent to which limited political consent among the disputants might affect the CIVPOL mission.

Mandate: The factor that determines whether the mandate can be executed successfully is the extent to which the parties actually consent to ends that CIVPOL seeks to serve. At the core of the "enforcement gap" was the fiction that all the parties consented to full implementation of the DPA. There were no effective sanctions to close the gaps in either law enforcement or compliance with the DPA, other than compellance by IFOR/SFOR, and this also had its constraints.

Clearly, the international community needs to develop instruments that can give it greater leverage in such circumstances. One interesting alternative would be to incorporate constabulary forces into the military force mix. Their mission would be to provide support to the IPTF so that it could more effectively carry out its tasks.

Recruitment of CIVPOL Monitors: The Bosnia experience highlights four deficiencies:

- An inordinate delay in mobilizing personnel.

- The caliber of monitors.

- The mix of ranks and skills required to perform the CIVPOL mission.

- The capacity of the IPTF to recruit monitors from democratic nations, who are capable of imparting the necessary skills of democratic policing. The ability of the IPTF to nurture a democratic transition in policing is proportional to its success in attracting monitors of this caliber.

To remedy these deficiencies, the following actions would appear to be warranted:

- Identify a cadre of CIV-POL personnel who are available on a "stand-by" basis, analogous to the arrangement the UN uses with military forces.

- Continue and expand the practice of sending Selection Assistance Teams to donor countries to screen volunteers prior to deployment.

- Identify for donor nations the skills and ranks desired for each mission. The constraint in this regard is not the United Nations, which has shown commendable flexibility, but rather the capacity to recruit additional personnel from stable democracies, especially from Europe. This will happen only if the nations involved understand this to be a priority.

VII. Information Activities[69]
Pascale Combelles Siegel

Introduction

When it comes to peace operations, many officers are convinced that victory is determined not on the ground but in media reporting. This concept has led to the development of information programs designed to influence public attitudes both at home and in the local population. This has also made information a critical element in the command and control of peace operations. As U.S. doctrine correctly states, "Public affairs is a fundamental tool of competent leadership, a critical element of effective battle command and an essential part of successful mission accomplishment."[70] This chapter examines the role of information in peace operations through the prism of IFOR operations in Bosnia-Herzegovina (December 1995-December 1996).

Information activities contribute in different ways to mission accomplishment. A successful public information campaign contributes to building and preserving public support for a military operation as it affects the prism (media reporting) through which the world and the local communities assess the events of peace operations. Indeed, media reporting provides the basis for the world's—including many in the political elite—judgment as to the success or failure of a peace operation.

Information activities also help commanders communicate to the parties their intentions and might, and get the local population to act friendly. With UNPROFOR and IFOR, major military operations were rare.[71] On the other hand, IFOR abundantly used information activities to deter the FWF from violating the military annex of the Dayton agreement and from attacking NATO's troops. IFOR also used information to convince the local population that a brighter future awaits them if the parties comply fully with the Dayton agreement.

During *Joint Endeavor*, IFOR Public Information (PI) ran an information campaign designed to "seize and maintain the initiative by imparting timely and effective information within the commander's intent."[72] The term information campaign refers to the coordinated and synchronized use of public information and psychological operations. The campaign was thus composed of two elements: a PI campaign designed to establish IFOR's credibility with the international media to gain international support of the operation; and a psychological operations (PSYOP) campaign designed to shape the local population's perception in favor of IFOR troops and activities. IFOR PI undertook the public information aspects of the policy, while the Combined Joint IFOR Information Campaign Task Force (CJIICTF) undertook the PSYOP aspects.[73]

Traditionally PI and PSYOP are separated. The strict separation stems from the different missions and philosophies.

- **Psychological operations** are an operational tool (under G/J3-operations-supervision) designed to shape target audiences' perceptions so that they create the least possible interference with friendly forces.
- **Public information**, on the other hand, has a dual function. First, public information is an operational tool designed to gain and maintain public opinion support for the operation; it is also used

as a 'public diplomacy' tool designed to pressure adversaries into a friendly course of action. Second, it is a democratic requirement. Public information is the means by which a commander reports to the people what their children and tax dollars are used for. This entails some obligations, such as truthful and timely reporting.

The nature of *Operation Joint Endeavor*, a peace-enforcement operation, made it possible to closely associate public information and psychological operations. IFOR PSYOP campaign consisted of convincing the local population and FWF of the benefits of the Dayton agreement by relying on truthful and honest arguments. It thus did not resort to deception or disinformation campaigns (two other facets of psychological operations). Under these circumstances, PI and PSYOP were open and transparent. Both operations relied on similar guidance, themes, and messages. Each of them was entrusted with reaching a specific audience. Public information dealt with journalists, while PSYOP carried IFOR's message to the local population without the mediation of journalists, through IFOR-owned media: a TV production section, 6 organic and 56 affiliated radio stations, a national weekly newspaper *The Herald Of Peace*, a youth magazine *Mircko*, posters and handbills.

This chapter examines the place of PI and PSYOP in peace operations through the prism of IFOR operations in Bosnia-Herzegovina. It presents a brief background on *Operation Joint Endeavor* the planning process and defines the key concepts for information activities throughout the operation. The following section shows how IFOR implemented these key concepts and how they affected command and control and mission accomplishment. The next section tackles some of the obstacles and problems that appeared during the implementation phase. The final section draws implications from the IFOR experience for future peace operations.

Planning

When SHAPE and AFSOUTH began planning for *Operation Joint Endeavor*, they did so with little up-to-date guidance. In fall 1995, the NAC was revising its public information strategy document to adjust it to the upcoming operation. The document was not completed in time to aid planning. At that time, SHAPE was also revising its policies on public information and psychological operations.[74] SHAPE, however, circulated its draft revisions to PI and PSYOP planners. Planning was thus based on newly drafted doctrines, and on previous planning for contingencies in former-Yugoslavia.[75]

Key Concepts

NATO commanders expected information to play a critical role in the success of IFOR's mission, by helping gain international support and by shaping local attitudes in favor of IFOR troops and operations. Following Admiral Smith's intent, planners established the need for a proactive, fully coordinated campaign which was synchronized with the major staff components. The key concepts of IFOR's information policies during *Joint Endeavor* were—

- IFOR was to run a transparent campaign, relying on truth and dispatching complete, accurate, and timely information to establish itself as a credible source of information and to gain and maintain public support for IFOR operations.
- IFOR was to coordinate messages internally with other operational elements in theater (especially with PSYOP and CIMIC) and liaise with major civilian agencies operating in Bosnia-Herzegovina.
- IFOR was to rely on information as a non-lethal weapon system to entice friendly behavior.

The public information campaign key concepts had consequences for the command and control structure. Indeed, plans sought to establish and promote cooperation and liaison, both internally (within the command staff components) and externally (with the civilian organizations). Plans authorized a functional information chain, allowing PIOs across the country to exchange information, thus speeding the information flow. Plans also called for a close integration of PI with operational staffs (mostly G/J3), and mentioned the possibility to closely integrate PI and PSYOP elements in a coordinated and synchronized campaign.[76]

Accurate and Timely Information

Providing IFOR's target audiences (the international and local media, the local population, and the local factions) with complete, accurate, and timely information was the key element of a policy designed to gain and maintain credibility with the international media. According to Capt. Van Dyke, USN, IFOR chief PIO, Admiral Smith felt that in an open and transparent operation such as IFOR, "if we [IFOR] know, they [the media] know."[77] Under these circumstances, disseminating relevant information—including bad news and mistakes—as quickly as possible was an absolute requirement. Achieving this goal had major command and control implications. To provide complete and accurate information to its audiences, PI needed to be tied into operations. To ensure timely information, PI needed to have knowledge of operations/incidents as they unfolded and to be allowed to quickly release information to the press. To achieve these requirements, IFOR closely integrated PI and PSYOP with other operational elements (mostly G/J2 and G/J3), established a functional chain of information, and delegated release authority to the lowest responsible level.

Integration of PI and PSYOP with Other Staff Components

To provide the media with complete and accurate information and to disseminate important facts and messages to the local population, PI and PSYOP personnel were closely integrated with operations staffs and enjoyed a close relationship with the IFOR commanders, especially at headquarters level.

At headquarters level, commanders organized a very close relationship with their public information officers. For example, Admiral Lopez, USN, COMIFOR in summer and fall 1996, held his first and last meeting every day with Capt. Van Dyke, USN, the IFOR chief PIO. COMARRC, LtGen Walker, UKA, usually chaired a daily ARRC information coordination group. Both ARRC and IFOR PIOs enjoyed an open-door policy with their commanders. They had regular one-on-one informal meetings when they needed. This close relationship allowed the PIOs to gain insights into the commanders' thinking and wishes. It also ensured that the commander knew what was developing in the news media.

In addition, throughout the operation most commanders made sure that PI had complete and timely knowledge of current and future operations, even if classified. The following mechanisms helped maintain the flow of information between PI and operations. IFOR PI had a liaison officer to the Joint Operations Center (JOC). At ARRC, MND(N) and MND(SW), PIOs had free access to the operations room throughout the operation. IFOR and ARRC PIOs attended COMIFOR and COMARRC staff meetings as well as the morning and evening conference calls. At headquarters level and at MND(N) and (SW), PIOs attended the morning staff meetings and the daily conference calls. These arrangements enabled IFOR PI to anticipate and prepare for incidents (through knowledge of plans) and difficult issues (through a clear understanding of HQ policy and thinking). The rapid link between PI and Ops, minimized the likelihood that a reporter would break a story about IFOR operations that PIOs were not aware of.

The Information Chain

To provide timely information to its audiences, PI needs to be aware of operations and incidents as they unfolded. This constitutes a tough challenge because reporting through a chain of command is time-consuming, as each authority level processes the information before passing it up. It is an even more time-consuming process in a multinational operation where each layer might speak a different language. This process does not adequately support PIO needs for timely delivery of accurate information. The stop-gap measure lay in a functional information chain linking public information officers throughout theater.

The challenge stems from the inherent imbalance between a journalist's ability to report on the spot and the military's need to verify and process information before it passes it up the chain of command. A journalist can provide viewers with personal impressions and judgments, while military reporting typically relies on verifying information. For the journalist, immediacy can override accuracy. For the military, accuracy usually overrides immediacy. The problem is compounded by the fact that journalists can relate any piece of news much faster than the military. While witnessing an incident, a journalist just needs to set up a satellite phone to break the news to his central offices. In a matter of minutes, the news may reach wide international audiences. By comparison, the military flow of information is much slower. The danger of this inherent imbalance is that higher headquarters learn about an operation/incident from the news rather than from its subordinate headquarters. The likely results are potentially important. Higher headquarters will often (angrily) turn to subordinate elements for confirmation. On occasions, it may affect decision making, either by providing a lasting impression or by forcing the commander to react in the heat of the moment.

IFOR's solution to this dilemma consisted of a vertical functional information chain linking all PIOs throughout theater. According to Colonel Serveille, annex P to OPLAN 40105 explicitly authorized a direct liaison between public information organizations at all levels of IFOR operations.[78] The chain of information worked in coordination with the chain of command. It allowed PIOs to communicate and exchange information without having to pass through all the layers of the chain of command, thus speeding up the information flow.

In case of a serious incident, the process was further decentralized. Division or headquarters dispatched a PIO to collect firsthand information and (eventually) deal with the press on-the-scene. This provision greatly reduced the amount of time necessary for PI to obtain operational information of potential media interest.

Delegation of Release Authority

The purpose of these arrangements would be defeated if, in the end, PIOs were not allowed to release the information to the media. Therefore, under IFOR, information release authority was delegated to the lowest possible level. As a result, COMIFOR had authority to release (or to delegate release authority to appropriate levels) all theater-operational information. In addition, IFOR PI was authorized to confirm news already obvious to the media without having to refer to higher headquarters. This provision greatly enhanced the PI's ability to react quickly to fast-breaking news.

Appropriate delegation of release authority ensured that PIOs throughout theater could react in a timely fashion to fast-breaking news without interference from higher echelons. The higher the release authority is, the longer it takes to confirm and release relevant information. In some cases, such delays can create tensions with the press and damage the military's credibility among journalists.

A Coordinated Campaign

Coordination was ensured through a variety of meetings where information policy and activities were discussed and IFOR's information strategy was established. Coordination occurred at several levels: internally (between various staff components), externally (between IFOR and the main civilian organizations operating in Bosnia-Herzegovina, such as the OHR, the UNHCR, the UNMIBH, the OSCE), and nationally (within national contingents).

Internal Coordination

Internal coordination was designed to enhance information flow between staff components, avoid duplication of efforts, and synchronize efforts so they mutually reinforced each other. Thorough internal coordination made it less likely that different staff components would develop diverging plans. Although IFOR and ARRC plans called for coordination between staff components involved in information activities, they did not set up specific mechanisms. Consequently, early in the deployment, IFOR and ARRC staffs created such mechanisms as necessities arose. As the enumeration below shows, the ARRC initiated most of the internal coordination mechanisms.

The Chief Information Officer: Shortly after deployment, COMARRC (IFOR land component commander) designated Col. Tim Wilton, UKA, as Chief Information Officer and tasked him with organizing the daily coordination between the PI and the CJIICTF staffs at operational level. On a daily basis, the chief information officer developed a centralized coordination process to ensure that all messages flowing out of IFOR conformed to the commander's intent, were coherent with one another, and reinforced each other.

The ARRC Information Coordination Group: Every morning, the ARRC commander (COMARRC) chaired an information coordination group composed of ARRC chief of staff, civilian political advisor, civilian media advisor, chief PIO, chief IFOR PIO, ARRC spokesmen, DCOMCJIICTF, and ARRC G3 and G5. In practice, however, IFOR PIO did not always attend the ARRC meeting. Every day, the ICG decided which message to put forward and chose the delivery system (media and/or PSYOP) and timing of the delivery. Typically, the ICG worked on a 1-day to 1-week horizon.

The ARRC perception group: Every Friday, the ARRC chief PIO chaired a 'perception group meeting.' IFOR PI, ARRC spokesmen, COMARRC media advisor, DCOMCJIICTF, ARRC G3, and ARRC G5 attended this weekly meeting. They looked at media coverage trends and determined how best to present and time IFOR's arguments to the media. The group worked on a 2- to 4-week horizon and produced a weekly information matrix summarizing all information activities throughout theater.

The ARRC Crisis Planning Group: This group met as crises erupted (such as Han Pisejak and Celic) for contingency planning. This meeting brought PI and PSYOP planners into operational planning at an early moment.

Though not as systematic as at headquarters level, coordination mechanisms were established at two of the three multinational divisions: MND(N) and MND(SW). The U.S.-led MND(N) held an Information Operations Council designed to bring together the key players relevant for information dissemination (PIO, G3, PSYOP, civil affairs). In the UK-led MND(SW), the chief PIO attended operational and civil affairs meetings, but did not organize a specific coordination forum. Coordination was mostly informal, through walk-ins and phone calls with relevant staffs. It is unclear whether the MND(SW) informal approach would have been more effective associated with formal coordination mechanisms.[79]

External Coordination

Coordination also took place with the major civilian organizations in charge of facilitating the implementation the civilian annexes of the DPA. In particular, IFOR established common activities and coordination mechanisms with the OHR, the UNHCR, the UNMIBH, and the OSCE.

IFOR quickly learned that coordinating with the civilian agencies was necessary. Early in the operation (by end of February 1996), IFOR PI realized that media interest was shifting to the civilian implementation of the DPA. However, at that stage civilian organizations attended, but did not take part in, the daily briefing. IFOR PI felt it was left in a position to talk about civilian issues outside its realm of responsibility. IFOR PI feared this situation could damage its credibility.

However, establishing coordination mechanisms with the civilian agencies was a challenging task. First, civilian agencies were slow to respond to IFOR's offers for cooperation as many arrived in theater well after IFOR. For a while, they were consumed by problems in setting up their own operations. Cooperation with IFOR was not their main concern. In addition, it seemed that some of the civilian organizations were reluctant to cooperate closely with IFOR out of fear they would lose their freedom of speech and be tainted by their association with a military force. As a result, widespread cooperation was only fully in place by mid-May 1996.[80] The coordination and cooperation mechanisms included the following:

The daily combined briefing: In early spring 1996, the OHR, UNHCR, UNMIBH, OSCE, and to a lesser extent the World Bank agreed to brief the press daily along with IFOR at the Holiday Inn. The IFOR Sarajevo press center thus became the focal point for dissemination of information about the international effort in Bosnia-Herzegovina. From then on, the international community presented itself to the world as united in a common effort in favor of DPA implementation. By mid-May 1996, civilian agencies agreed to chair the daily briefing three times a week. All of this served to publicly reinforce NATO's objective of gradually transferring military tasks to civilian agencies.

The pre-briefing meeting: Fifteen minutes before the daily briefing took place, spokesmen from IFOR and the civilian agencies held a pre-briefing meeting. At this meeting, each spokesman presented the information he had, what he intended to say at the press conference, and when required asked for additional information. Spokesmen then decided what information to release and in what order. The pre-briefing meeting helped spokesmen to share and compare information. This process helped reduce inaccuracies, and in some cases, helped de-conflict sensitive issues. It also helped the spokesmen to refrain from publicly criticizing each other and to tone down their disagreements.

The Joint Information Coordination Committee (JICC): Every week, IFOR and ARRC PI, CIMIC, CJIICTF, and the major international organizations' spokesmen met at the IFOR press center in the Sarajevo Holiday Inn.[81] The JICC provided a formal forum for key players in policy and communication to inform each other of current activities and future plans. The JICC allowed them to ensure that their messages did not conflict (or to de-conflict them if necessary) and to prepare common strategies. Through the JICC, IFOR tried to foster a unified message, a strong synergy between all players involved so that each effort mutually reinforced the others. According to Captain Van Dyke, USN, IFOR chief PIO, "during these meetings, everyone shared their latest PI plans and activities, striving to eliminate any potential conflicts in public policies which the former warring factions could then exploit. The corporate experience of the civilian agency spokespersons, and the close personal and professional cooperation that grew between them and IFOR spokespersons, were invaluable to our overall information operations. In return, the civilian agencies benefited greatly from our extensive support agreements."[82] LtCol Furlong, USA, deputy commander of the CJIICTF, echoed Van Dyke's sentiment: "The JICC was critical in enabling the international community to speak with one voice on controversial issues such as war criminals, mass graves, and repatriation."[83]

Informal cooperation process: As the combined press conference and coordination meetings developed, informal coordination and cooperation increased. Spokesmen would call each other up frequently to pass information, to seek confirmation or additional details. This process greatly enhanced the information flow between the main agencies working in Bosnia-Herzegovina.

National Coordination

IFOR was a 36-nation coalition placed under SACEUR's operational control. As a result, each contingent was expected to report daily to the NATO chain of command. But aside from the NATO chain of command, each nation expected its contingent to report to national authorities. Contingents fulfilled this dual requirement by sending Situation Reports (SITREPs) to IFOR and to their respective MODs. In a specific case, U.S. public information officers throughout theater were required to participate in a daily teleconference with representatives of the State Department, Department of Defense, and National Security Council.[84] Conversely, nations also expected their public officers in theater to follow national guidelines and directives.

In some cases, national requirements sparked difficulties with IFOR. For example during fall 1996, MND(N) heavily advertised the redeployment of U.S. units out of Bosnia. That line supported the U.S. official position that U.S. troops would come home after a 12-month deployment, but it contradicted IFOR's effort to keep the redeployment issue in low profile. In some cases, information was formally released to the international press, both by contingents in theater and by home nations, without IFOR prior knowledge. In a few instances regarding casualties incidents, nations even released information when NATO was the formal release authority.[85]

PI And IIC As A Non-Lethal Weapon

In peace support operations, where the outside force does not conduct traditional combat operations, the commander has to place a greater reliance on non-lethal weapons. PI and PSYOP are two critical non-lethal weapons. In Bosnia-Herzegovina, these two groups worked hand-in-glove to make each other's activities more effective in support of the commanders' objectives. PI and PSYOP are tools for the commander to communicate with adversaries, neutral parties, various factions, and the local population. The PI will do so through providing material to journalists while PSYOP will do so through controlled dissemination means (such as force-controlled radio stations or poster campaigns).

To be able to use these tools effectively, the commander had to have PI and PSYOP tied into the command and control structure. This occurred, in the obvious vein, through inclusion of both the IFOR PIO and the CJIICTF commander at the morning and other critical staff meetings. Both the PI organization and the CJIICTF had liaisons in the IFOR CJ-3 staff through officers assigned to the JOC. The coordination meetings discussed above were also crucial to ensuring effectiveness.

This tying of the PI and IIC (PSYOP) into the command and control structure made it possible for COMIFOR and other commanders to use these tools in support of objectives and operations. At headquarters level and in some divisions, information was systematically used to reinforce the appropriateness of IFOR's activities. Information was always on the commander's mind as one of his major tools for action. G3 was constantly aware of the possibility to use the media and PI was always aware of ongoing and future operations. For example, the MND(SW) commander often relied on press statements to lay blame publicly on the factions who violated provisions of the DPA to pressure them into compliance.[86] In a number of high-profile incidents, IFOR relied on its information campaign to influence the behavior of the local factions without having to resort to the use of force. In summer 1996, a Serb policeman fired a warning shot at an IFOR soldier and ordered his policemen to surround him. In response, COMIFOR approved an information plan (resorting to press statements and IIC products) to apply gradual public pressure on RS leaders to oust the chief of police. In another example, RS leaders refused to let IFOR troops inspect an ammunition depot in Han Pisejak. COMIFOR instructed IFOR spokesman to recommend that all NGOs pull out of RS since IFOR was about to use lethal force to inspect the depot. After a few days, RS leadership authorized IFOR to carry out its inspection mission.[87]

The PI and PSYOP organizations played another role as non-lethal weapons—they were sources of information for the operation at the same time that they released information. Journalists can provide, knowingly or unknowingly, a great deal of information to PIOs that is potentially critical to operations. The coordination and communication meant to give PIOs information also served as a means to transmit information back to the operation (specifically, the J-2 or J-3 elements). The IIC personnel, as well, had extensive contacts with the local populace and interpreters. These contacts always have the potential for providing HUMINT that will help the force commander understand the situation better and could provide critical operational information. In non-traditional missions such as *Joint Endeavor*, commands have to expand their concepts of intelligence and important information to capture the complex types of problems that exist in these operations. PI and PSYOP, like Civil Affairs, are far more important information sources in a peace support operation than in a wartime environment. With this in mind, the command and control structure/concept must have a means to feed their information back into the command as well as to feed them information for dissemination into the broader community.

Close coordination with operations enabled PI to play an expanded role in the operation. First, it enabled PI to provide the media with accurate and timely information. It also allowed for better timing of public information campaigns. Finally, it facilitated use of information as an operational tool. It allowed commanders to communicate directly with their 'adversaries' and with the local populations.

Limits and Problems

Differing Concepts of Operations

In a 36-partner coalition such as IFOR, room existed for different concepts of PI/PSYOP and how best to use them in a combined campaign. Even between the three major contributors (the United States, the United Kingdom, and France), there were significant differences in their approaches to information operations. The following outlines some of the most significant issues.

One major bone of contention was the nature and amount of information to be released to the media. For example, it seemed that IFOR and ARRC perspectives on this issue often conflicted. IFOR's policy, based on U.S. public affairs principles, was clear: all information likely to interest the media is to be released unless precluded by troop safety and/or operational security. Information already obvious to the media should be confirmed. For IFOR HQ, the question should always be: "Why should I not release the information?" The ARRC, especially at the beginning of the operation, seemed to strictly follow the British doctrine, according to which one does not talk about ongoing or upcoming operations. For the ARRC, the basic question seemed to be: "Why should I release this information?" The two doctrines regularly generated conflict between the two headquarters.

There also were frictions between IFOR and subordinate headquarters about the level and type of information that should be reported up the chain of command/chain of information. Differences of opinion in that domain also caused tensions. In some cases, contingents did not report as much information as IFOR felt it needed to effectively handle information operations. In some instances, contingents failed to report information that would reflect negatively on their attitudes/operations. In other cases, contingents failed to report details viewed as unimportant operationally. These details, however, could have helped IFOR spokesmen with the media.[88]

Some contingents failed to closely associate their PI with their operational staffs. For example, at the French-led MND(SE), commanders seemed to consider the PI as a support operation. During the first months of the operation, PI did not have easy access to the operations room, did not attend the conference calls, and was not associated with G2 or G3 activities. Things only improved slowly. Several months into operations, PIOs were tasked with presenting a daily press summary at the evening division conference call. By fall 1996, they gained unlimited access to the operations room. They then became more closely associated with operations as an organizational reform placed the PIO under G3 supervision. It seemed, however, that these reforms were too slow and incomplete to fully satisfy IFOR HQ PI.

Various contingents also shared different concepts of PSYOP. For example, the Spaniard and Italian contingents did not cooperate closely with the CJIICTF, although both contingents used information policies in support of their G5 (civil affairs) activities. The major difference of opinion occurred between the United States (who ran the CJIICTF) and the British. The U.S. has a rigid top-down approach to PSYOP with centralized planning and product development (at headquarters level) and decentralized execution by subordinate units. Bosnia fit this approach. During *Joint Endeavor*, the CJIICTF headquarters developed products and COMIFOR (then COMARRC) approved all products before release. Finally, subordinate units in the three MNDs disseminated the products throughout theater. The MNDs were able to provide inputs for future products, but they were not allowed to run their own campaigns. The top-down approach allowed IFOR to run a unified campaign across theater. According to LtCol Furlong, DCOMCJIICTF, unity of effort was especially important in regard to Bosnian Serb audiences, who were more hostile to the international community's effort than any other Bosnian group. This approach, however, conflicted with the British developing doctrine. In MND(SW), the British wanted a decentralized, grassroots product development on the grounds that local commanders knew better the local situation and could therefore develop products better to fit local circumstances. The British also thought the approval process (at COMIFOR's level) was too slow and cumbersome. They favored delegating approval authority to the lowest practical level. While some fixes occurred through IFOR to improve problems stemming from these different approaches, the basic tension remained.[89]

Political Sensitivities over Psychological Operations

Some of the nations participating in the coalition, among them the French (who led the multinational division in MND(SE), were reluctant to use PSYOP forces. For historical and political reasons, the French were very sensitive about the concept of psychological operations.[90] As a result, the French only allowed a six-man U.S. PSYOP team under a bilateral liaison agreement. The team manned an IFOR radio in Mostar and occasionally disseminated *The Herald Of Peace* and other CJIICTF products. For the most part of the operation, the division's staffs only had limited interactions with the U.S. PSYOP forces.[91]

Political sensitivities also led to PSYOP personnel remaining under national command and control. Based on a 1984 Executive Directive, the United States refused to place PSYOP forces under NATO command and control.[92] U.S. PSYOP forces (the bulk of the CJIICTF) thus operated under USEUCOM operational control. Refusal to place PSYOP forces under SACEUR's operational control generated several problems. The arrangement created a de facto dual chain of command, which contradicts basic military principles, as CJIICTF products had to be approved at IFOR and EUCOM levels. In practice, this requirement did not appear to slow down the approval process significantly, mainly because

EUCOM quickly agreed to a silent approval procedure.[93] Second, this arrangement created coordination problems because the CJIICTF, as a theater-level (mainly U.S.) command, did not always feel compelled to coordinate activities with the MND HQs. For example, a U.S. tactical PSYOP team showed up in MND(SE) unannounced for a dissemination mission and stumbled onto an anti-sniper operation led by the French division. Third, this arrangement also inhibited a flexible use of PSYOP elements at tactical level as the ARRC and the divisions had limited authority to instruct the PSYOP personnel to conduct specific activities. Finally, as each nation retained control over its PSYOP elements, *Joint Endeavor* set a bad example for future operations. As more nations strengthen their PSYOP assets, the multiplication of national chains of command constitutes a dangerous trend. In the long run, it may damage NATO's ability to achieve unity of effort. This issue needs to be readdressed in the near future.

Coordination Pitfalls

Though the coordination mechanisms established at IFOR headquarters levels proved to be beneficial (most notably by enhancing the information flow), they were not necessarily reproduced at division levels.

The French-led MND(SE) did not mirror the internal coordination mechanisms and forums set up at headquarters. The division had neither formal nor informal coordination processes. The division commanders seemed to consider information as a support activity. Throughout the operation, PI neither chaired nor participated in coordination meetings with other staff elements. Within months of the operation's start, the PI officers had established informal links with the American PSYOP unit, the G5 (civil affairs), and the G3. However, the coordination remained loose throughout the year.

All three divisions failed to reap the benefits that a close coordination with the civilian agencies might have given them. Apart from MND(SW), which tried to establish limited common activities with the civilian organizations (mostly regular briefings with the UNHCR), the other divisions did not seek to coordinate their activities with the local representatives of the civilian organizations operating in their AOR. In MND(N), the force protection rules seriously handicapped the PIO's ability to coordinate with outside organizations. CIMIC was the only interface with the local communities. In MND(SE), the PIOs did not hold regular coordination meetings or common activities with the civilian agencies in its AOR. In that case, it seems that strong suspicions about ultimate and ulterior motives remained on both parts.[94] Overall, at division level common activities and coordination forums between PI and the civilian agencies were rare.

Implications of the Bosnia Experience

Operation Joint Endeavor revealed the critical nature of information activities in peace operations. In a peace operation, media reporting plays a critical role in determining success or failure. A commander's information activities (mostly PI and PSYOP) are the best tools to gain support for an operation and to influence perceptions. The Bosnia experience provides several important lessons on how best to achieve a proper information flow and real coordination.

The information campaign was based upon principles that served well the commanders' and the public's needs. By providing complete, timely, and accurate information, IFOR established its credibility with the international media and the local public. Throughout the operation, reporters have publicly expressed their satisfaction with the arrangements made.[95] The requirement for dissemination of complete, timely, and accurate information was adequately supported by several internal arrangements:

- Allowing a functional chain of information linking PI officers throughout theater proved beneficial. It sped up information flow, allowing PI to provide the media with timely information. This flow was enhanced by the close integration of information staffs with other operational elements.
- PI and PSYOP close interactions with G/J2 and G/J3 facilitated their integration with other tools in the commander's arsenal. Close relations between PI and commanders allowed PIO to be fully aware of the commanders' wishes and thinking.

The widespread coordination taking place within operational staffs (especially G/J2 and G/J3) and with civilian agencies made it possible to develop a common information strategy, most notably by timing release of similar messages and themes. It also made it easier to react promptly and comprehensively to significant events and the commander's needs. Common activities and coordination mechanisms with civilian agencies were particularly beneficial to the operation. By accounts of civilian and military participants alike, and in comparison with earlier missions, this was perhaps the most extensive and effective civilian-military cooperation process for PI in a multinational operation. Most notably, the coordination mechanisms with civilian agencies enabled IFOR and the primary organizations to appear as united in a common effort on the behalf of Bosnia-Herzegovina. It provided a forum to exchange information, reduce inaccuracies, and de-conflict sensitive issues.

Adequate information flow and close coordination allowed the commander to use PI and PSYOP as a non-lethal weapon. It was one of the commander's major tools to communicate intentions, might, and resolve to the local populations and the FWF. Throughout the operation, commanders made extensive use of public information and PSYOP to help achieve operational goals. Those lessons should not be forgotten for the next time around.

VIII. Tactical PSYOP Support to Task Force Eagle
Mark R. Jacobson

Introduction[96]

Since December 1995 over 1,000 soldiers from the U.S. Army's Civil Affairs and Psychological Operations Command (USACAPOC) have supported IFOR and SFOR in the former Yugoslavia. The PSYOP component to this mission represents one of the largest and most comprehensive PSYOP missions in U.S. history. For the past 2 years, PSYOP units have operated under the guidance and control of the Combined Joint Information Task Force (CJIICTF), and have been one of the few weapons systems that were used every day of the operation.

U.S. and allied PSYOP soldiers have kept the peace on a complex and potentially volatile "psychological battlefield." The internecine conflicts in the former Yugoslavia were largely the result of the ability of nationalist leaders to effectively create a demand for war by disseminating divisive and deceptive propaganda.[97] In addition, by the time the CJIICTF began their own information campaign, the peoples of the former Yugoslavia had already had an additional 35 years of experience under Tito's rule within which to develop a sophisticated understanding of the nature and power of propaganda. Thus, U.S. PSYOP troops had to keep the peace in a media environment much more sophisticated than those previously encountered in Panama, Haiti, Somalia, or the Persian Gulf.

This chapter will examine the organization, use, and effectiveness of PSYOP in the former Yugoslavia.[98] Specifically, the chapter will describe the support provided by the CJIICTF to Task Force Eagle, the U.S.-led, multinational element responsible for operations in MND(N). The chapter will analyze tactical PSYOP support at the brigade and battalion task force levels, that is, the levels where U.S. troops "actively" kept the peace. The chapter as a whole will address both the failures and successes of PSYOP support based largely, but not solely, on the experiences of one of the three Brigade Psychological Support Elements (BPSEs) assigned to support Task Force Eagle.

In June 1996, BPSE 210, part of the 346th PSYOP Company (346thPOC) began their deployment to Bosnia along with other elements of the 15th PSYOP BN (15th POB), 2nd PSYOP Group (2nd POG).[99] In all the 15th POB deployed one Division Psychological Support Element (designated DPSE 20) and three BPSE's each with three enhanced Tactical PSYOP Teams (TPT's) to Task Force Eagle as well as elements to support the British forces in MND(SW). In addition, 7th POG personnel-manned "Red Ball" was a PSYOP element headquartered at the HQ CJIICTF in Sarajevo that served as a transportation element by delivering products to the various MNDs, and could be used to fill in gaps in the theater by doing dissemination as required. The deployment also included officers mobilized from HQ 15th POB and HQ 2nd POG who served in the Corps PSYOP Support Element and the CJIICTF with the Commander, 2nd POG serving as the COMCJIICTF (See figure 8-1).

DPSE 20 and its subordinate elements replaced elements from the 9th POB, 4th Psychological Operations Group, based out of Ft. Bragg, NC. BPSE 210 supported the 1st Brigade, 1st Armored Division—the Ready First Combat Team (RFCT), located in the sector north of Tuzla between the Russian and NORDPOL AORs (See figure 8-2). BPSE 220 supported the 2nd Brigade, 1st Armored Division while BPSE 230 first supported military police

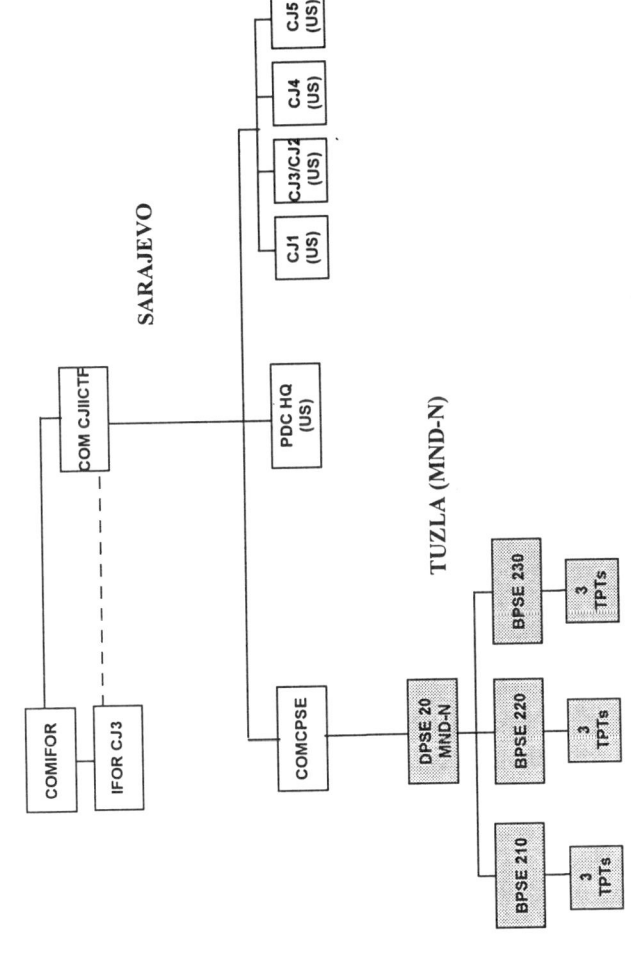

Figure 8-1. CJIICTF Organization

Figure 8-2. MND Areas of Responsibility

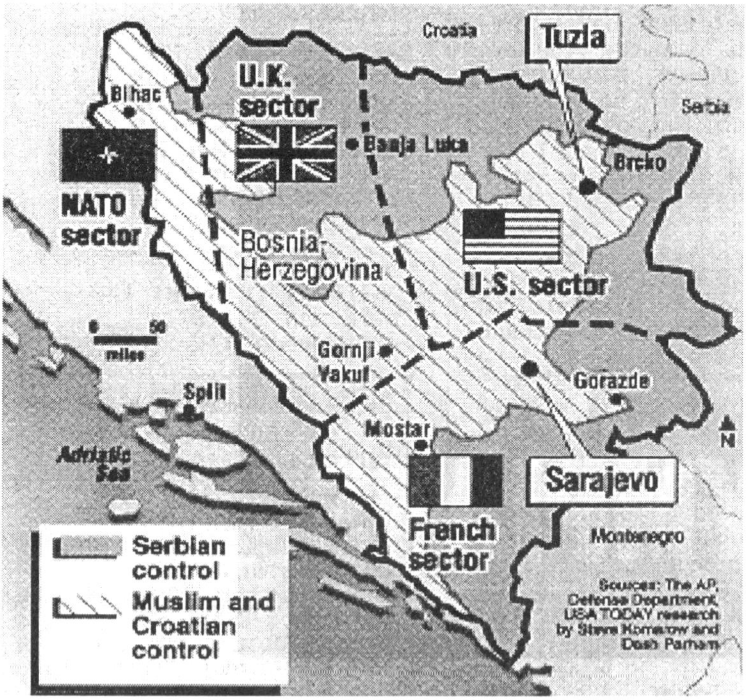

units in the area around HQ Task Force Eagle and would later support Nordic and Polish elements (NORDPOL) in Doboj, Bosnia.[100] In November 1996, after the 1st Armored Division turned control of the Task Force Eagle (TFE) AOR over to the 1st Infantry Division, BPSE 210 supported Task Force 1-18INF.

The significance of this particular case study lies in the both the strategic significance of the AOR and the nature of operations that took place in that area during the time in question. The AOR (hereafter the RFCT/TF 1-18 AOR), included the city of Brcko, the most volatile area within MND(N) and one of the two most significant potential flashpoints in Bosnia-Herzegovina. To this day Brcko has remained a sticking point in the drive toward a lasting peace largely, due to its strategic significance to both the Republika Srpska (RS) and the Muslim-Croat Federation. Specifically, the Serbs consider Brcko the linchpin to the Posavina Corridor, the small strip of land connecting the two halves of the RS granted to them under the GFAP in Bosnia and Herzegovina. The RS has made it clear that the loss of Brcko will mean war while the Muslims have been equally obstinate, declaring that a Serbian Brcko may entail a return to hostilities. Thus, as Major General Montgomery Meigs has cogently stated, Brcko is the "the strategic and geographic Gordian Knot..." that will determine the fate of Bosnia.[101]

The nature of the AOR required BPSE 210 to perform a variety of PSYOP missions, including disseminating, collecting intelligence, assisting Civil Affairs, preparing the population for the Brcko Arbitration decision, and planning for and actively preventing civil disturbances from growing out of control. During the IFOR mission Brcko was the role model for successful crisis management both in terms of IFOR/SFOR actions as well as for methods of NATO interaction with NGOs, IGOs, and more importantly the FWF military and civilian populations. Indeed Brcko was one of the only places in Bosnia where all three factions were regularly talking to each other at the same table.[102] Thus, an examination of this unit's particular operations provides a good gauge from which to look at other BPSE operations both in other sectors and during other rotations during *Operation Joint Endeavor/Operation Joint Guard*.[103]

194 Lessons from Bosnia

Although the documentary evidence indicates that the experiences of other BPSEs (during both IFOR rotations) resembled those of the BPSEs in MND(N), the reader should exercise caution with the analysis and conclusions of this particular study. This is indeed a study of one particular unit, at one particular time, and at one particular place. More importantly, just as previous U.S. operations did not prove to be perfect models for operations in the former Yugoslavia, future PSYOP operations will not simply need to mimic those of *Operation Joint Endeavor* in order to succeed. The "information battlefield" of which the PSYOP battlefield is a part is dynamic and thus the psychological environment may be unfamiliar even if the next mission involves a return to the Balkans.

The PSYOP Mission

The primary implied task of the tactical PSYOP teams in the TFE AOR was to disseminate IIC products per doctrinal convention and campaign guidance provided from higher headquarters. The CJIICTF and CPSE would coordinate the operational PSYOP campaign and execute PSYOP dissemination within the various MNDs through DPSEs, BPSEs, and TPTs, tactical elements designed for this task. Unfortunately, the nature of the mission combined with the particular task organization chosen by the PSYOP planners meant that tactical elements were often challenged to deal with operational issues as well as tactical ones. This placed the CJIICTF HQ in the precarious position of trying to support the MNDs while at the same time protecting the integrity of the PSYOP operational plan as espoused by the JTF CDR and the theater CINC. Likewise, the DPSE at MND(N) would have to try and support both the operational PSYOP plan and the particular needs of the Commander, Task Force Eagle (COMEAGLE), to whom the DPSE provided tactical PSYOP support.

The IFOR/SFOR information campaign has been massive both in terms of the quantity of materials disseminated and the variety of themes stressed during the operation.[104] Since December 1995, the CJIICTF has produced and disseminated close to 12 million products within the Federation and the RS. This includes handbills, pamphlets, posters, the *Herald of Peace*, (a weekly IFOR newspaper focusing on news and features of national interest) the Mirko teen-oriented magazine, as well as various radio, television, and miscellaneous products such as soccer balls, coloring books, and IFOR/SFOR logo pens.[105] These products have been developed to support the missions of the military and civilian components of the IFOR/SFOR campaign, to include NATO forces, the United Nations, Red Cross, OSCE, European Union, World Bank, and other miscellaneous IOs and NGOs. The CJIICTF sought to influence the attitudes and behaviors of targeted groups within Bosnia-Herzegovina in order to encourage cooperation with IFOR, deter resistance to peacekeeping activities, and encourage the return to normalcy within both the Federation and the RS. The guidance for the CJIICTF campaign at the theater level was expressed in the Information Campaign Operations (PSYOP) annex H to OPLAN-10405 (SACEUR Plan) and annex H to 40105 (IFOR/AFSOUTH Plan). In each of the division areas, the information campaign was guided by PSYOP annexes to the divisional Operations Orders (OPORDS).

Even before DPSE 20 took over responsibility for PSYOP operations in the TFE AOR, the ability of PSYOP to operate within the theater had been problematic. The entry of a new COMCJIICTF, COMCPSE, and DPSE within a few weeks of each other exacerbated the situation, primarily due to the failure of the incoming organization to conduct an adequate leader's reconnaissance. The conduct of a leader's recon is not only a basic tactical principle but also a prerequisite to effective operations. The absence of a leader's recon for key leaders and operators prior to the deployment of the PSYOP force-package in June 1996 resulted in unnecessary difficulties for the PSYOP elements in Task Force Eagle and thus their supported units.

The decision of the CDR 2D POG (who was the incoming CDR CJIICTF) to not support a leader's recon by key DPSE and/or BPSE leaders meant that prior to the force package as a whole entering the theater, there had been no one capable of assessing the current AOR situation and providing on-the-ground feedback to the rest of the deploying unit. Although the 346th POC made good use of open source material in order to provide PSYOP-relevant background information to the deploying troops, they received very little up-to-date intelligence or information on the type of operations taking place in the AOR. Reports sent by the CJIICTF through USASOC and USACAPOC to the 2nd POG had to be sent by regular mail (because of inadequate communications systems at the 2nd POG), and were weeks old by the time they reached the units preparing to deploy. Furthermore, the 2nd POG did not take advantage of those means available to contact the units they would replace. Elements down through the BPSE level could have contacted their counterparts via DSN, commercial telephone, electronic mail, and even video conference calls.[106] This would have enabled the deploying elements to obtain an up-to-date intelligence picture of the area, gain a greater understanding of the operational limitations and restrictions in the various AORs, and find out about living/working conditions and supply shortages.

No formal or informal mission statements were disseminated by the CDR 2nd POG or CDR 15th POB (later the COMCJIICTF and COMCPSE, respectively) prior to, during, or immediately after the troop deployment. The absence of a clear mission statement from the incoming COMCJIICTF to the fresh PSYOP soldiers in Bosnia equally hampered the ability of the PSYOP elements to integrate properly and effectively into the Task Force Eagle mission. A debilitating command climate fostered by the COMCJIICTF and communications difficulties made the development of a coordinated effort between the BPSEs, DPSEs, and CPSE even more problematic. Thus, despite periodic mission updates, annexes, and FRAGOs (fragmentary orders) developed by the CJIICTF staff, the PSYOP elements in MND(N) remained unclear about their own role in the CJIICTF mission.[107]

Thus, the BPSE never knew the commander's intent behind the PSYOP campaign. This limited the ability of the BPSE to accomplish its mission in several ways. First, the BPSE did not know what the priorities of effort were at a given time and this prevented effective prior planning and the ability to anticipate potential operational difficulties. Without a specified mission BPSE could not explain adequately to the local maneuver commanders the purpose of the various information campaigns Sarajevo ran in the RFCT/TF 1-18 AOR. Lacking clear guidance the BPSE found themselves pushed in conflicting directions by the supported unit, the DPSE, and the CJIICTF. Not until the final 60 days of the deployment did the PSYOP elements in the RFCT/TF 1-18 AOR even see a PSYOP annex to the ARRC, IFOR, or LANDCENT OPORDs or FRAGOs.[108]

Intelligence Operations

Operational requirements dictate that PSYOP is both a consumer and a producer of intelligence. As such, PSYOP elements must have a well established collection management architecture of its own and be firmly integrated into the various intelligence structures within the supported unit's organization. Effective PSYOP depends upon current and accurate intelligence provided through the intelligence cycle. Tactical PSYOP Teams and BPSEs will often collect the information needed to fill the "intelligence requirements" generated by both the PSYOP task force and the various supported units.

The experience of BPSE 210 during its 7 months in MND(N) demonstrated that PSYOP could contribute to the intelligence cycle as a key HUMINT source. Unfortunately, the integration of the PSYOP elements into the collection management architecture of the supported unit proved a hindrance to the processing of PSYOP relevant information and the dissemination of finished intelligence products to the PSYOP elements.

While Force Protection Teams (FPTs) made up of counterintelligence agents (MOS 97B) and interrogators (MOS 97E) were the primary HUMINT sources in the TFE AOR, the close contact PSYOP and Civil Affairs soldiers had with the local community meant that they too became key HUMINT collection assets.[109] Civil Affairs Tactical Support Teams were often the best sources of political intelligence at the local level. Likewise, Tactical PSYOP Teams became a valuable HUMINT asset due to the large number of contacts they maintained in the local civilian population, including key members of local political parties. About 95 percent of all PSYOP missions in the TFE AOR involved some sort of HUMINT collection. Most importantly, TPTs were the points of contact between the local IFOR commanders and the indigenous print and broadcast media personalities in the AOR.

Coordination between PSYOP elements and the Force Protection elements was inconsistent and depended mainly on the personalities in the FPT and PSYOP cells. A high level of coordination in RFCT Tactical Operations Center (TOC) helped to alleviate some problems at both the division and battalion levels. Specifically, daily coordination between the brigade PSYOP and the brigade HUMINT cell ensured the detection of "false confirmations" and conflicting reports. This did not, however, prevent the entire stovepiping problem. A great deal of PSYOP information seems to have moved up the PSYOP channels without ever reaching the supported unit's intelligence shops. The lack of synchronization between the DPSE and the 1st I.D. S-2 particularly affected the ability of PSYOP information to be turned into useful intelligence. Additionally, because the CJIICTF needed to collect as much information as possible for the purposes of product assessment and development, PSYOP SITREPs were often too long to be included in their entirety in the BN and BDE INTSUMs and daily commander's SITREPs. Thus, sometimes only a small amount of information would make its way directly to the supported unit's S-2 shops. In essence the tactical PSYOP elements would prepare two SITREPs each day, one for the supported unit and one for the PSYOP chain.[110]

One area in which CA, PSYOP, and Force Protection teams had a particular need for collaboration was in the development of area assessments that helped the BN and BDEs develop an understanding of the environment in which they operated. Area assessments included basic information about the geography, social dynamics, political environment, cultural, and economic factors in various communities in an AOR. Area assessments were basic tasks required of both PSYOP and CA teams as well as a mission for the newly created FPTs. Rather than developing separate CA, PSYOP, and FPT assessments, the teams at the BN and BDE sought to produce a single document, using all teams as agents for collection and thereby increasing the efficiency of the collection and production effort. Although reporting formats differed slightly, and each group sought to emphasize different considerations in their initial reports (e.g., Civil Affairs emphasizing economic factors and indicators), most of the information collected was easily assembled into a single report. Area assessments, however, are not static documents and must be updated continuously. Unfortunately, there was no standard operating procedure (SOP) common to all elements involved (S-2, PSYOP, CA, FPT) for the collection of assessment information, much less the management and updating of this information. Though the ad hoc system for updating the assessments did not destroy the value of these intelligence products, it did make their use and upkeep somewhat cumbersome.

In order to make some sense of the big picture, a commander will need intelligence from out of his AO. While in a conventional operation political intelligence might seem the province for echelons above Corps, in a peacekeeping operation political and other so-called "strategic intelligence" were essential to operations at the brigade and battalion level. Thus, in order for the commanders to maintain "total mission awareness," intelligence within the Task Force Eagle elements was generally pushed down to much lower echelons than would normally be expected. While the maneuver units were supplied with a great deal of the type of intelligence products needed to discern the big picture, the CJIICTF could not always provide its subordinate elements with the type of information they required. The CJIICTF was hamstrung in many ways by the nature of the stove-piped intelligence inputs into IFOR/SFOR.[111] Thus, retrieving information from the CJIICTF proved difficult. In particular, the CJIICTF was unable to provide the PSYOP elements at Task Force Eagle with Basic PSYOP Studies, Special PSYOP

Assessments, and other intelligence products such as USIA and BBC audience analysis surveys of media preferences in the former Yugoslavia.[112]

Dissemination Operations

Several operational problems with regards to the dissemination of PSYOP products existed during BPSE 210's tenure in the RFCT/TF 1-18 AOR. These problems included the appropriateness of PSYOP products to the target audiences and the timeliness with which these products were delivered to the TPTs for dissemination to the population. There is a great deal of evidence to suggest that these problems with product dissemination occurred throughout the CJIICTF AOR. Additionally, the comments of the supported unit and previous PSYOP rotations indicate that these problems existed during the initial 6 months of the IFOR mission as well.

The nature of the product development, approval, and delivery process greatly hindered the timely delivery of PSYOP products. Centralized product development and printing locations in Sarajevo meant that it would usually take more than a week to conceive, obtain approval, and deliver products from the CJIICTF to the TPTs. A "Red Ball" delivery element comprised of trained 37F personnel was supposed to transport the products to the DPSE at Tuzla Main approximately once a week.[113] Because the pace of missions in MND(N) as well as personnel and vehicle shortages at the brigade and BN PSYOP elements, the products would often sit in Tuzla for several days until the BPSE could arrange the support necessary to convoy to Tuzla and pick up the products. Once products arrived at the BPSE it might be an additional 2 days before the products would make it out on LOG/LNO runs or the teams themselves could arrange to come back to the BPSE and pick them up. The result was that time-sensitive information did not get to the population until the news was stale or the information had been taken over by events. In several crisis situations the products did not arrive until well after the situations had been resolved.[114] The CJIICTF attempted to use alternative delivery methods such as heliborne transport but the Bosnia weather, especially after October, made this sort of transportation a luxury. It is not clear whether or not the CJIICTF considered direct delivery by the Red Ball (a purpose designed delivery element) to the BDE and BN PSYOP elements that were not located in between Tuzla and Sarajevo. In any case, the number of missions devoted to the procurement of products took away from the TPT's ability to concentrate on their dissemination and intelligence collection missions.

Even if the CJIICTF had alleviated some delivery problems, the product development and Byzantine approval process alone would have challenged the ability of the CJIICTF to disseminate all its products in a timely manner. This process frustrated not only those in the tactical PSYOP elements but more importantly the supported unit whom the products served. As a result of the approval and delivery process, PSYOP products were simply not available at all times to support operations, despite several weeks lead-time for the preparation of such materials.[115] In the case of operations in the former Yugoslavia, the fact that products required approval at a multinational headquarters complicated the entire process (figure 8-3)[116] The key issue in regards to BPSE operations was that the process was deemed too slow to adequately respond to the needs of the Task Force Eagle peacekeeping mission.

From December 1995 until February 1997, the two BPSEs assigned Task Force Eagle frequently expressed their own, as well as their supported units' dissatisfaction, with the timeliness of products.[117] The RFCT and TF 1-18 commanders both quickly discovered that PSYOP products could not be developed quickly enough to keep pace with the changing operational and tactical landscape. Thus the supported units throughout the TFE AOR tended to rely upon the Mobile Public Affairs Detachments (MPAD) at the Combined Press Information Center (CPIC) at HQ Task Force Eagle to produce information products in contingency situations rather than on those developed by the PSYOP task force. What is particularly interesting is that in order to maintain message consistency, both

202   Lessons from Bosnia

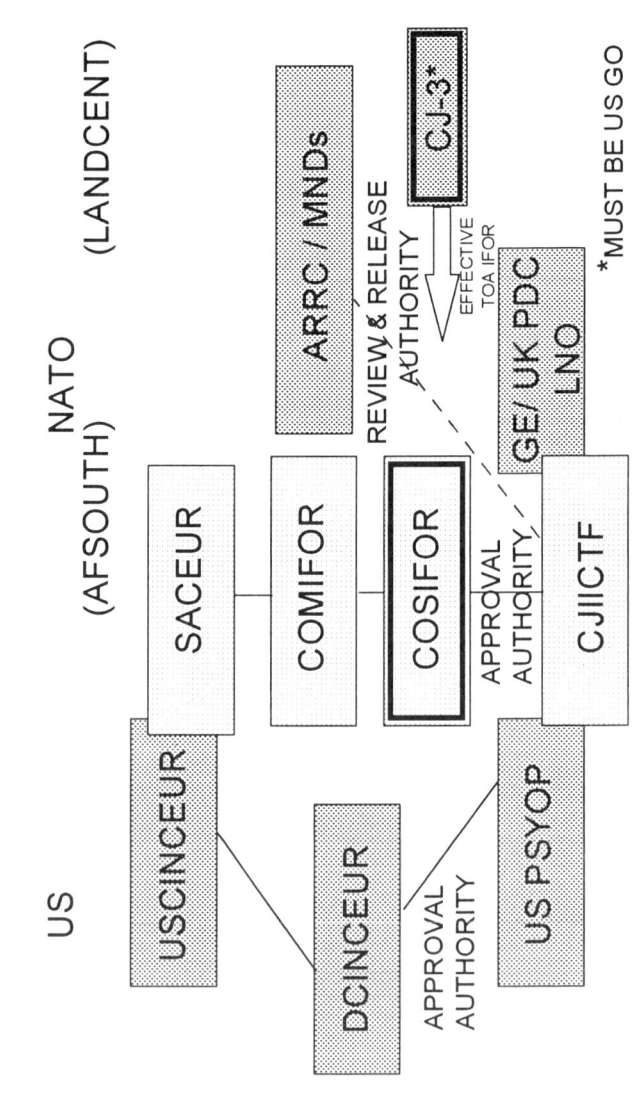

Figure 8-3. Product Approval Process

the MPAD and PSYOP missions were directed and guided by the same "Information Campaign Guidelines" at all levels. The Public Affairs components, at least within the U.S. sector, took advantage of decentralized execution giving authority to the JIB (Joint Information Bureau, later the CPIC (Combined Press Information Center)) chief at the division level to approve statements that would go out to the public. Meanwhile the PSYOP message, based on the same information campaign guidelines, would be going through a redundant approval process before being released, perhaps days later, to the PSYOP BPSEs.[118]

By the end of the BPSE's deployment, the situation had proven so untenable within the RFCT/TF 1-18 AOR that products that would normally be developed and approved by PSYOP, such as radio spots, announcements, and commanders' speeches to the population, were produced, developed, and disseminated through the MPAD's. Turnaround on most products would be a few days with approval authority coming within hours. The same product would have taken much longer to develop, approve, and disseminate through the PSYOP channels.[119]

In a PSYOP campaign, the information campaign guidelines must be viewed the same way that the combat arms view limiting stakes and ROE—they are parameters within which soldiers may operate without constantly seeking advice from above. There is a strong argument to be made that the MPAD method of having the division elements approve the products so long as they fall within the guidelines may be a better approach for some products. The problem was and is, however, that any product approved from one AOR such as MND(N) inevitably has a spillover effect in other AORs. Information by its very nature spreads quickly and permeates everywhere. Thus, it is important that an overall IO campaign continue to be centrally planned at the Task Force level. Robust communication systems and perhaps LNOs might have helped improve coordination as well as flexible and responsive product development and delivery.

Although tight centralized control might have been appropriate in the beginning of the operation or where the operational environment did not differ significantly from AOR to AOR, this was not the case during this time period in the former Yugoslavia. The CJIICTF would have done better to tailor its campaign by trying to more finitely divide its target audience selection rather than finding the common denominator.[120] The following analogy illustrates the problem with the PSYOP campaign approval process. When a BN is given a portion of the battlefield to defend, the commander divides it among his companies. Eventually, aiming stakes are set and each soldier is given limits of fire in either direction. When the battle begins the soldiers are trained to keep their fire within these parameters—they do not call up the corps headquarters when the enemy arrives and say, "I have three soldiers in my sights, one with a machine gun, one with a grenade, and one with a rifle. Who do I shoot first and where do I shoot them?"

What the soldier would use would be rules of engagement (ROE) designed to help the soldier determine when to shoot—his training would tell him where to place the round. In a PSYOP campaign, the information campaign guidelines are the limiting stakes and the guidance from the CJIICTF are the ROE used to help determine the parameters of operation for tactical PSYOP. There is indeed a strong argument to be made that the MPAD/CPIC methods of product approval and dissemination authority might be more appropriate to a Bosnia-type mission than those used by the PSYOP component of the CJIICTF. The problem is that PSYOP objectives and themes are approved at the NAC/SACEUR level. They cannot be changed by the COMCJIICTF, much less by division commanders and PSYOP DPSEs. Nor should they be, as it is essential that the IO campaign maintain consistency throughout the theater. What the PSYOP elements and the supported units can do, however, is adjust the disseminated product by "tweaking" the messages that come out as long as they are in consonance with the approved PSYOP themes.

The actual products used were, in the opinion of the DPSE and BPSEs in MND(N), not sufficiently targeted to change attitudes and shape the behaviors within the BPSE AOR. Too many printed products, especially the posters, reflected an orientation toward American pop culture rather than the more familiar European traditions. While the development of these products adequately represented the results of comprehensive pre-testing done in the Sarajevo area, many of the products contained themes and symbols (figure 8-4) that were not familiar to the more provincial target audiences in the areas outside of Sarajevo. Those products that had a sophisticated, European feel, such as the teenage magazine *MIRKO*, proved as successful in areas outside of Sarajevo in terms of audience receptivity and understanding. The proper use, however, of familiar American icons such as Superman helped to reach the children and adults targeted throughout the country in the IFOR mine awareness campaign.

The CJIICTF weekly paper, *The Herald of Peace (HoP)*, and the IFOR Radio campaign in the RFCT/TF 1-18 AOR raise doubts about the way in which CJIICTF conducted these campaigns outside of Sarajevo. The early *HoP* was a valuable tool in educating the masses about the details of the Dayton Peace Accords. After the first 5 months, however, the *HoP* began to fall victim to the relative success of the peacekeeping mission. As some degree of normality returned to the region, the large Bosnian, Croatian, and Serbian daily papers, as well as a host of regional and European papers, soon became available to the general public. Despite its objectivity, the relatively (but unavoidably) bland *Herald of Peace* eventually lost its appeal to that of the other papers.[121] The population quickly hungered for more sophisticated approaches to national (often controversial) issues as well as information on local events. Once post-testing indicated that the *HoP* was losing its appeal, the CJIICTF took steps to alleviate this situation, including the development of a sophisticated and catchy monthly to replace the weekly version of the newspaper.[122]

206   Lessons from Bosnia

Figure 8-4. In some instances, American cultural themes and symbols did not translate well into the Bosnian cultures. Though Monopoly may have been familiar to those in cosmopolitan urban centers, it proved alien to audiences in the more provincial areas of the country. In some instances the CJICTF production cell transplanted American advertisements into IFOR programs with varying degrees of success. The teenage magazine *MIRKO*, however, developed by some of NATO's European members, successfully integrated Western cultural icons into subtle propaganda platforms.

Similarly, the IFOR radio campaigns in the RFCT/TF 1-18 AOR lacked the ability to acquire, maintain, and thus persuade a target audience. The CJIICTF ran two radio stations in MND(N) for most of the first year of the campaign. Radio IFOR-Brcko's capabilities (the CJIICTF station in the RFCT/TF 1-18 AOR) as a PSYOP weapon suffered due both to technical and programming difficulties. The station had an extremely small broadcast footprint due largely to the location of the station (a function of force-protection considerations) and the terrain in the broadcast area. Additionally, while the majority of the listening audience tuned in to FM radio stations, Radio IFOR broadcast on the AM band.[123] The CJIICTF viewed the radio assets in traditional terms—as operational and not as tactical assets. The local PSYOP elements and their supported units, however, found several occasions where radio could and did serve as an effective tactical weapon.[124] As part of an operational campaign, the entertainment format of the radio station focused on children, teenagers, and young adults while the vast majority of messages (mostly in English and not Serbo-Croatian) were targeted at an older population. In short, even if the American rock and roll and pop music could have acquired a target audience, it would not have been the one that many of the messages were designed for.[125]

Part of the reason for the disconnect between the PSYOP products and their intended audiences was an inadequate regimen of pre- and post-testing. Products used in the RFCT/TF1-18 AOR were not pre-tested in that particular sector until November of 1996—almost a full year into the operation. The inability to send products down to the BPSEs as digital files meant that pre-test packages had to be sent down via the Red Ball. The associated transportation problems between Sarajevo and the TPTs in MND(N) meant that there was, at times, almost a 3-week delay between the initial submission of a product for pre-testing in MND(N) and the receipt of responses by the PDC from the TPTs conducting the pre-tests. In addition, some negative criticism of products at the BPSE level did not make it to the PDC at the CJIICTF.[126] The number of requests received by the DPSE in MND(N) for "roll-up" reports requiring the location where products were disseminated rather than the audience receptivity of those products indicates that the COMCJIICTF may have mistakenly believed that the physical proximity of a population to areas of dissemination was directly proportional to the degree of reception and understanding.[127]

For the PSYOP operators in the field, both pre- and posttesting alike were hampered by the fact that there was little guidance as to the particular target audiences, specific objectives, or desired behaviors that should be observed in the population as a result of the PSYOP materials. Many product action worksheets reflected the common denominator approach to targeting by referring to the audience as "population of Bosnia-Herzegovina," which flew in the face of the understanding that when you "target all you target none."

Although the sophisticated information environment made the tried and true methods of PSYOP more difficult to implement, one of the most effective PSYOP weapons in the TFE AOR was one of the oldest: face-to-face communication.[128] The ability of the TPTs to sit down, relax, and just talk with or "hang out" with locals—be it at a coffee shop, restaurant, or in private homes—allowed the soldiers to cut through the red tape and speak to the people in real terms. The ability to immediately assess the impact of statements on the target audience allowed for a great deal more to be accomplished in a shorter amount of time. Armed with talking points provided initially by the DPSE and later directly from local MPAD elements, the TPTs were able to provide the "party line" to the locals on even sensitive issues such as the Brcko Arbitration or War Crimes issues.[129] One particular TPTs discussions with local political parties in the Brcko area also resulted in the first and perhaps only series of "multi-party" meetings in Bosnia-Herzegovina. At these meetings, the local chapters of national Serb, Croat, and Muslim parties sat down and in a civilized manner discussed their differences and even possible solutions to the local problems that faced all of them. In addition, PSYOP TPTs proved themselves capable and reliable key communicators in crisis situations, such as those at

Zvornik, Mahala, and Celic. The success of the TPTs was not only due to their skills, but the ability of the teams to respond clearly and quickly to the needs of the supported unit.

Without a doubt, the BDE and BN commanders were the most potent PSYOP weapons in the TFE AOR. The success of the IFOR mission as a whole rested largely on their individual abilities to persuade the FWF that peace was the only alternative. Within each of their AORs, the FWF military and political leadership viewed the brigade and battalion as the voice of IFOR itself it because these particular U.S. commanders actively encouraged compliance with the GFAP whether through persuasion or coercion. For these reasons alone it was important that the BDE and BN commanders be highly visible in the AOR. Thus, the maneuver commanders enlisted PSYOP support in order to get their messages out through the indigenous media outlets.

In the RFCT sector, the most powerful face-to-face communicator was undoubtedly Colonel Gregory Fontenot. Fontenot, a brilliant soldier and scholar as well as an exceptional orator, was not given the Brcko sector because of his timidity. Fontenot was exactly the type of personality to keep the peace in the Posavina Corridor and truly understood the psychological battlefield, often using it to his advantage in order to prevent situations from getting out of hand.[130] Fontenot's subordinates similarly used face-to-face communication and personal preventive diplomacy to alleviate problems and encourage compliance with the GFAP. Through the use of radio interviews and "fireside chats," Colonel Fontenot's successor in the region, LTC Stephen Layfield strove to attain the same position among the population that his predecessor had in the AOR.[131] Unfortunately, by the time TF 1-18 INF took over the AOR, the PSYOP elements had been told by higher headquarters not to get involved with any activities involving local radio stations.[132] This technically included working with the maneuver commanders in order to help them get their messages out on the airwaves. Hence, the MPADs took over responsibility for this job as well.

Operational Constraints

Force protection requirements and limited C3I capabilities within the PSYOP organization in theater affected operations in MND(N). While PSYOP soldiers may have been more vocal about concerns over force protection, it appears as though the measures resulted in very few tangible difficulties. C3I problems, however, had a somewhat greater influence on the ability of the PSYOP tactical elements to conduct operations.

Strict force protection measures in MND(N) required that soldiers carry their personal weapons at all times and wear Kevlar helmets, flack vests, and LBEs both on and off base. The regulations also required that U.S. military vehicles would have to travel in convoys of four or more. The purpose of these measures was to decrease the possibility of small unit tactical defeats.[133] For the PSYOP soldiers in RFCT/TF 1-18 AOR, most of the force protection issues do not appear to have had a significant effect on the ability of the soldiers to complete their missions.

The four-vehicle convoy rule had the greatest effect on operations. Within MND(N), TPTs had one or two vehicles at most. Even if the TPTs had four vehicles, there was no way the three- and four-man teams could have provided drivers and assistant drivers for each of these vehicles. In order to alleviate personnel and vehicle shortcomings, PSYOP teams paired up with their Force Protection Team (CI and HUMINT personnel) counterparts who had to operate under similar restrictions. This required a great deal of coordination due to the OPTEMPO of FPT, PSYOP, and CA elements. In addition, scheduled and unscheduled maintenance problems left the PSYOP teams without vehicles from time to time. Maintenance problems increased during the winter months. The greatest effect the four-vehicle convoy rule had on operations came in terms of the inability to conduct missions as a result of vehicle maintenance problems late into the deployment.[134] The second greatest problem was that the four-vehicle convoy rule made the delivery of PSYOP products from the CJIICTF to the DPSEs, BPSEs, and TPTs more problematic.

The authority to allow PSYOP forces to travel in two-vehicle convoys in MND(N) lay with COMEAGLE. Although several requests were made to COMEAGLE via the ARRC for an exception to policy for SOF troops such as CA and PSYOP, the requests were not granted during the IFOR mission. Exceptions were made for JCOs and Special Forces personnel due to mission requirements. Although there were legitimate concerns about the force protection posture and the ability of CA/PSYOP soldiers to operate efficiently, the fact remains that COMEAGLE had authority over U.S. troops in his MND, which meant that he had the responsibility to ensure that these troops were safe. Furthermore, the U.S. NCA and DoD made clear their intentions that keeping U.S. troops safe was to be the priority throughout the operation. For an excellent assessment of how the four-vehicle convoy rule and other force protection measures affected Force Protection Team missions, see Perkins, "CI and HUMINT in Bosnia." Despite several requests from the BPSEs, the four-vehicle convoy rule was not lifted until February 1997.

In the absence of organic transportation assets, the TPTs would attempt to "hitch a ride" with Civil Affairs teams or regularly scheduled MP and mounted infantry patrols operating in the AOR. This limited the ability to make PSYOP missions the priority assignments as TPTs could not always "drive" the focus of these other missions. Additionally, the ability of the PSYOP teams to work within and around these constraints rested largely on the ability of the TPT chiefs to coordinate and interact with their counterparts at the battalion level. The greater the involvement of the TPT in the BN operations, the better the level of coordination and support and thus the more likely that PSYOP missions would obtain adequate outside support. In the end, the results were better in some BN AORs than others.

Frustration with the four-vehicle convoy rule was paralleled by a disappointment with the individual protection requirements in the U.S. sector. The need to look like, as British soldiers put it, "Ninja Turtles" or "prisoners of peace" certainly frustrated a great number of U.S. soldiers. At least in the RFCT/TF 1-18 AOR, however, this frustration was by no means universal and seemed more evident among "rookies" and lower-enlisted soldiers rather than among the NCOs or veterans of Haiti, Somalia, Panama, and the Persian Gulf, where many had learned, firsthand of the potential benefits of protective clothing. Some soldiers, especially Civil Affairs, FPT, and PSYOP soldiers who dealt face-to-face with the local community, felt that the enhanced force protection requirements may have had a negative psychological impact on the local population.

PSYOP TPTs did get consistent, albeit infrequent, feedback indicating that the population questioned the need for the U.S. soldiers to wear that type of equipment. Although local civilian and FWF military personnel had openly questioned the need for U.S. forces to maintain such a posture, at no time did any of the teams indicate that this affected friendly attitudes toward U.S. soldiers. Teams learned to work within and around these constraints in order to successfully accomplish their missions.[135] Not all American peacekeepers, however, felt that the force protection measures hampered the mission. As one American commander put it, "you can discuss reconstruction and resettlement just fine in a helmet and flak jacket." Also, the posture may have even helped to encourage FWF compliance with the GFAP. Both the local communities and the FWF military forces in the AOR felt that they should respect U.S. troops, as they were well armed and well protected.[136] Additionally, a legitimate concern existed at least within BPSE 210 that the PSYOP soldiers may not have had all the supplementary tactical training and experience required to handle hostile tactical situations with as few as three soldiers.

A greater understanding of the psychological and operational impact of force protection measures in peacekeeping operations is certainly needed, especially in light of the great variety of beliefs about the issue within the NATO community. What is important is not necessarily whether or not troops deploy subject to enhanced force protection measures, for that may rest on political decisions at the NCA level, but that the military and political leadership understand the effects of such measures on the perceptions of the local population. Indeed the bottom line is that the beliefs on force protection measures represent greater differences of opinion on tactics for the application of force and particular techniques of conflict termination that will always be present in combined (or even joint) operations. Finally, despite the complaints about the force protection posture taken by U.S. troops, the fact remains that at the present time U.S. casualties as a result of hostile action have been near zero and that sharp responses to FWF "tests" or "resolve checks" have proven effective within MND(N).

Physical communications problems, an uninvolved command organization, and lackluster command climate also constrained PSYOP mission performance. These problems not only affected dissemination operations but the ability of the BPSEs and TPTs to collect information and secure PSYOP specific intelligence products.

By relying almost solely on the supported unit for communications support, the PSYOP BPSE was frequently left without adequate means of communicating with higher headquarters. The PSYOP annex to the OPORDS at the division level stated that "FM communications" would be the methods of communication for the BPSE and TPTs. Due to METT-T constraints, particularly the geographic and environmental conditions in Bosnia, FM communication was at best extraordinarily inconvenient and at worst impossible. The supported units utilized other communications systems such as VSAT, INMARSAT, LAN, and MSE for routine communications. The BPSE had to "borrow" phones and computers, which often proved problematic due to the heavy usage of this equipment by all elements.[137] At times it could take several hours for the BPSE to reach the TPT's or the DPSE and vice versa. The most reliable means of communication, courier, often took days. This proved unacceptable to the DPSE, CPSE, and CJIICTF, though they could not provide the BPSE with any support to solve problems.

These difficulties were paralleled by communications problems within the TPTs. The urban environment required that the teams split up and conduct liaison with various individuals. These missions were dismounted and often indoor. At times the personnel were far enough away from the vehicles that they could not communicate without radios. In markets, the crowds often impaired visual or verbal communication at distances less than 100 meters. PSYOP was the only element in the RFCT/TF 1-18 AOR that did not have its own organic intersquad communications such as Motorola handtalkies or PRC 127s. This became a significant force-protection issue and was noted many times by the BPSE in its SITREPS.[138]

The particular command relationships between the CJIICTF and its subordinate PSYOP elements at the division and brigade levels exacerbated the C3I problems resulting from communications difficulties. The dual chain of command for PSYOP has been and continues to be confusing both for PSYOP elements and supported units alike. In practice, supported units will either have Operational Control (OPCON) or Tactical Control (TACON) of the PSYOP elements. In some commander's minds, there is no dual chain of command—the TPTs report to the BPSE, the BPSEs report to the DPSE, the DPSE to the CPSE, and the CPSE to the POTF (in this case the CJIICTF). PSYOP elements, however, must rely on their supported units for "beans and bullets," and other essentials required to accomplish the mission.[139]

One of the greatest tensions between the PSYOP task force and the supported units in MND(N) arose because PSYOP did not plug into the operations cells in MND(N), ARRC, and HQ IFOR as well as they could have. The problem at MND(N) was due primarily to the lack of a theater PSYOP asset at MND(N); the DPSE was a tactical asset designed to control tactical PSYOP elements. In the absence of a CJIICTF representative or liaison to MND(N), the COMDPSE also became the individual responsible for operational PSYOP planning in the MND. Thus, the DPSE commander had to try and please two masters who often had conflicting intentions and goals.[140]

The relationship between the DPSEs and the BPSEs demonstrates what could happen as a result of the failure of PSYOP to "plug in" to the operations of a supported unit. PSYOP missions and operations appear as annexes to BN, BDE, and divisional OPORDs. PSYOP BPSEs are given Fragmentary Orders (FRAGOs) through the division OPORDs. The two units that BPSE

210 supported looked to its own division OPORDs, annexes, and FRAGOs in order to determine the priority of effort and support. Without written orders the BDE and BN viewed PSYOP missions as routine, and thus no command emphasis was placed on completing or, more importantly, supporting these missions. Verbal communication of intent between the DPSE and the BPSE did not translate into the same clear statement of purpose for the TF battle staff—only a written OPORD could do that. Without these written orders, mission limiters hampered BPSE missions and prevented the ability of PSYOP to successfully integrate into the STABOPS in the RFCT/TF 1-18 AOR.

The ability to conduct successful military operations rests on how well that organization can master the OODA loop, that is, the ability to observe, orient, decide and act quickly, deliberately, and decisively in the operational environment. While intelligence-gathering facilities, communications nodes, and effective weapons systems will give a military organization many of the tools it needs to work through this loop, the abilities of key leaders and personnel will play a disproportionate role in the ability of a military organization to make decisions and take action in a timely and effective manner. Within the PSYOP organization, the quality of personnel in the C2 process and OODA loop proved one of the weaker links.[141]

The lack of quality personnel in some positions inhibited the ability of PSYOP to integrate and thus perform successfully in the theater as a whole. Even those in some senior positions seem to have been weak links in the organization as well. Perhaps most importantly, the lack of command visits to PSYOP elements in the Task Force Eagle prevented those in Sarajevo from understanding the difference between the "ground truth" and the impression of Brcko as seen from a distance. Those CJIICTF and CPSE personnel that visited the MND on visits of a few days or more often left in disbelief as to the degree with which PSYOP was integrated into COMEAGLE's overall vision of keeping the peace in the AOR. Command visits could have helped to bridge the real and perceived gap between the theater PSYOP support effort and the needs of COMEAGLE. Additionally, command visits would have also done a great deal to promote the teamwork and build the trust throughout the PSYOP organization that was visibly lacking throughout the deployment. The resulting disconnects between the tactical elements in support of Task Force Eagle and the CJIICTF had a deleterious effect on morale and operations alike.

The C3I system described above affected the ability of the PSYOP elements to successfully complete their dissemination and intelligence collection functions in the TFE AOR. The specific problems encountered indicate that despite technological advances in information management and communications systems, military C3I networks will remain "friction sensitive" due to the necessary presence of human operators in those systems. Additionally, the unintended consequences of technological advance will often result in the system breaking down or not performing as originally intended, thus highlighting the importance of competent operators and managers in such a system.

Operational vs. Tactical PSYOP Support to MND(N)

Several U.S. commanders, including General Crouch (COMSFOR), MG Nash (COMEAGLE, 1st A.D.), and MG Meigs (COMEAGLE, 1st I.D.), clearly expressed their dissatisfaction with the degree and nature of PSYOP support in their AORs.[142] Their comments were largely directed at what they deemed to be a PSYOP campaign that was not responsive enough to their IO needs in MND(N). The reasons for this disconnect seem to lie in the larger differences between the priorities of effort in the U.S.-run MND versus those of the combined-joint headquarters in Sarajevo. These differences in turn reflect differences in opinion between the NATO members involved in the IFOR mission.

The CJIICTF operational campaign strove to bill IFOR as a credible and trustworthy source of information and then to use this credibility in order to encourage compliance with the GFAP, thereby enhancing the safety and security of IFOR/SFOR soldiers and local civilians alike. The campaign would also contribute to FWF compliance with the GFAP by reinforcing the notion that IFOR was resolved to use force if required. Finally, a great deal of emphasis was placed on support to the NGOs, IGOs, and PVOs that were the civilian contribution to the overall peacekeeping effort in Bosnia. The success of the civilian programs and long-term reconstruction required the CJIICTF to focus on a campaign that supported medium- and long-term goals in the region. This was accomplished by focusing on younger generations (the 18-26 year old age group) in order to help instill in them a greater understanding of the benefits of democracy and peace. These programs, however, had little to do with the immediate short-term (6 to 12 month) needs of the U.S. military peacekeeping forces in MND(N), where the primary concern (as relayed officially and unofficially through the U.S.-only chain of command) was force protection. Thus, some of the theater operations, such as those that supported a quick return to complete freedom of movement, were not exactly the type of PSYOP support these units desired.[143]

The emphasis placed on supporting the NGOs, IGOs, and PVOs naturally diluted the amount of time and energy that could have been devoted to direct support for the Task Force Eagle mission within IFOR. Theater-wide products for IFOR that supported similar long-term and countrywide programs also received the highest priority. Long-term campaigns (such as those programs targeting the teenagers in the former Yugoslavia) may have been of strategic and operational value, but certainly had much less value for the BDEs and BNs than would have tactical PSYOP support to deal with immediate and often localized problems. While the British division in MND(SW) had its own organic PSYOP support to produce regionally oriented products for operational and tactical support, the U.S. structure did not. Essentially, the Joint Psychological Operations Task Force that would normally have supported the highest level of unified command (in this case Task Force Eagle) had as its primary mission that of a Combined Joint PSYOP Task Force, or the CJIICTF. Without a CJIICTF LNO to MND(N) or an American LNO to the CJIICTF, there were no conduits for advocating the needs of MND(N) to theater campaign planners. Thus, the demands of a combined operation sometimes subordinated the need for tailored PSYOP support at the Task Force Eagle level.

U.S. joint PSYOP doctrine stresses that one of the major purposes of the PSYOP community is to ensure PSYOP support to U.S. conventional and Special Operations forces and specifically to "maintain the capability to accomplish U.S. only objectives when PSYOP forces and capabilities are provided to allied or coalition commands." Furthermore, in order for PSYOP to support maneuver units as envisioned in joint operations doctrine and enshrined in the notion of combined arms warfare, a PSYOP task force must be able to integrate and support maneuver divisions and subordinate units on the "battlefield" regardless of the operational environment. What is ironic is that unlike in the past, complications were not just the result of the inability of the supported units to understand the nature of the PSYOP weapons system. Rather the Task Force Eagle commanders were keenly aware of the psychological impact that military operations could have as well as the potential power of PSYOP campaigns to assist them in achieving their military objectives.

Because Task Force Eagle could not always obtain the type of PSYOP support it desired, COMEAGLE turned to other organizations to convey information to the local population, most notably the JIB and the MPADs.[144] This type of independent, U.S.-only information campaign did not sit well with some in the CJIICTF who were concerned about the consistency of the IFOR message. Indeed, some might argue that the CJIICTF correctly emphasized tight control over the development, approval, and dissemination of products because the mission itself was so political that any mistake at the tactical level would have enormous implications at the strategic level. Though this argument correctly explains the effect that some tactical mistakes can make, it may exaggerate the influence that *every* tactical action will have on the operational and strategic environment. Ironically, more so than with most weapons systems, PSYOP can both adjust fire and correct mistakes that have been made. Furthermore, the degree of coordination at Task Force Eagle between the various IO weapons systems, ensured that potentially damaging deviations from the overall Information Campaign guidelines did not take place. Indeed, the level of coordination at Task Force Eagle may have surpassed that in Sarajevo due to the complexity involved in running a multinational HQ such as that of the ARRC or HQ IFOR.

In order to synchronize the Task Force Eagle information campaign with that of the overall IFOR campaign, COMEAGLE put together the Commanders Information Coordination Group (CICG). The Joint Information Bureau (JIB) offered the idea of the CICG to MG Nash based on a formula that had worked for General Schwartzkopf during the Persian Gulf War and was working for the ARRC in Sarajevo. Each morning, COMEAGLE would meet with his principal IO personnel and operations staff, to include PSYOP, JIB, PAO, G-5, POLAD, JAG, G-3, and CoS. In addition, the LNOs from the two U.S. as well as the Russian, Turkish, and NORDPOL brigades were present at the meeting. During this meeting, discussion and coordination would take place on the types of information "floating around" in the AOR as well as ongoing campaigns directed from Sarajevo and local activities (such as JMCs, radio interviews, international media events) that were taking place under the auspices of MND(N). More importantly, through the advent of these meetings COMEAGLE check his information campaign strategy against the guidelines of the CJIICTF, and could have his staff deconflict against those directives from the CPIC in Sarajevo and U.S.-only sources of public information guidance.[145]

In order to wage an effective PSYOP campaign in a STABOPS environment, PSYOP commanders must understand that war, conflict, and peace may all exist at once in the theater. In addition, although we tend to envision these states as appearing in a continuum, it would be better to view them as a kaleidoscope. While it is an old PSYOP maxim that operations should be centrally controlled with decentralized execution, perhaps the operational kaleidoscope suggests that a more flexible concept of operations would be better set to cope with changes in the environment. In order to adequately support U.S. forces in such a conflict, perhaps a combined PSYOP campaign requires more than a tactical control element, such as a DPSE, at the highest level of unified command. This would translate, in combined operations, into the need for some sort of "mini" POTF, or Mission Information Support Team (MIST) with limited approval and production capability at Task Force Eagle level.[146]

Observations and Conclusions

An evaluation of tactical PSYOP support to Task Force Eagle does reveal some real strengths, correctable weaknesses, and important implications about psychological operations and information campaigns that the PSYOP community and their supported units need to consider as they prepare for future operations. To recap some of the observations of this study—

· U.S. PSYOP soldiers operated on a complex and potentially volatile battlefield and in a highly sophisticated media environment.

· Due to the proportion of PSYOP soldiers in the Reserves, there are certain difficulties involved in mobilizing these soldiers. Thus, modern communications systems must be available at the Reserve units in order to expedite the ability of these units to begin the handover process while still in CONUS.

· The current practice of putting together ad hoc PSYOP forces rather than entire companies (to include active Guard-Reserve personnel in key positions) should be re-evaluated. Although this may help with some personnel issues, the subsequent breakdown in unit integrity may be detrimental to the mission as a whole.

· A leader's reconnaissance for the tactical PSYOP elements would have alleviated many of the difficulties posed by the short time available to transition at the Task Force Eagle and BDE levels.

- Information regarding the nature of the PSYOP mission did not flow uninhibited from either the 2nd POG to the deploying units or from the incoming CJIICTF to the troops once they were deployed. This was due to physical and interpersonal communications problems at all levels of the PSYOP task force.

- The nature of *Operation Joint Endeavor* meant that tactical elements had to perform operational as well as tactical PSYOP planning and dissemination. This forced the DPSE commander into a position where he had to support theater and MND operations that were often in conflict with one another.

- PSYOP was a valuable HUMINT source to the supported unit commanders. Coordination of PSYOP-relevant intelligence collection matrices with those of other collection sources will have a synergistic effect on the ability of commanders to acquire information about the AOR.

- The stove-piping of information detracted from the value that raw data from PSYOP had for the intelligence production cycle.

- The production of area assessments for the supported unit needs to be a coordinated venture between PSYOP, CA, HUMINT, and other intelligence collection assets. Additionally, a strong relationship between HUMINT/CI personnel and PSYOP personnel helps to better assess the effect of the information campaigns on the attitudes and beliefs of the target audiences.

- PSYOP-related intelligence products must be made readily available to PSYOP elements at the lowest levels during STABOPS.

- A tedious product approval process presented a great challenge to the ability of PSYOP to support operations. The lack of digital data transfer capability, the multitude of staff agencies in the approval process, and the difficulty with disseminating completed products meant that by the time they arrived at the TPTs, some products had lost their ability to make an impact on the target audience.

- The four-vehicle convoy rule presented a great challenge to mission accomplishment, particularly when combined with other factors such as personnel shortages and vehicle maintenance problems.

- Individual force protection remains a contentious issue. Because these decisions are often driven by political decisions by the NCA, PSYOP may have to learn to work within these mission parameters. Though the community must be cognizant of the message a warfighting posture can send to target audiences, there is a strong argument to be made that these measures did not detract from the ability to accomplish the PSYOP mission.

- The lack of intersquad communications posed a serious force-protection threat to the tactical PSYOP teams.

- Face-to-face communication proved one of the most effective platforms for PSYOP in MND(N). The importance of the supported unit commander to the successful conduct of a face-to-face PSYOP campaign should not be understated.

- Because IFOR troops in MND(N) provided the local population with the basic security needs they craved, the U.S. troops in particular became key communicators. The ability of the soldiers in the supported units to establish a rapport with the local population helped to establish the credibility of IFOR. Additionally, the use of line troops as adjunct disseminators of PSYOP products allowed them not only to "break the ice" with locals but to add to the overall dissemination capability of the CJIICTF.

- The sophisticated media environments of the Information Age demand an increased use of the "our message, their medium" approach to PSYOP, particularly in STABOPS.

- Communications difficulties exacerbated real and perceived problems between the various PSYOP elements and constrained mission capability and performance. PSYOP units must have state-of-the-art communication for voice and data transmission to include satellite communications, LAN, and telephone connections.

- A CJIICTF LNO, such as that provided by a TPSE or an American PSYOP LNO in Sarajevo, could have helped to better balance and coordinate the needs of MND(N) for PSYOP support with the demands of a theater PSYOP campaign.

- The command climate is one of the intangibles that can determine whether or not a mission will succeed. Thus, leaders must make timely decisions and take deliberate action in support of the information campaign. Commanders must avoid the tendency to stay "in the office" and must get out into the field.

- The supported units in MND(N) truly understood PSYOP and the role it could play in Task Force Eagle operations. PSYOP was without a doubt one of the key Battlefield Operating Systems for COMEAGLE.

- CICG provides an excellent model for coordination between various IO weapons systems, to include PSYOP and Public Affairs.

- The major complaint of the supported units revolved around their frustration with the responsiveness of the CJIICTF to the needs of the MND.

In the end the few successes within MND(N) may have been overshadowed by the supported unit's perception that the PSYOP campaign waged out of the CJIICTF was disorganized and detrimental to the Task Force Eagle Mission. Whether or not this criticism is completely accurate, it correctly reflects the *belief* of the supported unit commanders. Thus, the PSYOP community may need to adjust the way it responds to the U.S. customer in a multinational operation. At the same time, the supported unit commanders and the other IO entities must avoid the temptation of bypassing the PSYOP approval process. Even though coordinating bodies such as the CICG and LIWA may offer possible solutions to coordinating information campaigns, there is indeed a great danger in running several separate IO campaigns at once.

In an age where the various information technologies outpace the doctrine that guides their employment, the PSYOP community must remind itself that doctrine must remain adaptable to a variety of situations.[147] The PSYOP task forces must provide consistent, timely, relevant, and effective support to the commander because psychological operations do not win wars on their own. As a prerequisite, the PSYOP community must understand maneuver and operations doctrine well enough to rapidly integrate into the battle staff, assimilate to changing tactical and operational conditions, and provide PSYOP courses of action to support the commander's intent. In short, until conventional force commanders themselves believe that PSYOP units are indispensable to their own combat power, PSYOP will never be fully integrated into the military's operational capability.[148]

IX. Counterintelligence and HUMINT
David D. Perkins

In the past 48 months, DoD Counterintelligence (CI) personnel working with national and DoD Human Intelligence (HUMINT) personnel from strategic, operational, and tactical organizations have provided critical support to numerous contingency operations and overseas training exercises. Beyond the traditional missions of CI and HUMINT, ground force commanders have identified CI and HUMINT support as essential to accomplishing the force protection mission in operations from *Provide Hope* to *Joint Endeavor* and in locations as diverse as Somalia, Panama, Haiti, Macedonia, Rwanda, and Turkey. (See figure 9-1.)

The CI and HUMINT elements recently deployed in Bosnia were the largest such deployment since *Desert Shield/Desert Storm*. They experienced success and the full endorsement of their supported commanders. This was a result of the integration into current operational procedures of lessons learned from past operations and, most significantly, the ingenuity, tenacity, and adaptability of the soldiers and civilians sent to Bosnia to execute the CI and HUMINT mission. These soldiers and civilians used innovative tactics, techniques, and procedures to provide the necessary intelligence to conduct successful operations in the complex, unpredictable environment of Bosnia. The primary goal of CI and HUMINT activities in Bosnia, and during other recent deployments, has been

226 *Lessons from Bosnia*

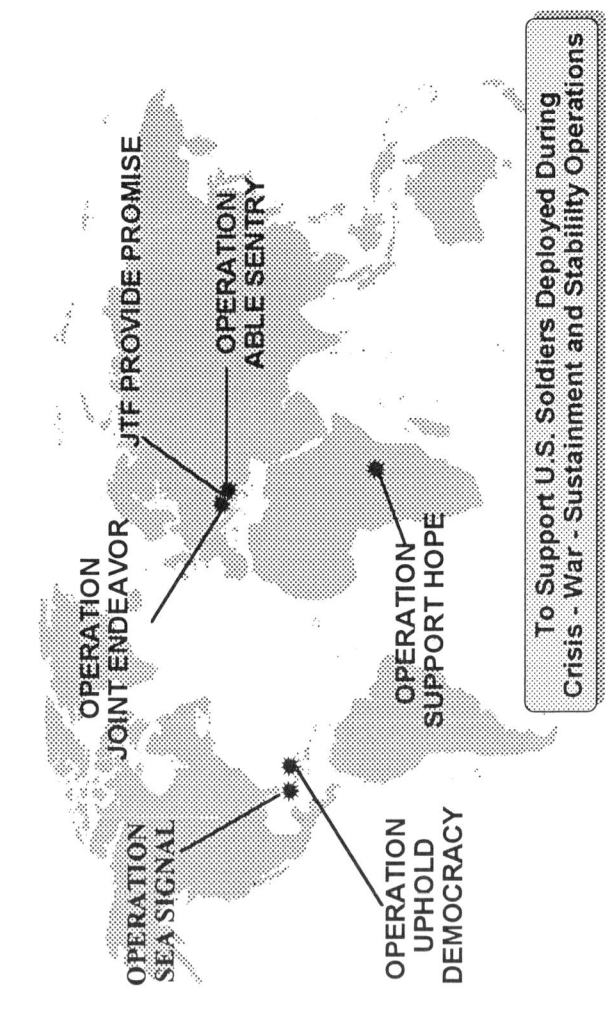

Figure 9-1. CI/HUMINT Support to Contingency Operations

to reduce risk to the force by providing the information and intelligence that the commander needed to effectively manage or avoid risk and still accomplish the mission. (See figure 9-2.)

This chapter provides an in-depth discussion of CI and HUMINT activities conducted in support of the U.S.-led ground Task Force Eagle or MND(N). The perspective will be that of the CI and HUMINT mission manager (G2X)—that element of the Task Force intelligence staff (G2) responsible for coordinating, deconflicting, and synchronizing all CI and HUMINT activities in the sector of operations of this multinational task force. CI and HUMINT worked together in support of Task Force operations and therefore cannot be addressed independently. Likewise, the multinational or combined aspects of CI and HUMINT operations will also be addressed.

Figure 9-2. The Force Protection Challenge

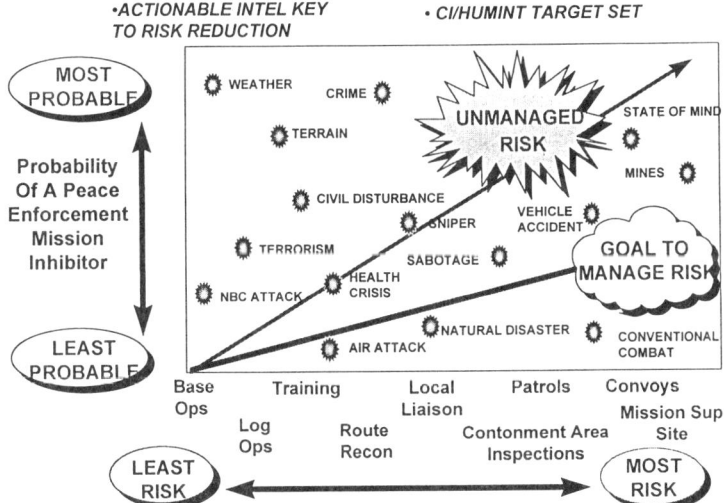

To appreciate the foundation upon which these activities were based, past operations and training must be briefly examined. The basic tactics, techniques, and procedures that worked in Bosnia were drawn from the past; developed, identified, or refined in other contingency operations; addressed in joint doctrine; practiced in local unit, non-doctrinal training courses; or developed, tested, and instituted on-the-fly by deployed personnel. Solutions came from many sources, but usually from the young soldier who understood both the requirement and the customer, the ground commander. The experienced soldier or civilian and the parts of the bureaucracy that would bypass red tape and provide the necessary equipment and expertise also proved to be essential to mission accomplishment.

This chapter will focus on the positive, constructive results of approximately 200 operators and a few leader-managers who, working as a team, accomplished an important mission.

Past Operations

Veterans of the U.S. Army Counterintelligence Corps (CIC) and the Office of Strategic Services (OSS) deployed throughout Europe during WWII and the aftermath, along with CI and HUMINT veterans of the Vietnam conflict, could provide a convincing argument that the tactics, techniques, and procedures used today, although somewhat refined with some information technology-based tools, are very similar or identical to those used in their previous operations. Sometime in the development of CI and HUMINT disciplines the focus on supporting warfighters was lost or allowed to go dormant. As the DoD prepared for the Cold War to go hot, CI and HUMINT took a backseat, while the other intelligence disciplines, which relied on systems built with high technology and could provide almost instant results, came to the forefront. Recent contingency operations such as Operations Other Than War (OOTW) (now referred to as Stability and Sustainment Operations (SSO)), have brought CI and HUMINT to the table with other intelligence disciplines.

Operation Restore Hope in Somalia set the stage for the importance of CI and HUMINT in future operations. The lessons learned there were significant and set the course for CI and HUMINT in supporting the warfighter. The requirement for joint doctrine and a computer-based information system with connectivity to the overall intelligence communication architecture had been identified as a result of *Desert Shield/Desert Storm*. Then, Somalia set in motion the first application of the draft joint doctrine. During this time frame, USAREUR began experimenting with the first version of the TRRIP. (See figure 9-3.)

The TRRIP was a prototype, notebook computer-based data acquisition, management, and communication system designed to CI requirements. The prototype TRRIP was deployed on an exercise called *Dragon Hammer 92* and then in support of the U.S. Army Hospital that deployed to Zagreb, Croatia, in December 1992. (See figure 9-4.) By deploying the TRRIP in support of the hospital, USAREUR began to develop the communications architecture that would be required to support a TRRIP deployed with the tactical forces. United States European Command (USEUCOM) also understood the utility of such a capability and stated the requirement for such a system on the theater commander's (CINC's) Intelligence Priority List (IPL).

In July of 1993, the requirement to send a battalion combat team to Macedonia was identified. The mission was, and still is, to monitor the border between Serbia and Macedonia. *Operation Able Sentry* was underway and CI and tactical HUMINT assets were deployed early to support the mission. (See figure 9-5.) Based on this deployment, USAREUR, in conjunction with the U.S. Army Intelligence and Security Command (INSCOM), developed the CI and Tactical HUMINT Contingency Operations Course. This course taught soldiers the tactics, techniques, and procedures necessary to conduct operations in the former Republic of Yugoslavia as well as in other OOTW operations.

The U.S. Army Intelligence Center at Fort Huachuca developed the CI Force Protection Source Operations Course to meet these evolving requirements. The Air Force and the Navy also be-

230 *Lessons from Bosnia*

Figure 9-3. CI/HUMINT Automation Toolset(CHATS)

Capabilities

Data entry (Robust Office Software Package)
Embedded Training
Excellent User Interface
Austere DataBase
Scanner
CD-ROM
Color Capable Printer
Digital Camera
Secure Fax
E-Mail Capable
Flexible Communications Interface
- International Maritime Satellite Terminal (IMARSAT)
- Mobile Subscriber Equipment (MSE)
- Defense Switched Network (DSN)
- Single Channel Ground and Airborne Radio System (SINCGARS)
- TROJAN Special Purpose Integrated Remote Intelligence Terminal (SPIRIT)
- Land Satellite Terminal 5-C/E

Formerly referred to as Theater Rapid Response Intelligence Package (TRRIP)

Figure 9-4. U.S. Army Hospital Deploys to Zagreb, Croatia

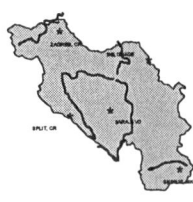
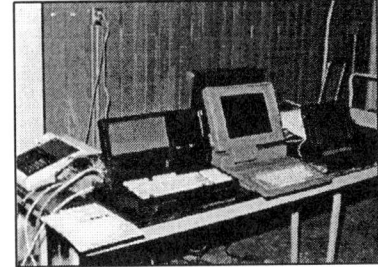

- Two Soldier CI Team Deploys Dec 92
- INMARSAT Communications
- Prototype TRRIP Deploys

Prototype Theater Rapid Response Intelligence Package (TRRIP) Deployed - Zagreb, Also Deployed During Dragon Hammer 92

Figure 9-5. Operation Able Sentry

- Support to Force Protection Mission CI/Tac HUMINT Team Deploys Jul 93
- Extensive Liaison
- Specialized Train-up of 5 Team Members Prior to Deployment

U.S. Contingent Base Camp   Zenith 286 Laptop

gan to develop courses to train their personnel in these specific skills. Although the Marine Corps already had trained their personnel in many of these skills, they developed tactics, techniques, and procedures to incorporate the use of a system like the TRRIP. Unfortunately, the number of soldiers who had received this specialized training was minimal.

Deployment of a Task Force CI Coordinating Authority (TFCICA) and support staff to Naples, Italy, to augment the joint intelligence staff (J2) of JTF *Provide Promise* was another event from which commanders and the intelligence community could learn how to employ these assets. This led to the deployment of a six person, joint CI team referred to as the Force Protection Branch to Zagreb, Croatia, to support JTF *Provide Promise* (Forward). Commander, JTF *Provide Promise* (FWD), Col. Quist, U.S. Marine Corps, stated in a letter to the USEUCOM Chief of Staff:

> The capability of the Force Protection Branch (FPB) is an essential part of the battlefield operating system on which I rely. In Operations Other Than War, the skills and method of operation used by the FPB are essential for successful, acceptable-risk operations. Without the services of the FPB I would lose a valuable asset which allows me to determine risk to our operations.

The second generation prototype TRRIP was then deployed. (See figure 9-6). This gave the Joint CI Team a significant capability. This deployment also provided USAREUR and INSCOM TRRIP developers critical input to the system itself and to the communications architecture necessary to support multiple systems in different geographical locations. Specialized software, a digital camera, and a scanner had been added. CI and HUMINT discovered that information was being delivered to analysts and to the decision makers faster and more accurately than had ever been experienced. TRRIPs were deployed in Naples, Italy; Skopje, Macedonia; and Zagreb Croatia. CI- and HUMINT-trained soldiers were on the ground and answering the commander's questions. Teams are still deployed in Macedonia and Croatia.

Figure 9-6. JTF Provide Promise (FWD)

- Joint CI Team Deploys April 94
- Support to Force Protection Mission
- Responsive CI Communications

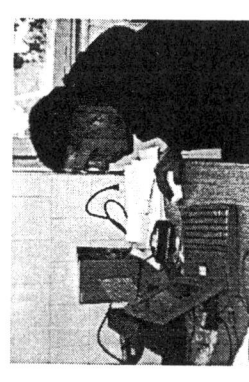

Theater Rapid Response Intelligence Package (TRRIP) Lite, Deployed - Zagreb

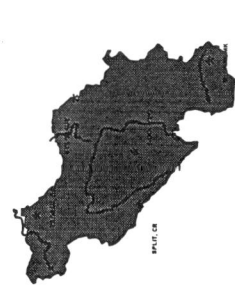

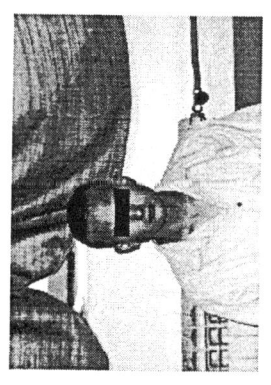

U.S. Army Deserter - Debriefed and Evacuated to the Theater Rear by JTF

Operation Support Hope (see figure 9-7) in Rwanda was flawlessly executed by the supporting CI and HUMINT soldiers. This short-fused operation required 36 operators with 6 TRRIPs to deploy rapidly to various locations in Africa to support the operation. The results were stunning, and the concept of using CI and HUMINT assets in OOTWs was cemented in USEUCOM. The investment in the capability continued and would pay off with the deployment to Bosnia.

CI and HUMINT operators provided critical intelligence during *Operation Uphold Democracy* in Haiti. (See figure 9-8.) The communications architecture was not stressed; however, input for the development of the TRRIP was obtained from the operators. Further definition and refinement of user requirements was taking place. CI and HUMINT were using real-world deployments as their Advanced Warfighting Experiments (AWE).

The Hard Road to Success in Bosnia

The Environment in Bosnia

The CI and HUMINT operators deployed to Bosnia faced some difficult challenges and very real threats. Three former warring factions, with significant combat power and robust intelligence collection capabilities, were waiting for the arrival of NATO forces. Local civilians hired as linguists, cooks, maids, handymen, electricians, and carpenters became an everyday concern of the CI and HUMINT operators. Terrorists, organized crime, and petty criminals were also part of the threat. Some of the toughest terrain in the world and formidable winter weather also posed significant challenges to everyday survival. Based on previous peace operation deployments, CI and HUMINT became the intelligence disciplines of choice for Bosnia, and for that reason CI and tactical HUMINT soldiers were deployed early with the advance elements of the Task Force.

Figure 9-7. Operation Support Hope

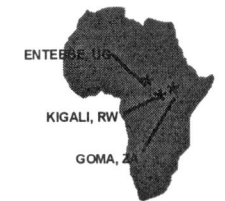

- Excellent CI Planning and Mission Execution
- Rapid Deployment - First in, CI/Tac HUMINT Teams Deploy JUL 94
- Extensive Liaison

BG Nix Signing Over U.S. Equipment to the UN High Commission on Refugees Representative

Entebbe Airport

Figure 9-8. Operation Uphold Democracy

- CI/Human Intelligence (HUMINT) was key to Success in OCT 94
- Extensive Collection and Reporting
- CI Force Protection Source Operations
- CI and HUMINT Successful Coordination

Haitian Detainee Screened by CI

CI/TAC HUMINT Area Recon

The Plan

The success of any operation depends on the plan. Operators are fast to explain that the plan is just that, a plan. In the execution phase any plan begins to lose coherence as branches to planned courses of action must be taken and sequels to operations must be conducted. Nevertheless, the existence of a plan ensures that everyone understands the objective and has a clear vision of the commander's intent. CI and HUMINT operations are no different. They require a detailed, flexible plan that would be understood at every echelon, especially the lowest echelon where it is said that "the rubber meets the road."

After arriving at Task Force Eagle headquarters in Tuzla, the operators were able to assess the situation and define in greater detail the CI and HUMINT mission. A detailed, all inclusive plan was written, including communication, report formats, annotation procedures, information flow, logistics, and command and control. This plan was to be the foundation of CI and HUMINT operations within the Task Force Eagle sector. Based on the corporate knowledge acquired from previous operations, joint doctrine, service doctrine, and capabilities, the plan for CI and HUMINT operations in Task Force Eagle sector was quickly approved and signed. The CI and HUMINT annex to the operations order (OPORD) was distributed to every battalion within the Task Force.

Having developed the plan as the foundation, there was more to come. The communications portion of the plan, which depicted the architecture used, took 3 months to build. (See figure 9-9.) The heroics of young soldiers, older warrant officers wanting to learn, and contractors working and teaching made this architecture come to life. The plan was working. A method for processing hand held digital imagery was developed. A Counterespionage Standard Operating Procedure was also written specifically for this operation. Requirements management, report numbering, quality control, database, and source management systems were just a few of the topics that had to be addressed. A method was established for tracking the operational readiness of the commercial-off-the-shelf (COTS)

Counterintelligence and HUMINT 237

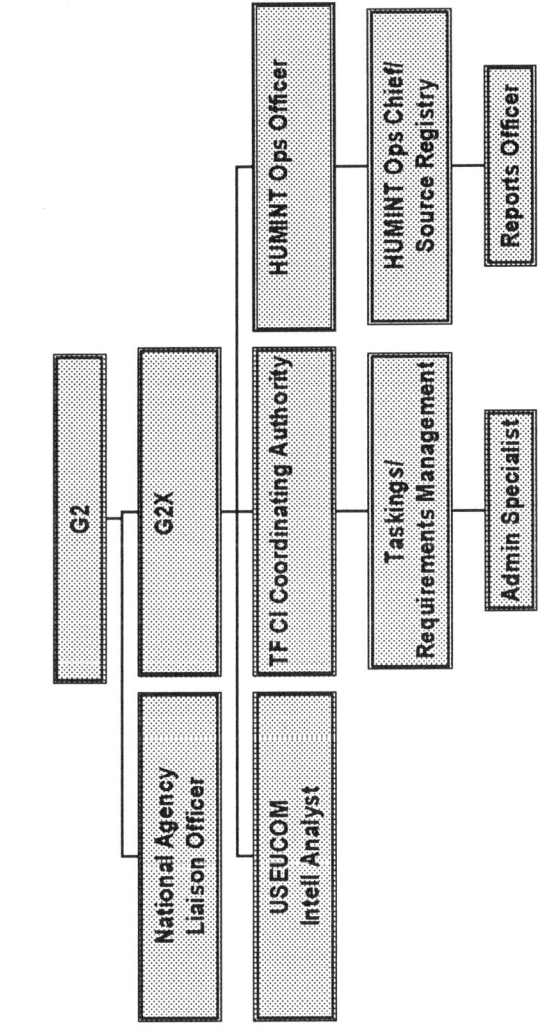

Figure 9-9. Counterintelligence Human Intelligence

hardware and software upon which the TRRIP was based. The plan was an 80-percent solution, which in a tactical operation will usually win.

The CI and HUMINT Force Package

At the height of IFOR operations, approximately 110 U.S. Army CI and tactical HUMINT soldiers were deployed in support of Task Force Eagle. Four-person teams, tactically tailored for a variety of missions, were deployed in direct support of battalions and in general support of the Task Force. Their ability to support force protection intelligence requirements effectively prompted the Task Force commander to request additional teams during the potentially disruptive elections in September 1996. Additionally, allied forces within Task Force Eagle quickly discovered the importance of the CI and tactical HUMINT capability and requested U.S. Army CI and tactical HUMINT support. As a result, teams were dedicated to support the Nordic brigade, the Polish battalion, and the Swedish battalion. This ensured timely exchange of force protection information throughout the Task Force Eagle sector. CI and HUMINT personnel provided the local commanders with information on threats to their units as well as their units' vulnerability to foreign intelligence collection and/or terrorist operations.

The G2X was critical to the success of CI and HUMINT operations. The requirement for such an element was derived from joint doctrine, which called for it to be located at the level of the JTF intelligence staff (J2). Thus, initially the G2X was considered the J2X. There was no JTF or J2 to augment, so the original concept underwent a significant metamorphosis. The end result was a small J2X element at the U.S. National Intelligence Center which augmented the ARRC in Sarajevo and a rather robust G2X in support of Task Force Eagle.

The G2X consisted of a Defense HUMINT Service (DHS) cell, a national agency liaison officer, an Army G2X, and an Army Task Force Counterintelligence Coordinating Authority, as well as Air Force, Navy, and Marine Corps personnel. (See figure 9-10).

Counterintelligence and HUMINT 239

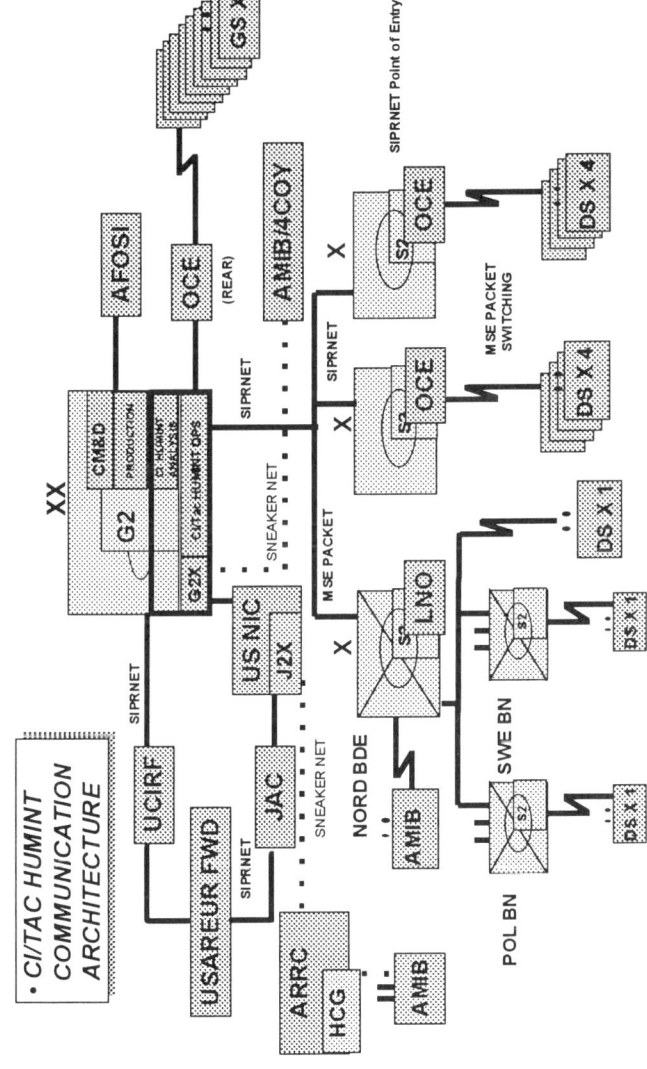

Figure 9-10. Counterintelligence Human Intelligence

An essential change to the original plan was that the G2X had no operational elements assigned. The G2X was strictly a staff element responsible for coordinating, deconflicting, and synchronizing the activities of multinational CI and HUMINT assets, U.S. national-level HUMINT assets, and DoD strategic HUMINT assets in the Task Force Eagle Sector. The G2X would also be responsible for coordinating with the ARRC HUMINT Coordination Group (HCG), now called CJ2X.

The G2X also evolved into the G2's quasi-collection managers for CI and HUMINT. This was more of an enabling function for the overall collection manager. It was a critical step to ensure CI and HUMINT were working in concert with other intelligence disciplines. The G2 saw CI and HUMINT just as any other collection discipline—an asset to be managed, synchronized, used to tip other collection means, and used to verify information collected via other intelligence collection disciplines.

The DHS cell within the G2X provided a critical function in refining the commander's PIRs into requirements against which DHS assets could collect. This cell also played an essential role in ensuring time-sensitive HUMINT was quickly processed, edited, and disseminated—first to the commander, second to the theater consumers, and finally to the national intelligence community. This usually was accomplished simultaneously.

DHS also provided significant support to the operations. Working closely with the allies, with the tactical elements, and independently, DHS provided a critical collection capability to the Task Force G2 as well as the theater- and national-level consumers. DHS flexibility, responsiveness, and focus on the ground commander's requirements made them an instant success. Other national-level agencies also provided essential support, giving Task Force Eagle an unprecedented, multiechelon, dedicated, responsive CI and HUMINT capability. Task Force Eagle would need it!

CI and HUMINT Operations

In an effort to counter the non-traditional threats confronted in this multinational peacekeeping operation, CI and HUMINT elements were called upon to provide, coordinate, deconflict, synchronize, and integrate an unusually wide variety of intelligence support. That support included counterintelligence collection, threat and vulnerability assessments, liaison with local law enforcement and foreign military security and intelligence services, CI Force Protection Source Operations, Technical Surveillance Countermeasures (TSCM), debriefing of U.S. and allied soldiers, debriefing and screening of displaced persons or refugees and detainees, investigations and analysis, exploitation of foreign documents and equipment, and timely dissemination of hand-held digital imagery. Accomplishing all of these efforts was a critical requirement with enormous ramifications, not only for the mission of enforcing the Dayton Accords but for protecting the soldiers assigned to the MNDs.

The operational tempo for the CI and HUMINT operators, both forward-deployed and in support, was extremely high. Initially, tactical teams were restricted in movement due to force protection concerns. Eventually the Task Force commander, understanding the importance of the CI and HUMINT team mission, authorized an exception to policy for CI and HUMINT Teams. He allowed them to travel in two-vehicle convoys, as opposed to the standard four-vehicle convoys, during daylight hours. Travel required a brigade or battalion commander's approval. Travel at night required general officer approval and four vehicles. This made liaison dinners a challenge, but they did get approved. CI and HUMINT operators at the division level and those teams assigned to the Nordic brigade were able to use this important exception to policy. U.S. brigade commanders, however, were not required to implement this policy and therefore continued to require their teams to travel in four-vehicle convoys. This did not deter the teams. They became experts at organizing a four-vehicle convoy of military police, civil affairs, or whatever kind of personnel they could find heading out of the base camp. This process might take 2 to 4 hours during the evening to organize for the next day.

Bosnia was, and still is, an environment where CI and HUMINT operators could show their value added. The threats were real and the PIRs were critical to the commander. This was not a so-called "sensor-to-shooter" environment. It was an environment of terrorists, criminals, and elements of the three FWFs, all of whom were hard to identify but were well-armed and had significant intelligence collection capabilities including HUMINT. To describe this as a complex and challenging environment is an understatement.

After the first 3 months of 18- to 20-hour workdays 7 days a week, the success stories began to be daily events. The quality of reporting significantly improved, the hand held digital imagery was superb—and the commander expected it. The analysts began to produce superior products, mostly based on CI and HUMINT reporting from the field. The responsiveness of the CI and HUMINT assets improved as the communications routing was used so much that it was considered "burned in" and soldiers became more familiar with the TRRIP. The CI and HUMINT community had reached a solid 80 percent solution.

The Usora bridge incident in early August 1996 is an example of timely, accurate, and high-quality reporting that was collected and processed faster by CI and HUMINT teams than the CNN. A smaller bridge built by the United Nations near the Usora bridge was badly damaged after a charge had been thrown from a moving vehicle onto it. A tactical CI and HUMINT team immediately responded to the incident and arrived at the scene, interviewed witnesses, took digital photographs of the damage and, within one hour, passed the brigade and the TF commander accurate information. The national intelligence community had the final Intelligence Information Report (IIR) with digital photographs within 4 hours, with most of that time having been taken for imagery annotation. Hence, the standard for CI and HUMINT teams was to beat CNN and tell the real story. (See figure 9-11). Source operations, coun-

Counterintelligence and HUMINT 243

Figure 9-11. Incident Vicinity of Usora Bridge

- *Four hours from time of incident to National Dissemination*
- CI/Tac HUMINT Reporting
- Small explosive charge placed on bridge

terespionage investigations, local hire screenings, vulnerability assessments, and TSCM services were activities the commanders understood and demanded.

CI and HUMINT Collection Management and Single-Source Analysis

Another element of the plan that would ensure that the best asset or combination of assets was used to answer the requirement was the collection management portion. The collection management process for CI and HUMINT assets became more refined as the analyst-to-collector dialogue was established. A tactical evaluation system was developed. Task Force Eagle analysts were taught how to write evaluations and how to integrate CI- and HUMINT-derived information into the common picture of the battlefield. Timely feedback to the collector provided instant results. After 6 months, the analysts understood the capabilities and limitations of CI and HUMINT assets. The CI and HUMINT operators understood what the analysts needed. This was not accomplished without some frustration on the part of operators and analysts. Collection management had also been formalized and refined with collection requirements linked directly to the commander's PIR. Reporting would indicate which PIR the collected information addressed.

Early in the deployment, both CI and HUMINT single-source analysis and reporting, as well as the incorporation of CI- and HUMINT-collected information or analysis products into the all-source analysis product, was happening by chance rather than by design. This occasional dual-reporting carried the potential for confusion and misinformation. The element responsible for this analysis and reporting function in a Division Analysis and Control Element (ACE) is normally four soldiers. With 24-hour operations, it was obvious that augmentation would be required. The amount of reporting quickly overwhelmed the analytical capability and this continued to be a challenge until the fifth month of the deployment. The soldiers selected to augment the CI/HUMINT analysis in the

ACE were usually personnel coming into theater on temporary change of station (TCS) orders and may or may not have had analytical experience. A senior analyst from USEUCOM trained other analysts on how to analyze CI and HUMINT information. Some soldiers quickly understood the requirement or had previous experience; however, this was the exception.

Unfortunately, due mainly to physical space limitation at Tuzla, the analytical effort was fragmented between the Division Main in Tuzla and the Division Rear in Lukavac. The Division Rear did not have workstations connected to the sensitive compartmented information (SCI) circuit referred to as DSNET 3. This severely limited their capability. They eventually did establish connectivity to the SIPRNET. This helped the situation. However, the analytical world for CI and HUMINT significantly changed in May. This was because the Division Rear CI and HUMINT analytical element, called the HUMINT Analysis Cell (HAC), moved to the Division Main. They were given SCI connectivity with the Joint Deployable Intelligence Support System (JDISS) as well as the U.S. Army WARLORD system. Also, in August the DIA, Defense Intelligence Threat Data Base System (DITDS) Program Manager, working with USAREUR and INSCOM, deployed a computer network server forward, providing for the first time automated link analysis capability, local storage for digital photographs, and another workstation which was needed for the CI and HUMINT analysts, sometimes called Multi-Discipline Counterintelligence (MDCI) analysts.

When the HAC, which had been constituted primarily from 165th Military Intelligence (MI) battalion personnel and TCSers, moved to Tuzla, it gave the Division ACE the extra capability that would prove critical in preparing for the September elections in Bosnia. They also provided other mid- and long-term analytical products for the commander. These products were impressive and could match the quality of any national- or theater-level product. Another important product read by the Task Force commander everyday was the "Night Owl." This was an open-source product, based on the translation of daily newspapers, television, and radio broadcasts throughout Bosnia. It selected articles or broadcasts which would be of interest to the tactical decision makers. Dissemination was made via the Non-classified Internet Protocol Router Network (NIPRNET).

The most challenging aspect of the total analytical effort was orchestrating who would produce what product and for whom. An all-encompassing distributive analysis plan was never written or executed. Some national analysts complained that the Task Force was not reporting all the information received from the field. They were correct. There was too much information and not enough time. Reporting from the field was sent up the chain and laterally to all echelons, faster and in greater quantity in the U.S. sector than during any other military operation in history. This included text reports, hand held digital imagery and frames from handheld video. Analysts deployed with Task Force Eagle were able to develop an understanding of the real situation in the field which could not be transformed into a text message or relayed via video teleconferencing or a digital photograph. This came from interacting with the CI and HUMINT operators, making visits to various locations throughout the area of operation, and being involved in numerous operational briefings.

Automation and Communications

The use of low-cost, COTS information technologies proved to be a critical tool for the CI and HUMINT operator. Technology had never been used on this scale to support CI and HUMINT activities. One of the most significant CI and tactical HUMINT innovations was the TRRIP, which has paid great dividends in Bosnia. The TRRIP hardware and software suite provided a robust automated/data acquisition package that ensured timely reporting and product dissemination to commanders at the battalion, brigade, and task force level, as well as to national and theater consumers. This prototype system consists of COTS software and hardware connected to mobile subscriber equipment (MSE). The TROJAN Special Purpose Integrated Remote Intelligence Terminal (SPIRIT), commercial telephone, or International Maritime Satellite (IMARSAT) provided extensive connectivity, greatly increasing the relevancy of the reporting to the warfighter and leveraging national and theater analytic assets to deliver unprecedented support.

The Army, Air Force, and Navy deployed with TRRIP-like systems. The connectivity provided by the Augsburg Hub, or server, was the critical link that enabled the CI and tactical HUMINT architecture to work throughout the theater. Access to the SIPRNET revolutionized the method by which CI and HUMINT information was processed and disseminated as well as how CI and HUMINT assets were managed. Linking the MSE network with the SIPRNET via the TROJAN SPIRIT was the critical step in ensuring connectivity to battalion level. TRRIP and SIPRNET have significantly changed the CI and HUMINT disciplines. These communities are just beginning to understand the full impact of these tools designed for the operator, not the analyst. The young CI and HUMINT soldiers in Bosnia have shown that they understand what these tools can and will do.

The database capability built by the DIA DITDS Program Office was known as the BLACKBIRD database. This was an operator's database used to file every spot report. In Task Force Eagle, these reports were called FPIRs and all were databased, no matter how insignificant. Allied reporting was also fed into BLACKBIRD. Information that normally would go into the battalion, brigade, or maybe the Task Force INTSUM would retain its individuality in the BLACKBIRD database, thus making the information much more powerful. This would prove critical in conducting link and pattern analysis or building association matrixes. This would also provide historical knowledge for the follow-on CI/HUMINT soldier.

Lessons Learned

The first lesson learned was that you will learn 100 things a day in the first 3 to 6 months of most contingency operations. The second lesson learned is that you must try to write down at least 1 of those 100 things you learned every day. The observers or the visiting professionals sent into the area for a short time to capture the lessons learned for you will not understand the essence of what you learned. You will be frustrated by reading their lengthy reports about what you did right, what you could have done better, and even how to fix it. They will not be accurate and it will irritate you because they have not recorded what you told them when you took the valuable time from your busy day to explain something to them. The bottom line is, if you are there from the beginning, living in miserable conditions, sleeping in your vehicle night after night, eating Meals Ready-to-Eat (MREs), filling sandbags, pulling guard duty, wondering when you might get a hot shower; **write down what you learned**. That is part of your job as a soldier. The CI and HUMINT soldiers, with their computers, were able to capture numerous lessons learned. The following are some of those lessons learned.

Detailed planning is necessary. During the planning phase, the leadership must bring in the experienced operators who have been on the ground and understand the task at hand. One seasoned veteran referred to this team as "the dirty thirty." The composition of this team must be carefully crafted to include the conceptual thinker, the pragmatist, the writer, the coordinator, the marketeer, the visionary, and the leader. They are all needed. One of the team must understand the Joint Operations, Planning and Execution System (JOPES). The others must understand the capabilities and limitations of the assets being considered to accomplish the mission. The plan must be straightforward and understood at the lowest echelon. Those at the lowest level must know that they can influence the plan with their input once they are in the execution phase. The success of executing the branches and sequels will depend upon this critical input.

Actionable intelligence must be provided. CI and HUMINT operators must understand that their information must be delivered to the customer immediately. In the Information Age the decision cycle becomes compressed; no longer can CI and HUMINT operators agonize over punctuation, format, and grammatical correctness. There should be limited locations in the architecture for quality control, preferably at the lowest level. Editing and vetting can be accomplished later, prior to the incorporation of the information into a national-level centralized database. The warfighter cannot wait for that. Speed and accuracy must prevail over form.

The demand for handheld imagery will increase. Handheld digital imagery, as well as handheld video, took on an importance that was predicted well before soldiers deployed to Bosnia. Unfortunately, database storage and retrieval of this information is still an unfullfillable requirement. Combat camera crews, the Task Force historian, soldiers manning critical checkpoints, and soldiers inspecting cantonment areas all had digital cameras along with every CI and HUMINT team. The product was demanded by the commanders. In SSOs the digital photo or video clip that is delivered quickly can have more impact than satellite or UAV imagery.

The J2X or G2X function is a must. This element is essential to all JTFs now and in the future, no matter what the mission. CI and HUMINT assets are essential to support the force protection mission. Joint doctrine must continue to be developed to further refine the integration of CI and HUMINT into joint and combined operations.

Modern information systems and communications are critical to the success of CI and HUMINT. CI and HUMINT had never before used computers and communications as a tool on the scale that they were used during *Operation Joint Endeavor*. Furthermore, it was accomplished without a dedicated, funded program. CI and HUMINT soldiers in Bosnia initially had 3-year-old systems because the USAREUR and subordinate operational commands had acquired funds, designed a system based on COTS, and fielded the capability they knew they needed. DoD and the services should ensure that the CI and HUMINT community can benefit from state-of-the-art technology. The need for a program office which responds to CI- and HUMINT-user defined requirements from the strategic to the tactical levels is evident.

CI and HUMINT single-source analysis is essential but difficult. Collecting information is easy compared to the task of telling the warfighter what it means and doing so in time for action to be taken. Reporting yesterday's news has limited utility. Predictive analysis is an art form. In the area of force protection, identifying periods of increased risk based on analyzed information may be the best the intelligence community can do. The Task Force commander will act when presented with a conclusion that indicates a greater threat at a certain time and place. These must, however, not be whims but well thought out analytical conclusions. CI and HUMINT require knowledgeable analysts who understand the collector.

Analysis maximizes the use of collection resources. The more analysts-to-collector interface, the better the collection effort. Analyst and collector dialogue, either electronically or face-to-face, paid dividends. The collectors understood that someone was actually interested in what they were collecting and they soon developed a keen sense of the type of information that the analyst was actually looking for. The collection manager's job became easier. The main task was ensuring that the best assets were going against the right requirement at the right time, a synchronization effort that included both CI and HUMINT collection assets. This is often given lip service in the overall collection planning cycle.

Assets must be focused and responsive. This is difficult with as many as 200 individual professional, collection personnel on the ground and approximately 20,000 more soldiers with eyes and ears interacting with the population. UAV's, satellites, and other technical collection systems are much easier to control and synchronize. Keeping the 200 professional CI and HUMINT collectors focused and responsive was a learning process, but eventually met with success. They all eventually responded to the Task Force commander's requirements first.

Investment in the training base is needed. Soldiers were deployed who were not trained with the skills that would be necessary to operate in this complex environment. CI and tactical HUMINT soldiers were trained in basic soldier skills. However, the bread and butter skills of a CI or HUMINT collector on the ground had been neglected. This was no surprise. The Army trains for the scenario with the most risk, the high-intensity battle. If mistakes are made on the battlefield, more firepower with creative and decisive maneuver can turn the battle. However, in a Bosnia-like situation, more firepower will not always work. Skills, including use of technology, must be taught before deployment. Skills such as how to anticipate requirements or how to think and undertake creative problem solving are important. The answer to the challenge is not usually in the manual.

Investment in training warfigthers must become a top priority. Giving the Task Force commander and his G2 25 CI and tactical HUMINT teams, assets from the DHS, multinational CI and HUMINT soldiers, and national agency assets was like giving a mechanic a new tool for working on a car and saying, this is a great tool and will make the car run better, but we are not going to teach you how to use it. Training the warfighter in Bosnia on how to use the CI and HUMINT assets available was at times a challenge. The Task Force commander quickly understood the capability and began to set high expectations. He had never had these assets available during any training exercise. Luckily, that did not seem to make a difference. Commanders at lower echelons reacted differently to using CI and HUMINT assets. The intelligence community must not forget to teach the warfighter about CI and HUMINT.

A solid, realistic plan with built-in flexibility is the key to success. The CI and HUMINT annex to the OPORD must be completed during the planning cycle, not after the operation has begun. CI and HUMINT must ensure that they are closely involved in the planning cycle and not on the outside looking in.

Know your players. Leading and managing a pick-up team is a difficult proposition. You must learn your players' capabilities as quickly as possible. Hopefully, you will be sent some known quantities who will make life a little easier. Set soldiers up for success as often as possible.

Good support is critical. The backend support is as critical as what is happening in the sector. Soldiers who are forward-deployed will always need something from the rear—get it to them.

Know your equipment. Check it, check it again, and if time allows check it again. This seems simple, but with new technology or inserted technology, this is a must. Leaders must ensure that there is time to conduct the appropriate checks, and then ensure the checks are done.

Common sense lessons learned are sometimes forgotten.

- Know and anticipate your customers requirements.
- Invest resources in high payoff activities.
- Always be considered a part of the team.
- Send the appropriate rank.
- Listen to the service experts, and seek more than one opinion.
- You will go with what you've got.
- Innovate—do not be concerned when given broad, non-specific mission guidance. Use the tools that you have and think.
- Comms, Comms, Comms, Comms.
- Treat your equipment with respect; the information you collect and send may save your life or another soldier's.
- Tailor your product to your commander.

The mission in Bosnia continues. The lessons learned continue. We cannot afford to make the same mistake twice in a highly volatile environment such as exists in Bosnia or in the next Bosnia. The CI and HUMINT soldiers deploying in as follow-on forces have benefited from the knowledge of those who have gone before.

As the DoD continues to do more with less in non-traditional, non-linear operational environments, the capability provided by CI and HUMINT soldiers must not be overlooked. Commanders at all levels will continue to call upon those resources to assist in developing the situational awareness necessary to ensure that U.S. soldiers embark upon operations with an acceptable level of risk. In Bosnia, the CI and tactical HUMINT soldiers adapted quickly to an unfamiliar operational environment not normally experienced at the National Training Center or during any other armored division training event. They proved their worth as they developed innovative and effective tactics, techniques, and procedures to meet the demands they faced. As a proven commodity, CI and HUMINT soldiers, as well as those responsible for managing both the CI and HUMINT programs, must be given the latitude to continue developing new doctrine, leveraging new technology, and refining current methods and procedures. They are a critical asset who must be protected and supported as they pursue positive change to meet the challenges of today, tomorrow, and into the 21st century.

X. Information Operations in Bosnia: A Soldier's Perspective
Kenneth Allard

My arrival at the headquarters of the US 1st Armored Division in Tuzla, Bosnia, in May 1996 came some 5 months following its deployment as the principal U.S. peacekeeping force committed to *Operation Joint Endeavor*. As the senior NATO observer for that sector, I participated in field and aviation operations in four of the five maneuver brigade areas, observing U.S. and allied contingents comprising MND(N) of the IFOR and paying particular attention to command and control issues. While no outside observer could acquire the in-depth knowledge possessed by the dedicated men and women who had lived this mission from its inception, the tradeoff lay in the insights gathered from soldiers at many levels, from the division to the foxhole and from units deployed throughout the area of operations. While these observations were inevitably snapshots, the issues highlighted here seem especially relevant as lessons for the future.

In assessing these very preliminary findings, however, it is important to provide an operational context, since heat rather than cold, and dust rather than mud, now affected the missions of *Operation Joint Endeavor*. Even more remarkable were the "life support systems" which had transformed the primitive mud pits of

January into the elaborate base camps of May—some of which rivaled or surpassed the facilities in Germany from which the troops had come. Above all, the political and social atmosphere of Bosnia itself was the constant backdrop to the mission. An uneasy calm prevailed throughout the region, with shooting largely confined to occasional incidents of "celebratory firing" by drunken members of the local populace, factional demonstrations in the form of cemetery visits or soccer rallies, and constant tension over the issue of apprehending war criminals. All the forces participating in *Operation Joint Endeavor* supported the various international teams delivering humanitarian relief, investigating war crimes, supervising elections, and preparing for the long process of reconstruction. But the principal IFOR military functions were to provide the security forces that controlled the countryside, patrolling the zone of separation between the former warring factions, and carrying out the force demobilization and weapons cantonment provisions of the Dayton Accords.

Inspections of each declared weapons site were ordered in specific instructions issued to the brigades. The results of those inspections (and weapons totals) were tracked through databases maintained by the division G-2. Despite this systematic approach, there were almost daily instances in which weapons—sometimes major ones, like tanks and air defense guns—were discovered outside cantonment areas. Some of these occurrences appeared to be the result of honest mistakes, but in others there appeared to be either creative bookkeeping by the factions or outright attempts at concealment. The most consistent estimate was that possibly 70 percent of these weapons holdings had been accounted for, since Bosnia has a history, culture, and geography favoring concealment from outside powers.

In carrying out these missions, the U.S. force commander was explicit in ordering that "all operations be deliberate, coordinated and documented." This guidance was strictly followed, with more similarities between the brigades than differences. Each patrol featured an effective combination of combat power, pre-planned air and fire support, multilevel communications, area knowledge, and at least some effort to appreciate the situation of the local populace. The only real differences were in the application of the principle of force protection. The four-vehicle convoy rule was rigidly enforced in every U.S. unit, but somewhat more relaxed in the multinational units, where one- or two-vehicle administrative movements were the norm. On patrols, however, three-vehicle convoys regularly featured at least three armored vehicles for consistent firepower and personal protection. And in both the U.S. and the multinational units, patrols consistently wore Kevlar helmets, flak jackets, and personal sidearms with magazines inserted.

Reality Versus Perception

The military tasks flowing from the varied functions of IFOR underlined both the importance of information in modern military operations and the difficulties of adapting traditional structures to new missions and technologies. The reality of Bosnia presented an uneven picture of progress and problems that contrasted sharply with inside-the-Beltway perceptions. Defense trade publications regularly featured stories about the high technology supporting the Bosnian operation—complete with seductive images of electronic maps, gigabytes of computer-transmitted information, and live imagery from UAVs. As one Washington-based official exclaimed, "...with huge bandwidths and powerful computers, we can get intelligence to where it is needed—Humvees, cockpits, ships."

Because information is the lifeblood of any modern military operation, an unprecedented amount of data indeed flowed from Washington to European headquarters and intermediate staging bases. A family of wide-area networks, for example, connected NATO headquarters with the IFOR in Bosnia, passing operational and intelligence messages to the 33 nationalities comprising the coalition. The Internet was also used for everything from "morale messages" exchanged between the troops and their families to home pages carrying frequent public affairs updates. A generation of painstaking efforts in the arena of NATO communications standardization had paid off as well, with systems that provided an essential baseline of interoperability for IFOR's coalition partners. In one memorable nighttime mission that I witnessed, a close air support mission over northern Bosnia featured British Harriers vectored by offshore NATO AWACS aircraft to Norwegian forward air controllers providing direct support to a Swedish-led brigade.

But elaborate information flows between higher command levels did not always translate into better support for the warfighter. In fact, life in Bosnia had not changed very much for the American soldier, because the information revolution largely seemed to stop at division level. Despite the techno-hype, subordinate brigades and battalions typically conducted operations much as they had 20 years before, with acetate-covered 1:50,000 maps, outdated communications gear, and only those sensor or reconnaissance systems organic to ground units. Unlike the popular image of a Tom Clancy "Ops Center," most tactical command centers (see figure 10-1) looked much as they had in other wars—usually housed in tents, semi-destroyed buildings, or the back ends of armored vehicles. To add in the effects of mountainous terrain (limiting line-of-sight communications), weather (either cold and muddy or hot and dusty), and computer viruses (sophisticated and ubiquitous) was to confront the new as well as the enduring qualities of military life in the field. In the apt summation of one U.S. Army general in Bosnia, "Soldiering is still an outdoor sport." And as always, the ingenuity and dedication of U.S. and NATO soldiers were critical in coping with these challenges.

Command and Control

It is important to recognize that the specter of the failed peacekeeping mission in Somalia pervaded much of what went on in Bosnia. In its aftermath, the fundamental question of "Who's in charge?" had become virtually synonymous with the dread specter of U.S. troops serving under foreign command. In practice, the 40-year history of NATO command arrangements had long since pro-

Figure 10-1. Tactical Command Center in MND(N)

duced the compromise of OPCON—a kind of leasing arrangement in which the designated NATO commander directed the actions of national elements while not interfering in their internal functions. NATO's first out-of-area operation nevertheless raised almost daily "rendering unto Caesar" questions as various national elements—the United States among them—carefully weighed alliance perspectives against national interests. But on the whole, these issues were well managed through military professionalism, with newly established soldier-to-soldier relationships being especially important in the integration of the Russian brigade attached to IFOR (see below).

In contrast, the largest single command and control problem in Bosnia was the failure of the Dayton Accords to designate a single authority to synchronize the military, political, and humanitarian aspects of the mission. As shown in figure 10-2, the relatively clean lines of NATO command and control contrasted sharply with the complicated and ambiguous arrangements handicapping the already difficult tasks of reconciliation and reconstruction. Especially in the American sector, civil affairs units (largely drawn from Reserve components) were used to good effect by brigade and

260   Lessons from Bosnia

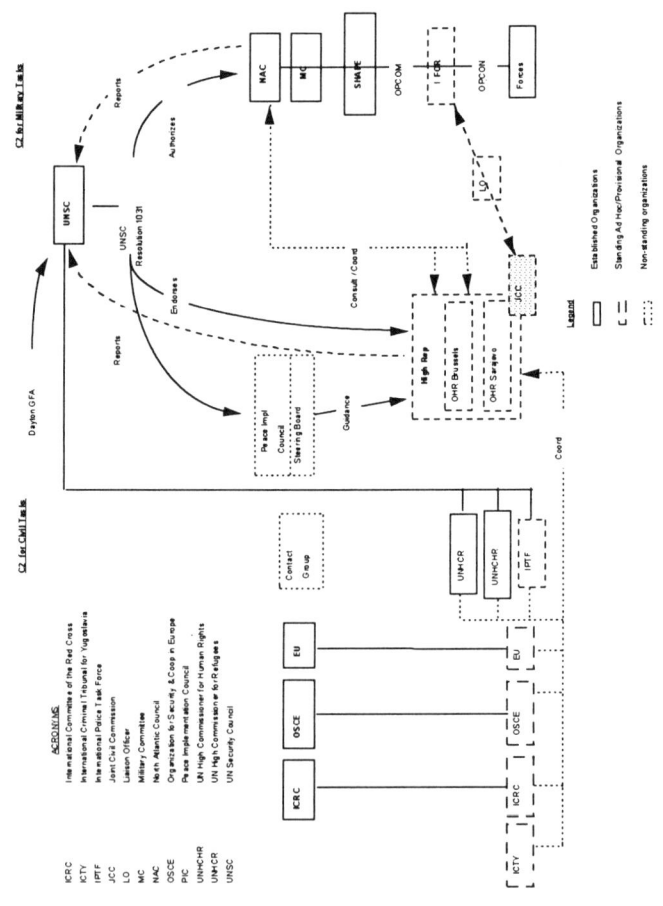

Figure 10-2.

battalion commanders whose culture emphasized initiative, accountability, and deadlines. Lacking either corresponding capabilities or these cultural attributes, their civilian counterparts were painfully slow in organizing the reconstruction efforts on which reconciliation ultimately depends. Not surprisingly, the humanitarian side of the mission consistently failed to keep pace with the improved security situation.

The Russian Brigade

I began an interview with the deputy commander of the Russian brigade by asking about the integration of Russian forces within IFOR. His indignant answer was, "What do you mean, integration?!" Rather than being integrated, the Russians regarded the formal relationship between the Russian brigade and the U.S.-led division as a friendly affiliation between equals. "They ask us to do things and we do them." This comment illustrates a not-well-understood aspect of Russian participation. The accompanying illustration (see figure 10-3a) of the NATO version of those command relationships shows an OPCON relationship connecting the Russian brigade to the SACEUR through his Deputy for Russian Forces. The relationship between the brigade and the U.S. division was described in the NATO documents as TACON, essentially the authority to direct tactical movements and missions. Also shown, however, is the Russian version (figure 10-3b) of this same relationship. Their word for OPCON is "operativny kontrol"—the same term used in Soviet military science to define military control at the operational level, particularly the control of those formations known as "operational maneuver groups." What NATO understands as TACON is translated by the Russians as "vzaimodestvya" or "interoperability"—connoting a relationship based on equality. As a practical matter, however, day-to-day operational matters were handled informally and effectively between Major General William Nash, the U.S. division commander, and Major General Alexander Lentsov—through a close personal relationship based on their com-

Figure 10-3. OPCON Relationships
Russian Participation in TFE

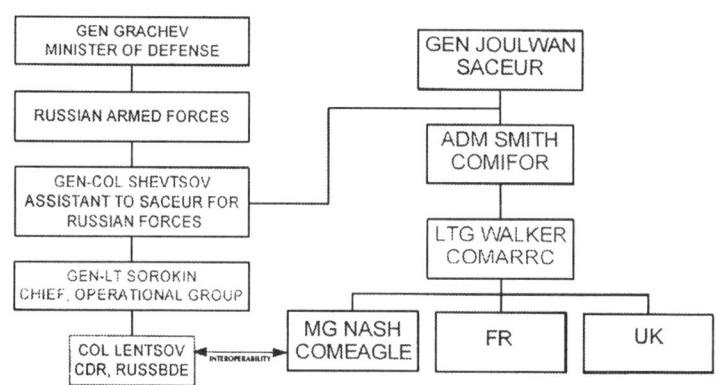

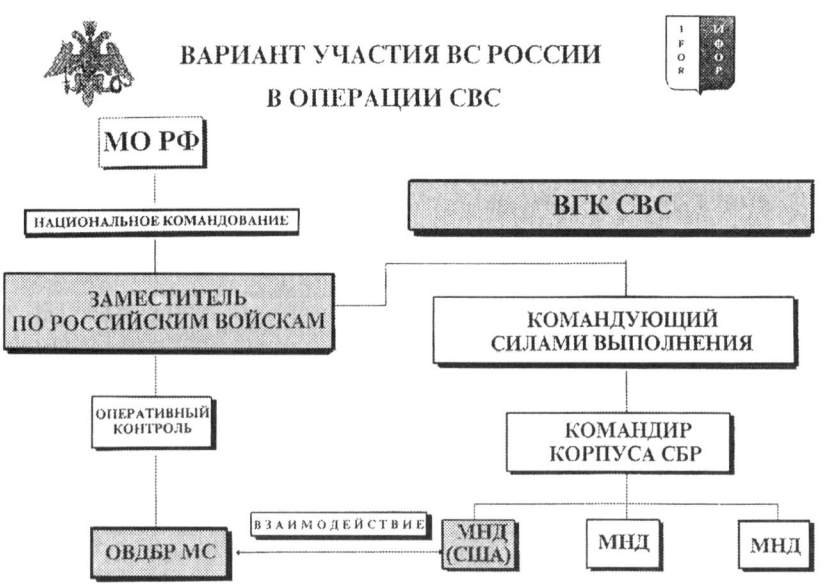

mon professionalism as soldiers. More difficult questions, such as the assignment of Russian soldiers away from their assigned sector, were resolved through the illustrated command relationships.

Whatever term might have been strictly applied, there was a high degree of operational integration between the Russian brigade and other divisional units. Aviation support, intelligence, reconnaissance, and surveillance were tightly coordinated as well as requirements for inspections and other missions. The Russians appeared to respond best to written orders, which they considered more binding than verbal instructions. And while many NATO armies routinely perform "implied and specified tasks" in any mission, this was emphatically not standard Russian practice. From General Lentsov on down, there was a notably "strict construction" in the way the Russian brigade defined and performed its military tasks. Given this emphasis, there were some otherwise routine civil affairs functions that either were not performed or not reported because the Russians saw no reason to do so, including water supply, home reconstruction, and personality profiles of key local leaders. Indeed, the ubiquitous American reporting style (up to six daily medical reports, for example) and paperwork burden had to be greatly simplified for the Russians—something which their U.S. counterparts could only envy.

Because they were hand-picked for this mission, the Russian brigade projected themselves as a tough, competent force. Their base camps were invariably well-chosen with competently sighted weapons and comprehensive entrenchments. In the field, their tactical communications tended to be slow and unreliable. The FM radios were made compatible with the American SINCGARS system by the simple expedient of turning the squelch off, an arrangement similar to that used between the Army and the Marines during Somalia. Oddly enough, the Russians typically featured less frequent and more decentralized reporting requirements, so that it was standard practice on some key missions to deploy a U.S. liaison officer equipped with a TACSAT radio with a direct link to division headquarters. On joint patrols, Russian junior officers were well organized and tactically proficient (see figure 10-4). However, they

Figure 10-4. U.S. soldiers and Russian paratroopers conduct a rountine joint patrol operation south of Brcko, Bosnia-Herzegovina, in the Russian Brigade's sector.

were often matter-of-fact about some things the United States takes more seriously: mission planning and briefings; delineation of specific objectives; integration of combined arms at the lowest levels; and after action reviews. Their cooperation and enthusiasm for working with NATO, were beyond reproach.

Use of Information

In both the NATO and U.S. contingents, reductions in headquarters and staffs have not matched post-Cold War cutbacks in force structures. While organizational featherbedding is often the first rule of combined operations, redundant hierarchies are no match for the speed and efficiency of decentralized electronic networks. Therefore, it was not unusual for information broadcast by these networks to be shared far faster than corroborating data successively reported through each layer in the chain of command. In a practice known as "skip-echeloning," both Washington-based commands and IFOR headquarters elements occasionally used these networks to bypass intervening organizations in order to exchange information requirements firsthand—sometimes leaving the broader community in the dark. The Division Chief of Staff described how on several occasions watch officers at the headquarters were directly called by the White House Situation Room and other higher headquarters to confirm information apparently available at those levels but not until that moment known by the on-scene commander.

These hierarchical structures and the intensely political nature of *Operation Joint Endeavor* prompted floods of information at the operational level. Put simply, data was the preferred means of disciplining American forces, often to the point of micromanagement. By the mid-point of the operation, some 1,200 "fragmentary orders" had been transmitted by the division to its subordinate units. And each evening at the U.S. headquarters in Tuzla, a "battle update briefing" prepared by the division staff covered the day's events in excruciating detail. More than 120 PowerPoint slides were typically used to highlight the latest operational and intelligence developments as well as to pinpoint a host of administrative issues, such as the number of sandbags used to protect base camps. These briefings and the accompanying slides were regularly transmitted back to the higher U.S. headquarters monitoring the operations. These set-piece briefings, so reminiscent of the "Five O'Clock Follies" of the Vietnam era, promoted a ubiquitous and even hyperactive reporting regime which regularly led to cultural clashes, only some of which were a function of different nationalities. According to one harried executive officer at a U.S. brigade: "During the last incident in our sector, seven of our nine phone lines were tied up answering questions from the division staff." Multiple taskings and overlapping reports were similarly cited as problems in both the U.S. and coalition brigades. However the multinational units at least found ways to cope with what they regarded as a uniquely American addiction to data requirements. "We take what we need," one allied brigade commander pointed out with exquisite tact.

Media and Public Affairs

The media—the quintessential network—suffused the entire Bosnian mission, provoking ambitious efforts by NATO and U.S. public affairs officers to make full use of information as a weapon of peace. Especially in the U.S. sector, with its 12-nation contingent, the formation of a joint information bureau was an important step in using information as a means to provide timely and accurate information as well as to influence compliance with the Dayton Accords. Not only was this bureau run with an international staff, but its director became central to the functioning of the command group, providing daily advice to the division commander and operating in close partnership with the operations, intelligence, and civic affairs elements. The importance of these relationships could be seen in a June 1996 incident, when the Associated Press wrongly reported that Serb General Ratko Mladic (an indicted war criminal) had faced down IFOR soldiers, forcing them to withdraw. Within minutes of the story's filing on the AP wire, alarm bells went off at headquarters from Sarajevo to Washington. Although the U.S. commander in Tuzla and his public affairs staff were instantly besieged with phone calls, it took more than 24 hours to ensure that an accurate version of this event had been reported. Because such an act of deliberate or accidental "disinformation" could take on a life of its own through a tightly wired global information grid, the management of perceptions became an important and continuing mission. Precisely for that reason, hard-pressed U.S. commanders regularly sought out local media opportunities, including, in one instance, a regular guest slot on a Bosnian radio call-in show. The lesson learned: in peace operations, as in other politically charged conflicts, perception is the reality.

Communications and Automation

The Army communications system generally worked well in Bosnia, but only at great costs in manpower and effort. As in the past, radio transmissions dominated tactical communications. Because most Army tactical radios operate on line-of-sight transmissions, it was essential to place repeaters and relays on mountain tops. But with large numbers of radio nets required for the 15 brigades operating in the U.S. sector, there was a real problem with interference ("signal fratricide"). Ironically, even in one of the world's most mountainous regions there was only so much high ground to go around. Since these critical relay sites had to be fortified and defended, support requirements typically consume 7-8 percent of combat manpower in addition to the U.S. signal brigade of over 1,100 soldiers. There was a sharp contrast between this "tooth-to-tail" ratio and the AT&T satellite phone system operated in U.S. base camps by roughly 24 company employees. Although the military communications system featured free morale calls, most U.S. soldiers phoned home with AT&T prepaid credit cards—expense outweighed by clarity and convenience. Their commanders often had similar feelings, in part because of the drain on already strapped combat manpower. "The former warring factions have better communications," snapped one U.S. brigade commander, "because they have cellular phones and I don't."

The brigades and battalions in the U.S. sector—(including the multinational units) were linked to the headquarters and each other by several baseline automation systems. The Maneuver Control System (MCS) is a vintage Army system that provided a secure means of transmitting orders, maps, diagrams, and classified e-mail. WARLORD, an intelligence terminal specially configured for this operation, handled most intelligence products, including imagery. However, a plethora of other automated logistical and administrative systems were also present, representing more a kludged-together operating environment than a "system of systems." Such ad hoc arrangements made it correspondingly more difficult to maintain computers and electronic equipment or to defend them. Heat, cold, humidity, and dust are traditional enemies of automation; but these challenges were magnified in Bosnia because there were so many computers, military supply lines were long, and there was little commercial infrastructure to take up the slack. A closely related and ominous development was the fast-growing problem of computer viruses. *While it is difficult to be precise, conventional wisdom among U.S. units was that 50 percent of their personal computers suffered from viruses of one kind or another.* Another problem was that large numbers of single-purpose, stand-alone databases made the integration of information incomparably more difficult, especially in the intelligence arena. Work-arounds were the order of the day, with heroic contributions coming from the most junior ranks, often augmented by technical virtuosos drawn from the Reserve components. The most common refrain: "Sir, this system was not designed for the job we're doing here. So we messed around with it a little, and it's not perfect, but we made it work."

Support to the Warfighter

Despite the imperative of supporting the warfighter, the river of information available to U.S. military forces in Bosnia often diminished to a trickle by the time it reached the soldiers actually executing peacekeeping missions. In one operation, a brigade commander who had requested overhead imagery of his area complained that "the system" took 3 weeks to provide photographs that eventually turned out to be 6 months old. The reasons are many: communications pipelines too narrow for efficient digital data transmission to the lowest levels; outmoded tactical equipment; and automation resources easily overwhelmed by what data was available. But these were only some of the more pernicious effects of an unwritten but well-understood rule: the higher the headquarters, the more elaborate the information trappings and vice versa. Such priorities meant, for example, that the decision to deploy a state-of-the-art intelligence system known as Trojan Spirit with the U.S. brigades was delayed until shortly before those units left for Bosnia. Although technology can provide a compelling way to enlarge the information highway to the lower echelons, such well-intended "fixes" must be balanced against the realities of Bosnia's 24-hours-a-day operations. As one tactical intelligence officer said, "We just don't have time over here for any more visits by the Good Idea Fairy." The larger point is that advances in information technology are of military value only to the extent that they are accompanied by coherent doctrine, organizations, equipment, and people, to say nothing of the time needed to make them function as a team.

One of the bright spots in this picture, however, was the stunning success of Army tactical aviation in Bosnia. The helicopters of the 1st Armored Division's Fourth Brigade combined speed and mobility in mountainous terrain—critical advantages in a region where every other factor conspired any external force. But innovations by Army aviation and intelligence soldiers also led to a new method of digitizing the Apache attack helicopter's gun-camera footage—all for an investment of less than $1,000 in commercial software and off-the-shelf equipment. The resulting photographs (see figure 10-5) documented Dayton Accord violations and—as unclassified imagery—were occasionally handed over to the former warring factions. Not only did these pictures display the exact time and location of such typical violations as tanks in the zone of separation, but they also featured targeting cross-hairs centered on the offending equipment—an unsubtle but highly effective means of compelling compliance.

Conclusions

There can be no question that the military mission in Bosnia has been a success and that the American soldier, supported by his Air Force, Navy, and Marine counterparts, has been the primary reason why it has been so. But the Bosnian experience should also remind us that our worship of technology in warfare must be tempered by a stronger sense of the human factor. Information technology is uniquely affected by people, their training, their procedures,

270 *Lessons from Bosnia*

Figure 10-5. Apache Gunship Camera Photo

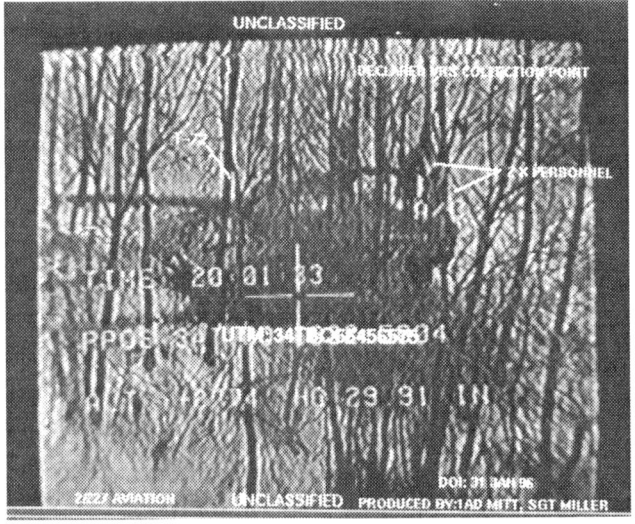

and the time they take to perform them. But the combination of these factors in combat or operational settings is constantly and curiously underestimated. We have barely begun to address the organizational implications of modern information technology in synchronizing the political and military sides of a peacekeeping operation, in reducing top-heavy headquarters, and in substituting commercial products and services for outmoded military equipment and redundant support structures. These are daunting tasks; but until they result in unshakable leadership commitments, our hard-won progress in Bosnia will fall short of the "sensor-to-shooter" potential that Information Age operations will demand on other fields and in other years.

XI. C4ISR Systems and Services[149,150,151]

Larry K. Wentz

The Challenge—Putting the Pieces Together

Effective C4ISR is a critical ingredient for the success of any military operation. Coalition operations such as *Joint Endeavor* present a complex set of challenges for the military C4ISR system planners, implementers, and operators. The most difficult challenge is the provision of integrated C4ISR services and capabilities to support the needs of ad hoc multinational military force structures and politically driven command arrangements. Although integrated C4ISR services are the desired objective, the realities tend to drive the solution to stove-piped implementations. In spite of technology advances, this will likely be the case for some time to come. There will continue to be uneven C4ISR capabilities among coalition members who will continue to rely on systems with which they are most comfortable—their own. For the IFOR operation, there were independent and separately managed NATO and national voice, message, data, and VTC networks; C4 systems and ISR systems; and so forth. This is simply the reality of coalition operations, with interoperability challenges and security disconnects that need to be dealt with. Agility and accommodation are truly keys to success in these types of operation.

In spite of formidable obstacles, NATO and its member nations were able to "put the pieces of the puzzle together" and installed and operated the largest military-civil communications and information system ever built to support a major peace operation—one of the success stories of *Operation Joint Endeavor*. The U.S. military CIS (communications and information systems) organizations (in particular, the U.S. Signal organizations such as 5th Signal Command) played a key leadership role in accomplishing the successful integration of the disparate NATO and national CIS systems. NATO, SHAPE, NACOSA, AFSOUTH, the IFOR CJ6, the ARRC, NC3A, and the United States, United Kingdom, and France all went through a very rapid learning curve, and many of the problems discussed herein were solved early into the IFOR operation by good will and good people working together for a common cause.

The U.S. Signal organizations also played a key leadership role in the establishment and staffing of the CJCCC (Combined Joint Communications Control Center) and the management of the IFOR CIS network. The United States provided 59 percent of the military communicators in theater at the peak of the operation. The prominent role of U.S. Signal officers in key positions in NATO, SHAPE, AFSOUTH, IFOR CJ6, EUCOM, DISA, USAREUR/5th Signal Command, USAFE, and other organizations was an important unifying factor. Many IFOR problems associated with system integration issues, ambiguous roles, incomplete doctrine, network and system management, and technical interoperability were successfully resolved through close coordination among these U.S. officers. The UK was also a key facilitator in this regard with important contributing players in NATO, SHAPE, NACOSA, AFSOUTH, the IFOR CJ6, the ARRC, and UK Signal units. The United Kingdom provided 32 percent of the military communicators in theater at the peak of the operation. NATO organizations such as AFSOUTH CISD (Communications and Information Systems Division), IFOR CJ6, SHAPE CISD, NACOSA, ARRC G6, and NC3A-the Hague rose to the occasion and provided untiring support to IFOR CIS installation, operation, and problem resolution activities as well.

Environmental Factors

In peace operations, it is necessary to be able to interface with the civil organizations such as the NGOs, PVOs, and IOs. In Bosnia there were more than 500 such personnel already operating in country when IFOR arrived and they relied on HF/VHF radios, regional Bosnia PTT telecommunications service where it existed, and to a large extent the UN VSAT voice network that supported UNPROFOR and other in-country UN elements. Some also had laptop computers, but none possessed the same level of communications and information system capabilities as the military.

The units deploying into BiH deployed into an area where the communication infrastructure had been destroyed and where the lack of cooperation among the former warring factions precluded the establishment of a BiH PTT-derived commercial communications capability to support or augment IFOR connectivity needs, especially cross-IEBL connectivity. In this regard, military owned and controlled primary connectivity was still a requirement for cross-IEBL and other essential C2 links.

The Bosnia population was literate and relatively well educated and was used to all forms of media that characterize an "information society." The local and international radio, television, and print media were everywhere, operating independently of the military and reporting incidents almost instantaneously, sometimes before they were reported to IFOR. This created challenges for IFOR staff and placed added demands on the CIS network to be able to get the right information to the right place at the right time to meet not only the operational needs but to also accommodate the "CNN" effect (unsubstantiated media reports).

There were hazards and risks that had to be dealt with during *Operation Joint Endeavor*. The terrain and weather conditions were extreme. The commercial power was unreliable or in many cases did not exist. There was a lack of public water and space for housing C4ISR support personnel. Dust and dirt proved to be a challenge for the deployed commercially based, high-technology

276 Lessons from Bosnia

PTT Damage

computer equipment that needed a relatively dust-free operational environment. Viruses also proved to be a problem for the computers and data networks, the main source being infected diskettes brought into the command centers by the staff. Minefields were numerous and added risk to all deployed C4ISR personnel. The force protection measures required soldiers to wear flack vests and helmets and travel in four-vehicle convoys, adding another challenge for those involved in the implementation, operation, and maintenance of the C4ISR systems.

There were other factors that influenced NATO and national activities in preparation for and execution of the IFOR deployment. The operation was occurring at a time when NATO and the nations were reducing force structures. Non-NATO and Partnership for Peace nations would be involved for the first time as well as the Russian Federation, and there was little guidance on how to proceed with these first-time events. In addition to the first out-of-area operation, it was also the first major ground operation ever. There were multiple OPLANs that added some confusion to the guidance for the CIS plans and management structure. NATO would be taking over from the UN and other peacekeeping agencies and this had some built-in uncertainties, including access to, integration of, and use of the already in-place CIS infrastructure of the UN, UK, and France. Deployment would take place in the depth of winter in an area of difficult terrain. The likelihood of hostilities was a major concern because of the fragility of the peace arrangements in Bosnia. There were effects on morale associated with deploying troops over the Christmas period. Therefore, one should not underestimate the degree of difficulty NATO and the nations faced as they prepared for and deployed to Bosnia in support of *Operation Joint Endeavor*.

Planning Considerations

CIS planning commenced more than 2 years prior to the Dayton Peace Accord being signed. Planning for OPLAN 40101 began in late summer of 1992 with the proposal of the Vance-Owens Peace Plan. The concept was to replace the UNPROFOR with

NATO forces. The ARRC was given the mission as the ground component commander and the responsibility to develop the scheme of maneuver. The plan matured and was re-designated as OPLAN 40103 in the fall of 1993, when it appeared that a larger replacement of UNPROFOR by a NATO force might be required.

In December 1994, members of USEUCOM staff met with AFSOUTH staff to discuss U.S. support for possibly assisting the UN in a withdrawal from Croatia and BiH. As a result of these discussions, preliminary planning for OPLAN 40104 began. By March of 1995, the political climate in Bosnia had deteriorated to the point that NATO planning for intervention resumed. OPLAN 40104 was developed for the sole purpose of withdrawing the UN from Bosnia and established the statement of requirements for the support of that operation. In September 1995, the political climate changed again; it appeared that peace was at hand in the region. As a result, in October 1995, NATO was directed by the North Atlantic Council to finalize plans for a peace-enforcement operation and AFSOUTH developed OPLAN 40105 to support this mission. NATO and national CIS organizations were thus left trying to hit a fast-moving political target and the changing operational plans did nothing to assist with the provision of "in time" CIS support. In fact, it made the situation more difficult.

Further complicating the planning was the fact that NATO had never attempted peace enforcement and it was its first ever out-of-area operation. Consequently, there was no doctrine, experience, or accepted practices to guide CIS planning and implementation—the NATO Combined Joint Task Force (CJTF) was just a concept and not doctrine. There were multiple NATO and national CIS organizations involved in the planning and implementation activities. The division of strategic, theater, and tactical CIS was less distinct for both NATO and national systems. AFSOUTH and SACEUR OPLANs reflected differing perspectives on CIS management and responsibilities. The Dayton Agreement assigned frequency management responsibilities to IFOR even though it had no established capability. These factors caused CIS organizational problems at the outset for IFOR CJ6. In order to address the shortfalls, a Theater Frequency Management Cell (TFMC) was created and a Combined Joint Communications Control Center (CJCCC) was established to focus the theater-level planning and management of the CIS aspects of the IFOR operation. The CJCCC also facilitated coordination of NATO, national, strategic, theater, and tactical CIS activities.

The operational scenario for *Joint Endeavor* was unclear at the outset and national planning was being kept closely held. Hence, who was going where, when, and with what equipment were unclear to the NATO planners. Also, a lack of timely political planning guidance caused last-minute changes to bring the CIS plan in line with new policy decisions. For example, there was a requirement for COMIFOR to be in theater but AFSOUTH had no mobile headquarters capability. Thus it was necessary to look for a facility first in Zagreb and then at the last minute in Sarajevo. Neither in-country facility was configured as an operational headquarters from a CIS perspective, and because space was a premium in Sarajevo, it became necessary to locate part of the headquarters in the rear, initially in Zagreb. A comparable rear area capability was established in Naples at the same time as well. This added unanticipated last-minute requirements to the CIS plan. The ambiguities in C2 arrangements exacerbated the CIS planning problems.

Delayed political decisions prohibited forces from performing any real reconnaissance of the Bosnia area of operation, which prevented headquarters, communications, and command center site surveys prior to deployment. Some reconnaissance was possible in Croatia. Hungary was a different situation, where U.S. reconnaissance was possible to prepare for the deployment of U.S. support elements. NATO had never worked operationally with the non-NATO nations scheduled to participate and there was no doctrine on how their needs and CIS capabilities would be accommodated and integrated into the IFOR operational network.

In spite of the highly uncertain planning and operational environment and a lack of established CIS requirements, NATO, IFOR, and the nations still needed to plan for deployment. They had to anticipate potential requirements and provide a CIS capability robust enough to accommodate unanticipated needs and surges should they occur. It was generally felt (at least by the United States) that it would be better to err on the side of providing too much CIS capability rather than not enough given the uncertainties of the operational environment. NATO was not fully supportive of an approach to "flood" with resources to overcome a problem.

Implementation and Operational Considerations

The NATO and IFOR framework member nation commands (i.e., NATO, SHAPE, AFSOUTH, ARRC, and the United States and United Kingdom, in particular) had to plan with a minimum of guidance and a lack of established requirements for the C4ISR capabilities to be deployed. The CIS contingency plans therefore had to be flexible enough to accommodate possible operational options ranging from assisting with the removal of the UNPROFOR, to peace enforcement, to peacekeeping, to war fighting. Furthermore, NATO lacked the CIS capability to deploy out of area. Limited military satellite bandwidth offered a major challenge as well. Two NATO satellites and one U.S. satellite were used but the bandwidth was still limited by space segment power and was inadequate to meet IFOR and national requirements. It was therefore necessary to rely on leased international vendor-provided commercial satellite services to fill the gap (e.g., IEC, SPACELINK, AT&T, and ITALIALINK).

The challenge facing NATO and the nations was to build a long haul and regional CIS network out of a mixture of military and commercial equipment that would vary widely in age, standards, and technology and would be built very quickly once given the order to deploy. Putting the pieces of the puzzle together (see figure 11-1) would most likely not result in a true "system of systems" for IFOR. Furthermore, there would be a need to interface systems that had not been planned or designed for interfacing. The independent national systems would be tied together, not engineered as a single system. Given the uncertainty of the situation it would most likely be a case of integrating what you get, not necessarily what

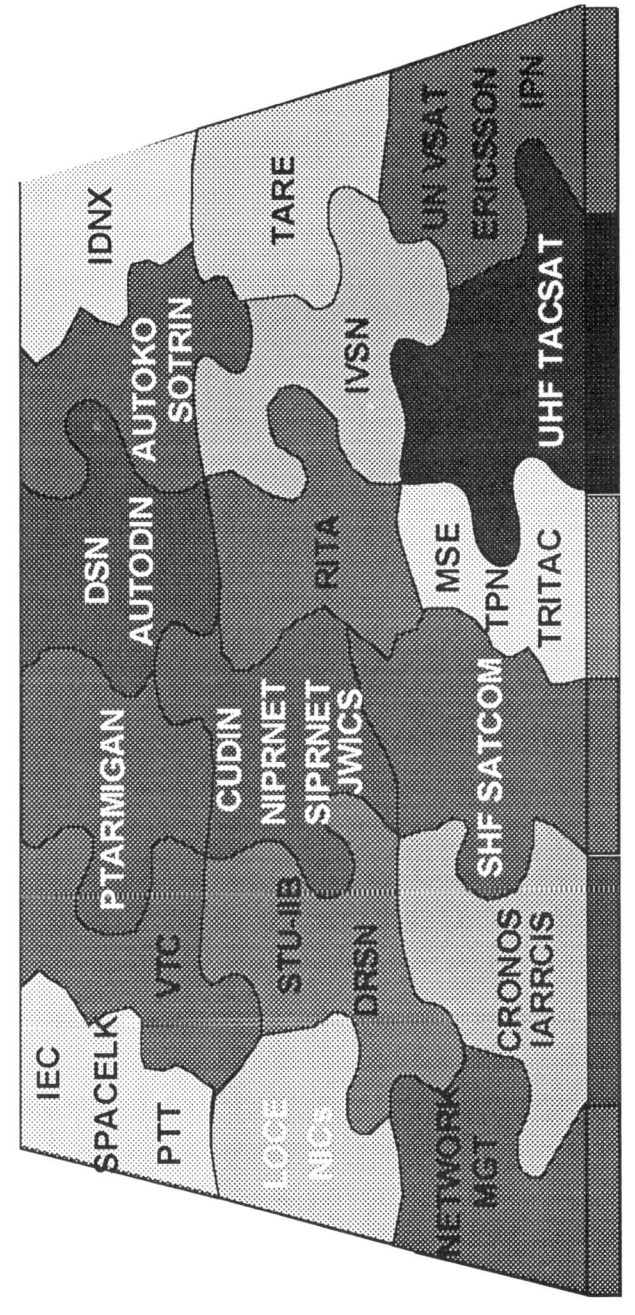

Figure 11-1. THE C4ISR Puzzle

you need, and then making the best of it. In addition, it would be necessary to support both mobile tactical command centers and fixed headquarters located in "buildings of opportunity," such as the Annex to the Tito Residence (see picture) in downtown Sarajevo, hotels in Ilidza, the 1984 Olympic stadium and ice rink in Zetra, a factory in Banja Luka, office buildings at the airfields in Tuzla and Mostar, and Croatian military compounds in Zagreb and Split.

No single NATO or national organization was capable of providing the entire CIS infrastructure to support the operation. In addition, NATO took time to build up the organization and structure to plan, implement, operate, and manage the integrated strategic, theater, and tactical CIS capability required for such a large out-of-area coalition peace operation. NATO turned to the nations

IFOR Headquarters, Sarajevo

to assist in the form of experience, staff, and CIS capabilities and the United States, United Kingdom, and France played lead nation roles in this regard. The timely and effective response of these nations and 9 months of pre-planning by NACOSA allowed AFSOUTH to quickly react to the signing of the Dayton GFAP and rapidly deploy enough CIS capability to allow IFOR to take command and control of the operation.

The U.S. military strategic, theater, and tactical C4ISR systems and services provided critical communications and information systems and services in support of the IFOR operation, especially the tactical SHF SATCOM (the United States provided 76 percent of the tactical SHF terminals). The U.S. Tri-Service Tactical Communications (TRI-TAC) tactical systems formed the basis for the IFOR strategic- and theater-level network and TRI-TAC/MSE were used to support MND(N) and the national units assigned to it. The British tactical systems were the other major player in the IFOR operation. The PTARMIGAN tactical system supported the ARRC and its connectivity with the MNDs and supported MND(SW) and the national units assigned to it as well. The UK tactical SHF terminals were key contributors to the IFOR backbone connectivity (the VSC-501s provided 22 percent of the tactical SHF terminals). The French tactical systems supported MND(SE) and the national units assigned to it. The French tactical SHF terminals only supported national connectivity needs. NATO-acquired CIS and leased commercial services provided a key portion of the rest of the IFOR capabilities extended into Croatia and Bosnia. The NATO TSGT (Transportable Satellite Ground Terminal) provided military SHF SATCOM access to the IFOR headquarters in Sarajevo.

Deployment into urban facilities provided interesting challenges for the implementation teams since they were required to wire these facilities for voice and data services from scratch. This included installing LANs and telephone lines; removing tactical equipment from their shelters and installing them in fixed facilities; installing cables in buildings and on compounds; installing VSAT terminals; and performing numerous other non-tactical installation functions. The installation activities stretched the abilities of the multinational teams deployed and required personnel with broad skills and training in order that they could be used for more than one task. The extensive use of commercial products (e.g., VSATs, IDNXs, routers, and ERICSSON telephone switches) meant that the military personnel needed additional training to engineer, install, and maintain this equipment as well. An IDNX course was set up at the NATO Latina, Italy, training facility to meet the IFOR need for installers and maintainers of this equipment. There were no "Tandy/Radio Shacks" in Bosnia so this put additional pressure on the support system for commercial equipment spares, repairs, and contractor assistance.

For any military operation, a certain amount of "learning on the job" is expected. However, the deployment into a generally urban environment (using office buildings for command centers), coupled with the extensive use of commercial products and services, created a need for more intensive on-the-job-training (OJT) than had been anticipated, both for the providers and users of the information services. OJT training programs were set up by the CIS providers not only to train their staff but also to teach command center staff how to use the information systems in the centers.

The proliferation of different information systems resulted in a situation where no one person was cross-trained to operate or maintain all of the systems in the command centers. Furthermore, the information system capabilities deployed were not being exploited due to the fact that the users lacked training and adequate understanding of the full potential of these systems. In many cases, information systems were simply used for word processing, e-mail, and PowerPoint briefings. SOCIFOR/JSOTF2 reported that the systems under their control could best be characterized as "too many, too duplicative."

There was a significant lack of trained data systems and network administrators. They were constantly in high demand and there were simply not enough of them to adequately meet the needs of the information networks deployed. The military also lacked experienced, system-level maintenance and network management personnel in theater to troubleshoot the complex information networks deployed. Contractor support and the professional skills of those at the SHAPE Technical Center (now the NATO C3 Agency, the Hague) and national elements such as 5th Signal Command and DISA had to be brought to bear to help solve complex system-level problems.

Training needs were not limited to information systems alone; there were shortfalls in the military SATCOM area as well, e.g., the ARRC lacked trained NATO Airbase System (NABS) SATCOM terminal operators and maintainers and had to be supplemented by USAFE technicians.

U.S. PSYOP and CIMIC operations experienced problems in communicating between headquarters and the deployed tactical teams. The tactical teams had to rely on services provided to them by the units they supported. In many cases, the supporting units did not have spare capacity to offer them, and therefore had to share access to the voice and data services. Such shared access was frequently not high on the priority of the supporting units, limiting the ability of the PSYOP and CIMIC teams to communicate effectively. In some cases, the teams deployed with laptops but could not access the U.S. tactical packet network due to the lack of Tactical Terminal Adapter (TTA) interface devices. The shortage of TTAs was only one aspect of this problem, and not the most important. The use of TTAs was also limited by a shortage of voice channels over the U.S. MSE. Finally, there were also problems experienced in the timely distribution of PSYOP products to the deployed tactical PSYOP teams since there was no automated PSYOP-provided information system dissemination capability to specifically meet these needs. Vehicle transportation means were relied upon to bulk deliver products (e.g., *The Herald of Peace*, handbills, and posters) to the MNDs for local distribution. Some transcripts for radio and TV broadcasts were sent electronically to the deployed tactical PSYOP teams.

The shortage of TTAs proved to be a broader U.S. Army problem since Combat Support Systems such as STAMIS (Standard Army Management Information System) deployed without appropriate interface devices and there was a general shortage of

TTAs in theater to support the demand for access to information services. It was reported that Task Force Eagle was short more than 300 TTAs and an average request of 3 users per week were being experienced at D+65. TTAs were used on an exception basis in MND(N). The preferred connectivity was via the Network Encryption System (NES) into the Tactical Packet Network that provided a security solution and concentration. The U.S. Army STACCS system also experienced some deployment problems as a result of the deploying units not providing the necessary modems for tail circuits off the NES—equipment was left in garrison.

Although there were high expectations that the soldier on the ground would benefit more from advances in information technology, this was not necessarily the case for IFOR, despite efforts to equip them with the latest capabilities. From a coalition operation point of view, however, significant progress was made in moving the "information revolution" to lower levels of the command hierarchy. In most instances, the IFOR CIS network provided better service and more capability than that available at NATO and the major NATO Command headquarters and at many of the IFOR troop contributing nations' home stations.

Unanticipated Requirements

The communications and information needs of operations such as the IFOR Public Information Office, IFOR Information Campaign, Engineers, PSYOP, CIMIC, Counterintelligence, and HUMINT were not completely formulated or necessarily fully understood at the outset of the operation. The need to be able to interface with and provide some limited support to the NGO/PVO/IO community was also underestimated. Therefore, the requirements were not adequately articulated to the IFOR and national CIS planners and providers so that the necessary service could be made available at the outset of the operation to support these activities. As an example, the IFOR CJCIMIC headquarters operation in the Burger building in downtown Sarajevo only had a few local telephone lines to conduct business in the early stages of operation. If they needed information services or a broader IFOR communications capability, they had to go to IFOR headquarters at the Tito Residency. The CIMIC and some HUMINT vehicles lacked radios for communicating while operating in the countryside. The engineers also generated a requirement for force protection communications since they too were frequently scattered throughout the country. The PIO needed more effective IFOR communications and information services at the Holiday Inn in Sarajevo and while traveling around the countryside in order to be able to quickly inform the chain of command of media-related, time-sensitive events and issues.

The IFOR engineers and legal and medical personnel needed to use the Internet to access reference material. The PIO also needed Internet access for media interaction. The Internet could be used to get English translations of Croatian and other international press releases and news articles. NATO policy at the outset of the operation did not support the use of commercial Internet services. NATO policy makers were often slow in accepting reality and the need for pragmatic change. The use of the Internet in NATO was an example of such a phenomenon. In contrast, Internet access was available to U.S. elements at almost all locations, even remote base camps in MND(N).

A significant change to the earlier OPLANs was abandoning the concept of a combined logistic support arrangement and making logistic support a national responsibility. This resulted in the establishment of three NSEs: the United States in Hungary, the British in Split, Croatia, and the French in Ploce, Croatia. The ARRC COSCOM commander was designated COMMZ Forward commander and located in Split, Croatia. He was given the responsibility of reporting movement into theater to the IFOR Commander for Support who was located in Zagreb, Croatia. This meant that providing communications between COMMZ Forward and the NSEs was a theater responsibility. For the United States it also added the requirement to support a U.S. NSE in Hungary.

Early Interoperability Considerations

Interoperability became a major concern when the total scope of the engineering effort for the IFOR network was realized. No one nation had committed to the integrated network engineering task that included terrestrial and satellite transmission systems; commercial PTT networks; and diverse systems of voice, video, and data of NATO and national strategic, theater, and tactical systems. It was decided to conduct a major interoperability exercise, called *INTEROP 95*, to get a better insight into the system integration and interface issues and solutions. *INTEROP 95*, held in April 1995, included more than 250 participants from 8 nations and tested all anticipated interfaces necessary to execute the AFSOUTH and ARRC OPLANs. System interfaces tested included the UN Ericsson commercial switch, the Olivetti commercial switch, the Italian tactical system SOTRIN, the U.S. tactical systems TRI-TAC/MSE, the UK tactical system PTARMIGAN, the U.S. strategic system DSN, and the NATO voice network IVSN. The N.E.T. commercial IDNX, the SHAPE TSGT and deployable reach-back communications capability REPLICA, the USAF TSSR (TROPO/Satellite Support Radio) LOS radio, and NATO and national tactical satellite terminals (U.S. TSCs, UK VSC-501 and NATO Air Base SATCOM (NABS) (USAFE deployed)) were tested as well. The results of *INTEROP 95* were so overwhelming that the U.S. Joint Interoperability Test Command (JITC) certified a number of the interfaces and published a NATO Interface Guide as a reference book. Lessons learned have shown that despite "standard NATO interfaces," interoperability trials still have to take place to reduce interface problems.

Exercises such as *INTEROP 95* and subsequently, *Mountain Shield I* and *II*, served to refine concepts of operation and work out many system integration and interoperability issues among various commercial and NATO strategic and national tactical switching and transmission systems. Among the 5th Signal Command learning experiences were difficulties in acquiring the NATO IVB satellite and poor-quality NATO satellite links (plagued with system hits). Subsequent U.S./NATO satellite testing revealed that

BPSK rather than QPSK transmission needed to be used on the NATO IVB to achieve the desired link performance. Unfortunately, BPSK requires more bandwidth so the satellite planners had to reengineer the planned satellite network that was already bandwidth constrained. This problem may also have been a training-related issue as well, in that the U.S. personnel may not have been adequately prepared for accessing the NATO satellite system. Pre-deployment exercises serve to help resolve problems such as these. They also provide excellent training for the participating coalition organizations that end up supporting the actual operation.

Based on field tests and exercises involving U.S., NATO, and allied communications systems, EUCOM J6 developed a EUCOM U.S./NATO/Allied Communications Systems Automated Interoperability Handbook. The handbook is on a laptop computer and is used to document known interoperable configurations that work. It provides a wiring diagram of the configuration, technical details, and other relevant information necessary to guide interface implementation in the field. An operator simply enters the configuration to be set up and if it has been accomplished before and documented, the computer provides the details necessary to implement, test, and operate the requested interface arrangement.

Evolution of the CIS Capabilities

One distinct advantage enjoyed by AFSOUTH was the time allowed in the lead up to the IFOR operation. During the planning of OPLANs 40103 and 40104 there was time to do some limited site surveys in Croatia and Bosnia and to coordinate CIS planning with NATO, SHAPE, and likely key participating nations such as the United States, United Kingdom, and France. It should be noted, however, that although there was a lot of time to plan the NATO CIS network to support the withdrawal of UN forces, there was little time to develop the theater contingency option to support the last-minute change to deploy into Bosnia for the IFOR peace-enforcement mission.

Fortunately, NATO had already taken action to extend its strategic CIS network into Croatia in anticipation of having to support the extraction of UN forces. The UN also had a fairly extensive network in place in Croatia and Bosnia to support UNPROFOR C2 needs. In addition, at the TOA (transfer of authority) from UNPROFOR to IFOR, there was also a considerable advantage in that the United Kingdom and France, two of the framework nations, were already in place as part of UNPROFOR. The fact that they were already in theater meant that they also had their CIS infrastructure operating in theater, including links back to their national support elements. These networks therefore became major players in facilitating the extension of NATO and national CIS capabilities to support the initial IFOR C2 needs in Bosnia.

The United States, on the other hand, was at a disadvantage in that it was required to essentially deploy its CIS capabilities from scratch when IFOR was activated. The establishment of the Headquarters IFOR, the C-SUPPORT Headquarters, and the ARRC CIS capabilities also experienced similar challenges at the outset of the operation.

The IFOR network implemented in Bosnia was basically a tactical military network which relied heavily on the tactical assets of the United States and the United Kingdom. Over time, the military network was augmented with commercial products and services. The IFOR plan was to phase out the military assets as soon as possible and rely more extensively on commercial services with a military overlay to support essential C2 needs. The commercial capabilities implemented were viewed as leave behind when IFOR withdrew and were therefore an integral part of the CIS exit strategy. When the decision was made in late 1996 to extend the NATO presence in Bosnia, the commercialization of the NATO CIS network in Bosnia and Croatia continued as a big element of the CIS strategy and the establishment of the so-called IFOR Peace Network.

TOA from AFSOUTH/IFOR to LANDCENT/IFOR occurred on 7 November 1996. The ARRC TOA to LANDCENT/IFOR occurred on 20 November 1996 and the TOA from IFOR to SFOR occurred on 20 December 1996. These TOAs were accompanied by a large personnel change and changes in the NATO and national CIS infrastructure. For the strategic and theater CIS connectivity, a rationalization and re-balancing of the networks was necessary to reflect the move of the IFOR operational center to Sarajevo and then to Ilidza where SFOR headquarters was established. Accompanying the reconfigurations were a greatly reduced role of AFSOUTH and downsizing of the CIS support to them.

LANDCENT had been planning for the transition for several months with "right seat" hand-over training initiated in late September 1996. In spite of an attempt to get up on the learning curve, LANDCENT still experienced many of the CIS implementation and procurement challenges seen in IFOR's initial deployment.

For the United States, there were also some unintended CIS reconfigurations as well. For example, due to the fact that Commander LANDCENT/SFOR was also Commander USAREUR, U.S. national CIS support systems had to be added to meet his U.S.-only requirements. The force structure downsizing associated with the IFOR TOA to SFOR also resulted in a major reconfiguration of the U.S. tactical satellite and switched networks supporting the NATO operation.

The UN Network

Prior to the IFOR operation, UNPROFOR had been operating in theater with a CIS network which consisted of VSAT, voice, secure and nonsecure fax, HF/VHF/UHF radios, and a system for convoy tracking and communications called LOGTRACKS. These assets were in place and some were available to support the IFOR deployment.

The UN VSAT network, depicted in figure 11-2, was already in place and provided voice connectivity to key locations to which IFOR deployed. It played a critical support role in not only

292   *Lessons from Bosnia*

Figure 11-2. UN VSAT Network

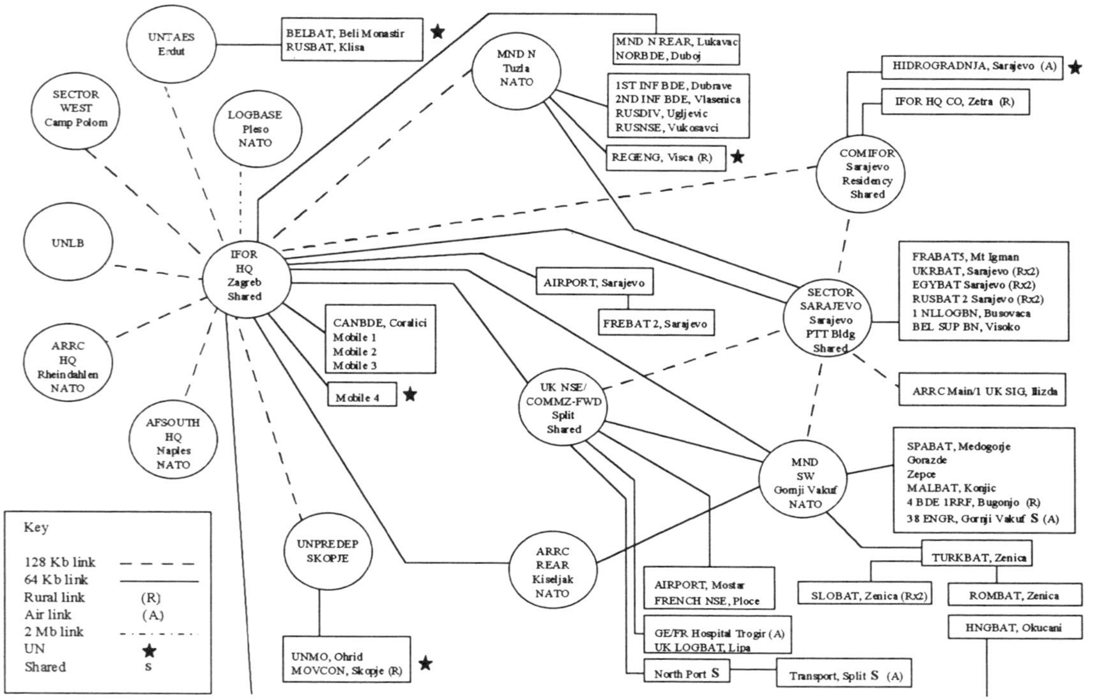

the deployment phase but also throughout the operation. The network consisted of ERICSSON switches interconnected by a commercial VSAT network. There were four standard access packages available: CORPS level—8 trunk lines and 80 extensions; division level—8 trunk lines and 30 extensions; brigade/battalion level—4 trunk lines and 10 extensions; and local access to 2 lines from local VSAT facilities. NATO leased the service from the UN.

The UN VHF radio network (Motorola) consisted of 40-watt base stations, 25-watt vehicle mounted sets, and 5-watt handheld sets. There were repeater stations throughout Croatia and BiH. ARRC-Main established a VHF "network of networks" to monitor election supervisor activity for the September 1996 national elections. The MND brigade operations centers performed the monitoring. The network was a combination of IPTF and UN assets with NATO-funded ARRC-Main assets used to fill in the gaps.

The NATO Network

In preparation for the execution of OPLAN 40104, the extraction of UN forces, a data network based on leased E1 (2mb/s) transmission bearers and using NATO-purchased IDNX smart multiplexers was extended by NACOSA and the United States into Croatia. The seven-node network connecting SHAPE, AFSOUTH, Vicenza, Brindisi, Zagreb, Pleso, and Split was approved and funded by NATO on 8 February 1995. Installation (with some assistance from DISA) began in March and was completed on 13 April 1995. In April 1995, the NAC approved the first-ever NATO out-of-area operation and authorized the deployment of up to 80 military personnel to install, operate, and maintain the E1/IDNX-based information network. The operation was dubbed "Mini-STEP 2" of a three-step process to extend NATO strategic communications and information services into the theater. On 26 April 1995, the first soldiers of the Southern Region Signal Regiment, AFSOUTH, began to deploy to Zagreb, Croatia. In addition to installing the interfaces to the E1/IDNX network, an operational WAN was established between the sites and LANs at Zagreb, Pleso, and Split. The plan also included pre-wiring and interconnecting designated buildings to be used by IFOR staff to permit rapid occupancy if the need arose. By the end of May 1995, the E1/IDNX-based strategic backbone information network was fully operational.

The NATO Transportable Satellite Ground Terminal (TSGT) was deployed to Camp Pleso (a UN compound collocated with the Zagreb international airport) and was used to provide a military path for the E1/IDNX network in the event of political instability in Croatia. The TSGT also supported the extension of SHAPE headquarters voice, message, and data services to the Zagreb area through the use of the SHAPE-provided REPLICA system. The REPLICA system was based on a prototype developed by the SHAPE Technical Center (now the NATO C3 Agency) and provided a reach-back service to SHAPE headquarters.

IFOR and Framework Nations Networks

With the signing of the Dayton Peace Agreement on 14 December 1995, the mission changed and Croatia and Hungary became the embarkation points for NATO troops deploying into the region. OPLANs 40105 and 10405 provided the guidance for the deployment of these forces and the supporting CIS infrastructure. However, because of C2 differences, the OPLANs were never harmonized and this led to disruption and discord between AFSOUTH and SHAPE staffs.

The CJCCC started to deploy elements of its organization to Zagreb in early December 1995 along with the main staff elements of the IFOR C-Support. By 17 December 1995, HQ IFOR JOC operations were being conducted out of Zagreb with a HQ IFOR (FWD) JOC at the Residency in Sarajevo. On 18 December 1995, the NATO TSGT and REPLICA were moved from Camp Pleso (Zagreb) to Sarajevo. The TOA from UNPROFOR to IFOR took place on 20 December 1995. At this time the Residency in Sarajevo had the following systems operational: UN VSAT, TRI-

TAC, REPLICA, DSN, PTARMIGAN, Defense Red Switch Network, WAN, Video Teleconferencing (VTC) (connecting the Residency, AFSOUTH, and Zagreb), TARE, Recognized Air Picture from the CAOC, and LOCE INTEL access. The ARRC too was up and operational at this time with connectivity to its MNDs, the NSEs (National Support Elements), and IFOR Headquarters.

The IFOR CIS network (figure 11-3) was based on a strategy to use national military tactical systems to extend the NATO strategic CIS network into the area of operation. When a period of stability was achieved, the plan was to replace the tactical systems with commercial capabilities. It had to be kept in mind that the IFOR mission was to be completed within a year. Therefore, the IFOR CIS infrastructure would need to be replaced, in any case, by commercial capabilities as part of the mission completion.

In addition to supporting the IFOR CIS network, the framework nations (the United States, United Kingdom, and France) also provided capabilities that would support their own forces committed to *Operation Joint Endeavor* (figure 11-4). These capabilities included strategic to tactical C2 and mission support networks, as well as national intelligence capabilities and supporting ISR networks that would provide intelligence support to the national commanders and provide IFOR-releasable intelligence to IFOR and the ARRC through the NICs (National Intelligence Cells). Tactical systems indigenous to the units deployed, such as the U.S. MSE, single channel TACSAT, and Combat Net Radio, were employed at division and below. The United Kingdom deployed SCRA, VHF, UHF, VSAT, leased PTT, and INMARSAT capabilities to support division to battalion voice and data services, including access to MENTOR, their strategic-level network (DSN equivalent). The French deployed a number of different capabilities to support division to battalion voice, telegraph, and data services: the SPARTACUS TACSAT, the SICILE/TANIT network that supported HF/VHF/UHF/PTT/INMARSAT and PTARMIGAN interfaces and services, and the SYRACUSE SHF SATCOM. The RTY network also provided telegraph services down to the battalion level. Ac-

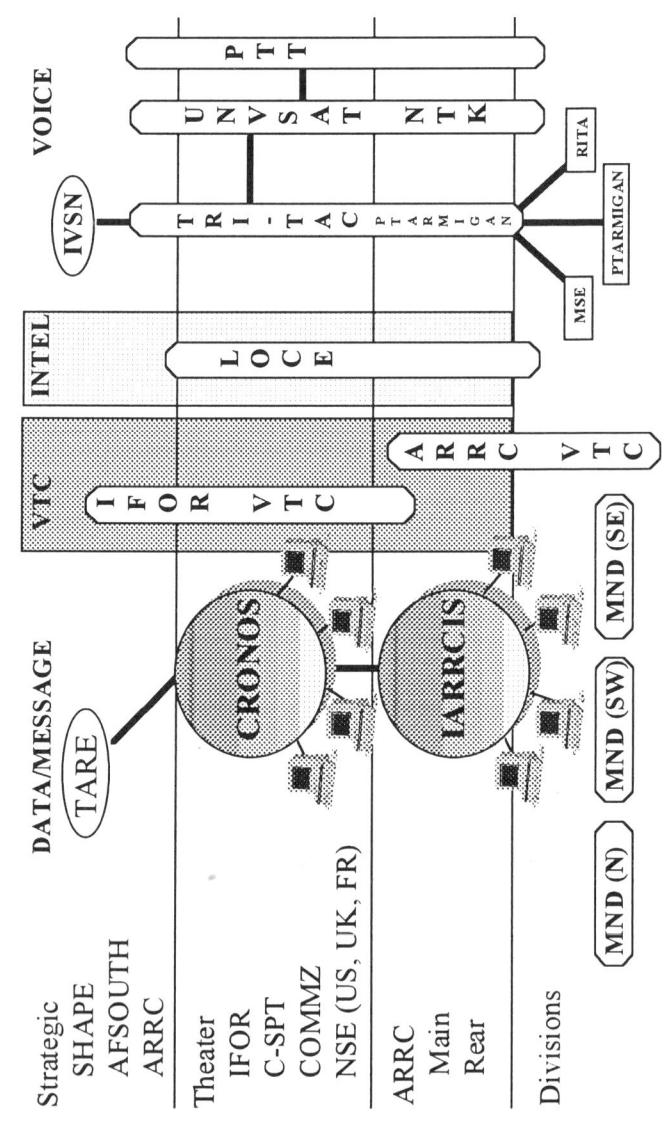

Figure 11-3. IFOR CIS Network

C4ISR Systems and Services

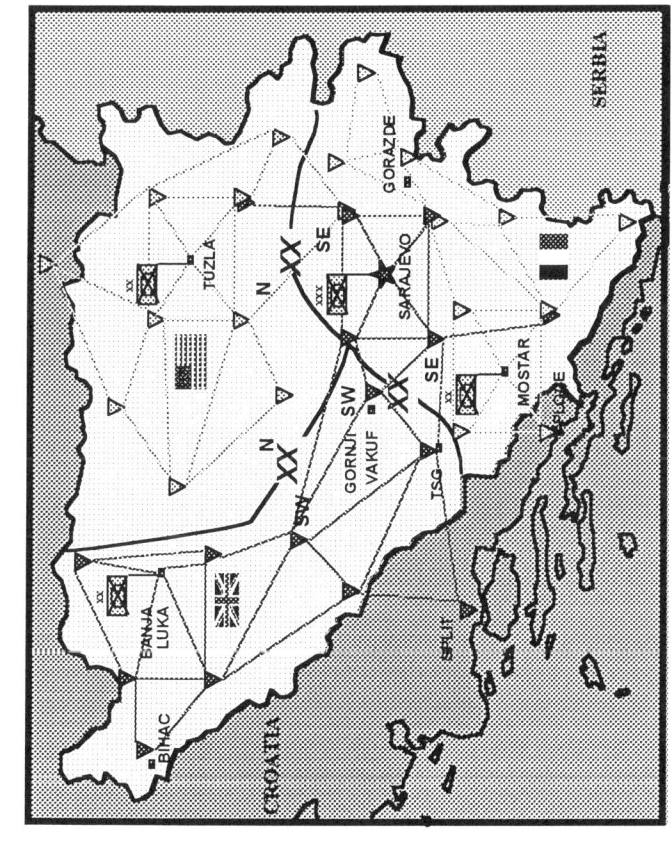

Figure 11-4. Framework Nations Network

cess to the French strategic-level system RITTER (DSN equivalent) was provided as well. The French tactical system RITA was not deployed until the March 1996 time frame.

The IFOR implementation strategy would undergo some change, however, with the fall 1996 decision to extend the NATO involvement for an additional 18 months and transition IFOR to LANDCENT/SFOR. Commercialization of the military network through the establishment of a commercial services-based, end-state network, the IFOR Private (Peace) Network (IPN), continued to be the strategy followed by IFOR and subsequently LANDCENT/SFOR. The replacement of IFOR with SFOR and the movement of SFOR headquarters from the Residency in Sarajevo to Ilidza (outside of Sarajevo) extended the reliance on military tactical systems beyond the time frame anticipated and also required the acquisition of additional NATO CIS capabilities to accommodate this change. Furthermore, the United States had to provide additional national communications to support a four-star general, who while serving as the LANDCENT/SFOR commander in Sarajevo also retained command of USAREUR.

IFOR C4I Systems and Service

Since NATO had no in-place ability to deploy forward its strategic C4I capabilities, IFOR had to rely heavily on the national tactical assets of the framework nations, the UN VSAT networks, and commercial products and services to extend connectivity into Bosnia and to provide information services to the deployed headquarters and forces. The pervasive use of commercial-of-the-shelf information products and services propelled NATO and IFOR into the Information Age.

Military and Commercial SATCOM

Due to the lack of Bosnia telecommunications infrastructure (and in particular, cross-IEBL connectivity), mountainous terrain, and the high cost of force protection for radio relay sites, national military SHF SATCOM was used extensively. It was used not only to provide the transmission bearers for the initial deployment but also to support connectivity throughout the IFOR operation (figure 11-5) as well. NATO only had one TSGT and it was deployed to Sarajevo to support IFOR Headquarters reach-back connectivity to SHAPE. Because NACOSA had SHF SATCOM expertise and NATO had SHF space segment capacity, it was possible for NACOSA to design and the CJCCC to implement a large and complex SATCOM network using the NATO and U.S. DSCS satellites and national tactical SATCOM terminal assets. The United States and United Kingdom provided the bulk of the military tactical SHF SATCOM terminals (U.S.: 35 TSCs and 5 NABS, UK: 9 VSC-501s) supporting IFOR, ARRC, C-SPT, the NSEs, and the MNDs. In order to achieve the desired bandwidth on key links, it was necessary for the U.S. Regional Space Support Center (RSSC) to engineer the U.S. loading of the satellite based on the use of 20-foot dishes (these dishes were in short supply).

The French provided military SATCOM (the SYRACUSE, TANIT, and SPARTACUS tactical satellite terminals) connectivity but only for the MND(SE) area of operation and connectivity to France. The SYRACUSE network used the French TELECOM II A and B satellites.

By late summer 1996, although the original NATO TSGT (designated T1) was still operating well in Sarajevo, there was increasing concern about the ability to keep the terminal operational (overdue for an upgrade) and spares to support it. Therefore, it was decided to deploy several of the newly acquired NATO TSGTs to Sarajevo to replace the old equipment. The first TSGT was deployed in September 1996 to replace the aging T1. Three more terminals were deployed over the next 3 months. Adding the new

300　Lessons from Bosnia

Figure 11-5. SHF Architecture

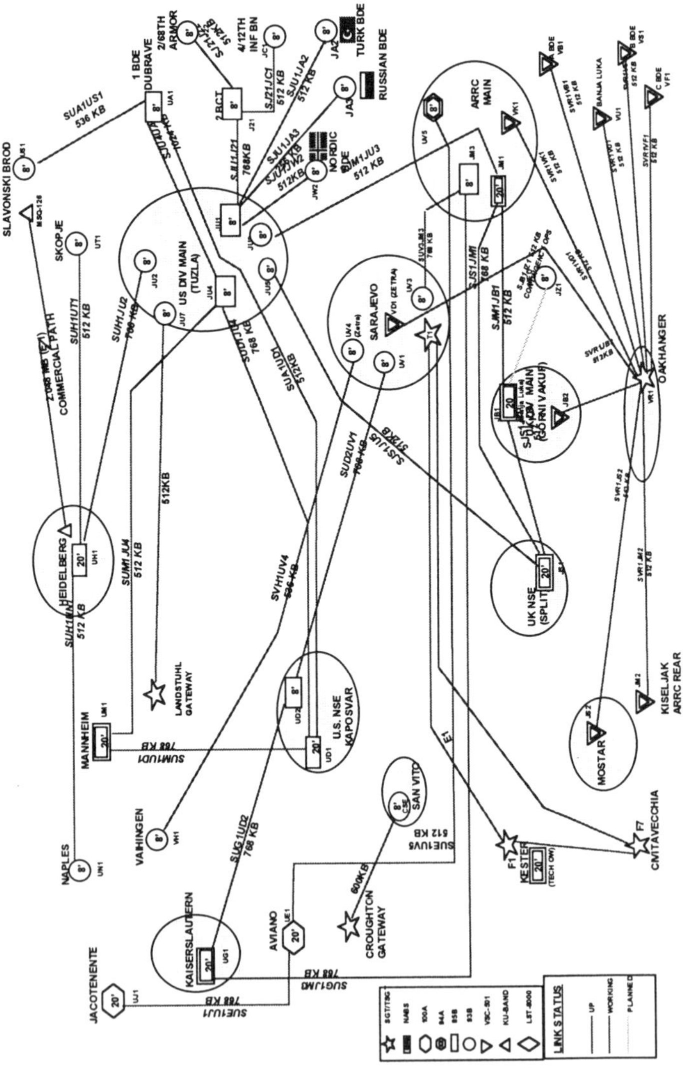

terminals also increased capacity and provided more robust NATO SATCOM connectivity in the area in anticipation of the transfer of authority to LANDCENT/SFOR.

The USAF terrestrial TROPO/SATELLITE Support Radio (TSSR) provided a 2mb/s line of sight (LOS) capability that was quite flexible and easy to set up. The TSSR was used to establish local connectivity where it was not possible to acquire PTT service. For example, it was used from the roof of the Tito Residency annex to Zetra stadium to link IFOR headquarters with the NATO satellite ground terminal and by the ARRC in Ilidza to connect to the UN VSAT network in Sarajevo.

Single-channel UHF SATCOM allowed commanders to overcome terrain and distance restrictions for broadcast radio networks. In particular, at the tactical level this capability allowed formations and units to operate voice nets over wide areas without deploying VHF FM rebroadcast stations. The distance, terrain, and ground security environment that the forces needed to operate over often did not allow the deployment of rebroadcast stations. TACSAT had the efficiencies of a broadcast network, allowing stations in the net to hear and respond simultaneously. The terminals were small and easily portable and allowed maneuver commanders to quickly establish communications. UHF SATCOM was a major player throughout the theater with 37 networks active out of a planned 48 (see figure 11-6). Establishing UHF access and allocation procedures was a first for NATO. Problems were worked out jointly between AFSOUTH, NACOSA, and USEUCOM. NATO leased 32 UHF channels from the U.S. satellite network (at a very high price from the NATO point of view). NATO also initiated action to procure 212 UHF TACSAT terminals (half LST-5E [wide and narrow band capable] and half PRC-117D [narrow band capable only with a separate crypto add-on]). The CJCCC established the initial set of UHF access and allocation procedures and closely managed the emerging network. The number of UHF channels available on the satellite limited the capability over a particular region. Addi-

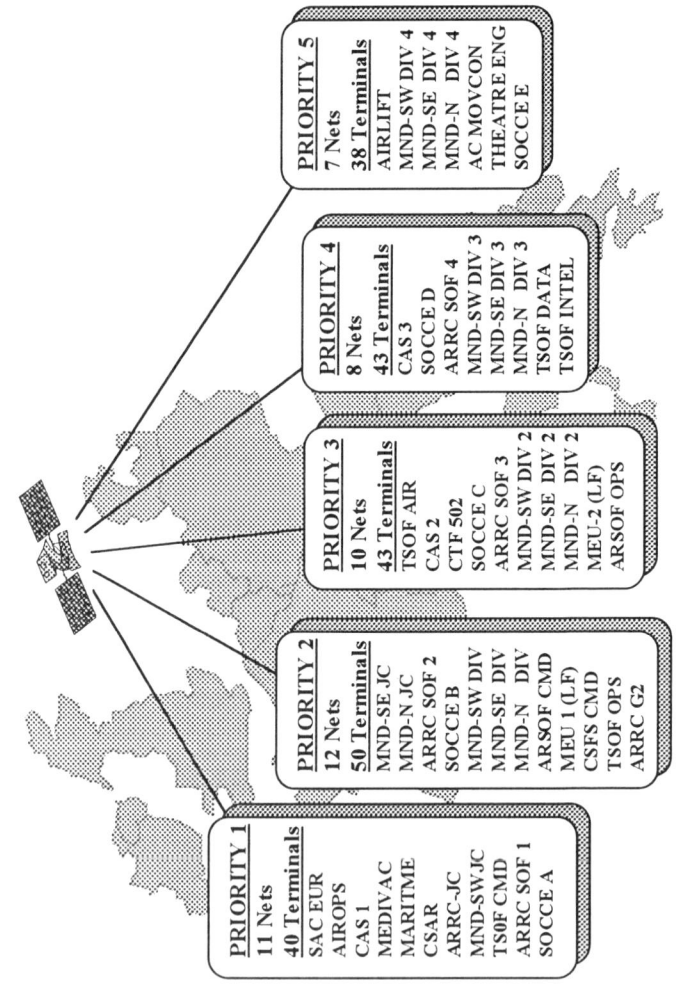

Figure 11-6. UHF SATCOM

tionally, there were some long lead time items in re-supply and repair because the UHF terminals were low-density items. This had some operational impact implications.

As the operation evolved, commercial VSAT services were extended into the area through contract services provided by IEC, SPACELINK, and HARRIS TELEDATA. IDNX smart multiservice bandwidth managers were interconnected by the military and commercial bearers and used to provide a robust transmission infrastructure that provided connectivity for the voice, data, and VTC networks. In fact, the combined IFOR and U.S. IDNX network was the largest military IDNX-based network ever implemented. The E1/SATCOM/IDNX network proved to be a flexible and capable system for *Operation Joint Endeavor*. Figure 11-7 shows the status of the NATO IDNX network at the end of *Operation Joint Endeavor*. The network supported communications services for 18 different geographically dispersed locations. A leased 2mb/s commercial SATCOM link, ITALIALINK, connected IFOR headquarters in Sarajevo with AFSOUTH headquarters, Naples. Commercial INMARSAT terminals were also used by IFOR, the ARRC, the MNDs, C-SPT, the NSEs, and national command elements.

Military Voice and Commercial Services

National tactical voice equipment was used to establish the IFOR Voice Network (figure 11-8). The U.S. TRI-TAC system provided a large portion of the strategic- and theater-level telecommunications infrastructure supporting organizations such as SHAPE, AFSOUTH, IFOR, C-SUPPORT, COMMZ, and the NSEs. NATO also provided some. The UK tactical system, PTARMIGAN, provided the telecommunications support for the ARRC (CORPS level) and between the ARRC and the MND headquarters. The United States, United Kingdom, and France used their tactical systems to support division-level communications including service to those forces assigned to their divisions. TRI-TAC/MSE equipment was employed in support to MND(N) and the U.S. NSE in Hungary. PTARMIGAN was used to support MND(SW) and the UK NSE in

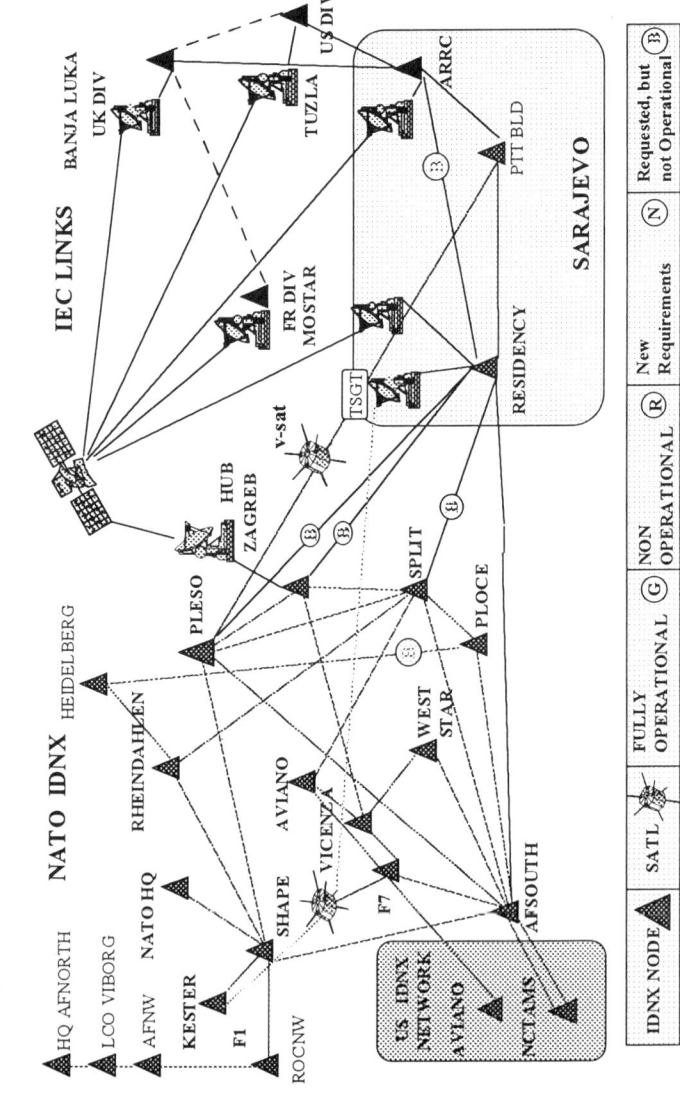

Figure 11-7. IDNX/IEC/SPACELINK/ITALIALINK Network

C4ISR Systems and Services 305

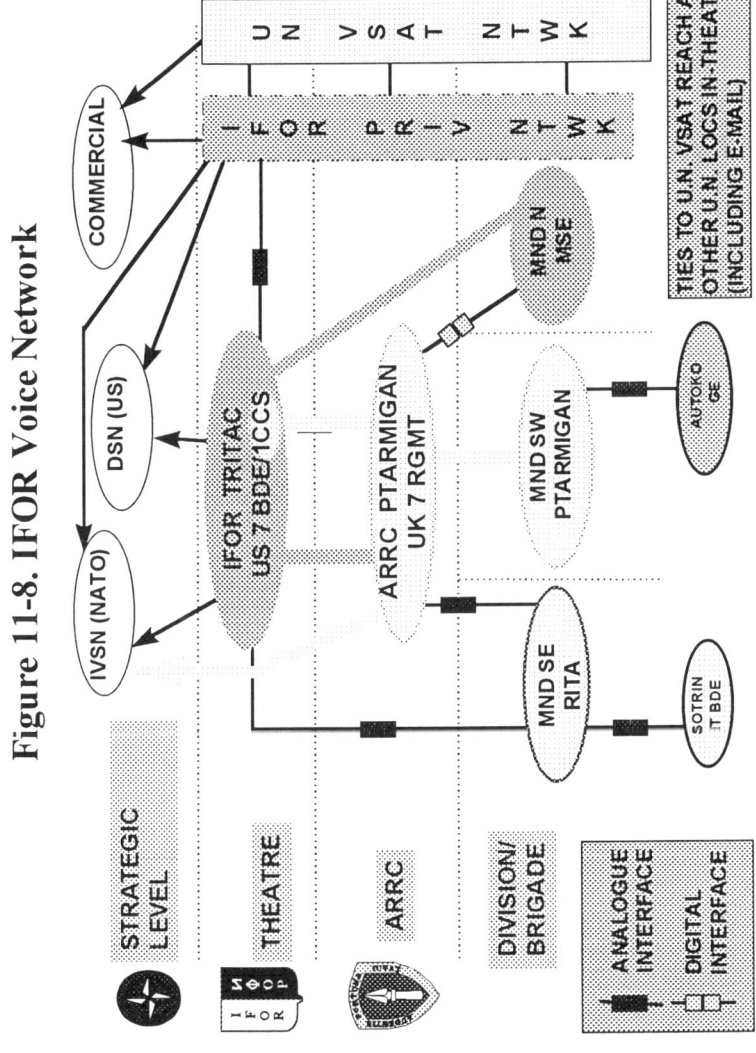

Figure 11-8. IFOR Voice Network

Split. French tactical systems already in place were used to initially support MND(SE). The tactical system RITA was deployed in the March 1996 time frame to provide additional support to MND(SE) and its NSE in Ploce. The Italian system, SOTRIN, supported the Italian brigade in MND(SE) and the German tactical system, AUTOKO, supported the German contingent in MND(SW). STANAG 5040 was employed to provide an analogue interface between the national, tactical, and strategic voice networks; between TRI-TAC and the NATO strategic voice network, IVSN; and between TRI-TAC and the commercial networks such as the UN VSAT and the Bosnia and Croatian PTTs where available. The Interim Digital Interface PTARMIGAN (IDIP), designed by the United Kingdom for this operation, was used to provide a digital interface between PTARMIGAN and the TRI-TAC/MSE systems. STANAG 5040 was used for the TRI-TAC to RITA interface as well as SOTRIN and AUTOKO interfaces with RITA and PTARMIGAN, respectively.

The OHR (Office of the High Representative) had a terrestrial UHF Motorola network that was installed to link major Bosnian cities. IFOR headquarters obtained a channel on this network to provide force protection communications for CIMIC and IFOR Information Campaign personnel in the field.

The Republika Srpska (RS) and the Federation telecommunications infrastructure were severely damaged as a result of the war. Some damage was also caused by the allied bombing campaign. Before the war, there were about 4,000 international lines but in December 1995 there were only 400. There were some 30,000 Federation and 27,000 RS trunks before the war but in December 1995 there were 8,000 and 4,000 respectively. As a result, only limited local and regional services were generally available. The international call completions went from a pre-war percentage of 35 percent to 2 percent in December 1995. There was no operational cross-IEBL connectivity even though physically some connectivity existed. For example, RS and Federation trunk switches were interconnected but software code blocks prevented dialing between the two networks. Commercial cellular communication was available in some areas of Croatia and towards the end of the IFOR operation, a limited coverage commercial cellular capability was implemented in the Sarajevo area.

AT&T and British Telecom provided a soldier Call Home commercial service as part of the military MWR (morale, welfare, and recreation) support initiatives. MCI also showed an interest in providing service, but due to the contract arrangement with AT&T this did not happen. AT&T implemented roughly a 20-node commercial satellite-based network to support the MWR service and to support other U.S. military needs in Bosnia, Croatia, and Hungary. The AT&T implementation at the outset was slower than the U.S. military would have liked it to be and DSN was used to provide limited support for MWR needs. In the case of AT&T there was a Military Saver Program under a contract with AFFEES that soldiers could join in order to get reduced rates. During the 1995 Christmas holiday period there was a promotion sponsored by AFFES, VFW, and AT&T that provided every U.S. soldier a free $20 calling card donated by these organizations.

There were various morale-call policies in place for NATO and national military personnel. The United States allowed deployed military to use the DSN for this purpose. There was, however, an IFOR-related unintended consequence associated with this practice. For U.S. personnel assigned to IFOR organizational elements, the only access to the DSN (at least in the Sarajevo area) was through the UN VSAT network. There was no NATO policy that prevented the use of the UN VSAT network for this purpose. As a result, the UN VSAT network, which was already overloaded with operational traffic, experienced additional loading from morale calls that interfered with the operational use of the network. The French used RITA to call back to France. The British forbade morale calls over their military networks. It was reported that staffs of all nationalities used the IFOR commercial access at the Residency in Sarajevo to make direct-dial international calls home. This too had IFOR-related unintended consequences. The calls interfered with bona fide mission traffic (since the commercial access could be used when UN VSAT and other networks were having problems or loaded with operational traffic). In addition, this service was expensive. NATO, which leased the service and ran the switch at the Residency, did not enforce a policy on use of this service and usage accounting was not performed on the switch in Sarajevo to check for abuse of the service.

IFOR Data and Messaging Services

IFOR data network service was provided by extending the AFSOUTH information system prototype designed by the SHAPE Technical Center (now the NATO C3 Agency, the Hague). The prototyping activities were carried out under project ECHO (Evolutionary Capability for Headquarters Operation). At the end of 1993, ECHO was a four-node commercial client-server-based architecture interconnected by a X.25-based Wide Area Network. The interconnecting links operated at 2.5kb/s. By February 1994 the network was expanded and migrated from X.25 to TCP/IP with enhanced security features (authorized to operate NATO SECRET system high). In May 1995, the functionality was further expanded and the network was declared operational and re-named CRONOS. The interconnecting links were upgraded and varied in bandwidth between 9.6kb/s and 64kb/s. The network supported Microsoft Office and e-mail services along with some functionally specific C2 applications such as the PAIS, CRESP, Allied Deployment and Movement System (ADAMS), and the RAP from the CAOC. The CRONOS network was extended to support NATO and IFOR strategic- and theater-level needs. The CRONOS LAN at IFOR headquarters had to be upgraded to switched Ethernet technology due to the volume of traffic received and generated by the Joint Operations Center.

UK CIS support to the ARRC included a tactical information system, the Interim ARRC Information System (IARRCIS). IARRCIS was a ruggedized equivalent of CRONOS and was used to support the ARRC and the data services between the ARRC and the MND headquarters. The CRONOS and IARRCIS networks (figure 11-9) were interfaced to provide seamless data and e-mail service between the NATO and IFOR strategic, theater, and tactical

C4ISR Systems and Services 309

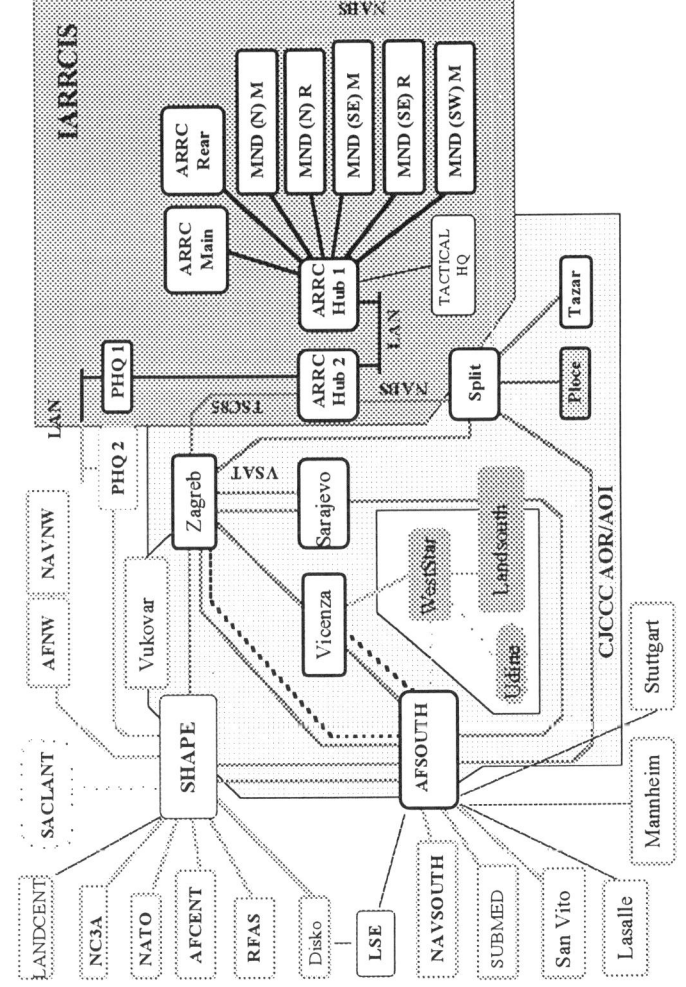

Figure 11-9. CRONOS/IARRCIS Network

headquarters and support organizations. There was no interface between the IFOR/ARRC data networks (CRONOS and IARRCIS) and the strategic, theater, and tactical data networks of the MND nations and other participating nations.

The ADAMS, also developed by STC (now the NC3A), was used to coordinate and track NATO and national deployments. The ADAMS provided three main elements: the network for secure communication and data exchange; the software to support the analysis, planning, and management of the actual deployment process; and the databases describing the forces, transportation assets, and mobility infrastructure. NATO and national access to the ADAMS hub at SHAPE were provided through the public ISDN network via a router, a NATO approved encryption device, a terminal adapter, and an ADAMS workstation located at the appropriate NATO and national movement staff headquarters. At the outset, the initial users were the three framework nations, SHAPE, and the NC3A but soon grew to accommodate all NATO troop-contributing nations. The SHAPE Allied Movement Control Center in Mons, Belgium, and the IFOR Joint Movement Control Center in Zagreb, Croatia, coordinated the detailed deployment plans (DDPs) inputted from the nations and monitored and reported on the actual deployment. DDPs were text files describing what, where, when, and how things were moving. By the end of the deployment phase a total of 217 DDPs from 20 nations had been processed. The frequency of updates varied greatly between nations. Most of the nations provided updates only in response to significant events or changes to the plan. The United States on the other hand used a software interface between its JOPES and ADAMS to provide daily updates whether or not there were significant changes. This proved to be especially helpful for reporting actual movements.

The decision was made early not to extend the NATO strategic message network, the TARE, into theater. Instead, it was decided to provide an interface between the NATO data network, CRONOS, and the TARE and wrap the formal NATO messages (ACP 127 format) in an e-mail and send them via the interface (figure 11-10). There was one exception to this policy; a TARE termi-

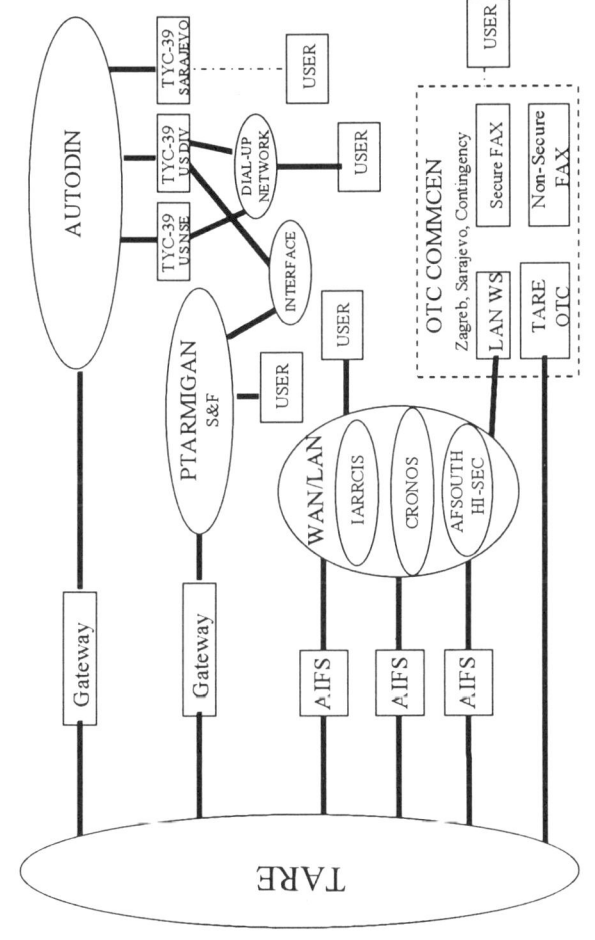

Figure 11-10. Message Network

nal was provided at the Residency in Sarajevo for messages of higher classification than NATO SECRET and to be used as a backup in case the CRONOS LAN failed. The CRONOS LAN was unstable for the first several months of operation and did fail frequently. The United States extended a limited Automatic Digital Network (AUTODIN) capability into theater. The fact that the NATO TARE and the U.S. AUTODIN systems were interconnected at the strategic level made it possible to support some over-the-counter NATO messaging services for IFOR in Zagreb and Sarajevo.

Internet Service

Unclassified Internet was used frequently and demands for service increased throughout the operation. IFOR use of the Internet was not planned; its use simply grew with user demand. In MND(N) and the U.S. NSE, Internet access was provided via the NES and Tactical Packet Network (TPN), and via Point of Presence (POP) routers. Internet access was more widely available to U.S. forces than to NATO elements.

A limited theater-level Internet access was provided by the U.S. Army to IFOR, but IFOR really needed its own access that made Internet services more readily available to a broader IFOR community. The Public Information Office (PIO) used it for media interactions and home pages were created to inform the press and public about the operation in general. The intelligence community used it for open-source assessments; legal and medical personnel used it as a reference tool; and the engineers used it for activities such as predictions for the height of the Sava River to adjust the pontoon bridges. Deployed military personnel used it to maintain contact with their home organizations. It also had value as part of the MWR support—e-mails to home.

Internet access allowed the staffs to obtain information directly from sources around the world. As a result of the demand for Internet services by IFOR, NATO reviewed and revised its policy on restricted NATO use of the Internet. Users accessed the Internet by dialing through the U.S. DSN and the UN VSAT network to gain access to the U.S. NIPRNET that had a gateway to the Internet. Access was also possible through other dial-in servers in Germany and in other locations. Later in the operation, the CJCCC provided an IFOR dial-up service to an Internet server connected to the Sarajevo UN telephone switch, which had a positive effect in off-loading the long data calls on the DSN and UN VSAT systems. Direct IFOR access to the Internet using the public network and commercial providers also became available.

IFOR Video Teleconferencing Service

Two Video Teleconferencing networks (figure 11-11) were established to support IFOR C2 decision making and to facilitate coordination, one for Commander IFOR and his command elements and the other for the Commander ARRC and his MND commanders. The ARRC also had a secure voice conferencing capability provided by the PTARMIGAN system. VTC was an essential element of the NATO command and control operations. The NATO VTC at the Residency in Sarajevo was booked regularly for most of the day. By August 1996, the network included Naples, Split, Zagreb, the USS *LaSalle*, ARRC-Main, SHAPE headquarters in Belgium, and LANDCENT headquarters in Germany. The United States also deployed an extensive VTC capability, it was the U.S. Army's C2 system of choice.

IFOR Intelligence Services

The overall intelligence architecture to support IFOR is depicted in figure 11-12. The figure shows the NATO, national, and lower level connectivity. The U.S. LOCE system was extended to division level to support IFOR intelligence needs. Nations also provided national intelligence support and services to IFOR through liaison officers and NICs. An ICC (Intelligence Coordination Cell) was also established at the Joint Analysis Center in Molesworth, England. The cell consisted of a number of different national representatives who helped respond to theater requests for information

314 Lessons from Bosnia

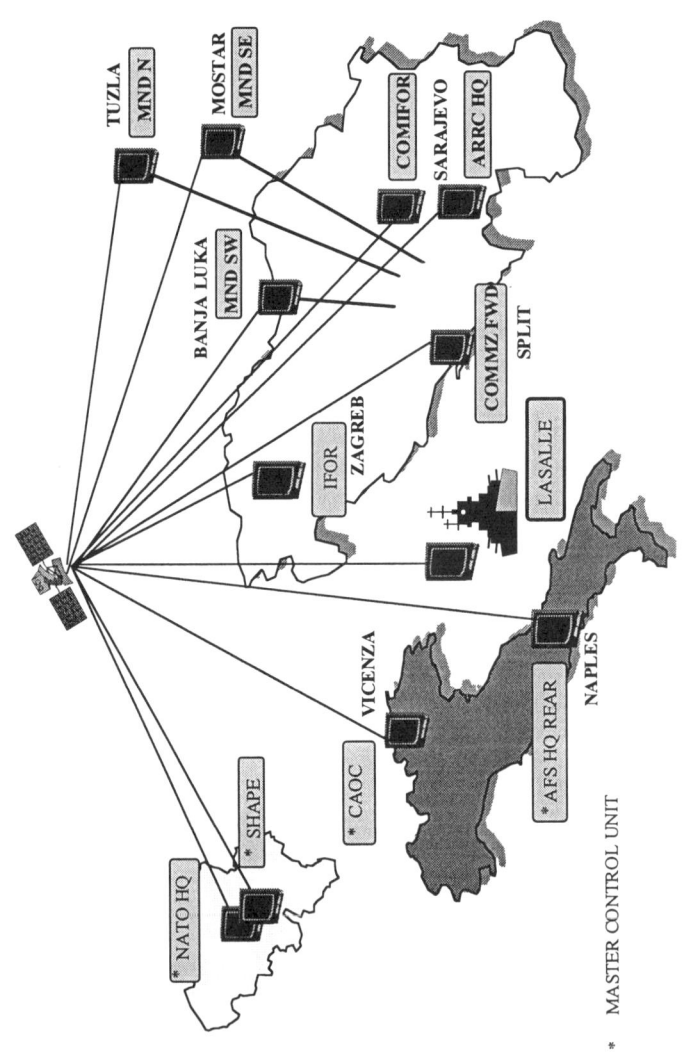

Figure 11-11. IFOR VTC Network

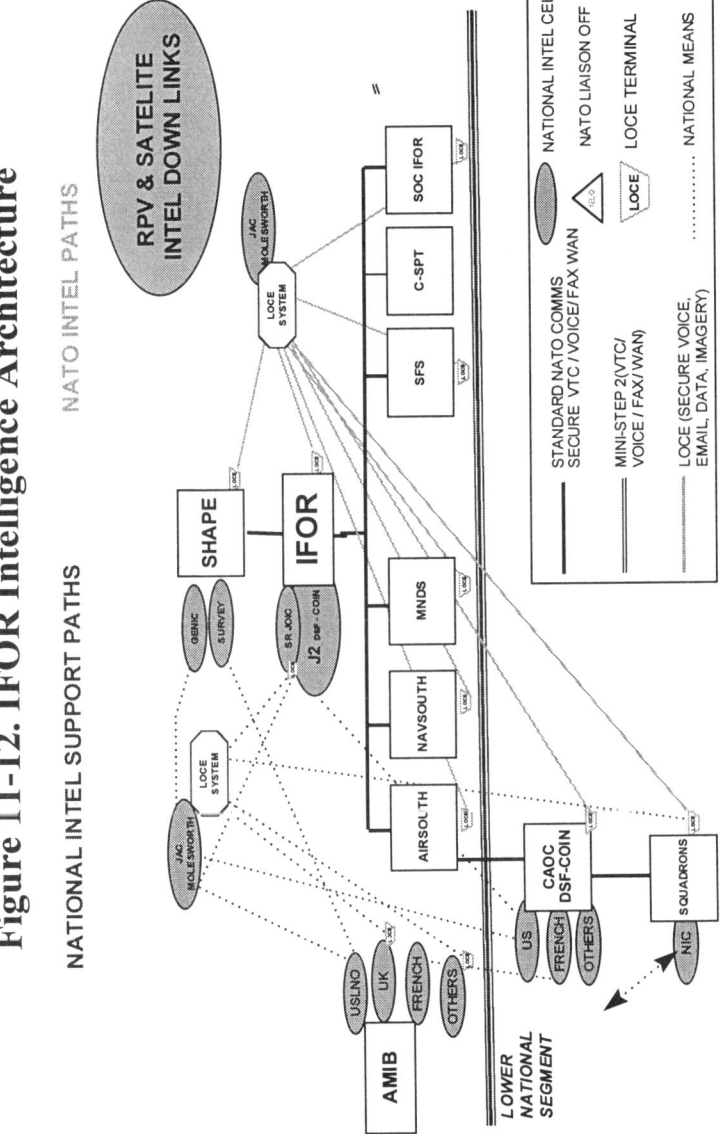

Figure 11-12. IFOR Intelligence Architecture

via the LOCE system. They also helped to clarify requests (language differences) from members of their national forces deployed in theater. The national representatives had direct communications access to their national intelligence sources for obtaining additional information to respond to specific requests from the theater and to add to the LOCE database for use by IFOR in general. The ICC was essentially a coalition "intelligence help desk." The LOCE network provided the means for initiating the requests and disseminating the packaged results, including populating the LOCE servers with national data released to IFOR.

The multinational coalition operation, which included members from non-NATO countries, required the establishment of an IFOR Releasable category for classified information to be shared with IFOR and its partners in the operation. In terms of sharing, the United States extended access to some of its national intelligence capabilities, such as ASAS WARLORD workstations, to units assigned to MND(N) like the Russian brigade.

IFOR Air, Naval, and Special Operations Support

CIS support for air and naval operations remained in place following *Deny Flight*, *Decisive Force*, and *Sharp Guard* and did not require special efforts to integrate them into the IFOR operation. Although a reserve force was never allocated to IFOR, the Marine Expeditionary Unit offshore remained an option and had to be considered in the development of the CIS architecture. The Special Operations Forces CIS support consisted of both IFOR and nationally provided C4ISR capabilities. For example, the Joint Special Operations Task Force, also known as the Special Operations Command IFOR, located on the San Vito Air Station in Italy had a number of different C4ISR systems serving the operation. They had IFOR and national voice, message, and data services including for the United States, both collateral and SCI LANs for access to national capabilities. They had access to LOCE. U.S. systems such as JDISS, ASAS-Warrior, TRRIP, SOFPARS,

JSTARS, TIBS, and SOCRATES METOC were provided. In fact, there was a significant overlap in capabilities deployed to support SOCIFOR operations.

IFOR Non-NATO Nations Support

The non-NATO troop contributing nations did not have direct access to the IFOR CIS network. In order to facilitate communications between and among NATO and the non-NATO troop contributing nations (e.g., Austria, Czech Republic, Hungary, Russia, and others) who supported the IFOR operation, it was necessary to set up a special network using the public switched network. The U.S. supplied secure telephones (KY-71E) so that these nations and NATO could communicate securely either by voice or fax. In order to participate in the IFOR operation, the non-NATO units were required to provide funding and security assurances to NATO and to allocate their units to one of the IFOR MNDs.

IFOR Election Network

The High Representative, Mr. Carl Bildt, stated that free and open access to the media had to be provided as one of the 12 conditions for establishing a framework for free and fair national elections. Very few independent broadcasting stations were operational in Bosnia with virtually all of them being controlled by either the governments or entities. To circumvent this, two projects were considered: (1) a nationwide television broadcasting network called the Open Broadcast Network and (2) an FM broadcasting network called the Free Elections Radio Network (FERN). Both the Republika Srpska and Federation governments were unwilling to cooperate. Of the two projects, only the FERN was implemented. The project was realized mainly due to the drive of the Swiss government and the Office of Security and Cooperation in Europe, for which Switzerland was chairman. To implement FERN, IFOR compounds were used since other locations for transmitters were most likely mined. In addition, the UN had experienced theft problems for radio sites that were not provided force protection. HQ IFOR, CJCCC, CIMIC, and IIC personnel were also utilized extensively for consulting, obtaining site access permissions, and verifying coverage patterns, frequency management support, and other services. In support of the elections, IFOR was responsible for protecting the election supervisors and IPTF personnel. As noted earlier, to accommodate this requirement ARRC communications personnel patched together a nationwide VHF Motorola network using IPTF, UN, and their own assets—if a nationwide cellular telephone network had existed in Bosnia, it would have been possible to provide communications to all election monitors.

IFOR Security Considerations

Security for the IFOR CIS network was provided through the use of approved NATO and national security devices. The CRONOS, LOCE, Tactical Voice, ADAMS, and VTC networks operated SECRET system high. STU-IIB secure voice units were available for use over the non-secure UN VSAT and PTT networks and on INMARSAT. Although the information networks were operated system high, other information protection measures, including network-level virus protection and intrusion detection and protection, were slow in implementation.

COMSEC management proved to be a challenge. Two theater distribution accounts had to be established to provide COMSEC support to IFOR forces—one to support Italy-based operations and one to support forces deployed to Croatia and Bosnia. The purpose of the accounts was to issue NATO material to those units who had no national distribution pipeline established in theater, to issue NATO crypto to national accounts, and to support national distribution in the event that national pipelines were not able to issue NATO cryptos to their deployed units. Normally crypto distribution is via the national pipelines to national units only. National regulations prohibit the issue of NATO crypto to other nations. The establishment of the special accounts was an attempt to streamline the process and ensure that cryptos would be distributed in a multinational environment to NATO users. STU-IIBs were used to electronically distribute key material. This worked reasonably well but was limited by the availability of data transfer devices and the quality of the Croatian and Bosnian phone lines. In the future, NATO needs one crypto pipeline that is capable of distributing NATO crypto throughout the force; can electronically transfer key material; is rapid and secure; and can ensure that the key will get to where it needs to go.

IFOR Network and System Management

In order to pull the CIS planning, implementation, and management together, the IFOR CJ6 established a new organizational element, the CJCCC, to work with NACOSA, the ARRC G6, the MND G6s, the C-Support G6, and the national control centers (figure 11-13). The CJCCC (first located in Zagreb, Croatia, and then moved to AFSOUTH headquarters in Naples, Italy) was also responsible for managing the IFOR theater-level CIS network. NACOSA (located in Mons, Belgium, at SHAPE headquarters) had the responsibility for managing the NATO strategic-level CIS network. The Kester, Belgium, NATO satellite control center supported NACOSA in the management of the NATO IV satellite system. There were overlaps in the responsibilities of the CJCCC and NACOSA because of the blurring of the boundary between strategic- and theater-level systems. These differences needed to be sorted out early in the operation but the SHAPE/AFSOUTH C2 differences precluded this happening quickly.

The CIS organizational elements supporting the IFOR operation exceeded 4,000 personnel at the peak of the operation and the CJCCC alone approached 300 personnel. The CJCCC and IFOR CJ6 set up operation in Zagreb in early December 1995 but the IFOR CJ6 moved to Naples in January 1996. The CJCCC did not move to Naples until May 1996 where it managed the theater CIS network for the rest of the IFOR operation. On 4 November 1996, command of the CJCCC was transferred from AFSOUTH to LANDCENT in preparation for the 7 November TOA from AFSOUTH/IFOR to LANDCENT/IFOR and the TOA of the ARRC

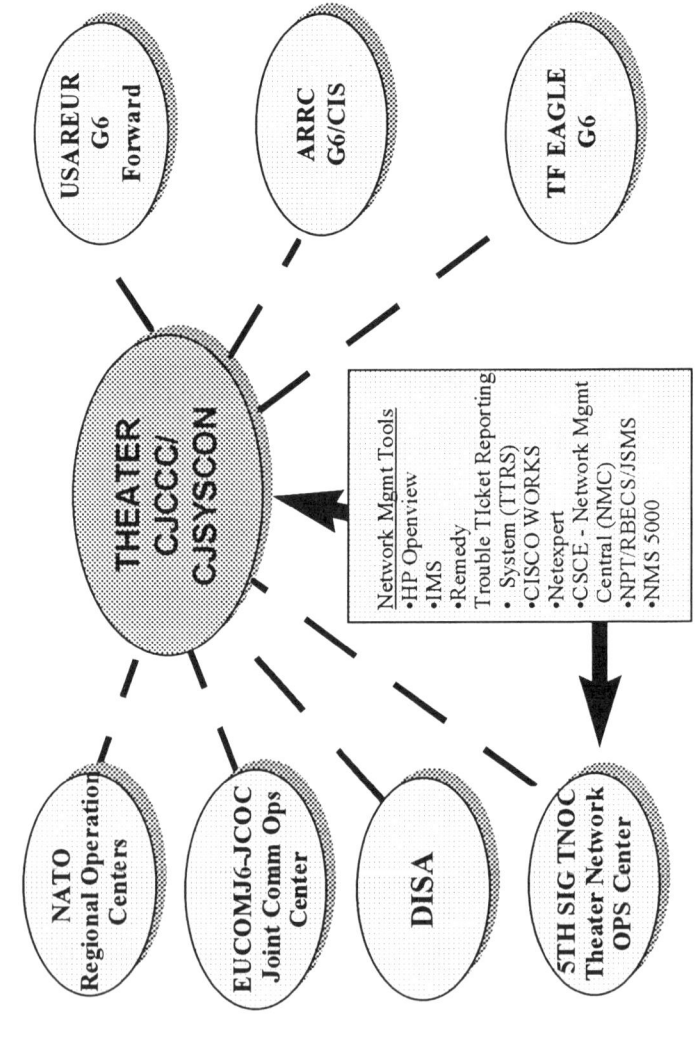

Figure 11-13. Network Management

to LANDCENT/IFOR on 20 November. On 20 December 1996, TOA from IFOR to SFOR was accomplished and as part of this transfer, plans were initiated to move the SFOR CJCCC to Sarajevo. The CJCCC was subsequently renamed the Communications Information Systems Control Center (CISCC) and moved to Ilidza to be collocated with SFOR headquarters.

In response to the Dayton Accord frequency management tasking to IFOR, a Theater Frequency Management Cell (TFMC) was established in Zagreb at the outset of the operation. The cell deployed from Naples with little information on units to be supported, their number (ORBAT), their locations, their requirements, or their equipment in theater. The only available database was that of ongoing operations for *Deny Flight* and other UN missions. There was no information on the available spectrum and no Status of Forces Agreement. UN units transferred to IFOR were already using frequencies and would either continue to use them or change to other frequencies because of location changes and operations under different commands. The Sarajevo area also presented a problem because of the large concentration of units and associated communications equipment. The ARRC colocated its Field Management Office with the TFMC to coordinate and manage the frequency requirements in BiH for all land forces. The TFMC used automated tools provided by the United States and NATO. A TFMC Forward was eventually established in Sarajevo to act as the agent for day-to-day coordination within BiH and with the ethnic factions. The TFMC and ARRC FMO were relocated to Naples with the CJCCC move in May 1996. Over time, the TFMC was able to manage the use of the spectrum quite well. Most of the problems faced were caused by the lack of information on unit deployments, by organizations not being aware of the TFMC and the need to coordinate with it, by poor planning, and by late entries of frequency requests. On the civil side, there were problems because the RS was using Belgrade as their recognized frequency management authority, not the BiH. For instance, Belgrade TV was being relayed illegally by RS transmitters. Also, the records of stations operating in BiH were inaccurate—few stations listed were still in operation, and many of the ones that were in operation weren't registered.

Logistic support under OPLAN 40104 was conceived as being a combined operation but because of national difficulties, it evolved into framework nations supporting their own forces and those allocated to them. Thus, the role of the Commander for Support became one of coordination and deconfliction and required changes to the CIS concept. A dedicated CIS logistics organization was established based upon the Southern Region Communications Logistics Depot in Lago Patria, Naples, which executed all logistical requirements in conjunction with forward sites in Zagreb and Sarajevo. Air transportation was provided by the IFOR shuttle flights and was a key element in the CIS logistic plan.

U.S. C4ISR Systems and Service

The C4ISR infrastructure provided by the United States to its deployed forces exceeded current Army doctrine. Capabilities included TRI-TAC/MSE, commercial telephone services at every base camp, and both secure and non-secure data network services at all base camps. MSE to DSN connectivity (more than 3 million calls completed), single channel TACSAT (supported operational, administrative, and logistic networks), INMARSAT for worldwide commercial telephone access, facsimile at base camps, and VTC to brigade headquarters were also provided. The MCS (Maneuver Control System), the ASAS WARLORD (intelligence), the WAN/LAN networks using Windows NT servers, and MSE communications connectivity formed the backbone information system for the division in MND(N). MCS was distributed to every major subordinate command element including the multinational units assigned to the division. The presence of MCS at each brigade level of command made the dissemination of information such as FRAGOs and OPORDs timely and efficient. MCS was also capable of providing multiple broadcasts of information to several C2 nodes using its

FTP capability. MCS was, however, somewhat complicated and not particularly user friendly. Furthermore, because of the inflexibility of its tools (e.g., mapping and word processing) to tailor the capabilities to meet needs particular to this mission, it was used predominantly as a communications hub rather than in its traditional role as a maneuver C2 system.

The U.S. communications and information systems deployment set a new standard for division and below. Doctrinally, only the brigade and separate battalions had voice and data capabilities. During the operation, all base camps had this capability and, in some instances, remote camps for isolated companies had the same level of support.

The 5th Signal Command was fully deployed by mid-March, with almost 700 personnel in country. *Operation Joint Endeavor* used the entire USAREUR theater-level multi-channel tactical satellite and large switch assets and still required augmentation with USAFE and commercial satellite and switching equipment.

U.S. Data and Messaging Services

Most of the messaging requirements, both administrative and C2, were satisfied with unclassified TCP/IP Internet-like networks connected with routers and hosts. E-mail could and did carry AUTODIN messages. Classified traffic was handled through AUTODIN and SIPRNET to TPN to C2 systems such as STACCS, MCS, and SIPR LAN servers at major headquarters (figure 11-14).

Especially innovative was the use of the IDNX equipment, routers (CISCO Series), NES, and other COTS technology to establish a network that provided Internet, NIPRNET, and SIPRNET access via the TPN to every base camp. The 5th Signal Command anticipated that the data needs of the operation would exceed the capabilities of the TPN planned and that it would be necessary to augment the TPN. The 5th Signal Command developed and deployed the Deployable Automation Support Host (DASH) to the U.S. NSE at Kapsovar, Hungary, to facilitate the augmentation of the TPN. The DASH included NIPRNET and SIPRNET routers,

324 *Lessons from Bosnia*

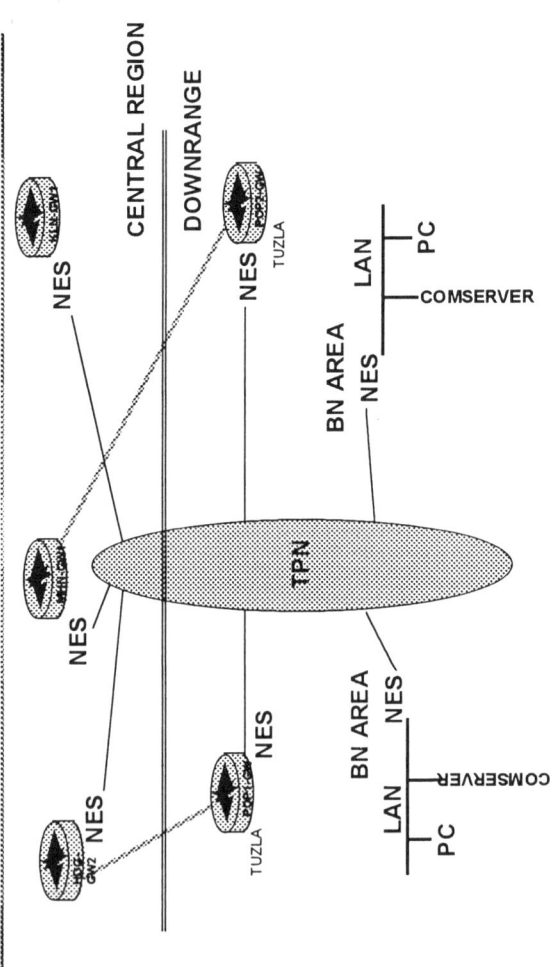

Figure 11-14. TPN/NES
Network Encryption System (NES)
(for 17 Battalion Areas)

hubs, direct-connect/high-speed modems, cables, small routers, TTAs, and other equipment and installer kits necessary to support implementation.

A POP router network augmented the DASH and incorporated both dial-up and LAN subscribers. The routers were networked through 56kb/s links. The POP and DASH router network was interfaced to the Common User Data Network (CUDN) via 256kb/s access links (figure 11-15). The CUDN provided NIPRNET connectivity to Army customers in Germany. Through CUDN gateways to NIPRNET, the deployed users had access to the worldwide NIPRNET, including access to the commercial Internet. The transportable command post, the MSQ-126 (borrowed from CINCPAC assets), was deployed to Supply Area Harmon in Slavinski Brod, Croatia, and provided NIPRNET access through a 128kb/s link with the Heidelberg, Germany, gateway node. USAREUR (FWD) in Taszar, Hungary, was provided access to the Heidelberg gateway through a POP router and 256kb/s link.

The POP router network employed the use of the NES to encrypt unclassified but sensitive traffic for transmission over the SECRET high TPN, thus protecting the TPN SECRET accreditation. The use of NES obviated the need for firewalls to allow unaccredited systems (e.g., used to overcome systemic problems of STAMIS accreditation) processing unclassified data to traverse the classified network, the TPN. The capability was fielded with nearly every Small Extension Node down to battalion level. Hence, the POP and DASH capabilities provided deployed users with a wide area network access through an Internet Protocol environment— another *Joint Endeavor* success story.

In the dynamic environment of *Joint Endeavor*, users arrived with a variety of operating systems and e-mail clients and different methods for accessing the network (e.g., dial-in and LAN). The Post Office Protocol-3 compliant server proved to be the most flexible and universal mail server standard available to deal effectively with the mix of capabilities deployed. Although this capability was not used for mail access, it was being considered for use in the future.

326 Lessons from Bosnia

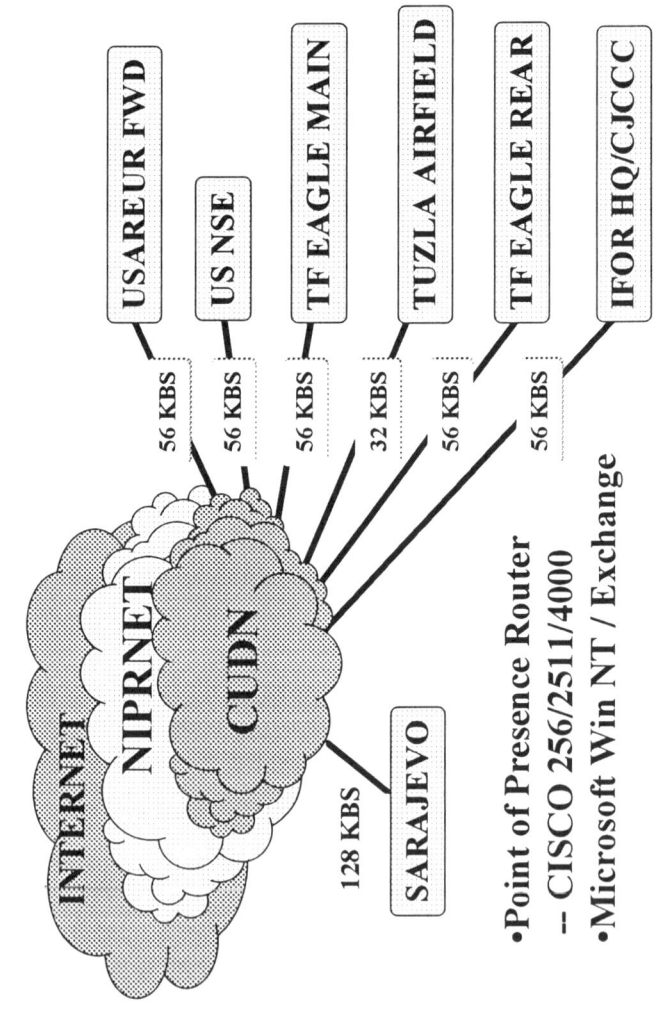

Figure 11-15. CUDN

U.S. Video Teleconferencing Service

The United States deployed two different VTC networks (figure 11-16) to support U.S. needs—an SCI level for intelligence operation use and a collateral level for V CORPS. VTC became the command and control system of choice, especially for the U.S. Army. LTG Abrams (Command, V CORPS and USAREUR (FWD)), the Commander MND(N) and Task Force Eagle, and the three allied brigades were tied together over the U.S.-provided VTC network prior to the NATO system coming on-line. LTG Abrams, who pioneered the active use of VTC in theater, pushed this particular arrangement. He created a "virtual headquarters" that linked the ISB in Hungary with the rear area operations in Germany (four locations) and CONUS, as well as with Task Force Eagle, its brigades, and the Sava river crossing site. The combination of e-mail, the file transfer of PowerPoint slides, and the VTC to discuss both command and staff decisions was a look into the future of a "virtual" command post, a key element of command posts of the future. LTG Abrams stated that e-mail and VTC made the difference in a successful deployment and execution in Bosnia. He compared them to the use of TACSAT and GPS (Global Positioning System) in *Desert Shield/Storm*.

U.S. Reach-Back Service

The use of an Army-provided Reach-Back capability to the Central Region proved effective in providing access to a broader range of voice and information services available through gateways with the U.S. strategic network, the Defense Information Infrastructure. The capability provided good access to Army activities in the Landstuhl, Kaiserslautern, Mannheim, and Heidelberg areas where a lot of the deployed active duty forces came from. It also served the needs of a large number of the CONUS-based deployed forces,

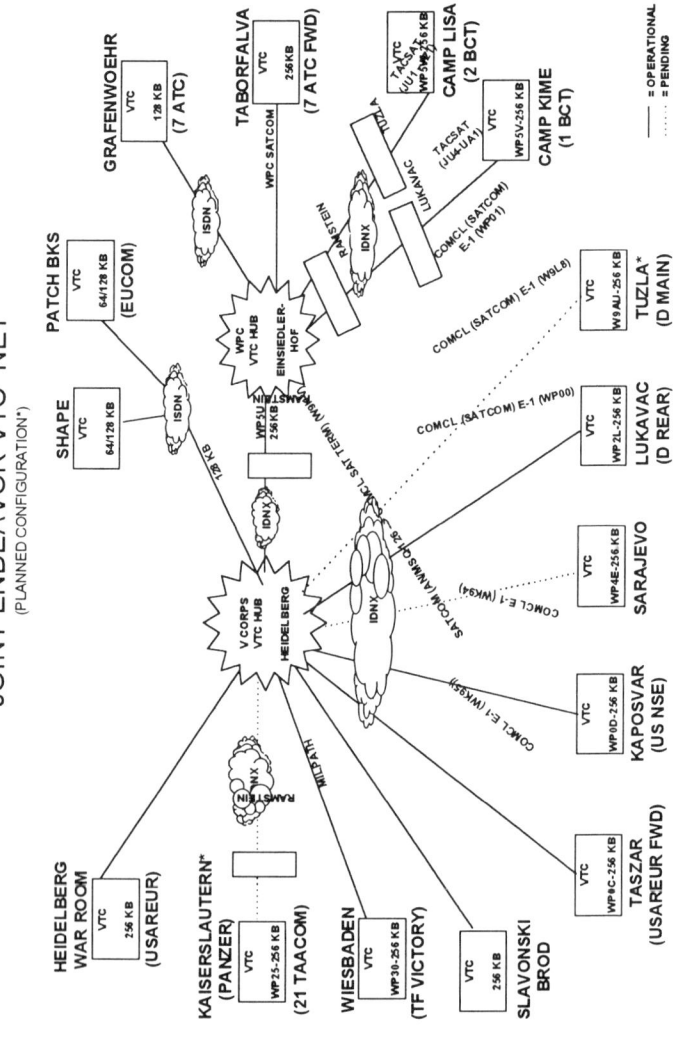

Figure 11-16. U.S. VTC Network JOINT ENDEAVOR VTC NET (PLANNED CONFIGURATION*)

such as the Civil Affairs and PSYOPS units. There was also a single-node Air Force Reach-Back capability to Ramstein AB, Germany.

The Army Reach-Back nodes (figure 11-17) were set up in Germany several days prior to the deployment of the tactical equipment to Bosnia, Croatia, and Hungary. Upon arrival in country, the first priority was to establish connectivity with the Reach-Back nodes. Tactical satellite assets were used for this purpose and enough assets were also deployed to ensure that dual and triple connectivity could be established to other TRI-TAC switches as well. The tactical networks were interconnected with the U.S. strategic network at three locations in Germany—Heidelberg, Mannheim, and Kaiserslautern. At the peak of the operation there were 228 trunks connecting the tactical voice network to the Defense Switched Network (DSN) alone.

Other U.S.-Provided C4 Services

The Global Positioning System (GPS) continued to be an important military capability and was used for marking of the IEBL and the ZOS, vehicle tracking, asset tracking, and precision navigation and position identification.

At the outset of *Operation Joint Endeavor*, almost every Air Mobility Command location reported inadequate communications capability to include the transmission of classified information. The operating units at both Rhein-Main and Ramstein ABs, Germany, were unable to communicate with the CAOC in Vicenza, Italy, on a required basis during the first several weeks of the operation. This resulted in frustration, as tasking was not received in a timely manner. Questions concerning missions and/or operations could not always be answered directly without extended delays. For example, at Vicenza it took weeks to get a STU-III in the Regional Air Movement and Coordination Center (RAMCC). The RAMCC also did not have a classified e-mail capability. The working environment needed to safeguard operationally sensitive information, especially when participating in combined operations.

330   *Lessons from Bosnia*

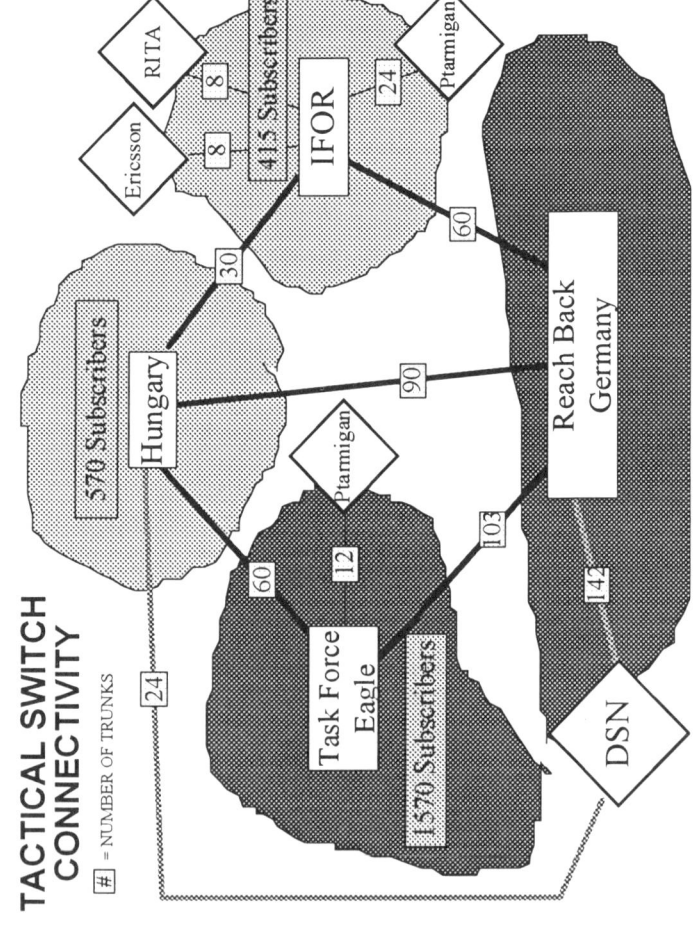

Figure 11-17. Reach-Back Capability

The Air Force C2 systems, the Global Decision Support System (GDSS), and the C2 Information Processing System (C2IPS) were undergoing upgrades when the operation was initiated. The systems were neither reliable nor user friendly. There were problems with the old and the new GDSS passing information to the old and new C2IPS. Some of the basic flight information was passed between systems, but remarks and comments were not. As a result, information about mission success, diversions, and cargo delivery was not always passed. The deployed operators also lacked adequate training to update and use the C2 systems and there were not enough trained personnel present and designated for ensuring that data was entered correctly and updated regularly.

Additionally, AMC resources were diverted from mission-specific tasks when duplicate requests for information were received from numerous agencies. There was a perception that the information being requested was for general information briefings and not decision making. For example, a request for a certain piece of information concerning aircraft reliability may have been pursued by three different divisions within the same directorate at AMC headquarters, as well as the TACC, the Air Staff and Joint Staff, and a variety of other organizations from the theater and throughout the DoD. As a result, deployed and headquarters personnel spent a great deal of time gathering and disseminating data and information instead of running the operation. This was a problem that was not unique to the Air Force but was pervasive across all IFOR and national organizational elements. Information requests must be managed carefully because they have the potential to grow and become more than just a burden on a given staff or organization.

The Air Force Mission Support System (AFMSS) was deployed to Rhein-Main AB. The AFMSS consisted of a deployable ground mission planning system and a portable system. The ground system was used for aircraft flight planning at the main operating base and the portable laptop system was used to plan missions at remote locations. The system deployed to Rhein-Main supported C-17 operations into Bosnia, including President Clinton and Secretary of Defense William Perry's visits to Bosnia. The C-17 crews planned and built their missions, downloaded the information, and then loaded it into the C-17's onboard computer. The aircrews cut the mission planning time to less than an hour. The use of high-resolution imagery and digital terrain elevation data allowed aircrews to fly their missions on the computer. The system also provided airfield orientation, high terrain, and threat awareness and tactics analysis. AMC's Tanker Airlift Control Center used charts and maps produced by the AFMSS system at AMC headquarters to plan the initial routes used in the Bosnia airlift operation. AMC aircrews used AFMSS in daily operations between Rhein-Main and Bosnia. Additional support was given in providing joint operations graphics and charts to the JSTARS operations.

The late and somewhat fragmented arrival of the Army Combat Service Support (CSS) elements, coupled with the arriving users being unprepared to set up their communications and automation equipment (the long-haul communications at the NSE were up and operating), put them at a disadvantage at the outset. March and April 1996 were spent establishing support areas and finally in May the logistics communications were established, supply support areas became operational, and supply backlogs were diminished. The Standard Army Management Information Systems (STAMIS), such as SAMS, ILAP, SARSS, SIDPERS, SPBS-R, ULLS, TAMMIS, and SAAS, supported the operation. Logistics also became a proving ground for advanced technology and concepts for developing automated systems to support force projection. Systems such as Total Asset Visibility (TAV), Intransit Visibility (ITV), Automated Manifesting System (AMS), Objective Supply Capability (OSC), Exportable Logistics System (ELS), and others were deployed to help improve the operation. An interesting Internet aspect was the use of the World Wide Web by ITV to determine locations of parts shipped in containers marked with RF tags. The ITV Home Page allowed managers to use a requisition query process imbedded in the Website. This helped managers estimate when parts arrived, thus preventing duplicate requisitions and setting priorities for receipt processing on arrival. The downside of deploying the prototype information systems was that the advanced technology outpaced the ability of the O/M support force to maintain the systems. The systems were also subject to environmental and human vulnerabilities that influenced their ability to provide reliable service, e.g., RF tags and bar codes missing, unauthorized software loads, untrained personnel trying to fix problems, freezing temperatures, high humidity, dust, and dirt.

U.S. ISR Systems and Services

U.S. intelligence, surveillance, and reconnaissance (ISR) support was the best that could be provided anywhere in the world. The United States leveraged its SIGINT, CI, HUMINT, OSINT, IMINT, and MASINT disciplines and capabilities and brought both its operational and advanced technology prototype systems to bear to provide the commander with "Information Dominance." Also key to the operational success was the contribution of many different intelligence organization elements—EUCOM J2; the analysis centers such as the JAC, UCIRF, and FOSIF; support activities such as the NICs and the National Intelligence Support Teams; and the CI/HUMINT teams on the ground in country to name a few.

Historically, weather has had a significant impact on military operations and *Operation Joint Endeavor* was no exception. The Balkans lacked a modern meteorological system and indigenous weather data was sparse. The 7th Weather Squadron and USAREUR weather staff provided accurate, timely, and relevant weather intelligence. The SWO provided numerous briefings and products that included satellite weather imagery of the Central Region and the area of operation, 24- and 48-hour forecasts, and weather impacts on operations. Thanks to the use of a German satellite communications weather broadcast system, the amount of real-time useful weather data to the troops in the field was the best in the history of the U.S. military. Weather personnel were deployed to IFOR, the ARRC, USAREUR (FWD), MND(N), and several base camps, but lacked sufficient manning to provide observers to other key locations. Remote weather support required more reliable communications from both the Air Force and Army to ensure climatologic data was received by supported units.

The JWICS (Joint Worldwide Intelligence Communications System), JMICS (Joint Military Intelligence Communications System), and Trojan Spirit systems were used to extend wide-band intelligence services into theater supporting SCI and collateral secure voice, data, facsimile, video, secondary imagery dissemination, and other intelligence-oriented information services. The Trojan Spirit extended 128kb/s service to the brigade level, 32 to 64kb/s for SIPRNET, and the remaining bandwidth for JWICS (DISNET-3) and for secure telephones. This in itself was a success story. It was not, however, envisioned that Trojan Spirit would be used to support a broader set of C3I needs. The capability was limited in the number of terminals and capacity per terminal and was really designed as an intelligence community asset. INTELINK and LOCE information networks were used to support intelligent dissemination of intelligence and other information. The U.S. INTELINK and INTELINK-S also provided Internet-like Web services and Netscape browser tools to facilitate collaboration, coordination, and search capabilities for improved information retrieval and dissemination.

The JDISS, DISE, TRRIP, and other intelligent workstations provided access to a core set of intelligence databases and applications. JDISS was the theater link to the rest of the intelligence world. TRAP, TIBS, and TRIXS broadcast and intelligence exchange services were provided. The ASAS-WARLORD workstations that supported all source data processing and manipulation formed the backbone of the division intelligence architecture and were used extensively. Access to ASAS-WARLORD was provided to the NORDIC and Russian brigades and the Turkish battalion supporting MND(N). UAVs, such as Predator and Pioneer, were used extensively for monitoring important areas of interest. NATO AWACS, JSTARS, U2, and other capabilities were employed to provide information that could be used to demonstrate to the FWF that they could be seen any time of the day or night and under all weather conditions. The message was clearly sent to the FWF that compliance would be closely monitored and enforced by IFOR.

There were innovative uses of deployed capabilities to meet operational needs. For example, the AH-64 gun camera tapes were processed through the MITT, which is normally a CORPS-level asset but was deployed to the division for this operation. Using the MITT frame-grabber capability and annotation software, it was possible to select an image or frame and exploit the still image. Hence, exploited unclassified images could be produced within 12 hours and given to the allies and the FWF. It was easy to convince the FWF to move tanks out of the ZOS when you could show them a clear picture with the AH-64 crosshairs on the side of the tank. Interestingly, in a 1992 Army after action report for *Desert Storm* it was noted that better use should be made of the helicopter gun cameras for intelligence purposes in support of the ground commander. It took a couple of innovative enlisted men several years later on the ground in Bosnia to recognize and use the new technology deployed for other purposes in a different way to bring it to a reality. The capability was also used with Combat Camera footage and amateur handheld video camera tapes.

Timely transmission of Combat Camera and CI/HUMINT digital camera products and the integration of these products into the information operations network were challenges faced early in the operation. Adjustments had to be made to accommodate these needs. One of these adjustments was the integration of the U.S. CI/HUMINT commercial notebook computer-based data acquisition, management, and communications system into the SIPRNET. The capability is referred to as TRRIP (Theater Rapid Response Intelligence Package). Linking the U.S. MSE network with the SIPRNET via Trojan Spirit provided connectivity to the battalion level for TRRIP users and significantly enhanced the operational effectiveness of the CI/HUMINT teams—a real success story. MSE in MND(N) was also linked to SIPRNET via the reach-back locations and this offered an opportunity to access a much greater capacity than the Trojan Spirit linking.

Another innovation based on commercially developed and available technology occurred in February 1996, when the CI/HUMINT team in Tuzla realized that the TRRIP too could play a role in exploiting Apache gun camera and other video sources to obtain images for the brigade commanders. By using the SNAPPY commercial freeze-frame product plugged into the back of the TRRIP, they could view video and do frame grabbing. The TRRIP lash-up did not have the annotation capabilities of the MITT but it could give the commanders snapshots of violations or other insights that they could then use with the FWF or otherwise. In this case, several SNAPPYs (high 8 video cameras, small-screen viewers, batteries, a freeze-frame printer, and power packs) were purchased by OSD(C3I) Office of Special Technology and provided to CI/HUMINT teams within 1 week of identifying the requirement. This COTS solution significantly enhanced the CI/HUMINT team capability at the brigade and battalion levels.

There were numerous other strategic and tactical ISR and communications capabilities deployed to support intelligence operations. Many of the systems deployed were stand-alone, and it was not clear to personnel in theater whether adequate consideration had been given to the integration of these capabilities in the operational environment. Division personnel felt that the burden of integration was placed on the units rather than having been done in advance of deployment as part of an integrated intelligence architecture. As a result, there were duplications and inefficient use of scarce bandwidth. This situation also contributed to training, maintenance, and logistic support problems as well as system performance and responsiveness to user needs. Furthermore, there was no one computer system that effectively balanced power, flexibility, and user-friendliness. The units had to determine the best machine to build a particular database on and the best format to put it in.

Bandwidth Limitations

In spite of the enhanced capabilities and broadband systems extended into theater, the warrior on the ground and on the move was still operating in the range of kb/s. Some were getting access to 64kb/s but most were still limited to something less than this and in many cases had to operate in the 2.4kb/s to 9.6kb/s range. The JSOTF2 was allocated 32kb/s access, which in their assessment was insufficient to meet the intelligence systems communications needs. The Task Force Eagle G2 After Action Review noted that the MSE was not powerful enough to handle the division intelligence dissemination needs and this impacted their production and dissemination operations. The Task Force's 26 WARLORD terminals were interconnected via the MSE packet switch network. The graphic presentations, maps, and images produced could not be easily disseminated to the brigades over this network because the interconnecting communications pipes were too small. Instead, the production method had to be tailored to meet dissemination needs. If products were to receive wide dissemination they would be produced in textual format to ease dissemination problems. If the products were to receive limited and specialized dissemination then graphics were the medium of choice. In either case, production and dissemination operations were being affected by the size of the communications pipes. DISA-Europe lessons learned also noted that the military tactical systems were unable to fully support the bandwidth demands (e.g., VTC, SIPRNET, NIPRNET, and telemedicine) and leased commercial service was the only way to provide the deployed commanders the same service they were used to in garrison. It was also necessary to use contractor personnel to fill the gap in trained military O&M personnel in country. The use of commercial products and contracted O&M personnel added training demands for both the military and the contractors.

U.S. Advanced Technology Systems

The advanced technology community stood poised to offer enhanced C4ISR capabilities for U.S. national and selected IFOR use. A wide range of the U.S. military's advanced technologies were deployed to the Bosnia theater which, among other capabilities, allowed the troops in MND(N) to electronically reconnoiter the landscape with a thoroughness that essentially allowed them to see day or night, in all weather, and in real time. The surveillance capabilities ranged from satellites in orbit to remote sensing devices buried in the ground, with an array of air and ground systems in between. If within an "area of interest" a phone call was made, a radio message was sent, or something moved on a Bosnia highway, the odds were it was known to the commanders and tracked by the systems.

Some of the advanced technologies were used before the IFOR deployment. For example, the PowerScene, a 3-D terrain visualization simulator (designed by Cambridge Research Assoc.) using computer-enhanced composites of satellite imagery, maps, and photographs, provided access to a "virtual Bosnia" that could be used to "fly" over the entire country and see realistic details down to one-meter resolution. The system was used for preflight rehearsals during the 1995 NATO bombing attacks and it was also a critical component of the Dayton peace talks. Tactically, the 1st AD used it to plan troop movements through a potentially hostile Bosnia countryside.

The Bosnia C2 Augmentation System/Joint Broadcast System (figure 11-18) was deployed in spring 1996 to provide improved wide-band connectivity and broadcast information services. These services accommodated intelligent push and pull of critical C2 information and services, such as intelligence, weather, broadcast news, and GCCS services to IFOR, the ARRC, and the MND headquarters. JBS was also used for real-time Predator video distribution.

The Army fielded the most advanced telemedicine system in history to provide medical care to U.S. forces in Bosnia, Croatia, and Hungary. The high bandwidth system supported applications

C4ISR Systems and Services 339

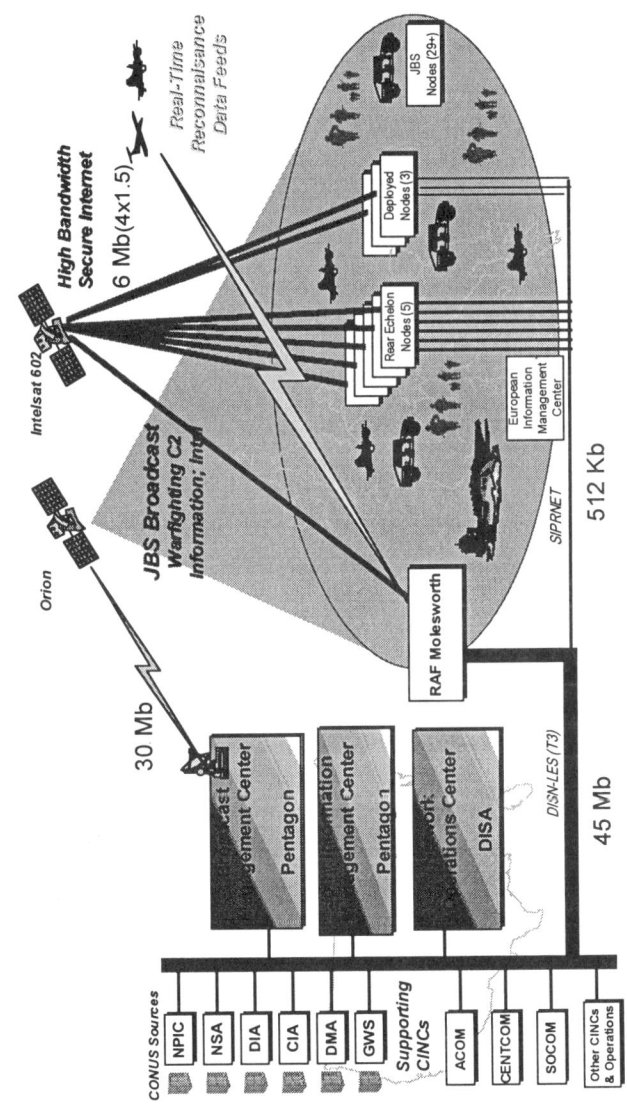

Figure 11-18. BC2A/JBS

such as telesurgery, telemedicine, telepsychology, and teledentistry. The Landstuhl Regional Medical Center in Germany, the Combat Support Hospital (CHS) in Tszar, Hungary, and the 212th Mobile Army Surgical Hospital (MASH) in Tuzla were linked to each other and to medical centers in the states. Internet access was also provided. It was reported by DISA that about 10 percent of the U.S.-provided bandwidth in the operational area was allocated to telemedicine activities. This focused attention on the need to reexamine the priorities for circuit preemption, since traditionally higher priority C2 and mission support users preempted telemedicine consultations either in progress or scheduled to temporarily restore failed circuits supporting their operations.

The Joint Total Asset Visibility (JTAV) system was another advanced capability deployed to Hungary and Bosnia to track assets on order from a supplier, in transit, or in storage. JTAV was not the only asset visibility system deployed. A system was developed by the Volpe Transportation Center that used RF tags and GPS, and the International Transportation Information Tracking (In-transit) system was also deployed. The Army also used a number of tiered logistics systems such as the Unit Level Logistic System, the Standard Army Retail-Level Supply System, and the Department of the Army Movement Management System.

U.S. Network and System Management

Network and system management was the glue that held all of the U.S. C4ISR pieces together. There were a number of different players on the U.S. side. The Joint Staff (J6Z) managed UHF and SHF SATCOM allocations and coordinated Joint Staff responses to CINC requests for additional contingency asset support. USEUCOM (J6) established a Joint Communications Operations Center to monitor and coordinate theater CIS activities. DISA-EUR managed the European theater Defense Information Infrastructure and extension of its capabilities such as DSN, NIPRNET, SIPRNET, and the IDNXs into Croatia and Bosnia. DISA and the Regional Space Support Center managed the DSCS satellite system. The DIA managed the Joint Worldwide Intelligence Communications System (JWICS) and its extension into the area of operation. USAFE established a network operations center in Ramstein, Germany, to manage Air Force assets supporting the operation. USAREUR/5th Signal Command managed the Reach-Back and the deployed voice, data, and VTC tactical networks from their Theater Network Operations Center (TNOC) in Mannheim, Germany. They were the principal provider of staff and expertise to the CJCCC and they also had network management capabilities and staff at USAREUR (FWD) in Hungary, Task Force Eagle in Bosnia, and other brigade and battalion network management operations. There were other organizations managing mission support systems for logistics, medical, personnel, and other activities. The intelligence community had a number of different organizations managing the numerous ISR systems and services supporting the operation, including the Joint Analysis Center in Molesworth, England, and the USAREUR Combat Intelligence Readiness Facility in Augsburg, Germany. Finally, DISA established a Joint Information Management Center in the Pentagon to manage the BC2A/JBS.

The Defense Information Systems Agency (DISA) reported that they processed more than 1,400 Telecommunications Service Order (TSO) requests for extension of Defense Information Infrastructure (DII) connectivity and services into the theater. Over 740 of these requests were urgent, with 400 of them being requested within the first month of the deployment.

Transfer of Authority—CIS Implications and Unintended Consequences

The redeployment of the ARRC was accompanied by the redeployment of the UK Signal Regiment (the United Kingdom was the framework nation supporting the ARRC) with its PTARMIGAN and IARRCIS CIS systems, including some other C2 capabilities. The U.S. TRI-TAC/MSE network was expanded to replace PTARMIGAN at the corps level and to provide connectivity to the

SFOR Multinational Forces. The IFOR CRONOS system replaced the IARRCIS as the C2 capability for SFOR. The EUROMUX system was deployed by the UK in MND(SW) to replace the PTARMIGAN system at the division level. The replacement of PTARMIGAN with the EUROMUX resulted in some interoperability problems between the EUROMUX and MSE and the TTC-39D that needed to be resolved. For example, at the conclusion of the IFOR operation, the EUROMUX interface to the U.S. systems was only working in one direction. Calls could be initiated from EUROMUX to the U.S. network intercept operator but calls could not be completed from the U.S. systems to EUROMUX. EUROMUX was a newer version of PTARMIGAN but with less functionality. EUROMUX had fewer switching capabilities than PTARMIGAN but was much more suitable for a smaller user base such as the new operation. The EUROMUX had an advantage over PTARMIGAN in that it was more modern and required much less manpower to operate. The SFOR configuration resulting from the redeployments is depicted in figure 11-19.

In addition to the withdrawal of the ARRC framework nation CIS systems (i.e., the UK PTARMIGAN and IARRCIS), the TOA to LANDCENT/SFOR also required some reconfiguration and redeployment of the IFOR-procured CIS infrastructure, some of which was destined for AFSOUTH's use. Part of the reconfiguration included accommodating the move of the headquarters SFOR from the annex at the Tito Residency to Ilidza and the modernization of the SFOR command center CIS support. Therefore, CIS equipment essential to the headquarters of the LANDCENT Component Commander and Commander SFOR had to be replaced in some cases and added to in other cases to meet SFOR requirements. In regard to the latter, the CRONOS local area network (LAN) established at the SFOR headquarters was extensive. Its LAN featured a 100mb/s backbone, 10mb/s links at the staff level, fiber optic links to the workstations, connections to 13 external wide area circuits, and a substantial population of workstations. Although most of the information distribution was by e-mail, automated data replication using the Public Folder tool and access via

C4ISR Systems and Services 343

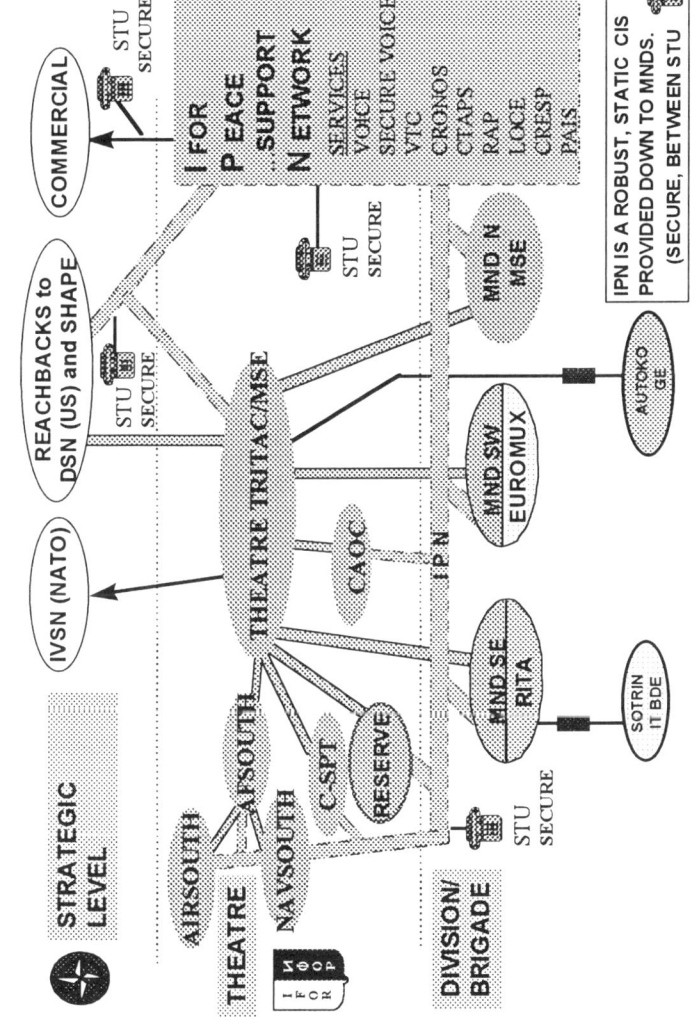

Figure 11-19. SFOR CIS Network

Web-based tools were also introduced. Expanded functionality for CRONOS applications such as PAIS and CRESP was included as well.

NATO HQ staff needed to be convinced that equipment already procured for IFOR could not be used in toto to meet LANDCENT/SFOR requirements. This raised the significant and ongoing challenge of equipment accountability. Despite the questions of eligibility, NATO common funding of CIS infrastructure was approved and procurement initiated to support the LANDCENT/SFOR requirements.

There were unintended consequences associated with the TOA to LANDCENT and the removal of the ARRC and the PTARMIGAN, IARRCIS, and other ARRC-provided CIS capabilities. EUROMUX and MSE did not entirely replace the functionality of PTARMIGAN. For example, there was no replacement for the PTARMIGAN secure voice conference capability and secure SCRA. The UK THISTLE system, which was used by the ARRC to build and distribute the ground order of battle, was pulled out. The ARRC's geographic support, which provided the map and boundary databases used by all IFOR command elements, was not removed but arrangements had to be made with the UK to lease the system to NATO. And finally, the CIS capabilities of the Allied Military Intelligence battalion were also impacted by the withdrawal of ARRC equipment. These capabilities either required replacement or enhancements to support the SFOR operation adequately. As a result, some confusion, difficulty, and expense caused a delay in providing minimum essential CIS to the new HQ SFOR in Sarajevo.

The TOA to LANDCENT/SFOR also had some unintended consequences for the U.S. military CIS providers. Since the commander LANDCENT/SFOR was also the commander USAREUR, it was necessary to provide additional CIS capabilities to support his national responsibilities. Some of the services that had to be extended to the new headquarters facility in Ilidza (outside of Sarajevo) were secure and nonsecure (including Internet) data network and e-mail services, extensions off the Red Switch in Stuttgart,

U.S. Secret mobile radio communications, and numerous DSN secure telephones. TACSAT and line-of-site communications, secure facsimile, U.S. television, and video teleconferencing were other capabilities that had to be provided. Simultaneously, Task Force Eagle downsized and transitioned from the 1st Armored Division to the 1st Infantry Division. The tactical network changed from the 22nd Signal Brigade and 141st Signal Battalion to the 121st Signal Battalion. The NATO and associated MND(N) downsizing (60,000 to 30,000 troops) and leadership change resulted in a major reconfiguration of the U.S. tactical satellite and switched network support to NATO throughout the area of operation as well.

Commercialization—A Key Player

Commercialization came in several forms. First, commercial products and services were used to augment the military systems deployed, as was the case with the IDNX and VSAT. In some cases, such as the NATO CRONOS network and U.S. NIPRNET and SIPRNET, they provided the strategic- and theater-level information services required for command and control operations. Commercial products and services were also an integral part of advanced technology capabilities deployed to theater, e.g., the U.S. BC2A/JBS information services and broadcast network. Commercialization played a role in the exit strategy when used as a means to replace tactical telecommunications systems with commercial capabilities such as the IPN for the IFOR telecommunications network and the Sprint contract to replace U.S. tactical systems in Hungary and Bosnia.

Use of commercial, off-the-shelf (COTS) desktop and laptop computers and use of Microsoft Office Professional and MS mail were crucial steps in achieving information standardization for the IFOR operation. Microsoft Mail was not a universal platform that lent itself well to a dynamic environment such as *Joint Endeavor* where different e-mail clients and operating systems were employed.

The only operating system that could be used to access Microsoft Mail remotely was Windows 95. Some users had to purchase Windows 95 so that they could access the system.

Information was easily exchanged using MS Word, PowerPoint, and Excel. MS Word was used by MND(N) to write FRAGOs, which were sent using FTP through the MCS to the subordinate commands. No comprehensive software users training was provided and so many operators had to learn on the job. Advanced training would have made it easier and faster for all users to learn MS Office Professional.

Using non-ruggedized hardware required special consideration. Daily cleaning and use of protective covers and power surge protectors were a must in the Bosnia environment. Handling of 3.5-inch diskettes and other removable data sources had to be done carefully as well. Disks needed to be kept clean to avoid loss of data. Double sources of storage when practical and disk covers and protective cases were also measures used.

The commercialization of IFOR communication systems was one of the goals for the overall improvement of the CIS architecture. The timing for withdrawal of the tactical systems was very much related to the success of the commercialization process. Tactical communications systems provided the advantages of mobility, flexibility, and security. Mobility and flexibility for communication systems became less important considerations as the operation continued and the headquarters remained almost entirely static. Security for the commercialized network could be met by means such as STU-IIBs for the voice network and operation of the secure data networks CRONOS and LOCE and the secure VTC network SECRET system high. Hence, it was possible to withdraw tactical systems once the commercial network was capable of satisfying the IFOR operational needs.

The military commercialization strategy must, however, take into account the disposition of the entity one plans to lease from or have a contractor operate in—both the political disposition (willingness) and the technical disposition (enough infrastructure to provide the service). PTT commercialization worked well in Croatia, but they were really "in the rear." In the Federation, the PTT was fairly cooperative, but didn't have the infrastructure. Contractor-provided service in these two areas worked fairly well, but was slow to deliver, especially since the bandwidth requirements were raised during and after acquisition of services. In the RS, nothing worked—PTT or contractor. Contractor support outside of IFOR compounds in RS areas was not obtainable because of lack of cooperation.

The IFOR plan for the commercialization of their communications network was also aimed at reducing the costs to NATO and reducing the IFOR dependence on the UN VSAT network. The plan was to install ERICSSON MD-110 digital switches at the major headquarters, expand the commercial VSAT/IDNX network, and lease E1 connectivity including cross-IBEL connectivity from the BiH and Croatian PTTs. The evolution of the commercial network, the IFOR Private (Peace) Network (IPN), was slower than IFOR would have liked. The main difficulties centered on the slow reconstruction of the BiH PTT infrastructure and the continued unwillingness of the FWF PTTs to provide cross-IEBL connectivity.

The United States also had major commercialization efforts in Taszar and Kaposvar, Hungary, and Tuzla, Bosnia. A 5th Signal Command contract with Sprint (supported by Lucent and MATAV) was used for this purpose. The voice part of the Taszar/Kaposvar effort was completed in two parts, approximately 50 percent in December 1996 allowing a return of 163 signal soldiers and the rest in February 1997 allowing the return of the remaining soldiers. The data part was finished in April 1997. The reduction in CIS personnel in MND(N) was a result of downsizing and to a lesser degree commercialization. The commercialization of seven base camps in Bosnia (completion scheduled for the spring of 1997) and the NATO force downsizing (about a 50-percent reduction) under *Operation Joint Guard* would contribute to a further reduction in the U.S. military CIS personnel in theater. It was estimated that the U.S. CIS military support personnel in country would be reduced from a high of more than 2,200 at the peak of the operation to just over 300 personnel upon completion of these actions.

There were some important lessons learned in the Army's commercialization efforts. First, the vendors could not respond quickly. One needs to plan on 120 days to contract and 5 to 6 months after that for the vendor to become fully operational. The problem is that vendors are not prepositioned or prepared to send mobile systems to operate in a field environment with an inadequate support structure. Second, the vendors are unable to hire technical personnel who are willing and able to match military personnel or DoD civilians in the field in technical expertise, dedication, and sense of urgency. This observation may run counter to conventional wisdom, but technical skills are in short supply in the workforce and commercial vendor personnel are not accustomed to the demands of the military in the field.

Contracting—Unexpected Challenges

NATO and national acquisition of products and services for use in the IFOR operation was not strictly centrally controlled, so there were inconsistencies in costs, spares, support arrangements, training, and documentation. For example, USAREUR did not coordinate its contracting with NAMSA (NATO Maintenance and Supply Agency), the NATO contracting authority in country; they used their own contracting officer. This required USAREUR contracting personnel to come from Germany and Hungary to accomplish the contracts mission when in-country NATO contracting officers could have accomplished the mission if an agreement with NATO had existed. There were few standing contracts to support contingency acquisitions. For example, at the outset DISA had a contract in place for use of the commercial space segment (the CSCI contract for transponder leasing). However, there was no DISA or other contract vehicle in place for providing earth terminals and for the installation of other equipment such as IDNXs, routers, and the O&M of installed equipment. The CSCI concept placed the responsibility for user access on the end users' CIS support organization. They were to provide the access arrangements such as a SATCOM terminal and access equipment to extend the service to the end user location.

Control of PTT costs was also a serious problem. There was no mechanism for logging commercial calls or recording usage of PTT access. Extensive operational use was made of available commercial PTT access. This was extremely expensive, but an essential way to do business, especially during the early phases of the operation. It is difficult to control the use of commercial PTT and prevent abuse, but some form of call logging and usage tracking would help.

Competitive bidding did not always realize the best product for price and in some cases did not work for IFOR. A lowest cost bid for a computer mouse bulk purchase resulted in the delivery of poor-quality equipment that failed after several weeks of use. A similar problem was experienced with the acquisition of tape for marking the minefield areas. It was also felt that the competitive bid for the NATO UHF TACSAT terminals led to different quality products (purchased 106 Harris PRC-117D and 106 Motorola LST-5E). The LST-5E narrow band performance was much better than the PRC-117D. In addition, the warranty repair cycle was much more responsive for the LST-5E (the theater experienced a period of 2 months of no spares for the PRC-117D before repaired sets were received through the warranty program, but did not have any spares problems for the LST-5E). Competitive bidding also did not necessarily work when dealing with the Serbs, since frequently there was only one source and price.

Vendor quality was also important, especially considering the environment in which IFOR operated. Vendor services and products did not always meet expectations. For some vendors, such as IEC, this was a new experience for them as well as NATO, so both were on a learning curve. NATO and national acquisition processes had to be streamlined in order to meet the time-sensitive needs of the deployment. Use of the U.S. FMS process was attempted to acquire IDNX equipment for NATO, but the process in the end proved to be too slow and cumbersome to achieve rapid acquisition. A contract between NATO and N.E.T. was used instead.

Spares and Repairs—A Steep Learning Curve

Providing spares was also an issue. Inadequate spares were purchased for equipment procured under emergency acquisitions. There were no Radio Shacks or Tandys in Bosnia to buy spare parts or other emergency off-the-shelf products. Vendor maintenance personnel of the right ethnic group did not always exist in the region of operation and special measures were necessary to get access to such personnel. Such a case was reported in MND(N) where a repairman was a Croatian and the U.S. military had to be used to get him through Serb territory to fix the equipment. In Bosnia, and the Sarajevo area in particular, all transactions were in cash and German DMs were preferred. Most vendors wanted hard cash up front and many preferred not to have formal contract arrangements.

Repair of commercial and military CIS equipment that failed in country presented some interesting challenges. Identification and evaluation of failed equipment was a problem, sometimes due to a lack of experience with the commercial equipment and in other cases due to inadequate training, documentation, and test equipment. There were warranty issues; for example, who does what repairs where? Most ADP equipment was under warranty and therefore no maintenance could be performed on it. Specific examples were computer hard drives and memory chips. Those used on SECRET LANs, for example, could not be sent back to the manufacturers for repair. For the LST-5E UHF TACSAT equipment, the antennas and handsets were not under warranty and could be repaired using operational spares; otherwise, the equipment had to be returned to Motorola for repair. There were issues related to getting the failed equipment out of theater to repair facilities and then back in country to the user, including tracking of the status of the repair process; shipping delays; repair turnaround time; and slow and often unreliable Customs processing. The repair turnaround times for assets under warranty were in many cases excessive and impacted mission capabilities.

Although USAREUR had done some thinking in advance of deployment, contractors as well as the military still found themselves on a steep learning curve once they deployed. There were issues related to where repair facilities should be located, e.g., at vendor repair facilities, at government repair facilities in Germany, at the Intermediate Staging Base in Hungary, or at facilities in Bosnia. The NATO supply system did not support NABS and TSSR equipment and special arrangements had to be made with the CJCCC to establish logistic support procedures. In this case, the equipment was sent to the 1st Combat Communications Squadron deployed in Tuzla, which then forwarded it to the Air Force repair facility at Ramstein AB, Germany. The U.S Army experienced problems with some 6,000 pieces of CIS equipment during the first 6 months of the deployment. These problems included software glitches, hardware failures, integration problems, crushed computers, dirty line printers, and computer mouse problems. Many of the issues were pervasive and difficult to solve in an operational environment.

Interoperability—Making Progress

Historically, interoperability has been one of the most difficult areas to deal with and this operation was no exception. Integration and interoperability of commercial and military systems were not always straightforward either. The IDNXs and VTCs required special interfaces with the military, PTT, and UN VSAT networks.

The analog-based STANAG 5040 was still the norm for interfacing strategic, theater, and tactical voice systems. The interface was slow, inefficient, and lacked functionality to effectively integrate the strategic and tactical voice networks to accomplish a true "system of systems." No digital interface existed for interfacing strategic and tactical digital networks. The TTC-39D experienced interface problems with the ERICSSON MD-110 switch used by the UN and IFOR. The Interim Digital Interface PTARMIGAN (IDIP) was designed by the United Kingdom specifically for this operation and was used to provide a more effective digital interface between the UK PTARMIGAN and the U.S. TRI-TAC/MSE tactical systems. Marc Space, a U.S. company, designed a special interface box to allow the PTARMIGAN store and forward to interface with the U.S TYC-39 tactical message switch—the interface was demonstrated at *INTEROP 95*. The EUROMMUX that replaced PTARMIGAN in the MND(SW) was not capable of accommodating a STANAG 5040 interface. Therefore, there were problems interfacing it with the TRI-TAC TTC-39D which replaced PTARMIGAN at the CORPS headquarters level (i.e., SFOR headquarters and its interfaces with the three MNDs) and the interface between MND(N) and MND(SW).

The IDNX deployment required the certification of some 50 different interface arrangements. There were no automated interfaces between the IFOR data networks (CRONOS, IARRCIS, and LOCE) and national data networks, such as the U.S. NIPRNET and SIPRNET. The CRONOS was not interfaced with LOCE or the ADAMS networks even though information was manually transferred between the systems. Network applications were not interoperable. The ADAMS movement control system and JOPES required a manual interface for exchanging information. The NATO and national intelligence systems were not directly connected and had to use manual exchanges to share information from one system to the other. For example, a correlation center was established at the JAC to populate the LOCE server with information from the United States, United Kingdom, France, and other national sources for distribution to IFOR elements. The STU-IIB, the NATO-approved secure voice equipment, was used extensively by IFOR, but a large number of the U.S. forces deployed to Bosnia with STU-IIIs that were not interoperable with the STU-IIB.

The U.S. intelligence processing system used at Echelons Above Corps (EAC) did not "talk" to the Echelons Corps and Below (ECB) systems such as JDISS. To fix the problem, an EAC processing system such as JDISS had to be deployed to ECB intelligence centers. The lack of connectivity between EAC and ECB systems was caused by security restrictions on certain intelligence information being processed with other kinds of intelligence information. Different levels of classifications and security accesses accompanied this information. Different kinds of intelligence data were compartmentalized and communicated to higher and lower users within their own stove-piped arrangements. This was a root cause of the proliferation of intelligence processing systems.

Liaison became a very important interoperability issue in IFOR. With 34 participating nations, it is easy to see that not all assigned personnel understood or spoke English, although English was the language of the operation. Therefore, liaison personnel were used to bridge the communications gap and facilitate coordination between organization elements. There were liaison cells in the CJCCC for representatives from the MNDs, ARRC, NACOSA, DISA, EUCOM, USAREUR, and USAFE. The intelligence and Special Operations Forces communities used and provided liaison personnel. The MNDs used liaisons with the forces assigned to them, such as the Russian brigade in MND(N), and between themselves and with IFOR and the ARRC.

Although interoperability is continuing to improve, there is still a long way to go to achieve seamless integration of NATO, national strategic and tactical, and commercially provided CIS systems and services.

NATO CIS Contingency Assets and Acquisition

The shortfalls in the existing NATO CIS infrastructure were known at the start of IFOR. The mechanism for overcoming the shortfalls was already in place and identified within the NATO CIS Contingency Assets Pool (NCCAP) concept. The NCCAP concept combined the Allied Command Europe (ACE) CIS Contingency Assets Pool, mainly for land and air users, with the Maritime CIS

Contingency Assets Pool, which was for naval users. Under the NCCAP concept, a pool of deployable CIS equipment would be procured and maintained for NATO and made available for contingency operations and exercises. Some equipment (new single- and multi-link TSGTs) was already being procured, but not delivered, when the operation started. In NATO, advance procurements are not generally planned for equipment with short manufacturing time scales in order to take full advantage of the latest commercial hardware and software technology. Contingency funding authorization is given to support rapid implementation on a need basis. The pool is enhanced where necessary with deployable assets made available by the nations. The provision of CIS assets for Bosnia was consistent with the NCCAP concept. Although the NCCAP concept was in place, there was initially very little equipment actually on hand. Furthermore, the detailed operational procedures for its use had not been finalized. Heavy reliance was therefore placed on the framework nations' national CIS assets, particularly those provided by the United States, and on leased PTT/VSAT/IDNX connectivity provided by NATO. In addition, greater reliance had to be placed on emergency procurement.

Generally speaking, NATO committees proved to be responsive and reacted flexibly to emergency CIS requests. There were some instances where the NATO CIS procurements failed to arrive in time to meet the operational commanders' requirements. In these cases, the NATO procurement cycle was too slow or unable to meet emergency requirements. In some cases, the contractor was unable to deliver and this resulted in failure to meet the operational requirement. One particular case in point was the failure of FLEXLINK to provide commercial SATCOM services. Due to the financial collapse of the FLEXLINK Company, it became necessary to find another vendor to provide the service. The Interstate Electronics Corporation (IEC) ultimately took over the contract from FLEXLINK and was responsible for providing an extension of NATO's E1/IDNX network into Bosnia to connect key IFOR locations via commercial SATCOM exclusive of the host nation's infrastructure. Because of the need to re-let the contract, the operational capability was implemented late. The implementation delay severely limited IFOR's ability to satisfy the bandwidth requirement for the operation. In May 1996, the IEC network became fully operational and provided the key services and necessary bandwidth down to the IFOR, ARRC, and MND levels.

International competitive bidding was only really imposed by the NATO Infrastructure Committee for the acquisition of the TACSAT terminals. Almost all other procurements were through Basic Ordering Agreements set up by the NC3A and AFSOUTH with a range of suppliers. In some cases, market surveys were employed before deciding on the most cost-effective provider. The time pressure imposed by the operational situation mandated a pragmatic balance between cost and delivery time in all cases.

For the IFOR operation, NATO authorized over $100 million dollars for CIS expenditures. More than $60 million was spent on communications alone, the major items being UHF/SHF tactical satellite terminals, UN VSAT service leases, commercial E1 leases, the IEC commercial SATCOM/IDNX network, and the UHF SATCOM channel lease from the United States.

C4ISR Performance

The pervasive use of COTS information products and services propelled NATO and IFOR into the Information Age and a new way of doing business. There was extensive use of e-mail and a reduced reliance on formal messaging systems. The formal message traffic (the NATO TARE message network) by volume (megabytes per day) was less than 10 percent of the total IFOR daily data network traffic. PowerPoint briefings were used to inform and were readily distributed over the data networks. The data networks were also used for collaborative planning and distribution of wide-band information such as images, although at times this was slow due to the limited bandwidth of the interconnecting links (64kb/s or less).

The bandwidth limitations were driven by NATO constraints on minimum cost solutions and unavailability of NATO-approved crypto equipment to run the links at higher rates.

Secure VTC was used extensively by IFOR and the ARRC for collaboration and coordination and as time went on, it became the medium of choice for conducting business. The VTCs were also used by subordinate IFOR elements to conduct day-to-day business. The VTC systems performed reasonably well when operating, but they were subject to outages due to SATCOM link bit error rates, crypto synchronization problems, and PICTURETEL software lock-outs. Numerous maintenance problems occurred and when they did, there was a lot of high-level pressure put on the maintenance staff to get them repaired quickly. Such pressure may have led to addressing the symptom and not necessarily the problem in many instances.

During the early deployment phases, different telephone handsets were present in command center locations. In some cases, it was reported that as many as seven different handsets were provided due to the multiple NATO, UN, and national voice networks. Although the various networks were interfaced and it was possible to progressively navigate through them, the networks were not integrated as a system with common numbering, routing, and signaling plans and directory services. Because of manpower shortages, time constraints, and constant change, telephone book and number management was a problem. There were multiple phone books at any one time (e.g., at least three phone books existed for the U.S. network: AFSOUTH, USAREUR FWD, and Task Force Eagle) and production coordination was sporadic. Phone book and dialing instruction distribution was a problem as well. As a result, calling from one network to another required some knowledge of the operational characteristics of each of the tactical systems, how they were interconnected, and the correct dialing sequence to progress from one network to the other. People frequently carried a dialing plan on a 3"x5" card in their pockets when traveling in Bosnia or found such a plan posted near the telephones.

The military tactical voice networks also were not very user friendly. The variety of multinational users at the theater and strategic levels found them difficult to use. The end-to-end network performance was also marginal, so users tended to default to using the UN VSAT network to do business since its operation was similar to a commercial telephone system. Unlike the military networks that were end-to-end security protected, the UN VSAT was not. One could use STU-IIBs on the UN VSAT but they were in short supply. Over time, a number of the tactical phones were removed, but there were still several different types of telephone handsets in the command centers.

The leased service offered by the UN to IFOR did not meet IFOR expectations. The UN VSAT network could not handle the load IFOR put on it. There were problems in getting priority responses from the UN to provide service for new IFOR subscribers/users and to take maintenance actions to resolve performance problems. There was no single UN focal point for actions in response to IFOR requests for service—the CJCCC element in Zagreb established a UN liaison position to facilitate working with the UN.

The new data network capabilities provided IFOR the opportunity to share information more efficiently and quickly (nearly simultaneously) at all levels of the command structure. This was a vast improvement over the previous procedures requiring the corroboration of data successively reported through each level in the chain of command. It was also possible to exchange information that bypassed ("skip echelon") intervening levels of the command structure. The ability to electronically bypass levels of command to obtain information firsthand was occasionally used in the interest of expediency and providing information up the chain of command, but sometimes at the expense of leaving others in the dark. Towards the end of the IFOR operation, the problem was not one of a lack of information but rather one of finding the useful details among the wealth of information available.

The CRONOS LAN and WAN management was evolving with the operation and had been the source of some problems during the early phases of the IFOR operation because of the need for

SOPs and trained network management and administration staff. There was also a conflict in the management responsibilities of the CJCCC and NACOSA caused by the SHAPE/AFSOUTH C2 differences. The NC3A, the Hague, maintained a CRONOS help desk that was connected to the network and was available to support requests for assistance from the theater.

Managing all of the information available to the commander and his staff was a difficult problem. Users lacked adequate tools to search for available information. Likewise, there were inadequate tools for managing information collection, storage, and sharing. This was particularly true early in the operation in the areas of coordinating, integrating, and fusing intelligence, surveillance, and reconnaissance capabilities and making this information available to the user. A mixture of NATO and national prototype and operational systems were used in an attempt to fuse various land, sea, and air pictures into a common tactical picture. The maritime and land pictures provided to the tactical commanders were of good quality. The air picture in the CAOC, made up from a variety of sources, was of particularly high quality. However, there was no overall integrated maritime/air/land picture provided to the commanders.

There were other sources of information such as the Internet and local and international media that needed to be incorporated into the IFOR information base. In terms of sharing classified information, security releasability was also an issue that needed to be addressed to ensure that information was put in the hands of those that needed it in a timely way without revealing sources and methods, but stringently protecting highly sensitive information.

Although extensive use was made of e-mail, VTC, and data network services, voice communications still played a major role in conducting the IFOR operation. This was true in spite of a grade of service that, at times, could exceed a 20-percent probability of blocking for call attempts during the early phases of the IFOR operation. The end-to-end voice quality was marginal especially if the call had to be routed through several different tactical switched networks. The UN VSAT network performance proved to be marginal, especially for calls out of the area of operation. Voice network performance improved towards the end of the IFOR phase of the operation, especially with the implementation of the IPN.

IFOR estimated that about 91 percent of the network capacity was dedicated to voice services, 6 percent for VTC, and 3 percent for data services. On the other hand, 5th Signal Command estimated that about 50 percent of the U.S. network was dedicated to voice services and 25 percent each for VTC and data services. If the U.S. intelligence network capacity were added to the U.S. statistics, data would certainly exceed 75 percent of the overall network capacity.

There were high hopes for extended use of cellular services in Bosnia, but effective coverage from the commercial networks could only be achieved in some parts of Croatia. A number of offers were made by cellular vendors to implement cellular services in Bosnia but were met with political opposition by the FWF PTTs. There was a proposal to operate from IFOR compounds. This had the added advantage of physical security. ARRC-Main was opposed to taking on such a responsibility because of the additional support and manpower implications. There was also a question regarding the effectiveness of the coverage of such a system. By the end of the IFOR operation, the PTT implemented a limited coverage cellular capability in Sarajevo.

Problems with viruses were experienced not only with the CRONOS and IARRCIS but also with most computers brought into the theater. The Center for Army Lessons Learned reported that within the first 60 days of operation nearly every Army computer brought into theater had been infected. Infected diskettes brought into the command centers and the swapping of diskettes (including infected ones) between the unclassified and classified systems were major sources of the problem and its proliferation. There was also a lack of personal discipline and standard operating procedures. Virus detection and correction measures were put in place along with a user information awareness campaign. Laptop computers were placed at the entrance to command centers with virus scan programs and a notice posted that all diskettes had to be scanned before being taken into the command center. Use of games on the command center computers—another source of viruses— was forbidden. C-Support in Zagreb used a diskette color-coding scheme to prevent confusion regarding classified versus unclassified. They also developed a set of operating instructions. Neither of the C-Support approaches were implemented IFOR-wide.

While most of the detected viruses were relatively benign, their ubiquitous presence underscored the vulnerability of the computers and data networks to systematic hostile attack. There was a need for improved intrusion detection capabilities for the data networks. A related issue was the lack of adequate data network configuration management and control. The CJCCC needed better configuration management tools and procedures. Security was an ongoing responsibility for which improvements were made over the duration of the operation.

Dust and dirt caused problems with disk drives and servers, creating the requirement for protective measures such as covering up computers when not in use and vacuuming the work areas and the computers themselves more frequently. Commercial power failures and fluctuations caused major CIS outages for those sites that did not have a UPS backup capability and power-line surge protectors. Sometimes the power failures were a result of planned outages. For example, the commander of the Croatia compound in Zagreb, where the UN and the IFOR C-Support were located, performed an unannounced base power outage. The interruption shut down the UN and C-Support CIS capabilities. Needless to say, swift action was taken to acquire a UPS capability to support the UN and IFOR C-Support CIS systems. Power was a serious problem that required high-level attention to get the necessary UPS capabilities deployed.

The extension of secure services to non-NATO coalition partners was also an issue that had to be dealt with by IFOR. Security policy modifications were required to accommodate the release of classified information and liaison teams were provided to non-NATO units assigned to IFOR, such as the U.S. INTEL team with the Russian brigade and the U.S.-provided narrow-band voice terminals for the PfP nations supporting the operation. IFOR CJ6 suggested that NATO might consider the use of commercially available security products to facilitate secure communications with non-NATO troop contributing nations in support of future peace operation security needs.

Network and system management of IFOR's communications and information network proved to be a major challenge (figure 11-20). An IFOR organization structure had to be created, agreed upon, and staffed quickly. The U.S Joint Pub 6-05 provided the basis for the establishment of the CJCCC to manage IFOR's network. System tools had to be acquired to monitor and manage the networks. There were multiple NATO and national players, such as SHAPE's NATO CIS Operating and Support Agency (NACOSA), the AFSOUTH CISD, the IFOR CJ6, the CJCCC, the ARRC G6, the MND G6s, and the national J6s. The roles, relationships, and activities of these organizations needed to be established and coordinated. Furthermore, overlaps in organizational responsibilities needed to be worked out since the distinction between strategic, theater, and tactical became blurred. SHAPE and AFSOUTH OPLANs and C2 differences did not help the staff attempts to resolve these overlaps. NATO communications and ADP were managed separately, and this needed to be accommodated by the CJCCC. Over time, these issues were resolved and the CIS system provided reasonable services. However, the CIS system for the most part was never heavily stressed during the IFOR operation. Therefore, the performance of the networks and the supporting management organization were never tested under more hostile or stressful conditions.

The management of the U.S. C4ISR networks was a challenge as well. C4 and ISR were managed separately as well as communications and ADP. The ISR systems were managed by different organization elements. The blurring of the strategic, theater, and tactical boundaries was a problem for the United States too. There was no doctrine defining the demarcation point between U.S. strategic, theater, and tactical systems. This had to be dealt with at the outset of the operation since strategic- and theater-level capa-

362 Lessons from Bosnia

Figure 11-20. CJCCC

bilities were deployed into the tactical area, resulting in overlapping responsibilities for the management organizations and no clear definition of who had end-to-end assured service responsibility.

The use of e-mail, PowerPoint briefings, PCs, and video teleconferencing not only dominated the mode of operation at division and above but was also beginning to penetrate below division as well. Tactical systems, however, still dominated at division and below. The maneuver units relied on tactical line-of-site communications. The use of non-tactical communications was at the commander's discretion. Commercial systems such as INMARSAT with STU-III and STU-IIB were used. There was also a desire for broader access to commercial services such as cellular and commercial SATCOM. Desktop and laptop computers were based throughout the tactical area. Early on these were 286 and 386 machines but it soon became necessary to deploy 486 and Pentium machines to handle the volume of data and accommodate the RAM needs of storage-hungry programs such as MS Office. Rotation of troops also added some unintended consequences. The arriving units would at times bring with them the latest version of software applications, contributing to some interoperability problems when trying to share products from different versions of software applications.

The IFOR information revolution largely stopped at the division headquarters level in Bosnia. In some cases such as MND(N) and the U.S. forces in Croatia and Hungary, higher bandwidth services were extended to the battalion level. Every U.S. base camp had telephone service and secure and non-secure data and e-mail capabilities. However, the communications and information system support to the IFOR warfighters changed very little, and the warfighters continued to operate much as they had in the past. Operations were conducted using acetate-covered 1:50,000 maps (see picture), outmoded tactical equipment, and sensor or reconnaissance systems organic to ground units.

The use of TCP/IP-based networks is proliferating for the unclassified military and commercial networks (the NIPRNET and Internet) and for the classified military networks (the NATO CRONOS and LOCE and the U.S. SIPRNET and INTELINK).

MND(N) Command Center

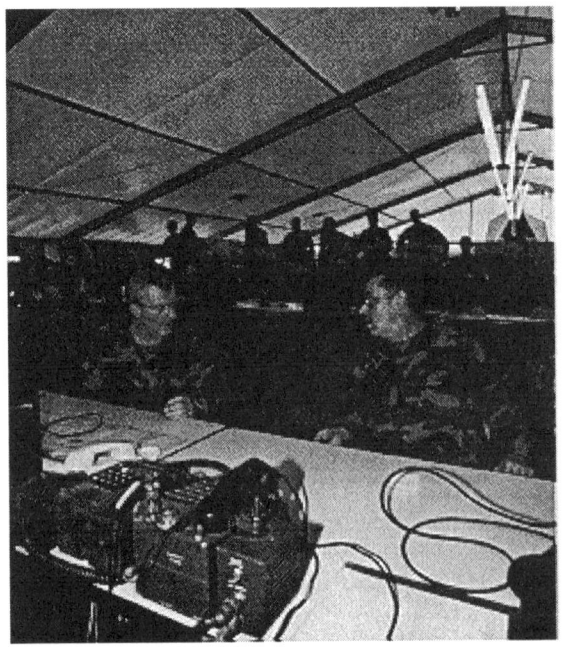

Furthermore, the data networks are increasingly being relied upon by the military for supporting operational C2 and intelligence traffic. Although the IFOR and national networks performed reasonably well overall, there were problems with congestion and assured service when equipment failures and traffic-loading situations were encountered at major nodes or operations centers. Under the stress of real hostilities, where one or more operations centers or nodes are attacked or destroyed or extreme traffic overloads are encountered, the networks could gridlock or fail, catastrophically denying service to essential C2 users. The redundancy, robustness, and resiliency of the IFOR network design and supporting network and system management structure were never really tested operationally. The IFOR network and system management capabilities and structure to support C2 traffic under extreme hostile conditions were not part of the design criteria, nor was such a capability implemented. It was tough enough to create a capability to manage the integrated peace operations network derived from NATO and national systems. Alternative (low bandwidth) fall-back systems (TARE/AUTODIN and C2 voice networks) were not implemented as a reconstitution or continuity of service capability even with the danger of open hostility, as was the possibility with the RS faction. The VTC network had similar weaknesses and was a "bandwidth hog" as well. If one or more nodes or operations centers were attacked, the bandwidth to support or reconstitute VTC service would most likely not have been available. Voice conference systems such as that provided for the ARRC by PTARMIGAN could have been used as a limited conferencing backup capability. There were a couple of satellite failures that highlighted the vulnerability of the IFOR network. Actions were taken to build in some additional redundancy and establish contingency plans for reconstitution of critical C2 links.

Technology Insertion

Although the deployed high-technology systems generally supported the headquarters far more effectively than they supported the soldier on the ground, there were, of course, exceptions. Many innovative uses were made of the U.S. military's array of advanced technologies (mainly in the area of ISR) to more effectively support the headquarters and the soldier on the ground. In fact, Bosnia (mainly MND(N) and the CAOC) became a model for the U.S. doctrine known as "Information Dominance" and technology test beds.

U.S commanders, in particular, reported that a virtual flood of new technologies followed their deployment to Bosnia. These technologies were generally inserted incompletely and imperfectly. Many of the new systems and technologies were deployed without doctrinal support, concepts of operations and training, and logistic support packages. As a consequence, they could not be fully employed. Moreover, because they had not been through full and systematic development and testing, trained military operators were not available. Initial operations and maintenance had to be provided by contractors or the government development team personnel. Even so, these new technologies reportedly still made excessive demands on military operator personnel who had to find the time to train, learn to maintain the equipment, and develop concepts of operation. In many cases, this meant that new systems were underutilized because their full functionality and potential were not understood.

The advanced technology capabilities deployed in Bosnia were essentially stove-pipe systems and capabilities that were overlaid on the operational networks. Hence, one of the major challenges the United States and IFOR faced was the integration of these capabilities and systems into the operation and then being able to exploit them to the maximum extent possible.

Air Force and Army initiatives were directed at trying to put discipline into the technology insertion process and facilitate the deployment of advanced technologies to the theater. In January 1996, the Air Force Electronic Systems Center at Hanscom AFB established a *Joint Endeavor* Laboratory, now the C2 Unified Battlespace Environment (CUBE). The laboratory replicated the C3I functionality of the CAOC in Vicenza, Italy, and was used for rapid problem solving and system integration testing of new capabilities before operational deployment to the theater. A 24-hour hotline was established to support technical assistance requests from the field. ESC also deployed technical assistance teams to the CAOC to help resolve on-site integration and configuration management problems. In December 1995, the Army Materiel Command established a Bosnia Technology Integration Cell (BTIC) to serve as a clearinghouse for critical technologies and the "nerve center" for tracking and integrating the technology community's efforts to support U.S. soldiers in Bosnia. The BTIC focused its efforts on prospecting for systems that would provide American forces with a technological advantage for operations such as anti-mine, anti-sniper, communications, and surveillance.

NATO too established an advanced technology laboratory to facilitate the introduction of new capabilities and functionality into the NATO CIS systems such as CRONOS and ADAMS. The laboratory facility at the NATO C3 Agency, The Hague (NC3A) replicated the NATO CIS systems deployed in support of IFOR and was used for rapid prototyping and system integration testing. A CRONOS Help Desk was established and manned 24 hours a day to provide on-line technical assistance and answer requests for help from the field. The NC3A also deployed technical assistance teams to help resolve problems in the field.

There were concerns expressed by other nations such as the United Kingdom and France that they could not keep up with the pace of U.S. technology and that this could have significant interoperability and operational implications for future coalition operations. A clear lesson from *Operation Joint Endeavor* was that advanced technologies are of military value and are suitable for deployment only when they are accompanied by coherent doctrine, organizational support, equipment, people, and the ability to effectively integrate them into the operational environment. It is also important to note that not all coalition partners can afford the latest

C3I technologies. Furthermore, some high-tech nations such as the United States may not be willing to share their latest capabilities with all members of a coalition of the willing, and not all coalition members use the technologies of these nations either. These are the realities of coalition operations and the way of the future. The push for the use of advanced technology will and should always be there and therefore needs to be more effectively accommodated.

Finally, as long as systems development and procurement lead times for military systems remain significantly longer than the rate of technological change in communications and automation, commercial products will be the only practical means of delivering state-of-the-art capabilities. So the challenges of augmenting military systems with commercial systems must be met and overcome.

Some Common Threads for Lessons Learned

A lot has been learned from *Operation Joint Endeavor* that can be applied to future peace operations. Some have particular significance for future NATO operations and the realization of the NATO CJTF and NCCAP concepts. Others can be applied to coalition peace operations in general. Some experiences are simply the realities of complex coalition operations. Others are experiences re-visited, and still others are lessons yet to be learned or in the process of being learned as a result of the IFOR experience. In the latter case, lessons learned are used in the context of the Center for Army Lessons Learned definition, "a lesson is learned when behavior changes." The following is an attempt to characterize some of the *Joint Endeavor* C4ISR experiences in these three categories. There is no priority of importance implied by the sequence in which they are presented.

Realities of Coalition Operations

- Participants must integrate what they get, not necessarily what they need.

- Forces should expect stove-piped system implementation with associated interoperability and security disconnects.

- The planning environment will be dynamic and confusing.

- The theater-level PTT infrastructure will be inadequate to support operational needs.

- Coalition partners will have uneven capabilities and experience.

- Command arrangements and force structures will be politically driven and implementation will be behind the power curve.

- Participants should expect to learn "on the job."

- Participants must keep it simple.

- Agility, adaptability, and innovation will be the norm.

Experiences Revisited

- U.S. military strategic and tactical C4ISR systems and services once again provided critical communications and information systems and services in support of a major coalition operation.

- The division of strategic, theater, and tactical C4ISR systems has become less distinct and planning and operational staffs and commanders will have to learn how to deal effectively with a pervasive communications and information system environment.

- Centralized network control was essential for the success of the communications and information system operations. Lack of this for IFOR early on in the operation resulted from SHAPE and AFSOUTH C2 differences.

- Standing contract arrangements for acquiring products and services in support of contingency operations were needed.

- All requests for communications and information services were urgent during the initial build-up phase. An adjudicating authority was needed to sort out priorities and validate coalition requirements.

- The size of the communications pipes was not sufficient to meet the demands of the operations (experienced at all levels—strategic, theater, and tactical).

- Independent and separately managed communications systems supported the C4 and ISR systems. There was a need to be able to more effectively share these capabilities in the operational environment.

- The operation could not have been successful without the extensive use of military satellite capability that only the United States, United Kingdom, and France forces could provide.

- Interoperability continues to be a challenge. Even though progress is being made, there is still a long way to go to achieve seamless operation of the coalition communications and information systems.

- Reliance on commercial products and services needs to be more effectively incorporated into the CIS architectures, planning, procurement, contracting, O&M, logistics support, and training.

- Training for commercial products and services has two aspects to be considered: training the military on commercial systems and training the contractor to work in a military environment.

- Contractor support and related O&M and logistic support arrangements for military use of commercial equipment and services still need to be understood in terms of operational implications and the ability to ensure continuity of service in a hostile environment.

- Commercialization of military systems supports an exit strategy aimed at the early withdrawal of military tactical systems. However, the commercialization strategy must take into account the disposition of the entity you plan to lease from, i.e., vendors must be positioned to provide the support, and there is a FWF PTT assured service risk that needs to be accommodated. A military overlay needs to be maintained to provide assured C2 connectivity.

- Dust, dirt, and commercial power failures continue to affect operations.

Lessons Yet to Be Learned or Being Learned

- The U.S. military played a key leadership role in the provision of IFOR CIS services and the integration of disparate NATO and national systems to realize and operate the largest military-civil communications and information system ever built to support a major peace operation.

- The prominent role of U.S. Signal officers in key positions in NATO, SHAPE, AFSOUTH, DISA, USAREUR/5th Signal Command, USAFE, and other organizations was an important unifying factor. Many IFOR problems associated with ambiguous roles, incomplete doctrine, and technical interoperability were successfully resolved through close coordination among these U.S. officers.

- NATO organizations such as AFSOUTH CISD, SHAPE CISD, NACOSA, ARRC G6, and NC3A, the Hague, rose to the occasion and provided untiring support to IFOR CIS installation, operation, and problem-solving activities.

- The United Kingdom was a key contributor to IFOR CIS systems, services, and problem resolution with important players in NATO, SHAPE, NACOSA, AFSOUTH, the ARRC, and UK Signal units.

- E-mail is largely replacing the formal messaging handling systems such as the U.S. AUTODIN and NATO TARE.

- VTC is becoming the C2 system of choice, especially for the U.S. Army.

- Information management and management of the use of information require careful consideration as NATO and the nations move into the global Information Age.

- Given the heavy reliance on the use of data networks and VTC to support operational C2 and intelligence requirements, consideration needs to be given to designing and implementing more robust operational networks in support of real-world operations; improving network and system management systems and structure so that continuity of service to essential C2 users can be ensured under stress conditions; providing low-bandwidth backup capabilities for essential C2 users for contingency use; and improving the management of access to and use of information network resources by non-essential C2 users under stress conditions.

- Despite the myriad of voice systems present, telephone service supporting the IFOR Joint Operations Center was still inadequate. Multilevel precedence and preemption down to the soldier in the field may be the only way to ensure that a common user system can be used for C2, especially in a damaged network.

- Network and system administrators are in high demand and there is a lack of trained military personnel to meet this demand. System-level troubleshooters for complex information systems are also lacking.

- Access to commercial Internet service and its use are required to support C2, mission support, and intelligence operations.

- Coalition operations dictate the use of collateral vice SCI classified material and facilities for the promulgation and reporting of intelligence information. At the tactical level, personnel are generally not cleared for SCI, nor is the security infrastructure available to support it.

- Proliferation of different information systems to support C2, mission support, and intelligence introduces unnecessary duplication and inefficient use of scarce bandwidth. Furthermore, no one individual in a command center was cross-trained (nor should they necessarily be expected to be) on all systems to either use them or maintain them.

- The CIS requirements of the PIO, CIMIC, PSYOP, CI/HUMINT, and other special activities such as NGO, PVO, and IO organization interfaces and support need to be made known up front so that adequate CIS services can be planned for and provided.

- There was no agreed baseline of NATO CIS services and information requirements for out-of-area operations.

- Inability to conduct proper reconnaissance for political reasons and last-minute changes resulted in deployment with incomplete planning and understanding of requirements.

- There needs to be an interoperable digital interface between national military tactical systems and between strategic civil and military systems and military tactical systems.

- Reach-back is an effective means for connecting deployed forces to the broader services of the strategic CIS infrastructure. NATO did not have such a capability per se (it only had a simple reach back to SHAPE for extension of headquarters services). The installed strategic-tactical digital network (STDN) gateway for the U.S. DII was not sufficiently capable to support *Joint Endeavor* needs. As a result, U.S. tactical switching and transmission equipment had to be employed at the strategic level (in Germany) to accommodate reach-back services and interfaces with the DII.

- Intelligence activities in support of peace operations require much more flexibility in databasing. More flexible and efficient information discovery and retrieval tools are needed.

- The technology insertion process is incomplete and imperfect and requires a more coherent and disciplined process to ensure that military value is achieved. Advanced technologies are of military value and suitable for deployment only when they are accompanied by coherent doctrine, organizational support, equipment, people, and the ability to effectively integrate them into the operational environment.

- Not all coalition partners can afford the latest and planned U.S C4ISR systems. The United States may not be willing to share its latest C4ISR systems with all elements of "coalitions of the willing." Furthermore, not all coalition partners use U.S. systems.

- The Information Age has arrived for NATO but largely stops at the division level. The Information Revolution needs to be extended to lower levels of the command structure to effectively support the troops who are actually executing the mission. The troops also need to be trained in how to prevent "information overload."

- Advanced information discovery tools need to be developed and provided in order to improve the ability of the commander and his staff to find the useful details among the wealth of information available.

- NATO needs the ability to more effectively deploy forward communications and information systems in support of peace operations. The roles and relationships of the network and systems management organization elements need to be clearly defined and made a part of the operations order.

- The artificial separation of communications and data processing responsibilities needs to be removed in the Information Age.

- More extensive sharing of information and collaboration has become the norm for doing business in a coalition operation.

- NATO needs to establish COMSEC accounts to support multinational operations down to the unit level. COMSEC/INFOSEC for non-NATO partners also needs to be addressed.

- NATO's peacetime procurement process is too complex and slow to meet the demands of a live peace operation. Nations must be able to have their say but care must also be given to national preferences that can complicate operational priorities. The situation did improve dramatically over the course of the IFOR operation.

- Tight CIS configuration management and control and a workable integrated logistics support plan are essential to support contingency operations.

- Major operational decisions (e.g., SFOR replacement of IFOR) should include active NATO CIS community involvement before the timelines on the move are finalized. IFOR/SFOR experience highlighted problems in this area.

- Software viruses caused problems for IFOR operations and appropriate detection and protection mechanisms need to be factored into the planning for information system enhancements. Also, there needs to be NATO policy guidance and enforcement.

- NATO and the nations need to carefully examine the defensive information warfare needs of future information systems and incorporate the necessary defensive capabilities (e.g., intrusion detection and protection) to reduce their vulnerabilities to potential hostile actions.

- Exercises and training demonstrated the value of setting up the expected C4I configurations in advance of the deployment to sort out integration and interoperability problems. The exercises also served to train and do some team building for those personnel who would deploy.

- NATO needs a proper organization for planning, implementing, and managing the communications and information networks required for out-of-area peace operations. The NATO CJTF concept and the IFOR CJCCC are building blocks for developing an appropriate capability. NACOSA is an established NATO organization responsible for planning, implementing, and managing the strategic CIS networks.

- Liaisons proved to be an effective means for facilitating coordination, collaboration, and cooperation among the many different NATO and national organizations participating in the management of the IFOR CIS network.

- A Frequency Management capability needs to be provided as part of the network management operation.

- Enhanced system and network management tools need to be made a part of an improved capability for NATO CIS network management.

In summary, the experiences from Bosnia reinforced the importance of information dominance. Getting the right information to the right person at the right time has significantly improved but has not yet reached or impacted the soldier on the ground to the same extent that it has changed the way business is done at higher headquarters. C4ISR interoperability continues to be a challenge, not only among the military coalition systems but also with commercial products and leased services and the systems used by the IOs, NGOs, and PVOs. Operational use of advanced information technologies and commercial products and services has become a reality and needs to be factored into the planning and training for peace operations. Innovative training and exercises and adherence to international standards are means to improving this situation as the world moves into the global Information Age.

One should not forget, however, that potential adversaries of the NATO alliance and the United States, in particular, will not be so foolish as to neglect glaring weaknesses in the C4I networks implemented in support of the IFOR operation. Active countermeasures against these networks may be the case in future operations. Doctrine and tactics based upon an assumed information dominance and freedom to communicate may not be sufficient the next time around, even for peacekeeping operations.

In conclusion, agility and accommodation continue to be keys to success, as well as some plain old good luck. Let us not forget, however, that the success of the IFOR C4I and national C4ISR network implementation and operation was in the final analysis because of the professionalism, dedication, and ingenuity of the men and women who were there and those who supported them. Good people make it happen.

XII. NDU/CCRP Bosnia Study
Larry K. Wentz

Background

Recognizing that the deployment and operation of C4ISR capabilities in support of the complex coalition peace operation in Bosnia provided a unique opportunity for learning, Mr. Emmett Paige, Jr., ASD/C3I, tasked the CCRP at NDU on February 15, 1996 to simultaneously collect experiences and lessons learned and to perform an analysis of the effectiveness of command arrangements and supporting C4ISR.

CCRP's charge was broad, covering both the effectiveness of command arrangements and the effectiveness of supporting C4ISR. Hence, the study addressed all of the classic issues of C4ISR, including structures, functions, capacities, doctrine, and training. Furthermore, CCRP was tasked to pull together the related ongoing C4ISR community activities and build a coherent C4ISR story, including lessons learned. The study charter was introduced to the Joint Staff through the J-6 (Director, Command, Control, Communications and Computer Systems), and was subsequently coordinated with the J-3 (through the Vice Director for Operations). Both endorsed the effort, and the decision was made that the J-3 would be the official Joint Staff point of contact for the effort.

380 Lessons from Bosnia

The CCRP Bosnia study charter listed three major tasking areas: (1) document the build up and evolution of C4I systems and capabilities provided to all echelons; (2) document command arrangements (both formal and informal) as they evolve and the rationales for changes; and (3) assess the effectiveness of command arrangements and C4I systems and the adjustments made to them over time. Command arrangements of interest specifically included those (a) associated with joint operations, (b) within and among U.S. Government (USG) organizations, (c) among military organizations (NATO, Russians, and others), (d) between the United States and NGOs and PVOs, and (e) with local governments and organizations. In addition, CCRP was tasked to unify the C4ISR community activities and put together a coherent lessons learned story.

CCRP was sensitized to the need to be unobtrusive and to minimize demands on military organizations in the theater of operations. In-theater travel and visits, while necessary for some aspects of the study, were limited to those required to support a quality product. Research activities were initiated in February 1996, and it was expected that they would continue for at least 6 months after the exit of major U.S. forces from Bosnia. With the transition of IFOR to SFOR on 20 December 1996, the NDU effort was adjusted to focus on putting the IFOR story together as a first priority. The collection of SFOR experiences and lessons learned was to continue but at a much lower level of effort.

The NDU study was designed to produce a variety of products, and a final report will summarize all of the findings on C4ISR Lessons Learned. Study results have been briefed at C4ISR community symposia and workshops such as AFCEA, MILCOM, the NDU INSS-sponsored NATO symposium, and the Pearson Canadian International Peacekeeping Centre workshop on peacekeeping and conflict resolution. Findings were also presented at the Swedish Naval Warfare Centre-sponsored Partnership-for-Peace lessons learned workshop, the NATO Panel 7 workshop on IFOR data collection and analysis, and the CCRP-sponsored International C2 Research symposium.

Using CCRP's approach of crafting balanced Mission Capability Packages (figure 12-1) to deal with emerging issues and opportunities, key findings will be provided to doctrine developers in the joint community and the services. In addition, the results will be used to develop professional military education (PME) materials for use at all levels of professional schooling. Finally, NDU/CCRP will select the most important topics and findings for publication as articles in *Joint Forces Quarterly* and other visible periodicals as well as books through the NDU Press.

Study Team

CCRP brought together a multidisciplined, diverse group of analysts and researchers to carry out the major tasking areas of the Bosnia study charter (figure 12-2). A core team was established under the leadership of the Director of the CCRP and consisted of participants from NDU/CCRP, Evidence Based Research Inc (EBR), C4I Integration Support Activity (CISA), MITRE, and Decision-Science Applications Inc. The core team was augmented, as required, with subject area experts from organizations such as DISA, JITC, SOCOM, J2/DIA, and J6Z. Staff from the Center for Naval Analysis (CNA) and Institute for Defense Analysis (IDA) also provided advice and inputs to the effort.

Approach

Operation Joint Endeavor was well underway before the NDU study effort was initiated and it was quickly determined that a number of other organizations had initiated efforts that would provide important information that the NDU effort did not need to duplicate. Therefore, CCRP made identifying all related efforts its

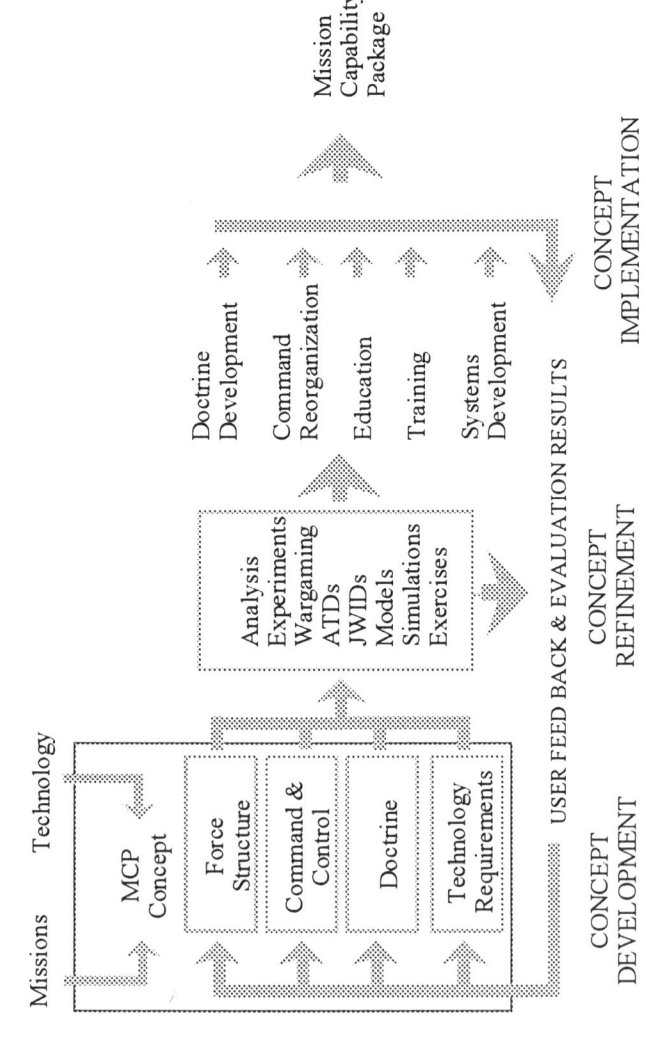

Figure 12-1. Mission Capability Package

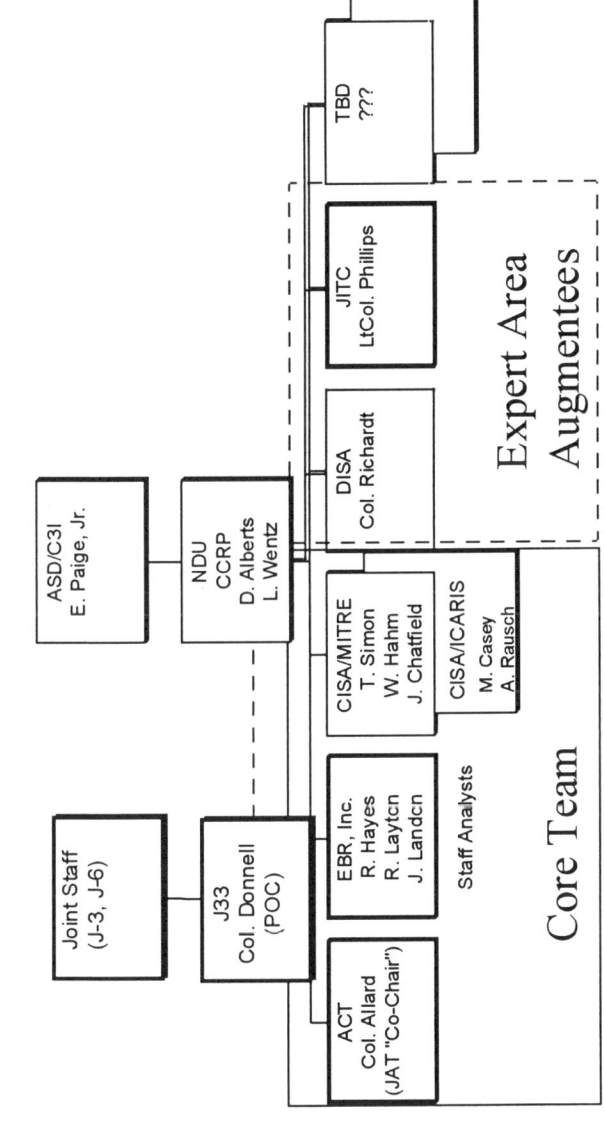

Figure 12-2. NDU/CCRP Bosnia C4ISR Team

first priority. These included lessons learned activities, research efforts, and assessments of C4ISR performance in Bosnia. The roundup of all relevant efforts was a key element of CCRP's four part, highly leveraged plan for accomplishing the mission of assessing C4ISR effectiveness and collecting lessons learned.

CCRP achieved its goal of a highly leveraged effort based upon attention to four principles: coordination, collaboration, integration, and focused research. **Coordination** allowed CCRP to avoid duplication, minimize demands on the commands in the field, and maximize the return on its own focused data collection efforts. **Collaboration** permitted the effective use of access and expertise in other organizations while also allowing CCRP's expertise to be used efficiently and effectively. **Integration** of all the work performed, whether by CCRP personnel, those working on their behalf, or those operating under very different charters, allowed CCRP to add value to the work of others and to provide a unique and important contribution. This included collecting products from all sources; comparing and contrasting them to test for consistency of findings across time, space, levels of command, and analyst perspective; and looking across the range of available evidence in order to detect larger patterns. Integrating the mass of material generated and being able to examine it from a relatively neutral perspective, the CCRP team was in an excellent position to detect the trends dominating the Bosnia experiences and the structures and processes that drive them. **Focused research** by the CCRP team was reserved for key issues that (a) were central to the charter from ASD/C3I and CCRP priorities, (b) focused on topics where CCRP had or could get expertise and relevant evidence, and (c) were not being adequately covered by other agencies or organizations.

Coordination

CCRP looked beyond conducting its specific technical analyses and developing specific products to helping the community at large do a better job of learning the lessons of the Bosnia experience. Therefore, CCRP devoted some of its efforts to create forums and mechanisms to encourage and facilitate studying the exchange of data, information, and ideas among the many organizations involved in studying the Bosnia experience. Formal and informal exchanges of drafts, professional discussions, workshops, publication of results, and the CCRP C2 symposia and community development programs were and will continue to be used to enrich the study and leverage its impact.

The most successful CCRP coordination initiative was the creation of a "Bosnia C4ISR Roundtable" (figure 12-3), where a range of U.S. activities involved in lessons learned and assessment of performance in Bosnia were brought together in a constructive atmosphere to encourage sharing and cooperation. The first meeting took place on April 10, 1996, with 21 activities involved. This session was an immediate and significant success. Virtually everyone present learned for the first time about one or more activities directly related to their own. Some initial findings were reported orally and consensus existed that the Roundtable should meet regularly. Participants readily agreed that the Roundtable should serve as a mechanism for reviewing draft materials and disseminating products on lessons learned and C4ISR performance.

Immediately after the first Roundtable meeting, CCRP published a directory of the organizations who had attended. This directory included the addresses (including telephone, fax, and e-mail) of the points of contact and a brief description of the relevant activities and interests of each of the organizations. An e-mail network was established to facilitate collaboration, coordination, and sharing of information. This network proved to be very beneficial to all of the participants. Follow-up meetings with a variety of Roundtable participants indicated that they had subsequently made a number of direct contacts with other members of the group and had been able to coordinate and focus their activities much better because of these new linkages.

The second meeting of the Bosnia C4ISR Roundtable took place on 30 May 1996. More than 30 activities or organizations asked to be represented, an increase of more than 50 percent from the first meeting. The agenda included presentations on several

Figure 12-3. The Bosnia C4ISR Roundtable

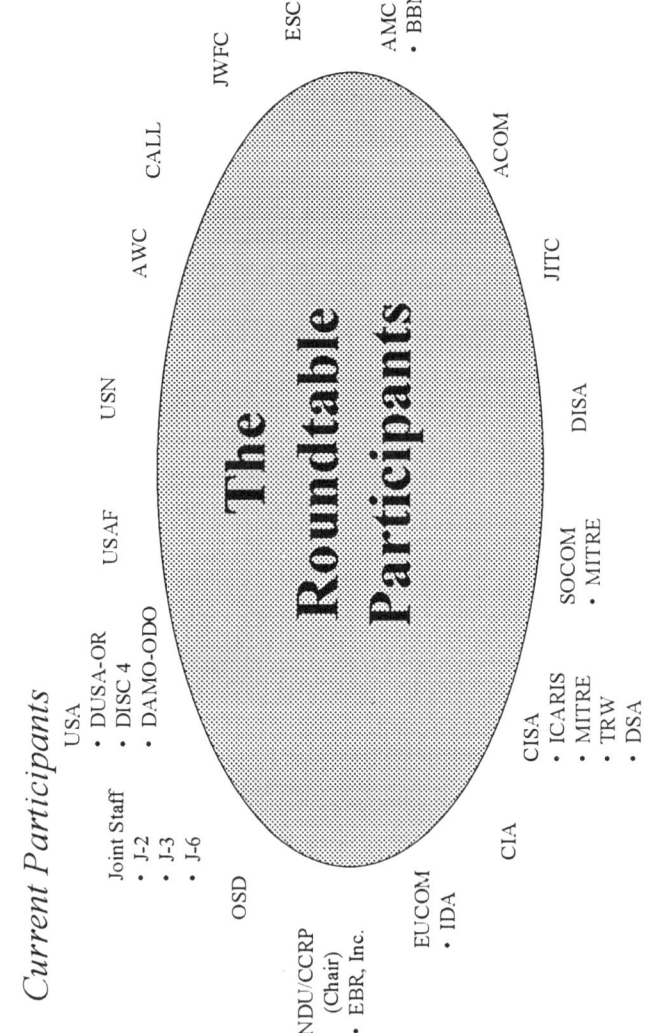

efforts that had reached preliminary findings. CCRP briefed the progress of efforts, IDA briefed their charter and first-order conclusions (largely on the planning and deployment phases) from their lessons learned effort for European Command (EUCOM), the Central Intelligence Agency (CIA) covered findings from their analysis of policies and procedures for intelligence sharing in the context of the Bosnia operation, and the CISA team briefed the progress of its C4ISR laydown. The first results of a study by the Center for Army Lessons Learned (CALL) were reviewed. Substantive discussion among different agencies was encouraged and proved highly productive.

As implied by its name, the Bosnia C4ISR Roundtable was a meeting among equals. All those U.S. organizations with a charter to collect data or lessons learned related to C4ISR, either in terms of command arrangements or supporting systems, were welcomed, as were those agencies or organizations who were potential consumers of the results of those analyses. CCRP served as the chair of the Roundtable. The organizations listed in figure 12-3 were all self-nominated by declaring that they had a role in Bosnian C4ISR and an interest in its assessment.

Taken together, the Roundtable was a major asset to the broad task of developing valid and meaningful lessons learned on the Bosnia C4ISR experience. While participation was voluntary, the value of the information exchange created a very real incentive for joining and attending. CCRP continued to use the Roundtable for the duration of the IFOR phase of the Bosnia operation. It was a useful mechanism to coordinate efforts and to ensure cross-checking of facts and findings within the community.

Collaboration

The rich set of lessons learned and effectiveness assessment activities already underway (figure 12-4) when the CCRP study started represented both major opportunities and potential problems. On the one hand, the opportunities for synergistic work were obvious. Moreover, as CCRP made contacts in the theater and the U.S.

community, virtually everyone indicated a willingness to cooperate and a positive attitude toward working together. Every organization involved in lessons learned or performance assessment also recognized that many different activities were underway. Almost all of them also expressed a strong desire for efficient and effective information exchange in this arena.

At the same time, there was a potential for problems to arise from the number and variety of activities underway. Overlapping missions and redundancy of data collection efforts were the most obvious. The demands on the time of key officers and staff in the field commands and operational headquarters were already high and a multitude of visitors became a significant burden. From the IFOR Joint Analysis Team (JAT) headquarters to the field commands, CCRP's analysts heard complaints about "IFOR Tourism" almost from the first contacts in theater. Some of these comments were pointedly directed at the United States, which reportedly had the largest number of visitors in the theater. Moreover, NATO sensitivity about national access to materials within NATO commands remained high and, reportedly, had not been well handled by U.S. and other national activities.

CCRP's approach was heavily influenced by attempts to take advantage of ongoing efforts where it could focus its limited resources on collecting data and conducting analyses of key issues. Considerable progress was made. By stressing collaboration, working closely with the JAT and selected U.S. activities, establishing mechanisms for cooperation and information exchange, and positioning itself to address key issues in command arrangements and C4ISR, CCRP was able to put an efficient and productive process in place and bring a coherent picture into focus. Having set up the necessary data collection and sharing mechanisms, CCRP became fully engaged in documenting the Bosnia C4ISR experience and identifying and researching key issues.

Three major thrusts existed (figure 12-4) in the IFOR lessons learned arena: NATO's formal effort, the NDU effort directed by ASD/C3I, and the relatively uncoordinated set of initiatives underway within the overall U.S. community. There were also na-

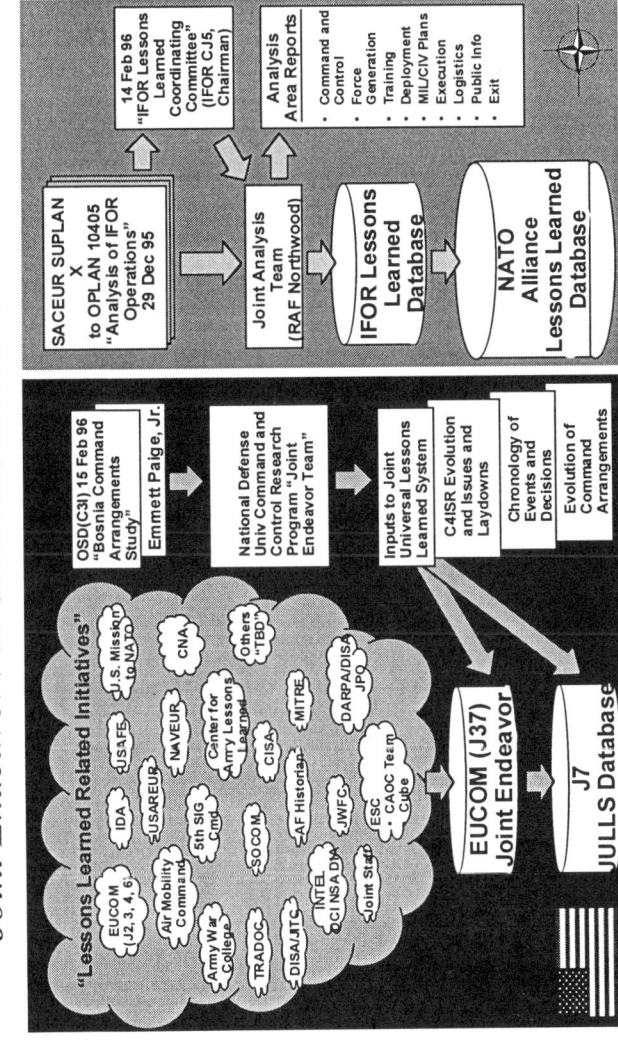

Figure 12-4. Collaborative Opportunities
Joint Endeavor / IFOR Lessons Learned Activities

tional efforts undertaken by the French and British, but these were not discovered until well into the CCRP study. The NATO process had a formal and relatively integrated structure. The charter of the JAT was explicitly derived from SACEURs Operations Plan (OPLAN), SUPLAN X. The JAT's charter focused on nine issue areas, including several related to C4ISR, particularly C2, force generation, military-civilian plans, execution, public information, and exit. The JAT also had the formal right to locate observers in NATO and IFOR headquarters and command centers in theater and had already done so. While the JAT viewed its charter as limited (primarily at the operational level and above, focused on its nine issue areas), they had the lead in NATO for IFOR operational lessons learned. This enabled them to collect information and conduct interviews on-site and in locations where unobtrusive presence was difficult. The JAT also maintained an extensive automated database on IFOR operations. They produced three interim reports (March 1996, June 1996, December 1996) which were forwarded to SHAPE and COMIFOR for distribution. A final report on IFOR lessons learned was sent to SHAPE in April 1997. In accordance with SUPLAN X, an IFOR/SFOR Lessons Learned Database was established and implemented on CRONOS. This database was the first of its kind in NATO to support an ongoing operation and it continued to be available for SFOR. In regard to the latter, the JAT charter was extended to June 1997 to accommodate the collection of lessons learned associated with the transition of IFOR to SFOR.

Clearly, a constructive interface with the JAT and the formal NATO process represented an important opportunity for collaboration, and this was an immediate priority for the CCRP team. An agreement was arranged between the director of JAT and the director of the NDU/CCRP study team. Under this agreement, CCRP provided both observers and analyst support to the JAT in return for access to data, information, and the Bosnia theater of operation for firsthand collection of experiences and insights. The CCRP and JAT collaborative effort proved to be extremely beneficial for both organizations.

NDU/CCRP Bosnia Study 391

In addition to the JAT, CCRP collaborative efforts were pursued with U.S. organizational elements such as EUCOM, USAREUR, U.S. Air Force Europe (USAFE), JAC at Molesworth, Electronic Systems Center (ESC), Air Mobility Command (AMC), AMC/BTIC, CISA (which became an active member of the CCRP core team), DISA/JITC, SOCOM, J2/DIA, CIA, NSA, CNA, IDA, the Air Force Historian, CALL, and the Army War College Peacekeeping Institute (AWC/PKI). The CCRP team had varying degrees of success in this regard, but in all cases, received numerous lessons learned reports and briefings from these organizations. Briefings and reports were also obtained from NATO organizational elements such as the JAT, the IFOR CJ6/CJCCC, the ARRC, the MND HQs, the IFOR Commander for Support (C-SPT), and several other sources.

CISA also undertook two major studies as part of its support to the CCRP effort. An IFOR C4ISR laydown was developed and is now available from them on a CD-ROM. A communications lessons learned assessment was done and is documented in their report, "Compendium of Operation Joint Endeavor Lessons Learned Activities," May 1997. An assessment of BC2A/JBS implementation lessons learned was also done for the CCRP effort by BAH in support of a DARO offer of help to CCRP.

CCRP contacts have also been made with the British and French lessons learned activities. Overall, the number of opportunities for collaboration was very large and potentially overwhelming for the modest size of the CCRP team. However, every effort was made to find and develop efficient mechanisms for collaboration. No significant effort was ignored and all relevant products were captured to ensure that CCRP's analyses and lessons learned were based on the best available insights and evidence.

Integration

CCRP assembled, reviewed, and integrated a large quantity of CCRP and non-CCRP briefings, reports, and other material. Products from a wide variety of sources were assembled first, so they would be available to support CCRP's analyses and reduce the effort that was required to create a comprehensive picture. Assembling the variety of views contained in these products put CCRP in a position to see what they had in common, to identify differences, and to assess their relative reliability and validity, as well as the comprehensiveness, reliability, and validity of the overall body of work. Moreover, CCRP was able to both use these products as sources of information in its own analyses and also develop the larger picture of C4ISR experience and performance.

The products covered the entire field of C4ISR. For example, the intelligence community undertook a number of assessments and lessons learned efforts. The CCRP team received inputs from the Task Force Eagle G2 on intelligence operations and ISR system performance in MND(N). Inputs were also received on the U.S. NIC operations in Bosnia and JAC support activities. Very early in the deployment SOCOM sent a team to inventory intelligence systems in the field and assess their contribution to SOF missions. The DCI organized a lessons learned activity that generated several significant reports on information releasability and dissemination. DIA and NSA also conducted their own review of the Bosnia experience. Virtually every intelligence organization with presence in the theater was seeking to place its own experience in context. These efforts were very valuable inputs to CCRP's understanding of the overall C4ISR issues. In addition, the Defense Science Board Bosnia Task Force report on the Application of Intelligence to the Battlefield was also made available to the CCRP team.

More focused efforts were underway from a number of other perspectives. The U.S. research and development community, particularly those elements led by DARPA and the DARPA/DISA JPO through various technology demonstration programs, was assessing the performance of leading-edge services and the process by which they were introduced into the *Operation Joint Endeavor* command structure. These were valuable sources for lessons learned in the technology insertion process. The Air Force established a Bosnia-oriented integration activity (referred to as the CUBE) at ESC to simulate the network of C2 systems controlling air operations in the theater with a particular emphasis on the CAOC. This allowed them to examine proposals for changes and assess the integration and introduction of new C2 capabilities before deployment into the Bosnian theater of operation. The ESC and Air Combat Command (ACC) also coordinated with the CAOC to assist with decision support system integration and air operation processes enhancements. The ESC lab also provided a Help Desk for dealing with real-time integration issues. The Army's AMC/BTIC served as a clearinghouse for critical technologies and the "nerve center" for tracking and integrating the technology communities' efforts to support U.S. soldiers in Bosnia. The SHAPE Technical Center (now the NATO C3 Agency, the Hague), who was responsible for technical support to NATO's C2, logistics, and transportation decision support systems as well as the new information systems used to support NATO's C2 operations (e.g., CRONOS) in-theater, was also collecting lessons learned and provided valuable insights to the CCRP team. Some of the contractors involved in bringing new technology into the theater and supporting it there were also learning important lessons and they too were documenting their experiences. N.E.T. provided CCRP lessons on the IDNX deployments and EDS provided lessons on the deployment of the IARRCIS.

SHAPE NACOSA and Communications and Information Systems Division (CISD), IFOR CJ6, the CJCCC, the ARRC G6, the MND G6s, and the C-SPT G6 provided insights on the deployment and management of the NATO communication and information networks, including lessons learned. IFOR CIMIC, Public Information, and PSYOP organizational elements provided insights to the CCRP team in the areas of civil-military operations and the IFOR information campaign. IOs, NGOs, and PVOs were also interviewed as a means to better understand the civil-military aspects of the operation.

The doctrine community was also watching operations in Bosnia closely, particularly for lessons learned in coalition C2 as well as civil-military relations. CALL deployed dozens of personnel with the U.S. troops supporting Task Force Eagle and issued four (a fifth in final review) volumes on findings and lessons learned. While largely at the tactical level, this work was very important to capture the U.S. experience. The U.S. Air Force had considerable interest in the Bosnia operation and began a vigorous effort to examine the problems associated with generating an integrated air picture in the theater, but then recognized that this was only a subset of the larger and more crucial issue of generating an integrated battlespace (air, ground, and maritime) picture and was deeply involved in that effort. IDA worked with the Air Force on issues related to air management, largely in the context of the CAOC. The Army War College Peacekeeping Institute held two After Action Reviews (AARs) to examine Title 10 issues that impact on the Army in the Bosnia context. These AARs have been made available to the CCRP study as well.

The AMC completed an analysis of its experiences in supporting the Bosnia deployment. The C2 elements of that report were valuable in the context of NATO lessons learned on this same topic and assisted CCRP in ensuring a balanced appraisal. EUCOM ECJ37 was designated by the Joint Staff J7 to be the theater manager for Joint Universal Lessons Learned System (JULLS). IDA was contracted to support EUCOM in this regard and to do an in-depth analysis of the planning, deployment, sustainment, and redeployment phases of the operation. These efforts provided the CCRP team with insights and a channel for monitoring a broader set of inputs relevant to C4ISR. The in-theater commands themselves held lessons learned conferences and meetings covering the deployment, sustainment, and transition of IFOR to SFOR phases of the operation. The results of some of these activities have been provided to the CCRP team in the form of briefing material.

The historians in NATO and U.S. commands were generally well informed and only a few days or weeks behind real-time capturing of important events. The NATO and IFOR historian's material and chronology were accessible through the JAT. The IFOR historian had recorded thousands of hours of interviews with all levels of the command structure. Activities of the other historians were generally releasable by the commands themselves. CCRP has initiated contact with the USAREUR, EUCOM, and Air Force historians to get access to their findings and databases.

Assembling the documentation in itself has created a valuable resource for future research and analyses. By actively reviewing and integrating these materials, CCRP has been able to make a meaningful contribution to the overall national and NATO lessons learned activities. By acting as a clearinghouse for the exchange of such materials, the Bosnia study has also contributed to the coherence and quality of the overall U.S. lessons learned activities.

Focused Research

CCRP's priorities were based on the needs and missions of the C4ISR community. They took two different perspectives: organizational and international. Organizational priority was given to OSD and the Joint Staff, with a recognition that the needs of the CINCs and services were also important priorities. At the same time, however, NATO's needs as a coalition and issues important to the non-NATO coalition partners were not ignored. Rather, they were picked up in the context of U.S. national needs. At the international level, U.S. issues were examined as well as issues that related to U.S. operations in the NATO context, NATO operations, and IFOR or NATO operations involving non-NATO partners. C4ISR was seen first as a military issue, but was also examined in terms of civil-military relations at all levels. CCRP's focused research addressed areas such as support to the warfighter, coalition command arrangements, C4ISR system performance and vulnerabilities, information operations, technology insertion, civil-military cooperation, and the lessons learned process.

Theater Visits

The ASD/C3I tasking for the Bosnia Command Arrangements Study was signed out on 15 February 1996 and study data collection began in the March/April 1996 time frame. The early phase of the CCRP study focused on data collection. Monthly visits were made to the JAT to gain insights and to review the database they were putting together on the IFOR operation. In addition to the data collection activity, CCRP also provided analyst support to the JAT during these visits. This too provided useful insights from a NATO perspective. Extensive visits were also made to supporting commands and to the theater of operation. These visits included EUCOM, DISA-EUR, the JAC, the 66th MI, USAREUR, USAFE, NATO, SHAPE, and the SHAPE Technical Center (now the NC3A the Hague). Two extended visits were made under the umbrella of the JAT observer corps to Bosnia and Croatia. In regard to the latter, visits were made to IFOR and the ARRC in Sarajevo, MND(SW) in Banja Luka, MND(SE) in Mostar, C-Support in Zagreb, and COMMZ (FWD) in Split. Visits were also made to the IFOR CJ6 and the CJCCC in Naples. NDU/CCRP also provided two observers to the JAT for duties at MND(N) in Tuzla and at IFOR (FWD) in Sarajevo. In addition, an NDU/CCRP observer and analyst was also provided to the JAT to focus on the area of IFOR information operations. This support included two extended visits to Bosnia and Croatia as well as visits to NATO, SHAPE, and the UN HQs in New York. The NATO and national insights gained through CCRP participation in the JAT observer and analyst activities have been invaluable.

The Future

The CCRP team continues to collect experiences and lessons learned from the IFOR portion of the operation, including those emerging from similar activities of the other two framework nations—France and the United Kingdom. Collection activities have also included the SFOR portion of the operation but at a significantly lower level of effort. It is planned to extend the IFOR database and library of lessons learned reports to include those of SFOR and any follow-on NATO activities. As new insights and findings emerge from the ongoing CCRP study activities, these will be documented in professional publications and shared through symposia and other professional forums.

XIII. Lessons Learned About Lessons Learned
Larry K. Wentz

Many NATO and national initiatives have attempted to collect Bosnia insights, assess the effectiveness of the IFOR, and assemble lessons learned from the Bosnia experience. Most of these activities were not well coordinated and no overarching set of issues or functions drove the independent activities. Furthermore, no one person or organization was given the responsibility for setting the agendas and priorities of these efforts. Hence, there were redundancies and overlaps in the related activities. The initiatives also varied in complexity and depth, duration of the efforts, and focus of the areas of interest. NDU was tasked by the ASD (C3I) to attempt to pull together an appropriate collection of ongoing activities and put a coherent C2 and supporting C4ISR picture together, including lesson learned. A by-product of this effort was firsthand experience with the numerous ongoing lessons learned activities and their strengths and weaknesses. This chapter discusses findings and experiences from both a U.S. and NATO perspective, including some national perspectives. This chapter discusses NDU's efforts to act as a clearinghouse for Bosnia study activities, to facilitate collaboration and cooperation among the related community initiatives, and to integrate the C4ISR community experiences and lessons learned into a coherent picture.

Approaches To Lessons Learned

As soon as CCRP began organizing its effort and seeking to assemble a list of ongoing activities, it became clear that a multitude of organizations and agencies were either already engaged in lessons learned activities in Bosnia or planning for them. CCRP alone had more than 40 U.S. Organizations participating in its Bosnia C4ISR Lessons Learned Roundtables. There was also a variety of approaches being employed to collect insights, assess operations, and assemble lessons learned (figure 13-1). These approaches ranged from more formal and structured arrangements such as the IFOR JAT, CALL, and the JULLS process employed by USEUCOM, USAREUR, and USAFE, to ad hoc arrangements such as the Air Mobility Command and DCI quick-look assessment activities. There were also other structured approaches such as the NDU/CCRP study, the Army War College Peacekeeping Institute After Action Reviews, the IFOR CJ6/CJCCC, C-SPT and ARRC lessons learned activities, and the activities of the historians (USEUCOM, USAREUR, USAF, SHAPE, IFOR, and others). The French employed a more ad hoc (individual collection and hot debriefing of returning commanders) approach to collecting their lessons and the British used a more structured (team) and unifying approach for their national effort. There were longer term strategic thinking-oriented assessment activities such as those being conducted at the George Mason University (GMU) Institute of Public Policy, the Army War College Peacekeeping Institute, the National Defense University Institute for National Strategic Studies, the Naval War College, and the Pearson Canadian International Peacekeeping Centre. These activities employed workshops and modeling and gaming techniques to examine policy, strategies, and options for the future.

The formal approaches tend to be long-term efforts that employ highly structured processes with collection, analysis, dissemination, and action resolution phases. They use subject area experts to collect information and insights through interviews, after action reviews, unsolicited inputs, and formal reporting such as JULLS. They also use a collection plan to focus and guide their

Lessons Learned About Lessons Learned

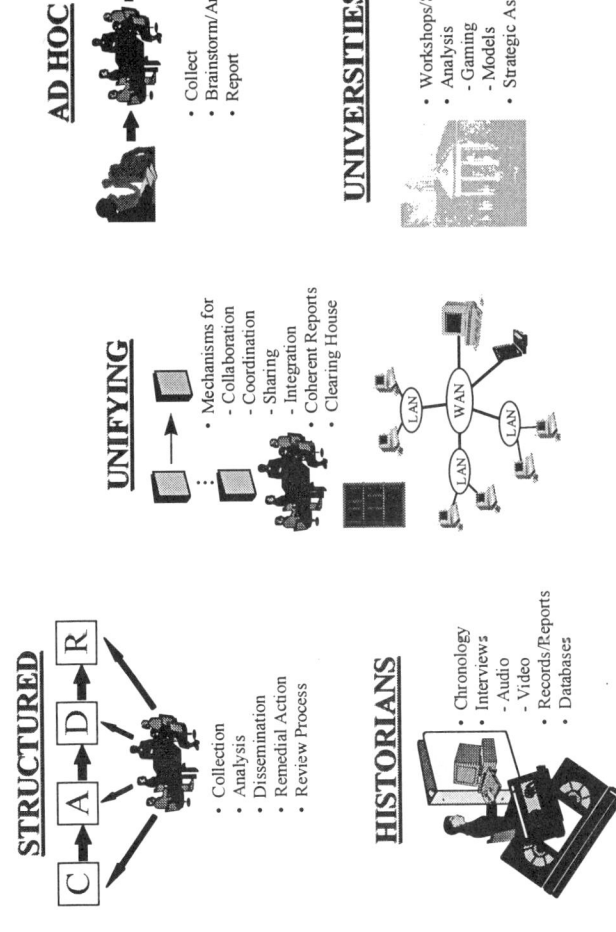

Figure 13-1. Approaches to Lessons Learned

activities. Professional analysts are used to assess the insights and experiences and to derive the lessons learned and recommend actions to resolve outstanding issues. Extensive databases are maintained on findings and recommendations. A review process is employed to ensure consistency and quality and to provide direction and guidance to the overall effort as appropriate. Results are disseminated in the form of formal reports, pamphlets, memorandums, bulletins, newsletters, customized reports, and Web home pages (both Internet and military networks). Finally, in some cases, a remedial action program is used to task organizations to fix problems and to track the resolution of outstanding actions.

The ad hoc activities tend to be less structured and of shorter duration. Subject area expert teams are formed and quick-look assessments using detailed theater interviews and brainstorming sessions are employed to drive out the key findings and recommendations. As an example, this was the approach used by the Air Mobility Command. The actions from ad hoc efforts tend to be focused on fixing near-term problems.

The other efforts are somewhere in between in terms of complexity and duration. For example, the JITC put a team of subject area experts in Bosnia for 3 months to collect insights and develop the communications baseline and associated interfaces and interoperability issues. Two months were then spent documenting and briefing their findings and recommendations, and a final report was published for broader distribution. The Army War College Peacekeeping Institute convened subject area experts, specifically those with Bosnia operational experience, for two different 1-week intensive after action reviews. The AAR outputs were briefings and reports with actionable items that were strategically oriented, i.e., things the Chief of Staff of the Army needed to be aware of and could take an action on. This effort was mainly focused on Title 10 issues but some other C2 issue areas were also addressed. The NDU/CCRP effort employed a small team of professionals oriented toward leveraging community activities to put a coherent story together that addressed strategic, operational, and tactical issues. The products were and will be briefings, reports, symposia and workshop participation and papers, and books and other material for the professional military education program. The IDA study done for EUCOM employed a small team of professionals to review, document, and analyze the U.S. participation in the Bosnia operation. Their reports addressed strategic- and operational-level issues related to the planning, deployment, sustainment, and redeployment phases of the IFOR operation.

Many of the commands involved in Bosnia had staff historians who were also seeking to document their commands' participation in the operation. The SHAPE and IFOR historians, in particular, had rich access and developed valuable material on the command history. The EUCOM, USAREUR, USAF, SHAPE, and IFOR historians were valuable sources for the NDU study. The historians used both audio and video taping extensively as the principal means for recording insights and experiences.

The commands, including the combat support organizations, also tasked their own headquarters to assemble lessons learned and to perform assessments. There were a few organization elements who, because of resource limitations and pressures of the operation, were unable to devote the level of effort necessary to do as complete a job as they would have liked to do. These units were, however, willing to work with unifying activities such as the NDU/CCRP effort to help them, but their lessons learned story together. IFOR held meetings of senior officers to review phases of the operation and to look ahead at future challenges. Indeed, virtually every level of command established similar tasking to ensure that lessons were both recorded and acted upon in the near term. Some of these reviews included specific review of performance issues, but their major focus tended to be on process improvement.

Finally, the universities and the military education community also monitored Bosnia. GMU's Institute of Public Policy (Program on Peacekeeping Policy) used their Conceptual Model of Peace Operations to examine issues related to Brcko. As noted earlier, the Army War College Peacekeeping Institute held two After Action Reviews focused on Title 10 issues. NDU's Institute for National Security Studies has been engaged in political-military analyses based on its expertise in prior peacekeeping efforts such as Somalia and Haiti. They have held workshops and used the NDU gaming facility to examine Bosnia issues related to civil-military operations, Brcko, IPTF, and conditions for exiting Bosnia. The Naval War College has also used its Situational Influence Assessment Module (produced by SAIC) to examine exit strategies. The Pearson Canadian International Peacekeeping Centre has sponsored a number of workshops and symposia on conflict resolution.

IFOR Lessons Learned Experiences

Despite the number of organizations involved in the lessons learned effort, no one, has yet been able to pull all of these activities together into a coherent "big picture" story for the military aspects. Furthermore, since little to no collection of lessons learned has occurred in regard to the political, civil reconstruction, nation building, and economic recovery aspects, an integrated picture of the "Dayton Perspective" has not even been attempted and it is not clear who would put such a perspective together in any case.

The IFOR JAT observers noted that many nations had fielded teams of analysts in various HQs, so there was the potential for much duplication of effort. Additionally, there was the burden placed on the staff in these HQs by a multiplicity of queries for essentially similar information. If a more coordinated approach had been possible from the outset, perhaps greater value might have been achieved to the benefit of all parties.

Lessons learned are multidimensional. In addition to the doctrine, policy, processes, procedural, and training aspects, there are also technical, system, operational, and command structure perspectives. One can look at them from NATO and national points of view or from the civilian, military, and humanitarian aspects. There are mission and function cuts that can be looked at as well as the planning, deployment, sustainment, and redeployment phases of the operation. The point is that no one organization covers all aspects of an operation in a way that puts a coherent big picture story together. For example, the IFOR JAT did not address the intelligence aspects of the operation. The IFOR CJ6 and CJCCC focused mainly on communications. The IFOR Commander for Support focused on functions such as movement control, legal, medical, and contracting but also covered some C2 structure and communications and information support aspects. The Air Mobility Command focused mainly on the airlift support for deployment. CALL, USAREUR, and the Army War College focused on the Army role in support of the operation. EUCOM and its IDA study looked at the U.S support to IFOR. The French and British focused on their national roles. The NDU/CCRP effort tried to pull a bigger picture story together, but again its guidance was C2 structure and the supporting C4ISR. There are lessons to be learned from the political, economic, and humanitarian activities in support of the Dayton Accord but it is not clear if anyone will be collecting insights and lessons learned for these aspects of the operation.

Clearly, broad participation has considerable benefits. The recognition of the importance of learning from the Bosnian experience, the active participation of both C4ISR producers and consumers, and the involvement of many agencies and organizations in both issue identification and problem solving are signs of learning and adaptive organizations. Hence, this bodes well for the future.

The current "catch as catch can" broad participation lessons learned system also has some very positive attributes. Lessons learned were sought throughout the operation and its supporting activities. The variety of actors involved meant that a broad range of perspectives were being considered. Moreover, because the operators were deeply involved, lessons were not generally collected and forgotten, but rather became the subject of specific actions to correct them. Obvious examples included the vigorous follow-up after LIWA reported vulnerabilities in unclassified LANs to USAREUR and the intelligence community's review of dissemination policy and follow-on aggressive action to change the field practices to improve the service to the coalition operation.

However, the lessons learned process had its problems. First, overlap and redundancy existed, which led to excessive demands on operator time. One senior NATO officer identified nine separate occasions when he had been interviewed by U.S. lessons learned efforts. Second, to the extent that lessons learned activities were performed within operating organizations, they tended to have parochial agendas and results. Third, no overall set of integrating issues or functions was created, so the lessons learned suffered from gaps on key issues and lacked systematic data collection efforts and sharing of lessons and insights. Finally, while lip service to information exchange was plentiful, many products were still held closely by their originators. The players in Bosnia lessons learned represented almost every organization or agency involved in or supporting *Operation Joint Endeavor*. The most important lessons learned activities were those of the commands and headquarters themselves, both U.S. and coalition partners, because they typically involved vigorous action programs to resolve the issues identified and because they represented the difference between the anticipated operating environment and the one actually encountered.

NDU's efforts to assemble a coherent lessons learned picture highlighted several difficulties as well. The most important problem encountered was the uncoordinated collection of information. In an effort to reduce demands on operators and simplify the situation, some commands granted "official" status to some collectors. For example, the IFOR JAT was given official monopoly on collecting lessons learned for NATO. Unfortunately, the focus of the formal IFOR effort was limited to the nine items in the JAT charter (see chapter 12). Furthermore, the quality of collection and analysis was dependent upon the specific officers the member nations were willing and able to provide the JAT for this tasking (it was necessary to augment the JAT with observers and analysts provided by NATO member nations). Only a fraction of the JAT team were trained analysts, and data collection tended to be more idiosyncratic than systematic. EUCOM granted similar "official" status to its IDA team. CALL functioned as the primary activity for

U.S. Army collection. Allied efforts were seldom as systematic as those used by U.S. commands. All in all, the high level of activity did not translate into systematic coverage of key issues.

Many of the lessons learned efforts have also proven parochial. They tended to focus on the relatively minor and technical issues that made day-to-day operations inconvenient or difficult rather than on more fundamental questions. There was a natural tendency to avoid putting one's own command on report so this resulted in a careful documentation of external factors without a balanced recognition of internal problems. Moreover, internally identified lessons learned had a tendency to focus on symptoms rather than causes. As a simple example, analyses of problems with computer systems viruses focused more on installing better virus protection devices rather than changing the behaviors that caused them to proliferate.

The most serious problem in lessons learned has been the inability to create an overarching set of issues or functions. While most lessons learned charters were very broad, no single person or organization had been given responsibility for setting the agenda. This resulted in gaps in coverage, particularly where the issues were potentially embarrassing or resided near organizational boundaries.

The lack of an overall structure for lessons learned collection and sharing was reinforced by the multiplicity of nations, organizations, and agencies involved and the inability to freely share findings and experiences. As noted earlier, the NATO JAT charter was limited to nine specific functional areas. C4ISR issues that cut across levels or national boundaries were particularly difficult to analyze because the charter seldom existed to examine the causal factors at work. Finally, broad community information exchange was more difficult than anticipated. The players were willing to orally discuss issues, insights, and lessons learned but few were willing to pass on formal or draft documentation until it was appropriately staffed and/or approved by their respective organizations for more general release. This reflected parochial agendas, NATO sensitivity to national access, and the lack of a central, authoritative lessons learned organization to facilitate information exchange and provide issue-focused guidance to the various efforts.

The Way Ahead

The need to capture lessons learned from real-world operations and use them for subsequent remedial actions is widely acknowledged throughout the international community. The need to build a more coherent story and more effectively collaborate and coordinate the collection and sharing of experiences and lessons learned may not be as widely accepted. Certainly, the international community needs to consider putting some mechanism in place to better focus, facilitate, and encourage the coordination, collaboration, and sharing of lessons learned activities and findings. The ability to enforce remedial actions also needs to be a part of this consideration. In order to accomplish this, an international organizational element needs to be granted some degree of official status and authority to perform the role. It also needs a staff of appropriate subject area experts and professional analysts, adequate funding, and an agreed process to guide the participation of the international community. NATO would be a logical organization to establish such a capability. If NATO were to provide such a capability, it would need to go beyond the level of effort and capability the JAT established to support IFOR and the NATO Permanent Maritime Analysis Team that supports maritime exercises and operations. Furthermore, it would need to not only be a BI-Major NATO Command (MNC) initiative that addresses the military aspects but also include the political aspects of NATO as well.

The NDU/CCRP approach to facilitate coordination, collaboration, and sharing through the use of the Bosnia C4ISR Roundtable was quite successful. This coupled with the special relationships formed with the IFOR JAT and U.S. command elements significantly helped CCRP's attempts to build a coherent story out of the various independent lessons learned activities. CCRP has been able to perform the role of clearinghouse with a reasonable degree of success. A lot of perseverance and community willingness to cooperate was necessary to pull off the successes to date. The effort is now bearing fruit.

The use of a unifying organization is certainly one way of pulling the community and their activities together. In the end, this may be the best way to approach improved collaboration, coordination, and sharing in order to ensure that a more coherent story emerges from the large number of activities triggered by a major international operation. It is certainly not a technology issue; the information networks of today provide the means to the end. It is an issue of political will. There is certainly a need to do this but the issues of who, where, level of effort, staffing, ability to enforce remedial actions, and funding of such an activity are yet to be fully addressed for either national or international initiatives. The system is broken and needs to be fixed.

There is an encouraging sign on the horizon. The lack of a standing NATO Joint Analysis capability, which led to the creation of the ad hoc JAT, also prompted discussion on the requirement for a permanent JAT. As a result of SHAPE's experience with IFOR, there is a BI-MNC proposal in front of the NATO Military Committee to consider the establishment of a BI-MNC Joint Analysis and Lessons Learned Centre. The stated purpose of this center is to be NATO's central agency for the operational analysis of exercises and real-world operations, and for the coordination of the related lessons learned and the associated remedial action process. It is the view of the two MNCs (SACEUR and SACLANT) that these three activities—analysis, lessons learned, and remedial action process—are closely connected and mutually supportive. This is certainly a step in the right direction to fixing the system for NATO and possibly for multinational operations as well.

XIV. Summary
Larry K. Wentz

NATO Comes of Age

The NATO Alliance proved that it can be flexible and adaptable and showed that with clear political guidance, the operational military arm can accomplish tasks given to it by its political authorities. The successful deployment of the NATO-led IFOR in support of *Operation Joint Endeavor* can be attributed to a number of factors. First, there was the pressure of world opinion to take action given the massacres in the country, the previous failures of the UN, and the opportunity for achieving a more permanent settlement provided by the Dayton Peace Accord (DPA). Second, relative to other international organizations (UN, WEU), NATO had an effective military and political structure. NATO had exercised its capabilities both politically (in the Partnership for Peace program) and militarily (in *Operations Deny Flight* and *Deliberate Force*) to bring stability to this part of the world. Finally, NATO had an intact command and control system, one based on 45 years of cooperation and refined during NATO operations in support of the UN in Bosnia.

Influencing Factors

The first ever out-of-area operation for NATO was a military success, but there were a number of key issues that IFOR had to address early on to ensure that it would happen. First, the Dayton Accord did not designate a single authority to synchronize the military, political, economic, and humanitarian aspects of the mission. Ad hoc arrangements were initially employed to facilitate collaboration and cooperation and more formal arrangements were employed later through participation in the Office of the High Representative (OHR)-established Joint Civil Commission (JCC).

Second, the civil-military activities in support of peace operations were new for NATO. There was no common understanding by commanders and staff at all levels of IFOR of the capabilities, roles, and mission of Civil Affairs units and personnel, referred to as Civil-Military Cooperation (CIMIC). Furthermore, the civil-military aspects did not receive sufficient attention during the planning and initial execution phase of the operation due to the heavy emphasis on the military enforcement aspects of the Dayton Accord and force protection.

Third, information operations for peacekeeping were also new for NATO. The NATO and SHAPE doctrines on public information and PSYOP had just been revised. National PSYOP doctrine differed and the command and control of PSYOP contingents remained with the participating nations (mainly the United States with participation from the United Kingdom, Germany, and to a lesser extent France) and was not placed under NATO C2 during the IFOR operation. The public information, civil affairs, and PSYOP aspects of the IFOR information operations required special attention to ensure coordination and synchronization of related activities. Ad hoc committees were established at the IFOR and ARRC levels to facilitate coordination.

Fourth, NATO had no in-place ability to deploy forward its strategic C4I capabilities. There was little to no Bosnia telecommunications infrastructure because it had been destroyed by the war and NATO air strikes. NATO, therefore, had to rely heavily on the national tactical assets of the framework nations—particularly the United States (the major contributor), the United Kingdom, and to a lesser extent France. The UN VSAT network, which was already in place, was used extensively and commercial products and deployable commercial SATCOM services were employed to extend NATO's strategic network connectivity into Bosnia and to provide information services to the deployed headquarters and forces.

There were other factors that influenced NATO and national activities in preparation for and execution of the IFOR deployment. The operation was occurring at a time when NATO and the nations were reducing force structures. Non-NATO and PfP nations would be involved with NATO in a real-world operation for the first time as well as the Russian Federation and there was little NATO guidance on how to proceed with these first-time events. In addition to being the first out-of-area operation, it was also the first major ground operation ever. There were multiple OPLANs that added some confusion. NATO would be taking over from the UN and other peacekeeping agencies and this had some built-in uncertainties. Deployment would take place in the depth of winter in difficult terrain. The likelihood of hostilities was a major concern because of the fragility of the peace arrangements in Bosnia. There were morale problems associated with deploying troops over the Christmas period. Therefore, one should not underestimate the degree of difficulty NATO and the nations faced as they prepared for and deployed to Bosnia in support of *Operation Joint Endeavor*.

Threat Environment

The threats in Bosnia were real. Three former warring factions, not only with significant combat power but also with robust intelligence collection capabilities, were waiting for the arrival of NATO forces and it was not clear how they might react to the IFOR deployment. The FWF also had a propaganda and disinformation campaign in operation and targeted against IFOR. Terrorists, organized crime, and petty criminals were also part of the threat. Finally, minefields were numerous and added risk to deployed personnel.

The local, national, and ethnic media were well established and generally trusted. The population of Bosnia was to a large extent literate and relatively well educated and used to all forms of media that characterize an "information society."

Making a Difference

Upon arrival in country, IFOR made it very clear to the FWF at the outset that they were there to enforce compliance with the Dayton Accord and would use force if necessary. Checkpoints were bulldozed, road blocks shut down, the FWF separated, and their forces and equipment placed in cantonment areas and barracks. Violations were experienced from time to time: weapons were discovered in unauthorized locations, soldiers and tanks in the ZOS, and unauthorized police checkpoints. Such violations were not tolerated and swift actions were taken when the FWF tested IFOR's resolve. The IFOR information campaign was also a powerful tool in getting the message to the FWF and the local population.

In the end, the Bosnia theater was more peaceful than expected. Except for a few overt physical attacks on facilities and personnel, the FWF were generally in compliance with the GFAP. One must be reminded, however, that the situation could have changed for the worse at a moment's notice.

Certainly, IFOR's tremendous military firepower was a deterrent but the military also put a lot of faith in the deterrent power of information dominance. IFOR was able to make it clear to the FWF that they could monitor them any time of the day or night and under any weather conditions. The ability to see, understand the situation, and strike with precision no doubt had its effect in deterring aggressive actions on the part of the FWF. In the words of MGEN William Nash, Commander MND(N), "We don't have arguments. We hand them pictures and they move their tanks."

The Fog of Peace Operations—Bosnia Experiences

Operation Joint Endeavor was, of course, an Operations Other Than War (OOTW) with all of the associated ambiguities, complexities, and challenges. As experienced in other OOTWs, these operations tend to be frustrating because the structure that militaries take for granted, such as a unified chain of command and clear, simple rules of engagement, are lacking.

For many reasons, OOTWs are usually messy and almost always involve ad hoc coalitions of the willing with politically driven command arrangements. More often than not they involve, at least in practice, a consultative environment in which key parties need to develop and maintain a common understanding of the mission, issues, and progress toward meeting the end state. Planning and executing such operations are complicated by factors such as short time lines, a highly dynamic environment, and uneven capabilities and experience among coalition members.

In almost all instances, OOTW operations are not able to rely on the in-country infrastructure to support their C2 needs and require augmentation of the limited indigenous capabilities with national tactical military systems. Given that a number of different players are usually involved and given their desire to use systems they are comfortable with, these operations typically begin with a "Federation of Systems" with the inevitable interoperability challenges and security disconnects. These are simply the realities of such operations and were true for *Operation Joint Endeavor* as well.

Force Protection

Bosnia was a somewhat schizophrenic operational environment. In MND(N), force protection measures were strictly enforced and troops were required to wear full battle gear and travel in four-vehicle convoys. For other parts of the area of operation, the force protection measures were less severe. The headquarters facilities were located in urban and/or open areas and many employed limited traditional lethal and physical protection such as heavily armed guards, tanks, barriers, sandbagged bunkers, and obstacle courses in access areas.

Protection for U.S. forces will always be a significant issue. In Bosnia, U.S. force protection took on a higher degree of importance than had been seen in other U.S. military peace support operations. It was a formal part of the OPLAN mission statement and permeated all aspects of mission execution. Many non-U.S. IFOR participants believed that U.S. force protection measures were politically motivated and not based on a realistic threat assessment. MGEN Nash, Commander MND(N), defended the tough self-protection standard as important for both safety and discipline reasons. Furthermore, in his view, "the American soldier today is...more of a target than soldiers of other countries and they deserve all the protection I can give them."

Enforcement of force protection was inconsistent between U.S. service members serving under a U.S. command and those under NATO control. Civil agencies were concerned that this inconsistency was sending mixed signals to the warring factions. The stringent U.S. force protection measures hampered civil-military cooperation activities and the ability of U.S. soldiers to move away from the peace-enforcement-only mindset. It appeared to many that the second- and third-order effects of the stringent force protection measures were neither fully understood nor properly anticipated. Some easing of the rules occurred over time as the operation evolved and more civil affairs work was performed off post.

Security Challenges

OPSEC was particularly challenging for the IFOR operation. The operational environment was reasonably stable for Bosnia and the lack of an obvious threat created the possibility of a relaxed security posture and increased complacency. Other types of OPSEC risks had to be managed as well. There were numerous television and print journalists questioning soldiers. On a daily basis, hundreds of local national workers entered IFOR areas of operation. It was a challenge for the CI and HUMINT operators to keep a close eye on these daily visitors.

There were COMSEC and INFOSEC issues that had to be dealt with as well. Although the military communications and information systems operated SECRET system-high, there were other systems that were not secure. The UN VSAT network, INMARSAT, cellular, and the commercial PTT telephone systems were not protected and they were used frequently for command and control purposes. The commercial Internet was also used frequently. Configuration management and information protection measures were slow in implementation. An enormous amount of classified and unclassified material was produced; extra care had to be taken when dealing with mixed classifications of information. There were releasability issues related to sharing information and capabilities among 30 plus nations. Diskettes were shared between classified and unclassified systems and there was a lack of discipline and standard operating procedures to effectively control the situation.

Security was an ongoing responsibility for which improvements were continuously made over the duration of the operation.

Information Activities

In today's high-technology environment, information can determine the success or failure of the military operation. The "CNN effect" (i.e., unsubstantiated media reports), coupled with the "information revolution," created formidable challenges for the military. In Bosnia, there was media presence throughout the country when IFOR arrived. The information networks serving the media, IFOR, and its coalition member nations provided the ability to share information at a speed and efficiency never before experienced. Frequently, media reports of incidents would reach the home country and/or higher headquarters before the commander on the ground was aware of the situation and able to react.

There were e-mails to home from the troops in the field and Internet home pages were used by the NATO and national public affairs organizations to inform and update the general public on IFOR operations. The ease with which information could be shared fostered active, and sometimes lengthy, reporting (such as daily situation reports). Higher headquarters were constantly apprised of matters both large and small. Occasionally, headquarters and other command elements would use the networks to bypass intervening organizations in order to get information firsthand, sometimes leaving the broader community in the dark. The problem soon became one of finding the useful details among the wealth of information available rather than a lack of information. Because of the improved ability to inform and influence, the Public Information Office and the IFOR Information Campaign (IIC) became important tools of the Bosnia operation.

As noted earlier, in some areas of Bosnia, such as those occupied by the Serbs, an information campaign targeted against NATO was already in full operation when the IFOR troops arrived. Hence, the IIC was at a disadvantage at the outset because it had to compete with an already established and effective campaign that could get inside of the IFOR decision loop and outmaneuver some of the initial IFOR efforts. A contributing factor was NATO rules of engagement for the IIC. The campaign was forbidden to use disinformation and deception and could not take actions that undermined the factions, take sides, or directly refute FWF disinformation activities.

IFOR also had some problems adapting to the local population's media consumption habits. While IFOR relied primarily on printed material (*The Herald of Peace* and *Mircko*, posters, and handbills) and radio to start with, the Bosnian's preferred medium was television. Also, IFOR radio transmitted on AM and the Bosnians listened mostly to FM radios. Adjustments were made to accommodate other media forms such as FM radio and television, including the use of local radio and television facilities as well. The

U.S. PSYOP platform, Commando Solo, was not deployed until the SFOR phase of the operation to support the September 1997 election activities.

The IIC proved to be a difficult task for IFOR and the jury is still out on its overall success. It was certainly a success in the first 9 months of the operation in support of force protection and Dayton Accord compliance activities and for the September 1996 national elections. There were also some other successes such as the raid on Fortica (terrorist training camps) and *Operation Volcano*, the destruction of 250 tons of Bosnia Serb munitions. The success on the civil, economic, and humanitarian side of the operation was not as obvious. A top-down driven campaign plan with top-down driven products was viewed as an important contributor to the military successes.

Intelligence Considerations

The intelligence community also faced challenges unique to supporting a coalition peace operation. Traditionally, intelligence tends to focus on the enemy. However, it is not always clear who the enemy is in a peace operation.

The bulk of the national intelligence systems supporting IFOR were designed for go-to-war, not peace, operations. The NATO intelligence doctrine, principles, and practices were being revised at the outset of the operation. In the case of the United States, "force protection" and the Army maneuver warfare doctrine drove the U.S. intelligence architecture put in place for *Joint Endeavor*. In reality, though, the IFOR operational environment was relatively benign and the peace support operation was not maneuver warfare.

The Bosnia intelligence operating environment was marked by large areas of operation and interest, difficult terrain, and poor weather conditions. There were multiple belligerent factions and a "front line" that was 360 degrees. The operation had to adapt to differences in NATO and national methodologies and procedures. The operation had to monitor a wide spectrum of threats, including the FWF, criminal activities, extremists, civil disturbances, and terrorism. FWF equipment storage sites and barracks, the ZOS, mass gravesites, and potential "hot spots" caused by freedom of movement, resettlement, and inter-ethnic conflicts had to be monitored as well. The nature of the operation muddled any clear division among strategic, theater, and tactical levels. Finally, equipped to function in a tactical fight, NATO and the national tactical intelligence capabilities were less prepared to function in a peace support role. Doctrine, CONOPS, procedures, intelligence preparation of the battlefield, and intelligence, surveillance and reconnaissance (ISR) capabilities had to be adjusted and augmented to accommodate peace operation requirements.

Experience with other OOTWs also clearly demonstrated that although non-intrusive means of collecting information were especially useful, HUMINT was usually key. In Bosnia, the man and woman on the ground collecting firsthand information about political leaders, business people, the condition of roads and bridges, withdrawal of forces from the ZOS, weapons and ammunition in cantonment areas, freedom of movement violations, and demonstrations and ethnic incidents proved invaluable. Over time, HUMINT became the dominant player in the IFOR intelligence operation.

The other intelligence disciplines proved important as well. SIGINT provided warning and a hedge against conventional threats. IMINT used the full spectrum of traditional assets from handheld to U.S. national to monitor verification sites and for the surveillance of "hot spots" and FWF compliance activities. There were also some non-traditional IMINT sources such as the Combat Camera Crew products, the AH-64 gun camera tapes, and the OH-58 cockpit tapes that proved invaluable. In addition, downlinked UAV imagery provided near real-time surveillance support. Many areas had land mines or were difficult to access from the ground; hence, the use of the advanced surveillance and reconnaissance capabilities avoided the need to put soldiers in harm's way. OSINT provided indications and warning of increased tensions in local areas, supported predictive analysis efforts, and helped focus other collection efforts. The "Night Owl," which was produced by the United

States at Camp Lukavac in MND(N), provided a daily summary of news and media commentary—a Bosnia version of the Pentagon's "Early Bird." Through its publication and use, commanders and staff were able to gain a better appreciation for the political, economic, and cultural environment. MASINT was used to support treaty compliance, early warning, and force protection.

The cumulative effect of the intelligence operation sent a clear signal to the FWF that IFOR was capable of knowing all and seeing all—Information Dominance. The U.S. military's phenomenal array of technology on the ground, in the air, and in space helped keep a risky operation relatively casualty-free. The counterintelligence and HUMINT activities in Bosnia were also essential to accomplishing the force protection mission by providing the information and intelligence the commander needed to manage and avoid risk and still accomplish the mission.

Civil-Military Aspects

The real "peacekeepers" in a peace operation are the humanitarian relief organizations that provide aid for the present and hope for the future. They are there before the military arrive, remain during the military presence, and stay after the military leave. Although Bosnia was a mature theater of operation for them, the military planners gave little (minimum) consideration to their experience, expertise, and activities in preparing for the IFOR operation. As a result, the military support to the humanitarian aspects of the operation was more reactive than proactive, especially during the early stages of the operation.

Military interaction with civilian organizations was more than civil-military cooperation. Civilian agencies (NGOs, PVOs, and IOs) had developed a network of influential contacts, compiled historical and specialty archives, and established relationships with local leaders and business people. They understood the infrastructure of the region, as well as the political and economic influences. These civilian agencies and centers of operation were both sources and consumers of intelligence information.

The humanitarian relief organizations tend to have limited communications and information system capabilities, especially in the theater of operation. Typically, they will use the in-country telecommunications infrastructure to the extent possible but many also have their own HF and/or VHF radios. These radios, however, may or may not be interoperable with the military systems they come in contact with during peace operations. In Bosnia, the NGOs/PVOs/IOs had reasonably good communications capabilities since many had already been in country for at least 4 years. They had access to the UN system and some of the regional PTT services in the country could be used as well.

Communicating and sharing information with the NGOs/PVOs/IOs was a new experience for NATO. The humanitarian relief organizations bring with them cultural and language differences that need to be understood and dealt with by the military in order to avoid misunderstandings, unnecessary competition, and mistrust. The need for the military and civil organizations to work together toward a common goal in Bosnia was not fully appreciated by the military at the outset. The emphasis by IFOR and the U.S. forces, in particular, on the military aspects of the Dayton Accord inhibited early progress in developing the civil dimension. Many of the new civilian agencies such as the OHR were consumed with problems in setting up their own organizations and cooperation with IFOR was not their main concern.

Civil-military activities prior to IFOR were very narrowly conceived by NATO and were generally regarded as "rear area" activities associated with host-nation logistic support and alleviating refugee interference with military operations. This combat-oriented doctrine had little relevance in the Bosnia context. The essence of the IFOR mission was to maintain a safe and secure environment so that reconciliation and reconstruction could take place. Since mission accomplishment depended upon effective civil-military cooperation (CIMIC), such cooperation and the CIMIC organizational element, in particular, became a vital "front line" asset. Widespread civil-military coordination and cooperation did not really occur until the May 1996 time frame. To quote Admiral Leighton Smith, COMIFOR, "In November we never heard of CIMIC. We had no idea what you did. Now we can't live without you."

Accommodating Differences

Coalition peace operations are accompanied by other doctrine, cultural, and language differences that challenged the overall coordination of the mission and ability to achieve unity of effort. Although a common language (such as English or French) was needed to participate, many of the players were not able to speak or understand the language used, placing an added burden on the coordination activities.

In Bosnia, PSYOP and CIMIC doctrines differed. The U.S. approach to PSYOP was to centrally manage and control at the highest level of command, whereas other nations such as the United Kingdom favored delegation to lower levels of the command structure, e.g., division headquarters. For CIMIC, there was no common understanding or approach at the outset of the IFOR operation. The ground commanders lacked a basic understanding of the role and value of CIMIC. This lack of understanding led to misperceptions that the CIMIC activities were contributing to mission creep and resulted in some unanticipated constraints being placed on their operation until their value became more apparent to the commanders. Unofficial doctrine and practices were essentially developed as the operation progressed. In the end, both the PSYOP and CIMIC operations were run out of their respective headquarters in Sarajevo.

Finally, with more than 30 different nations participating, it was a significant challenge to merge the cultural perspectives to achieve unity of effort and avoid cultural clashes. Liaison activities became very important and were used effectively to facilitate coordination and to bridge the language gap.

Putting the IFOR C2 Structure Together

NATO's ability to influence events during the early preparation for IFOR deployment helped avoid problems encountered by UNPROFOR and ensured a clearer definition of military tasks under a unified chain of command. Consequently, the language hammered into the General Framework Agreement made it clear that IFOR would "operate under the authority of and subject to the direction and political control of the North Atlantic Council through the NATO chain of command." UNSC Resolution 1031 provided NATO with the mandate and the necessary political authority to direct NATO and non-NATO forces under IFOR. However, NATO's robust military terms of reference highlight the paucity of authority for the civil activities of the High Representative—the weak link in the implementation of the Dayton Accord. In any future operation that depends on the success of both military and civil tasks, NATO will want to ensure that its civil counterpart also enjoys a commensurate amount of authority to fulfill its responsibilities.

The lack of unified political direction for the overall peace implementation process was a risk to the success of IFOR. The General Framework Agreement established three structures for implementation: an Implementation Force for the military aspects, a High Representative to coordinate civil tasks, and Donors Conferences to stimulate reconstruction. Given the UN's reluctance to take the lead, there was no internationally recognized political organization providing overall political direction. Consequently, the three structures remained virtually autonomous, operating within a loose framework of cooperation and without a formal structure for developing unified policy. The absence of a standing political organization with which the North Atlantic Council could coordinate policy exacerbated the inherent difficulties of synchronizing the civil-military implementation of the peace process at the strategic level and NATO's role in implementing the Peace Agreement.

There were some NATO and U.S.-related command arrangement shortfalls. Command and control differences existed between SHAPE and AFSOUTH/IFOR and between IFOR, the ARRC, and the Multinational Divisions, the most significant being with the U.S. MND(N). There was the need for a better definition of the command relationships between NATO, USCINCEUR, and USAREUR. Forces in a multinational environment operate with two chains of command: one for operations and the other for command, administrative, and logistical matters. The absence of a clear definition led to some inefficiencies and confusion during the operation. At the center of this issue was how the Army (Component) fulfilled its Title 10 responsibilities. The root cause of the problem was the absence of a U.S. Joint Task Force command equivalent that had the authority, expertise, and staffing to sufficiently provide U.S. C2 and coordinated logistics for out-of-sector U.S service members. In addition, in accordance with National Security Decision Directive 130, the U.S. PSYOP forces were not placed under IFOR C2. These forces remained under USEUCOM control. This caused some problems in the product coordination and approval process and limited the flexible use of PSYOP elements at the tactical level. The U.S. Civil Affairs and IFOR/ARRC CIMIC elements experienced command and control problems as well. Furthermore, having two headquarters (IFOR and ARRC) in the same local area of operation created problems not only for CA/CIMIC activities but also for the Public Information Offices too. Another important C2 shortfall was inadequate early coordination with humanitarian organizations, particularly the NGOs and PVOs already in country.

IFOR Command Arrangements

The AFSOUTH was made the operational-level headquarters for *Operation Joint Endeavor*. However, AFSOUTH was neither staffed nor equipped to lead an expeditionary land force into combat. The ARRC, NATO's rapid reaction force, was established as IFOR's corps-level land component command. The three framework nations (the United States, United Kingdom, and France) formed the basis for the multinational divisions (North, South West, and South East, respectively). OPCON and OPCOM of the divisions were also assigned to the ARRC. IFOR headquarters was split between Naples and Sarajevo and the ARRC's headquarters was located at Ilidza near Sarajevo, placing two major command headquarters within a few miles of each other. The U.S.-led MND(N) was the largest division and included brigades from Turkey, Russia, and a third non-U.S. brigade referred to as the NordPol brigade (made up of troops from Finland, Sweden, Norway, and Poland). The British-led MND(SW) was built around a British brigade along with troops from Canada, the Netherlands, and Denmark. Finally, the French-led MND(SE) was the smallest division and was comprised of troops from France, Italy, and Portugal. Both the British and French already had a large number troops in Bosnia in support of UNPROFOR and the Rapid Reaction Force. Hence, the bulk of the deployment activities for IFOR were the NATO command unit forces, the U.S. forces, and the forces of the non-NATO participating nations.

Maritime and air operations were run through COMNAVSOUTH, COMSTRIKFORSOUTH, and COMAIRSOUTH. The command of air operations was achieved by designating the IFOR Air Component Commander as the Joint Force Air Component Commander. A single-layer C2 structure was established at the CAOC in Vicenza, Italy, and was responsible for the entire air effort, simplifying the C2 for air operations. Collection management authority for aerial intelligence platforms (such as Predator) was a CAOC responsibility as well. The IFOR Regional Air Movement Control Center that was collocated with the CAOC exercised airlift movement control. This facilitated coordination with the other air operations. The air tasking process brought together all of the different tasking requirements and unified them in a single order, the Air Tasking Message.

The U.S. SOF established a Special Forces operating base in San Vito, Italy, and a forward operating base in Sarajevo under IFOR. Liaison control elements were assigned to coalition and NATO units to integrate intelligence, operations, communications, close air support, and medical evacuation. SOF also assisted in surveying and monitoring the zone of separation, supported civil-military activities, and provided liaisons with the FWF. Commander,

Special Operations Command Europe (also Commander, Special Operations Forces, IFOR) assumed OPCON of all SOF elements in support of *Operation Joint Endeavor* except for SOF afloat, PSYOP, and CA forces. U.S. PSYOP forces remained under USEUCOM C2 and CA forces under USAREUR command. As noted earlier, the command relationships of the U.S. PSYOP and CA forces were not clearly defined at the outset of the operation and this caused problems for the deployed forces. There was a Combined Joint Special Forces Operations Task Force located in Sarajevo which the U.S., UK, and France SOF elements supported. The United Kingdom and France also had their own national SOF units supporting MND(SW) and MND(SE) respectively.

An IFOR Commander for Support (C-SPT) was established in Zagreb, Croatia. His responsibilities included coordinating the sustainment, movements, medical, engineering, and contracting operations of the national logistic elements; and commanding selected IFOR units in support of the deployment, execution of peace implementation, and redeployment of IFOR. C-SPT was also designated as the single point of contact for all IFOR matters pertaining to relations with the Croatian government. The NATO Maintenance and Supply Agency (NAMSA) established a field office in Split, Croatia. They were responsible for all NATO common-funded contracting and contracting for all scarce resources in theater. They provided liaisons with C-SPT and the framework division headquarters. NAMSA headquarters in Luxembourg held all contracts for the theater. The ARRC COSCOM commander was designated the COMMZ Forward Commander and was located in Split, Croatia, as well. He was responsible for reporting movement into theater to C-SPT. Finally, three National Support Elements were established to support the framework nations' movement activities: the United States in Kaposvar, Hungary, the British in Split, Croatia, and the French in Ploce, Croatia.

Special Arrangements

Some of the IFOR C2 relationships were politically driven. For example, a special agreement was required between the U.S. Secretary of Defense, William Perry, and the Russian Minister of Defense, Pavel Grachev, for the employment of Russian forces in IFOR. This agreement provided SACEUR (General Joulwan) control of the Russian brigade through the Deputy Commander of IFOR for Russian Forces, Colonel General Shevtsov. COMARRC exercised tactical control (TACON) of the brigade through the Commander MND(N) in whose area the brigade operated. OPCON remained with the Russian chain of command. As with other politically dominated C2 structures, this arrangement would be problematic under stress, particularly if new missions were required. It did, however, initiate military cooperation between Russian and NATO forces.

IFOR established a Joint Military Commission (JMC) as the central body for commanders of military factions to coordinate and resolve problems. Two or more FWF military representatives (usually commanders) attended meetings under IFOR supervision to coordinate joint activities, disseminate intent and instructions, and resolve differences. COMIFOR delegated routine JMC chairmanship to COMARRC who issued instructions to ensure the parties' compliance with the military aspects of the GFAP. Below the COMARRC level, the MNDs, their subordinate brigades, and battalions established subordinate military commissions. At these lower levels, the JMC activities included disseminating policy, issuing instructions to factions on policies and procedures, coordinating GFAP-required actions, resolving military complaints or questions, coordinating civil-military actions where appropriate, and developing confidence-building measures between the parties.

The integration of the Partnership for Peace (PfP) nations and other non-NATO nations under NATO C2 was a success for several reasons. First, NATO already had experience dealing with the PfP nations through the NATO PfP Program and related exercise activities. Second, innovative command arrangements were employed at several levels. For example, national officers were brought into the multinational HQs and senior national officers were "dual hatted" as deputy commanders.

The command arrangements for the Public Information Office (PIO), PSYOP, and CIMIC operations and some aspects of the intelligence operations (e.g., CI /HUMINT) also required innovative adjustments to effectively integrate them into the overall IFOR command structure and operation. OPLAN 40105 called for PIO and coalition press and information centers with each of the major IFOR headquarters. In Sarajevo, IFOR and the ARRC decided to share a single press center located in the Holiday Inn but this caused confusion in the chain of command because of the dual command relationship and sometimes conflicting guidance. At the multinational divisions, the commanders preferred to bring their own national PI assets to run the PI program and this too introduced some confusion into the IFOR PI operation due to conflicting IFOR and national doctrine, procedures, and guidance on the nature and amount of information to be released to the media.

Putting the IFOR C4I Puzzle Together

In spite of formidable obstacles and a somewhat chaotic beginning, NATO and its member nations installed and operated the largest military-civil Communications and Information Systems (CIS) network ever built to support a major peace operation.

NATO had never attempted peace enforcement. Consequently, there was no doctrine, experience, or accepted practices to guide CIS planning and implementation—the NATO CJTF was just a concept and not doctrine. Furthermore, there were multiple NATO and national CIS organizations involved in the planning, implementation, and management activities related to the IFOR deployment. AFSOUTH and SACEUR OPLANs reflected differing perspectives on CIS network management. The Dayton Agreement assigned frequency management responsibilities to IFOR even though NATO had no established capability. These factors contributed to CIS organizational problems at the outset for the IFOR CJ6. As a result, it was necessary to create a Theater Frequency Management (TFM) capability to address the Dayton Agreement tasking and a Combined Joint Communications Control Center (CJCCC) to facilitate NATO and national coordination and focus the planning and management of the CIS aspects of the IFOR operation.

Dynamic Requirements Base

The communications and information needs of operations such as the Public Information Office, IFOR Information Campaign, Engineers, PSYOP, CIMIC, CI, and HUMINT were not completely formulated or necessarily fully understood at the outset of the operation. The need to be able to interface with and provide some limited support to the NGO/PVO/IO community was also underestimated. Therefore, the requirements were not adequately articulated to the CIS planners and providers so that the necessary services could be made available at the outset of the operation to support these activities. The CJCIMIC operation in the Burger building in downtown Sarajevo only had a few local telephone lines to conduct business in the early stages of operation. If they needed information services or a broader IFOR communications capability, they had to go to IFOR headquarters at the Tito Residency several blocks away. The CIMIC and some HUMINT operations vehicles lacked radios for communicating while operating in the countryside. The engineers also generated a requirement for force protection communications since they too were frequently scattered throughout the country.

Established NATO policy precluded the use of the Internet for operational purposes. However, the engineers and legal and medical personnel needed to use the Internet to access reference material. The PIO also needed Internet access for media interaction and more effective communications and information services to be able to quickly inform the chain of command of media-related, time-sensitive issues. The PIO could use the Internet to get English translations of Croatian and other international press releases and news articles. The NATO policy makers were slow to make a change regarding the use of the Internet.

The timely distribution of Combat Camera and CI/HUMINT digital camera and other video products was a problem faced early on in the operation. Adjustments had to be made to accommodate these needs. One of these adjustments was the integration of the U.S. CI/HUMINT commercial notebook computer-based data acquisition, management, and communications system into the SIPRNET—the capability is referred to as TRRIP. Linking the U.S. MSE network with the SIPRNET via Trojan Spirit provided broader bandwidth connectivity to the battalion level for TRRIP and other intelligence users and over time significantly enhanced the operational effectiveness of the CI/HUMINT teams in particular.

Extension of NATO CIS Capabilities

NATO's existing CIS infrastructure was not able to satisfy the requirements for this first out-of-area operation. The so-called NATO CIS Contingency Assets Pool (NCCAP) concept, which envisaged a core of deployable and earmarked national equipment, pre-authorized funding for contingency purchases, and use of national assets, was not sufficiently mature to support the operation. Significant enhancements were needed to extend NATO systems to the deployed forces and to improve the in-area CIS capabilities. Heavy reliance was placed on the framework nations' tactical CIS assets, particularly those provided by the United States, and the lease of PTT/IDNX connectivity by NATO to extend services into Croatia initially and later into Bosnia. Pragmatic and unconventional steps were taken to procure CIS capabilities. In addition, service was leased from the UN VSAT telecommunications network, which was already in operation in Bosnia and Croatia, and used by IFOR to support both the deployment and sustainment phases of the operation. Other systems and services were acquired through "emergency" acquisition procedures and leasing.

CIS support for air and naval operations remained in place following *Deny Flight*, *Decisive Force*, and *Sharp Guard* and did not require special efforts to integrate them into the IFOR operation. There was a similar arrangement for the Special Forces CIS support. Although a Reserve Force was never allocated to IFOR, the U.S. Marine Expeditionary Unit offshore remained an option and had to be considered in the development of the CIS architecture.

Due to the lack of Bosnia telecommunications infrastructure and cross-IEBL connectivity, mountainous terrain, and high cost of clearing land mines and providing force protection for mountain-top radio relay sites, an extensive tactical military satellite communications network was deployed to provide the required connectivity into the area of operation. The network used U.S. and UK national tactical satellite ground terminals that were placed in or near urban areas where the headquarters facilities were located and were provided force protection commensurate with these facilities. NATO only had one TSGT at the time of deployment and it was deployed to Sarajevo to support HQ IFOR. As the operation evolved, commercial VSAT services were extended into the Bosnia area of operation as well.

Unanticipated Training and Contracting Considerations

For any military operation, a certain amount of "learning on the job" is expected. However, the deployment into a generally urban environment, coupled with the extensive use of commercial products and services, created a need for more intensive on-the-job-training than had been anticipated. The CIS staff had to be prepared to operate in both a fixed (rewire buildings for telephone and LAN services) and tactical environment. In many cases, it was necessary to pull tactical equipment out of the vans and install it in a commercial office-like environment. Staff was required to operate across multiple disciplines (e.g., pull cables and install LANs). The use of commercial technologies such as VSATs, IDNXs, VTCs, ROUTERs, digital switches, and other data network products and services added training requirements. In fact, it was necessary to establish a special training program at the NATO Latina training facility for the IDNXs. Dealing with contractors and the Croatian and BiH PTTs also provided new challenges. Both the military and the contractors were on steep learning curves. Inadequate spares were purchased for equipment procured under emergency procedures and the repair time for assets under warranty was excessive. In the early phases of the IFOR operation, CIS was in a permanent state of flux. CIS personnel at all levels worked on improving the CIS infrastructure with remarkable enthusiasm and initiative. The success of the CIS implementation and operation was, to a large degree, due to their abilities and dedication.

The IFOR C4I Puzzle

In preparation for the execution of OPLAN 40104, the extraction of UN forces, a leased E1 (2mb/s) network was extended by SHAPE/NACOSA into Croatia and the United States into Hungary. By the end of May 1995, an IDNX-based strategic backbone information network was fully operational. The NATO TSGT was deployed to Camp Pleso (Zagreb) and used to extend SHAPE headquarters voice, message, and data services to the Zagreb area through the use of the REPLICA system, a SHAPE reach-back capability. With the signing of the Dayton Peace Agreement on 14 December 1995, the mission changed and Croatia and Hungary became the embarkation points for NATO and national troops deploying into the region. OPLANs 40105 and 10405 provided the guidance for the deployment of these forces and the supporting CIS infrastructure.

A complex mixture of NATO, national, UN, and civilian and commercial networks and components provided IFOR CIS services (i.e., voice, message, data, and VTC services). National tactical equipment was used to establish the core IFOR telecommunications infrastructure. The U.S. TRI-TAC system provided a large portion of the strategic- and theater-level telecommunications infrastructure supporting organizations such as SHAPE,

AFSOUTH, IFOR, C-SUPPORT, COMMZ, and the NSEs. NATO also provided some. The UK tactical system, PTARMIGAN, provided the telecommunications support for the ARRC and between the ARRC and the MND headquarters. The United States, United Kingdom, and France used their tactical systems to support division-level communications including service to those forces assigned to their divisions. TRI-TAC/MSE equipment was employed in support of MND(N) and the U.S. NSE in Hungary. PTARMIGAN was used to support MND(SW) and the UK NSE in Split. French tactical systems already in place were used to initially support MND(SE). The tactical system RITA was deployed in the March 1996 time frame to provide additional support to MND(SE) and its NSE in Ploce. The Italian system, SOTRIN, supported the Italian brigade in MND(SE) and the German tactical system, AUTOKO, supported the German contingent in MND(SW). The data and VTC networks were largely derived from commercial products and services. Commercial VSAT and IDNX products and services supplemented the tactical satellite backbone connectivity provided by the U.S. and British tactical satellite systems.

STANAG 5040 was employed to provide an analogue interface between the national tactical and strategic voice networks, between TRI-TAC and the NATO strategic voice network, IVSN, and between TRI-TAC and the commercial networks such as the UN VSAT and the Bosnia and Croatian PTTs. The Interim Digital Interface PTARMIGAN (IDIP), designed by the United Kingdom for this operation, provided a digital interface between PTARMIGAN and the TRI-TAC/MSE systems. STANAG 5040 was used for the TRI-TAC to RITA interface as well as by SOTRIN and AUTOKO interfaces with RITA and PTARMIGAN respectively.

The NATO CRONOS Wide Area Network and the Interim ARRC CIS network (both client-server architectures, employing Microsoft Office for office automation and providing M/S e-mail service) provided valuable crisis response and command and control capabilities for the IFOR operation. However, they lacked common standard operating procedures and needed more efficient network management. VTC was used extensively by IFOR and the

ARRC and as time went on, it became a key element in conducting business. VTC was also the C2 system of choice for the U.S. Army forces.

INMARSAT was used extensively and commercial cellular services were available in some areas of Croatia and towards the end of the IFOR phase of the operation in the Sarajevo area as well. Unclassified Internet was also used frequently and demands for service increased throughout the operation. Internet use by NATO, IFOR, and national elements was not planned; its use simply grew with user demand. An interesting side note, the Internet was used by the factions to tell their story (e.g., Serbs used it for their disinformation campaign). The UN and humanitarian relief organizations also made extensive use of the Internet to inform the international community of their actions.

The U.S. LOCE system was extended to division headquarters level and above to support IFOR intelligence needs. Nations also provided national intelligence support and services to IFOR through liaison officers and National Intelligence Cells (NICs). A mixture of prototype and operational systems were used in an attempt to fuse various land, sea, and air pictures into a tactical picture. The maritime and land pictures provided to the tactical commanders were of good quality. The air picture (referred to as RAP—Recognized Air Picture) in the CAOC, made up from a variety of sources, was of particularly high quality. However, there was no overall integrated maritime/air/land picture. The CRONOS network was used to distribute the RAP to the IFOR C2 nodes.

Network and system management of IFOR's communications and information networks proved to be a major challenge. An IFOR CIS organization structure had to be created, agreed upon, and staffed quickly. The U.S. Joint Pub 6-05 provided the basis for the establishment of the CJCCC to plan and manage IFOR's networks. System tools had to be acquired to monitor and manage the networks. There were multiple NATO and national players (e.g., SHAPE's NATO CIS Operating and Support Agency (NACOSA), the AFSOUTH ACOS CISD, the IFOR CJ6, the CJCCC, the ARRC

G6, the MND G6s, and national J6s) whose roles and relationships needed to be established and their activities in support of the operation coordinated.

C4I Integration and Interoperability Considerations

There were overlaps in network and system management organizational responsibilities that needed to be worked out since the distinction between strategic, theater, and tactical became blurred. NATO communications and ADP were managed separately and this needed to be accommodated by the CJCCC. There were stovepiped network implementations that had to be accommodated as well. The NATO and national C4 and I and national ISR systems were managed separately. Coordination and collaboration became key ingredients in the evolution of the IFOR network management structure and capabilities. Over time, these issues were resolved and the CIS system provided reasonable services. However, the CIS system for the most part was never heavily stressed during the IFOR operation. Therefore, the performance of the networks and the supporting management organization were never tested under more hostile or stressful conditions.

Historically, interoperability has been one of the most difficult areas to deal with and this operation was no exception. The analog-based STANAG 5040 was still the norm for interfacing strategic, theater, and tactical voice systems. No digital interface existed for interfacing strategic and tactical networks. The TTC-39D experienced interface problems with the Ericsson MD-110 switch used by the UN and IFOR. The STU-IIB is a NATO-approved secure voice equipment and was used extensively by IFOR. A large number of the U.S. forces that deployed to Bosnia brought with them STU-IIIs that were not interoperable. The Interim Digital Interface PTARMIGAN (IDIP), designed by the United Kingdom for this operation, was used to provide a digital interface between the UK PTARMIGAN and the U.S. TRI-TAC/MSE tactical systems. The IDNX deployment required the certification of some 50 interface arrangements.

There were no automated interfaces between the IFOR data networks (CRONOS, IARRCIS, and LOCE) and national networks. The CRONOS was not interfaced with LOCE or the ADAMS networks even though information was manually transferred between the systems. The main reason for this was security considerations. There were no approved secure guard gateways that could accommodate an automated interface. The ADAMS movement control system and JOPES required a manual interface for exchanging information. U.S. intelligence processing systems used at echelons above corps (EAC) did not "talk" to the echelons at corps and below (ECB) systems. To fix the problem, some EAC systems such as the U.S. Joint Deployable Intelligence Support System (JDISS) had to be deployed to ECB intelligence centers. Exercises such as *INTEROP 95* and *Mountain Shield* helped to work out many of the integration and interoperability issues in advance of the deployment and also provided excellent training for the organizations that deployed in support of the operation. However, while interoperability is improving, there is still a long way to go to achieve seamless integration of CIS systems and services.

IFOR Information Services

The pervasive use of COTS information products and services propelled NATO and IFOR into the Information Age and a new way of doing business. There was extensive use of e-mail and a reduced reliance on formal messaging. The formal message traffic (the NATO TARE message network) by volume (megabytes per day) was less than 10 percent of the total IFOR daily data network traffic. The VTC was used daily by IFOR and ARRC command elements for collaboration and coordination. For USAREUR and its deployed commanders, VTC became the C2 system of choice. The VTCs were also used by subordinate command elements to conduct day-to-day business. PowerPoint briefings were the medium of choice for presentations and were readily distributed over the data network. A cottage industry of "PowerPoint Rangers" emerged, as the presentations became very sophisticated. The briefing packages frequently exceeded a megabit in size and placed heavy loads on the data networks as they were distributed around the theater. The data networks were also used for collaborative planning and distribution of wide-band information such as images.

The new capabilities provided the opportunity to share information efficiently and nearly simultaneously at all levels of the command structure. This was a vast improvement over the previous procedures, requiring the corroboration of data successively reported through each level in the chain of command. It was also possible to exchange information that bypassed ("skip echelon") intervening levels of the command structure. The ability to electronically bypass levels of command to obtain information firsthand was occasionally used in the interest of expediency and providing information up the chain of command but sometimes at the expense of leaving others in the dark.

Managing all of the information available to the commander and his staff was a serious problem. Users did not have adequate tools to search for available information. Likewise, there were inadequate tools for managing information collection, storage, and distribution. This was particularly true in the area of coordinating, integrating, and fusing intelligence, surveillance, and reconnaissance capabilities and making this information available to the user. There were other sources of information such as the Internet and local and international media that needed to be incorporated into the IFOR information database. In terms of sharing classified information, security releasability was also an issue that needed to be addressed early in the operation to ensure that information was given to those who needed it in a timely way without revealing sources and methods, but stringently protecting highly sensitive information. There were 36 coalition partners, some of which NATO had never shared classified information with before. A special category, IFOR-releasable, was established for the operation.

Although extensive use was made of e-mail, VTC, and data network services, voice communications still played a major role in conducting the IFOR information operation. This was true in spite of a grade of service that, at times, exceeded a 20-percent probability of blocking for call attempts. In addition, the end-to-end voice quality was marginal if the call had to be routed through several different tactical switched networks.

The IFOR information revolution largely stopped at the division level in Bosnia. In some cases, such as MND(N) and for the U.S. forces in Croatia and Hungary, higher bandwidth services were extended to the battalion. Every U.S. base camp had telephone service and secure and non-secure data and e-mail capabilities. The U.S. intelligence community extended 128kb/s service to brigades via Trojan Spirit II deployments to the brigade level. On the other hand, the communications and information system support to the IFOR warfighter, in general, changed little and they continued to operate much as they had in the past. Operations were conducted using acetate-covered 1:50,000 maps (seen in all command centers), outmoded tactical equipment, and sensor or reconnaissance systems organic to the national ground units. The command centers were located in urban buildings, tents, semi-destroyed buildings, or the back of armored vehicles.

Although the deployed high-technology systems generally supported the headquarters far more effectively than they supported the soldier on the ground, there were exceptions. Many innovative uses were made of the U.S. military's array of advanced technologies (mainly in the areas of ISR) to more effectively support both the headquarters and the soldier on the ground. In fact, Bosnia became a model for the U.S. doctrine known as Information Dominance. The operation also became an advanced information system technology test bed for both NATO and advanced technology-driven nations such as the United States.

IFOR CIS Commercialization

IFOR commercialization efforts came in several forms. First, commercial products and services were used to augment the military systems deployed, as was the case with the IDNX and VSAT. The NATO data network CRONOS and the U.S. data networks NIPRNET and SIPRNET were based on commercial products and provided the strategic- and theater-level information services required for C2 operations. The NATO and U.S. VTC networks were also based on commercial products. Commercial products and services were also an integral part of advanced technology capabilities deployed to theater, e.g., the U.S. BC2A/JBS information services and broadcast network. Commercialization played a role in the IFOR exit strategy and was used to replace tactical military telecommunications systems with commercial products and services.

The use of commercial products and services had its challenges. Competitive bidding did not always realize the best product for price. Contracting arrangements differed among the different factions. There were no Radio Shacks/Tandys to buy spare parts or urgent capabilities. Maintenance support was complicated both in terms of adequacy of repair facilities, excessive repair cycles for assets under warranty, ready access to spares, and quality and use of vendor maintenance personnel. The latter included ethnic constrains such as the inability to easily use a Croatian maintenance person in a Serb area. Most vendors in theater would deal in cash only. Documentation and training packages in many cases were inadequate. Integration of commercial and military systems was not always straightforward. In spite of these difficulties, commercial products and services were used extensively and in many cases quite successfully.

IFOR's plan for the commercialization of their communications network was aimed at reducing the costs to NATO, allowing for the timely withdrawal of tactical systems, and reducing IFOR's dependence on the UN VSAT network. The plan was to install ERICSSON MD-110 digital switches at the major headquarter locations, expand the commercial VSAT/IDNX network, and lease E1 connectivity from the Croatian and BiH PTTs where available. The evolution of the commercial network (referred to as the IFOR Peace Network (IPN)) was slower than IFOR would have liked. The main difficulties centered on the slow reconstruction of the BiH PTT infrastructure and the continued unwillingness of the FWF PTTs to provide cross-IEBL connectivity.

The United States also had major commercialization efforts in Taszar and Kaposvar, Hungary, and Tuzla, Bosnia. In both the NATO and U.S. commercialization initiatives, a tactical military overlay system remained to support essential C2 requirements.

Some Unintended Consequences

There were unintended consequences associated with the TOA to LANDCENT and the removal of the ARRC CIS systems. The UK EUROMUX tactical system and the U.S. MSE tactical system did not replace the functionality of ARRC's PTARMIGAN system, e.g., secure voice conference capability and secure SCRA. The UK IARRCIS and THISTLE information systems, which were used by the ARRC to build and distribute the ground order of battle and other C2 and intelligence information, were pulled out and replaced with the NATO CRONOS and its prototype C2 and intelligence applications PAIS and CRESP. The ARRC's geographic support, which provided the map and boundary databases used by all IFOR command elements, was not removed but arrangements had to be made with the United Kingdom to lease the system to NATO. And finally, the CIS capabilities of the Allied Military Intelligence Battalion were also impacted by the withdrawal of ARRC equipment. These capabilities all required replacement to adequately support the SFOR operation.

Opportunities for Behavior Change— Lessons Learned

According to the Center for Army Lessons Learned, "A lesson is learned when behavior changes." Many of the IFOR experiences were not new and therefore were lessons yet to be learned. A major factor contributing to this situation was the inability to effectively share lessons already learned. The process is flawed. This point was made many times over by those interviewed by both the NDU/CCRP study team and the IFOR JAT. Frequently the observation was made, "if I had only known this before I deployed." Today's information technologies certainly provide the means for enhanced collaboration, sharing, and knowledge building. For example, IFOR-related home pages on INTELINK (e.g., EUCOM and INTEL community) and the commercial Internet (e.g., IFOR, SHAPE, and Task Force Eagle) are excellent examples of capabilities in place to serve selected community needs. The real issue is one of community will, and of who assumes the leadership role to put such an enhanced capability in place to serve the broader community needs as a whole.

Certainly NATO and the participating nations have learned a lot from the IFOR experience. Some experiences have particular significance for future NATO operations and the realization of the NATO CJTF and NCCAP concepts. Others can be applied to coalition peace operations in general. Whether these experiences become lessons learned is yet to be determined, but some of the more important IFOR-related experiences to be considered are as follows.

- Warfighting and peace operations require different skills and capabilities. The go-to-war oriented doctrine, CONOPS, tactics/techniques/procedures, C4ISR capabilities, and intelligence operations had to be adapted to meet IFOR peace operation requirements.

- Information operations require a comprehensive and integrated strategy from the inception of the operation.

- The division of strategic, theater, and tactical became less distinct for—
  - C4ISR systems and services
  - Intelligence operations
  - Information Campaign

- The Information Age arrived and significantly changed the way NATO and the military conducted operations:
  - E-mail replaced the formal message handling systems

- VTC was used extensively for C2 and decision making
- PowerPoint briefings were the medium of choice for presentations
- Enhanced collaboration and information sharing took place

- In spite of progress, interoperability continues to be a challenge:
  - C4ISR systems and services (military and civil systems)
  - Intelligence operations
  - Doctrine, CONOPS, and TTP
  - Language differences
  - Cultural differences
  - NGO and IO interfaces

- The size of communications pipes was not sufficient to meet the demands of the Information Age operation (problems were experienced at all levels—strategic, theater, and tactical).

- Coordinated public affairs, civil affairs, PSYOP, and CI/HUMINT initiatives demonstrated synergistic value-added for intelligence operations and the information campaign in support of peace operations.

- Civil Affairs came of age, especially for NATO and the framework nations the United States, France, and the United Kingdom.

- CI/HUMINT became the intelligence source of choice for the tactical commanders.

- PSYOP use of leaflets, loudspeakers, and radio broadcasting has been overtaken by global television for "information societies." The Internet has also emerged as a player.

- News media influence on peace operations—the "CNN Effect"—was experienced from the outset of the operation and must be accommodated by the military.

- Information Dominance was achieved and demonstrated. Commander and staff information overload was also demonstrated. This was especially true for the U.S. forces.

- Implications of modern commercial information technology has yet to be fully understood:
  - Operational C2 and decision making
  - Organizational structures and virtual headquarters
  - Insertion into and substitution for go-to-war capabilities
  - Human factors and use of information
  - Information discovery tools
  - Information protection
    - Lack coalition releasable COMSEC/INFOSEC capabilities
    - Lack configuration management and network virus and intrusion detection/protection capabilities

- Exercises such as *INTEROP 95* and *Mountain Shield* helped to work out many of the integration and interoperability issues in advance of the deployment and also provided excellent training for the organizations that deployed in support of the operation.

- Information management and management of information needs require careful consideration.

Bosnia was, in many regards, a living prototype of a post-Cold War operation. It was the kind of operation we may expect to see more of in the future and if we learn the correct lessons from the operation and act upon them, the payoff could be considerable. One should not forget, however, that potential adversaries of the NATO alliance and the United States, in particular, will not be so foolish as to neglect glaring weaknesses in the C2 and intelligence arrangements and C4ISR systems and services implemented in support of the IFOR operation. Doctrine and tactics based upon an assumed freedom to communicate and information dominance may not be sufficient the next time around, even for peacekeeping operations.

The experiences from Bosnia reinforced the importance of information dominance and the information campaign as force multipliers in peace operations. The public information campaign and the IFOR Information Campaign in support of force protection and implementation of the military aspects of the Dayton Accords were successes. The IFOR Information Campaign in support of civil reconstruction, economic recovery, and humanitarian activities was less successful. No one organization was responsible for orchestration, an integrated information campaign that addressed the political, civil, economic, and humanitarian aspects of the operation.

The political, civil, economic, and humanitarian aspects of peace operations require close cooperation between the civil organizations and the military. This, too, was reinforced by the Bosnia experiences.

Agility and accommodation continue to be keys to success as well as some plain old good luck. Overall, the IFOR operation was a military success because of the professionalism, dedication, and ingenuity of the men and women who were there and those who supported them.

End Notes

[1] CNN World Wide Web home page: The Balkan Tragedy, 1996/7.

[2] LTC David Perkins, USA, and Mark Jacobson, USAR.

[3] Col. Kenneth Allard, USA (Ret.), Col. Michael Dziedzic, USAF, Pascale Siegel, and Larry Wentz.

[4] Fellow Travel, an end of tour paper by Tony Boardman, UK, Headquarters SFOR, 1997.

[5] *The World Factbook* 1992 and 1995, Central Intelligence Agency.

[6] "Policing the New World Disorder: Peace Operations and the Public Security Function," Robert Oakley, Michael Dziedzic, Eliot Goldberg, NDU Press, 1997.

[7] "Policing the New World Disorder: Peace Operations and the Public Security Function," Robert Oakley, Michael Dziedzic, Eliot Goldberg, NDU Press, 1997.

[8] "Policing the New World Disorder: Peace Operations and the Public Security Function," Robert Oakley, Michael Dziedzic, Eliot Goldberg, NDU Press, 1997.

[9] Chapter 6, *Bosnia and the IPTF*, Col. Mike Dziedzic and Andy Blair.

[10] IDA report: *Operation Joint Endeavor-Description and Lessons Learned*, November 1996.

[11] Bosnia Country Handbook Peace Implementation Force (IFOR), DoD-1540-16-96, December 1995.

[12] IFOR Fact Sheets and IDA report: *Operation Joint Endeavor-Description and Lessons Learned*, November 1996.

[13] IDA report: *Operation Joint Endeavor-Description and Lessons Learned*,

November 1996.

[14]IFOR Fact Sheets and IDA report: *Operation Joint Endeavor-Description and Lessons Learned*, November 1996.

[15]There were numerous after action reports, lessons learned briefings, and interviews that served as the basis for this chapter. Those of particular importance were *USAREUR Headquarters After Action Review (1997), After Action Report Operation Joint Endeavor 1st AD Intelligence Production (1996)* (Capt. Rhonda Cook, USA), Center for Army Lessons Learned reports, U.S. Naval War College report on IFOR C4I and Information Operations, Army War College After Action Reviews, JS (J2) BOSNIA Intelligence Lessons Learned Working Group, IFOR Joint Analysis Team reports, SOCOM SOF Mission Support Lessons Learned, USEUCOM Lessons Learned reports, DCI report on IFOR Intelligence Sharing: Successes and Challenges, Defense Science Board Task Force on Improved Application of Intelligence to the Battlefield, Chapters 5 through 10 of this book and their authors and other interviews and reports.

[16]The author would like to thank the many individuals who commented on this chapter in its various stages of development and specifically Lt. Col. Bob Butler, USAF; LTC Mike Furlong, USA (Ret.); Col. Dave Hunt, USA; Col. Don Klemm, USA; LTC Dave Perkins, USA; CAPT Wayne Perras, USN (Ret.); and Tom Rausch, MITRE.

[17]USAREUR Headquarters After Action Report, *Operation Joint Endeavor*, May 1997.

[18]General Framework Agreement for Peace in Bosnia and Herzegovina. Art. I, § 2.

[19]General Framework Agreement for Peace in Bosnia and Herzegovina. Art. VI, § 3.

[20]"Combined Joint Civil Military Cooperation (CIMIC)," Briefing to Admiral T. Joseph Lopez, 24 July 1996.

[21]"Combined Joint Civil Military Cooperation," IFOR AFSOUTH Fact Sheet, August 20, 1996.

[22]David R. Segal and Dana P. Eyre. *U.S. Army in Peace Operations at the Dawning of the Twenty-First Century*. U.S. Army Research Institute for the Behaviour and Social Sciences, May 1996, p. 24.

[23]COMARRC Policy Guidance Number 8 - Civil Tasks, March 1996. Page 2, ¶ 4.

[24]The 96th Civil Affairs Battalion, which was to act as the U.S. CIMIC enabling force, was scheduled to deploy at D-13. Deployment did not occur until D-Day.

[25] We wish to acknowledge the careful scrutiny and incisive suggestions we received on earlier versions of this chapter from Deputy IPTF Commissioner Robert Wasserman, Maj. Don Zoufal, Col. Larry Forester, Jim Hooper, Lynn Thomas, and Glen MacPhail.

[26] Article 1, Annex 11, General Framework Agreement for Peace.

[27] Observations provided by Deputy Commissioner Robert Wasserman.

[28] On 25 Sep 1996, Mr. Ed van Thijn, Coordinator for International Monitoring, publicly asserted that the postponed municipal elections should be put off for at least 4 more months until the minimal essential conditions could be satisfied. OSCE Mission Chief, Amb Robert Frowick, in contrast, has insisted on going forward with the elections in late November. "Monitor Wants Bosnian Elections Postponed," *Washington Times*, 25 Sep 1996.

[29] The "Principals" were the High Representative, IFOR/SFOR commander, IPTF commissioner, and the Special Representative of the Secretary General who leads UNMIBH. In addition to this core group, when the issues of the day concerned the OSCE or the UNHCR, the heads of these organizations were also included.

[30] "Report of the Secretary General Pursuant to Security Council Resolution 1026 (1995), Document No. S/1995/1031, 13 December 1995, p.7.

[31] If one does the math, this comes out to 1,492. Presumably the additional 229 monitors were added because of a planning assumption that roughly 13 percent would be sick on leave or otherwise unavailable for duty. It is also worth noting that this figure was not adjusted after the Federation downsized from 32,750 to 11,500. Indeed, some 200 officers were added to create a superstation in Brcko after the decision was made in March 1997 to place that contested city under international administration.

[32] Kevin F. McCarroll and Donald R. Zoufal, "Transition of the Sarajevo Suburbs," *Joint Forces Quarterly*, Summer 1997, pp. 7-10.

[33] Memorandum for the Record, Subject: "UNMIBH Logistical Support to IPTF," from D/Chief logistics Officer to IPTF Deputy Commissioner, 29 July 1996, pp. 2 & 9.

[34] Ibid., p. 8. The impact of these logistical shortcomings was also chronicled by an IFOR officer visiting Kiseljak in late June. In his estimation the IPTF station there was "severely under-equipped," the number of vehicles was inadequate, and the commander lacked the means to communicate with officers on vehicular patrols. Consequently, patrolling had been restricted for safety reasons. IFOR Memorandum, 26 June 1996, "Discussion with IPTF Officer in Kiseljak," p. 3.

448   *Lessons from Bosnia*

[35]Ibid., p. 7.

[36]Ibid., pp. 4 & 8.

[37]Op. Cit. in Note 3, p. 7.

[38]"All shortages reflect the minimum number to marginally accomplish the mission using common assets, and presuming no equipment failures, losses, or repairs." Ibid., p. 10.

[39]Ibid., p. 10.

[40]Ibid., pp. 4 & 7.

[41]IPTF Memo, "UNMIBH Logistical Support to the IPTF." p. 7.

[42]Memorandum for the Director, Joint Logistics Operations Centre, from Chief of the Supply and Services Division, "Support to the UN Mission in B-H (UNMIBH), 27 Jan 95.

[43]FAX No. 151-2275, from Chief Medical Officer UNTOFY, to SRSG UNMIBH Sarajevo, "Medical Support to UN Personnel UNMIBH/UNIPTF," 15 Mar 1996.

[44]Interoffice Memorandum to the Special representative of the Secretary General and the Civ-Pol Commissioner, from United Nations Peace Forces Headquarters (FMEDO), "Medical Support to UN Mission Areas in the Former Yugoslavia after 31 January 1996," 25 January 1996.

[45]Op. Cit. in Note, pp. 1 & 6.

[46]Ibid., p. 6.

[47]*The Dayton Peace Accords*, Annex 1A, Article I, Paragraph 1.

[48]Kevin F. McCarroll and Donald R. Zoufal, "Transition of the Sarajevo Suburbs," *Joint Forces Quarterly,* Summer 1997, p 8.

[49]*The Dayton Peace Accords*, Annex 11, Article III. In addition, the Report of the Secretary General to the Security Council of 13 December 1995 prior to the deployment of the IPTF states that "..International Police Task Force monitors may be involved in local mediation if conflict arises as a result of actions by local police." Report of the Secretary-General Pursuant to Security Council Resolution 1026 (1995), Document No. S/1995/1031, 13 December 1995, paragraph 27.

[50]The following incidents, summarized by Somers and Reeves, are illustrative:

An example of such a violation is the groundless, ethnically motivated arrest of the Bosniac police chief of Jablanica by Croat police officers on 18 July

1996 after having been brought to Croat-dominated territory for an official police coordination meeting. The Chief was immediately arrested and detained by Croat authorities in West Mostar. An investigative judge commenced criminal proceedings while the Chief remained in detention. IPTF was required to stand by helplessly and attempt to negotiate his release from this ethnically motivated human rights violation. No form of police disciplinary action or prosecution against these Croat officials has resulted from this incident.

In a separate but equally illustrative incident, the Police Chief of Pale, in the Republika Srpska, while intoxicated in a public restaurant, fired his pistol through the windows and doors while other restaurant patrons were present. He subsequently used his loaded pistol to push another patron out of a chair by pushing the pistol against the patron's cheek. Again, no criminal charges were filed. No police disciplinary action was taken against this officer, even after the IPTF Commissioner wrote a strongly worded letter of protest to high ranking government officials.

The ongoing case of the four Serbs who were reported as missing persons on the Trnovo Road in Federation territory in July 1996 is illustrative of the continuation of ethnic hostilities through abuse of the criminal justice system. These four persons were discovered accidentally by IPTF monitors in October to be in the Sarajevo Centar Jail. They were being held without charges or bail. As of the date of this study, these persons have neither been charged nor released. It appears that the Federation police may have abducted or directed the abduction of these people for the purpose of conducting a future prisoner exchange. It is even more disturbing to note that one of these persons had been seriously wounded in the abduction and was denied medical attention for a significant period of time. Somers and Reeves, pp. 17, 24-25.

[51]As the Secretary General noted in his 13 December 1995 report to the Security Council prior to deployment of the IPTF, "Its effectiveness will depend, to an important extent, on the willingness of the parties to cooperate with it in accordance with Article IV of annex 11 to the Peace Agreement." Report of the Secretary-General Pursuant to Security Council Resolution 1026 (1995), Document No. S/1995/1031, p. 7, paragraph 27.

[52]Somers and Reeves, pp. 17-18.

[53]The IPTF Commissioner's Guidance calls upon Bosnian police forces to investigate police misconduct and discrimination scrupulously, and to use external auditors to ensure that written policies are enforced in practice and an independent review mechanism for allegations of police misconduct. Commissioner Guidance, pp. 2, 9, 16, 18.

[54]Interview with Maj. Fred Solis, member of the IPTF Special Projects Division,

450   *Lessons from Bosnia*

which had responsibility for the vetting program. September 1996.

[55]Confirmation of the "re-vetting" process as an IPTF power is found in the Commissioner's Guidance for Democratic Policing in the Federation of Bosnia-Herzegovina, Part 1, May 1996. This document specifically states that all police officers "not selected for duty in that Canton or its Opstinas, or selected for duty at the Federal level, will be demobilized." P. 5.

[56]AMEMBASSY SARAJEVO Message, Date-Time Group 051727 AUG 97, UNCLASS SARAJEVO 005266.

[57]The training consisted of a 1-week "Human Dignity" course and a 3-week introduction to international policing standards and the reorganized Federation police structure. IPTF Workshop conducted at the National Defense University on 26-27 June 1997.

[58]Pre-election briefing in CIMIC headquarters by IFOR Liaison Officer assigned to the IPTF, 13 Sep 96.

[59]They still had to depend on their own comm net: 73 base radios with 10-mile radius, and 178 hand-held radios, one-mile range.

[60]3 October 1996 Memorandum from LTC Mike Bailey to Amb Oakley, Subject: "To provide you with thoughts regarding the IPTF."

[61]26 September 1996 Memorandum from LTC Mike Bailey to Mr. Michael Arietti, Subject: "Bosnia Trip Report."

[62]"Commissioner's Guidance Notes for the Implementation of Democratic Policing Standards in the Federation of Bosnia-Herzegovina," in *Commissioner's Guidance for Democratic Policing in the Federation of Bosnia-Herzegovina* (Sarajevo: United Nations Mission in Bosnia-Herzegovina, 1996), pp. 1-2.

[63]*Commissioner's Guidance for Democratic Policing in the Federation of Bosnia-Herzegovina*, (Sarajevo: United Nations Mission in Bosnia-Herzegovina, 1996), p. 1.

[64]Ibid.

[65]Ibid.

[66]"The human rights abuses take many forms, ranging from willful blindness toward enforcing laws to overt criminality. A common form of misconduct is police participation and/or complicity in the kidnapping of members of ethnic minorities in order to amass candidates for the prisoner exchanges which occur on a regular basis with the full knowledge of the international community, including IPTF." Somers and Reeves.

[67]"The pre-trial period of the criminal process is, in most cases, subject to abuse, fails to conform to the European Convention on Human Rights, and requires the most immediate corrective measures." "As long as prison officials continue to allow limitless periods of detention of uncharged individuals, without bring this detention to the attention of judicial authorities, rule of law will elude the Entities." "...we were concerned that approximately 50 percent of judges from Republika Srpska and Bosnian Croat courts were not aware of the European Convention on Human Rights and the fact that the fundamental freedoms set out in it were to be incorporated into the legal system. A common response to questioning on this point was that the system already had appropriate safeguards on the subject of Human rights. We found it did not. We also found in general terms that there was a lack of continuing education for judges and possibly as a result of this, a lack of knowledge on the part of all judges concerning changes in the legal system brought about by GFAP, specifically the role of the Human Rights Chamber and its relationship to the legal system."

[68]HQ ACE, p. 23, Section 11.1.1.

[69]In this article, the author refers to information activities to describe the coordination and synchronization of public information and psychological operations in support of *Operation Joint Endeavor*. The author chose the term information activities instead of information operations for two reasons. First, NATO does not have an information operations doctrine. Second, according to the U.S. Army's FM 100-6, information operations refers to operations linking together public affairs, civil affairs, psychological operations, command and control warfare, and electronic warfare. Such encompassing information operations did not take place during *Operation Joint Endeavor*.

[70]Department of the Army, *Field Manual 46-1: Public Affairs*, draft version, November 1996.

[71]During UNPROFOR and IFOR missions, major military operations were rare. One of them took place in March 1996, when IFOR seized arms and ammunitions from the Bosnian government. IFOR also seized many documents linking the Bosnian government to Iran. Since then, IFOR military operations have been limited in scope. For example, IFOR is backing up IPTF's inspections of police stations.

[72] Colonel Tim Wilton, UKA, ARRC chief Public Information Officer, Sarajevo, October 1996.

[73]The PSYOP campaign was called IFOR Information Campaign because of po-

litical constraints. During the planning phase of *Joint Endeavor*, it appeared that the term "psychological operations" generated reluctance among some of the partners in the coalition. To ease those concerns, the PSYOP campaign was labeled IFOR Information Campaign. There is, however, no doubt that the IFOR Information Campaign was a PSYOP campaign. The CJIICTF only comprised PSYOP personnel and assets and conducted operations according to NATO's definition of Psychological Activities. Interview with LtCol John Markham, USA, SHAPE PSYOP staff officer, Mons, 19 December 1996.

[74]The PI and PSYOP policies in use at the time of planning were outdated. Both documents dated back to the 1980s and were more relevant to conventional warfighting in central Europe than to a peace operation in the Balkans.

[75]When AFSOUTH and SHAPE began planning for *Joint Endeavor*, two contingency plans already existed: OPLAN 40103 (NATO support for implementation of the Vance-Owen peace plan) and OPLAN 40104 (NATO support for a UN withdrawal from Bosnia-Herzegovina). Both plans were extensive. According to interviews conducted in theater, PI planners relied heavily on annex P to OPLAN 40104.

[76]Some of these concepts were not new and had already been tested in real-world operations (during *Operations Restore Hope* and *United Shield* in Somalia, for example). The requirements and mechanisms were more complex and more comprehensive, however, during *Joint Endeavor*.

[77] Interview with Capt. Mark Van Dyke, USN, IFOR chief PIO, Sarajevo, 17 October 1996.

[78]Interview with Colonel Serveille, FRA, IFOR deputy chief PIO, Sarajevo, 22 October 1996.

[79]While the MND(SW) operated in an intimate and rather collegial atmosphere, it is notable that the PI office was in a separate building from most of the command groups.

[80]According to Colonel Charles de Noirmont, FRA, IFOR deputy chief PIO, Admiral Smith threatened the major international organizations with withdrawing IFOR support for the Holiday Press Center (where the daily briefings were organized) before the agencies agreed to take partial charge and chair the daily briefing three times a week. Interview with the author, Paris, November 1996.

[81]On rarer occasions, U.S. embassy personnel attended the JICC.

[82]Captain Mark Van Dyke, USN, IFOR Chief Public Information Officer, "Public Information In Peacekeeping: The IFOR Experience," paper presented

before NATO's Political-Military Steering Committee Ad Hoc Group on Co-operation in Peacekeeping, Seminar on Public Relations Aspects of Peacekeeping, Brussels, Belgium, NATO Headquarters, 11 April 1997. Available at http://www.nato.int/ifor/afsouth.

[83]LtCol Furlong, USA (Ret.), Deputy Commander CJIICTF, comment to the author, September 1997.

[84]Interview with Colonel Icenogle, USA, MND(N) Joint Information Bureau Director, Tuzla, October 1996. However, some of the U.S. officers in NATO posts did not participate in this teleconference.

[85]For example, ordnance exploded in a tent, killing and wounding Italian and Portuguese soldiers. In such a case, where two nations were involved in the incident, only NATO had authority to release information about the circumstances of the incident. In that case, both nations issued statements describing the incident and pointing the finger at the other for responsibility. Interview with LtCol Hoehne, USA, SHAPE chief media officer, Mons, 18 December 1996.

[86]Interview with LtCol Paul Brooks, UKA, MND(SW) chief PIO, Banja-Luka, October 1996.

[87]In this case, however, IFOR's public announcement angered the IO/NGO community because they did not receive advance warning from IFOR.

[88]On 9 January 1996, a Bosnian Serb sniper shot a woman on the Sarajevo tramway. The French immediately fired back at his position. At the daily briefing, the press accused IFOR of standing by and not doing anything. At first, IFOR PI could not counter those accusations because it was not aware of the French response. When they finally became aware of it, the issue was no longer of interest to the media and was reported incorrectly internationally. Simon McDowall, Sarajevo CPIC director, interview with the author, London, February 1997. (For an account of the incident, see Olivier Tramond, "Une mission inédite executée par le 3e RPIMA à Sarajevo: La création d'une zone de séparation en milieu urbain," *Les Cahiers de la Fondation pour les Etudes de Défense*, 6/1997, p. 53.)

[89]This conflict also reflected the somewhat traditional tension between higher and subordinate headquarters. For example, it seems that the ARRC concurred with the U.S. approach that a unified campaign against the Bosnian Serbs was the best approach. Meanwhile, all divisions felt they should have more freedom to conduct operations relevant to their respective AORs. For example, in summer 1996, Gen. Jackson, UKA, MND(SW) commander, refused to disseminate an edition of *The Herald Of Peace* (approved by COMIFOR and COMARRC) featuring a front-page article on indicted war criminals with photographs of Mladic and

Karadzic. Gen. Jackson felt the article was insensitive to the Bosnian Serbs. After flag-level involvement at IFOR, ARRC, and EUCOM, it was decided that a division could no longer unilaterally block the dissemination of COMIFOR's approved products. In that case, COMARRC sided with the CJIICTF against the division's commander.

[90] The French reluctance stemmed from political and historical reasons. After the defeat in Indochina (1954), the French military constituted a PSYOP capability and used it extensively during the Algerian conflict. When many of the PSYOP officers supported the *coup des généraux* in 1961 (a rebellion against the legitimate government), the Ministry of Defense dissolved all the PSYOP units. This issue remains extremely sensitive to many government officials and general officers. However, as a result of IFOR operations, the French command for special operations (Commandement des Opérations Spéciales—COS) is now developing a PSYOP doctrine and capability.

[91] Interview with Major Chris Bailey, USA, PSYOP liaison officer to MND(SE), Mostar, October 1996.

[92] The Nation Security Decision Directive (NSDD) 130 states: "While U.S. international information activities must be sensitive to the concerns of foreign governments, our information programs should be understood to be a strategic instrument of U.S. national policy, not a tactical instrument of U.S. diplomacy. We cannot accept foreign control over program content." Under this directive, DoD has consistently refused to place its PSYOP forces under 'foreign' control. The definition of 'foreign' has been extended to include NATO.

[93] When LtCol Furlong briefed the Deputy Commander in Chief of U.S. Forces in Europe (DCINCEUR) on 6 December 1995 regarding the IFOR product approval process, DCINCEUR agreed to delegate approval authority to COMIFOR and to rely on COMCJIICTF's day-to-day judgment in case of conflict between the NATO and U.S. operations. If a conflict of interest appeared between IFOR and EUCOM's (i.e., USG) PSYOP campaigns, DCOMCJIICTF was to call EUCOM J3 to raise the issue and promote a mutually satisfying solution. According to LtCol Furlong, only one conflict occurred during *Joint Endeavor*.

[94] Ariane Quentier from the UNHCR thought the French (who headed the division) wanted to control her message. On the other hand, PIOs working at the division thought that cooperation was only possible if all speakers agreed to a common message.

[95] For example, Nik Gowing (BBC TV) and Kurt Schork (Reuters) publicly praised IFOR efforts to provide relevant information in a timely fashion. Rémy Ourdan, reporter for the French daily *Le Monde*, thought that IFOR had

been forthcoming with its operations. A *New York Times* reporter commented that *Joint Endeavor* was the "better military-media relationship he had ever seen."

[96]The author would like to thank the many individuals who commented on this chapter in its various stages of development: LTC James Treadwell; LTC Anthony Cucolo; LTC Mike Furlong; Major Steve Collins, JFKSWCS; Major Wayne Mason, JFKSWCS; Major Chris Ives, 2D POG; Major Richard Gordon, Royal Army Education Corps; Major Jack Guy, ACOM; SFC David Gates, 321st POC; SFC Robert Drennan, and SGT Jason Sherer, 346th POC (A); and the students and instructors at the Military Psychological Operations Course, Class 3/97 (Defense Intelligence and Security School, UK). While their guidance and assistance have helped the development of this chapter, I alone am responsible for its failings and shortcomings.

[97]Even though the larger conflict is over, the propaganda methods that helped to inflame it have not disappeared. See Jane Perlez, "Serbian Media is a One Man Show," *New York Times*, Sunday, August 10, 1997. For a more complete overview of the use of propaganda during the war in the Former Yugoslavia see Mark Thompson, *Forging War: The Media in Serbia, Croatia, and Bosnia-Herzegovina*, London, 1994 and Pedrag Simic, "The Former Yugoslavia: Media and Violence," *RFE/RL Research Report*, Vol. 3 No. 5, February 4, 1994.

[98]PSYOP are "Planned operations to convey selected information and indicators to foreign audiences to influence their emotions, motives, objective reasoning, and ultimately the behavior of foreign governments, organizations, groups, and individuals. The purpose of psychological operations is to induce or reinforce foreign attitudes and behavior favorable to the originator's objectives." *Joint Pub 1-02*. Indeed, one contentious issue for the PSYOP units in Bosnia was that NATO and USEUCOM did not allow the use of the term "PSYOP." Instead, PSYOP elements were given politically acceptable euphemisms such as Military-Civil Relations or Information Operations, and in the case of the PSYOP Task Force (POTF), the term Combined Joint IFOR Information Task Force (CJIICTF).

[99]Though the majority of the personnel deployed to support Task Force Eagle were assigned to the 346th POC, a significant number of personnel from the 321st POC and the 350th POC deployed as part of the 15th POB force package. Elements from the 7th POG were also attached. The practice of patching together ad hoc force packages from available reservists rather than maintaining strict unit integrity has been standard during reserve PSYOP deployments in recent years.

[100]During the IFOR mission there was no direct PSYOP support to the Russian

brigade in MND(N). The Russian LNOs at HQ TFE would receive IIC products to that Russian troops could disseminate them in their sector. Additionally, in some instances that were approved by the Joint Chiefs of Staff (JCS), U.S. loudspeaker teams supported Russian troops during crisis situations in Jusici and Celic. Another problem that the PSYOP community will have to consider is the role that "Command Information" platforms, such as the Finnish and French radio stations (not to mention the U.S. AFRTS and AFN) system, play in the information campaign. After all, there is no way to prevent the local population from picking up these broadcasts as well and thus they may impact upon the same target audiences as the PSYOP campaign.

[101] MG Meigs took over from MG William Nash as COMEAGLE when the 1st Infantry Division took over from the 1st Armored Division in November 1996. MG Meigs made these comments during an interview on the ABC News program, *Nightline*, aired on June 3, 1997. The particular segment focused on the difficulties involved with keeping the peace in Brcko, Bosnia.

[102] Recent incidents in Brcko (August 29, 1997), where SFOR troops eventually had to use non-lethal means to break up a public disturbance, should not detract from the successes during the IFOR mission. They may indeed be the exceptions that prove the rule.

[103] Much of this paper is based on the operations and intelligence files of BPSE 210 and DPSE 20, including not only materials that originated in the DPSE but those documents sent down from the CJIICTF to the DPSEs and CJIICTF. BPSE and DPSE SITREPS are available at the History and Museums Division, U.S. Army Special Operations Command, located at the JFK Special Warfare Center and School, Ft. Bragg, NC. Additional information was acquired through interviews and discussions with personnel from the 2nd and 4th POG.

[104] For a focused discussion on the overall IFOR Information Campaign see the preceding chapter by Pascale Combelles Siegel.

[105] CJIICTF Product Dissemination Summary, 20 May 1997. *The Herald of Progress*, a more sophisticated monthly periodical, replaced *The Herald of Peace* in February-March 1997.

[106] The outgoing DPSE commander had forwarded his e-mail address through 4th POG to 2nd POG but because 2nd POG did not have any e-mail capability, this information was not passed down to the deploying units. The 11th POB, on the other hand, made great use of electronic mail and conducted a leader's reconnaissance prior to their deployment to Bosnia in January 1997. This resulted in a much smoother transition than the previous rotation had encountered.

[107] Some at the CJIICTF believed that the CJIICTF and the CPSE had briefed the incoming tactical units. This definitely was not the case. Those stationed in Sarajevo at the CJIICTF often had different perceptions about what happened in MND(N) than those stationed in MND(N) and vice versa. This certainly reinforces this author's belief that clear and concise communication of intent between the COMCJIICTF through his COMCPSE to the COMDPSE in MND(N) was at best problematic.

[108] This disconnect between not only the CPSE and the DPSE but between the DPSE and the BPSEs reflects not only the lack of organic communications equipment within the tactical PSYOP units but the difficulty PSYOP had working within the CJ-3 to S-3 channels in a combined-joint operation. It also may indicate a failure on the CPSE's part to ensure that its subordinate elements had access to all information that it sent out over communications systems such as WARLORD.

[109] For an assessment of the role of Force Protection Teams see David D. Perkins, "Counterintelligence and Human Intelligence Operations in Bosnia," *Defense Intelligence Journal* 6-1 (1997): pp. 33-61.

[110] Furthermore, a look at the DPSE and SITREPs indicates that a great deal of information passed on to the DPSE did not always make it to the CPSE and CJIICTF. Attached elements such as FPTs and Civil Affairs had a somewhat better reporting system. Reports were made to the supported unit the same way any organic staff element would. While summaries of the day's events went up, details were sent as separate reports. In the case of FPTs each summary referenced a specific FPIR. This report was sent under separate cover but could be accessed by all if required. This meant that the same daily SITREP was sent to all concerned.

[111] In particular, each nation had intelligence that was releasable only to its own military. Some intelligence was only releasable to NATO and not non-NATO members participating in IFOR/SFOR, such as the Russians. Although there was a great deal of intelligence available through U.S.-only channels, because of the coalition nature of the mission the CJIICTF did not have direct access to the JDISS or other assets usually available in a SCIF. The only access the CJIICTF had to this traffic was by sending a representative to the NIC in order to "pull down" useful intelligence—often a difficult process in itself.

[112] Former CJIICTF personnel insist that some of this information, to include Basic PSYOP Studies, was sent down to DPSE level. If this was the case, the DPSE was not aware that such information was available. In any case the information was not readily available to either the BPSEs or the supported units in MND(N). Still, some CJIICTF personnel indicated that they did not think such information was useful at the tactical

level. This again reflects the lack of solid communications between the elements of the PSYOP task force and the problems of continuity inherent during the rotation of forces into and out of theater. Interviews with CJIICTF personnel, May and September 1997, and with DPSE 20 personnel, 1997.

[113] One issue that will have to be discussed within the PSYOP community is the requirement to have trained 37F personnel act simply as "drivers" for PSYOP products, especially given the personnel-intensive nature of this operation and the shortage of trained and deployable 37F personnel. Despite clear personnel shortages in MND(N), there were never any replacements or additional TPTs provided by the CJIICTF using the Red Ball soldiers. It is the opinion of this author that this use of PSYOP troops, given the operational situation in theater, was not the most efficient use of valuable resources.

[114] In some instances, however, products were delivered within a matter of days if not hours. In MND(N) this was sometimes done by sending products such as loudspeaker or radio scripts via electronic means from the CJIICTF through the CPSE and to the DPSE.

[115] Despite the availability of some products announcing the Bosnian elections of September 1996, guides intended to explain the voting registration process did not arrive in MND(N) until after voter registration had ended. In addition products requested in July 1996 to support the RFCT's "Spirit of the Posavina" campaign (a campaign designed to promote multiethnic unity and Civil Affairs actions in the Posavina Corridor) did not arrive until late November 1996 after the RFCT had already re-deployed to Germany. Likewise, after incidents involving IFOR soldiers and RS soldiers at Donja Mahala and Zvornik in late 1996, PSYOP elements in MND(N) waited 2 days before receiving approved scripts to give to local radio stations (and the IFOR station in Brcko). In the meantime local RS radio stations had already put their own "spin" on the story and broadcast it to listeners in the AOR.

[116] There is also some confusion as to whether or not products produced and developed specifically for NGOs and IGOs such as the UNHCR and the OSCE had to go through the same approval process as products developed specifically for IFOR units. To the best of this author's knowledge, these products did not have to go through the approval process but were still disseminated by U.S. TPTs.

[117] On at least two occasions, supported unit commanders refused to allow the HoP to be disseminated in their AOR. In one case this was due to an article discussing the deadline for voter registration appearing in an issue that was delivered several days after the deadline for registration had

already passed. Similarly, one HoP article highlighted that the start of the "Atlanta 96" Summer Olympics was near. This article, however, appeared in an issue that was dated after the Olympics had already come to a conclusion. Although some CJIICTF members insist that the DPSE had the authority to keep products from being disseminated in their AOR, the DSPE commander was not aware of this authority if he did have it.

[118]Though some would argue that this set a dangerous precedent by deliberately trying to bypass the PSYOP product approval process, the fact remains that these PAO "products" were approved properly albeit through a different approval chain. In addition, by November, 1996, the CJIICTF gave PSYOP units the authority to use "open source" press releases as legitimate messages that did not have to be screened through the usual approval process. The PSYOP community will have to wrestle with this potentially volatile issue and in conjunction with its counterparts in the Public Affairs (not to mention LIWA and JC2WC) community discover solutions. If no solution is found, it is likely that such "work arounds" will be utilized in future situations that mirror the ones in Bosnia.

[119]What the BPSE did in these instances, with the approval of the DPSE commander, was to assist and guide the MPAD's development of the BN commander's radio addresses to the local population—in essence a mini Information Control Group run by the PAO at the BN level. After the BN Commander approved the script (using of course the "guidelines" given to him by his own superiors) the messages were sent to Task Force Eagle (Division) for approval by the Joint Information Bureau (JIB). Using this method the BNs were even able to develop "pre-approved" scripts for contingencies and these scripts could be adjusted and altered as necessary so long as they fit within the "information campaign" guidelines. The reason that these "work arounds" were possible is because to a great degree the PSYOP messages and the "open source" press releases were (or would have been in contingencies) identical. This is often the case with U.S. "white" propaganda operations that have historically been straightforward information campaigns.

[120]In defense of the Product Development Center, finding themes, symbols, language, and grammar that would not offend any one segment of the local population was a lose-lose proposition. The purposeful politicization of the language and grammar in the Balkans meant that no matter what dialect IFOR chose to use, *someone* would take offense.

[121]The *HoP*, as with all IIC products, usually seemed somewhat bland when compared with the local competition. This is because the local papers were often shrill and polemic and not interested in objectivity. The lengthy approval process also tended to water down content.

[122] The prototype of the monthly *Herald of Progress* (unnamed at the time of development) was begun at the end of September by the CJIICTF. The full production of this product was delayed by the deployment of LANDCENT, which directed that *The Herald of Peace* should continue unchanged through at least December 1996. Another program that developed during this time period was the "our message, their medium" approach, whereby weekly contact would be maintained through articles printed by local newspapers. The British responded to this with the publication of a regional product designed for MND(SW). The popularity of *MOSTOVI* (Bridges) among the local population resulted in the newssheet becoming a full-blown newspaper by mid-1997.

[123] One of the local, family-owned FM stations seemed to have increased its listening audience by broadcasting in stereo. Casual listeners tuned into the station because as they were scanning through their channels the "FM Stereo" light went on their receiver and that attracted their attention. A technical note—there are ways to broadcast and make the stereo light go on individual receivers without actually broadcasting in stereo.

[124] The ability of the PSYOP elements within the 2nd BDE, 1st A.D. AOR to get messages to a local radio station during the Mahala-Zvornik civil disturbances in early Autumn 1996 prevented a small incident involving Serbian Police and IFOR troops from turning into a potentially bloody military confrontation and civil disturbance. Likewise, in the RFCT/TF 1-18 AOR, planning for some contingencies included use of both local and IFOR-run radio stations for tactical purposes.

[125] Throughout the deployment the issue arose within TFE as to whether or not the local population would be more receptive to messages broadcast over local radio stations (in line with the concept of "our message, their medium"). Within the RFCT/TF 1-18 AOR, the local radio stations had larger audiences, greater technical capacity, and more suitable entertainment formats for reaching a number of different target audiences. The PSYOP elements in the RFCT/TF 1-18 AOR sector had brief success by using the local stations, but this effort was hamstrung and eventually ended by directives from the CJIICTF. Subsequently, the local commanders turned again to the Public Affairs organizations in order to put out information over the local radio stations.

[126] Interviews with PSYOP personnel and a look at BPSE and DPSE SITREPS indicate that on several occasions in November and December 1996, the DPSE did not forward negative criticism of products to the CPSE and CJIICTF.

[127] Though the members of the CJIICTF staff vehemently disagree with this assessment, neither the COMCJIICTF nor the COMCPSE during this time

End Notes 461

period gave any indications that they had any more than a basic understanding of the dynamics of planning and executing an information campaign. In addition the CJIICTF was likely hamstrung due to budgetary and time constraints and thus had to take the common denominator approach to target audience analysis.

[128]Though there was no use of the Internet—one of the newest media for PSYOP—as a dissemination platform during the IFOR mission, the CJIICTF did consider the problem. This may have been an excellent medium for dissemination to certain key (urban elite) communicators. Students in Serbia have already had limited experience with the Internet as an effective means of persuasive communication, and called their recent uprising in Belgrade "the Internet revolution." See "The Internet Revolution," *Wired Magazine*, May 1996. The use of the Internet by the CJIICTF was held up at one time over the legality of using it because by law PSYOP products may not be available to the United States and the U.S. public could easily have accessed PSYOP Internet sites. Other assessments by the CJIICTF determined that the audience might have been too small to be worth the effort. Other U.S. Government entities, however, did use the Internet as a platform for dissemination. During the SFOR mission, the 1st Infantry Division considered its World Wide Web home page as one of several ways to convey information to target audiences. See LTC Garry J. Beavers and LTC Stephen W. Shanahan, "Operationalizing IO in Bosnia-Herzegovina," *Military Review* (forthcoming).

[129]Guidance on complex issues was often lacking, particularly in the latter part of the deployment. For example, many Muslims and Serbs in the RFCT/TF 1-18 AOR were very upset at the announcement that German troops would be arriving en masse in Bosnia. The typical response was, "you might as well send the Ustache," a reference to the Croat Fascists puppet state of the Nazi Reich. Despite several requests for the "party line," the BPSE could get no answer from the DPSE, CPSE, or CJIICTF on what to say. Eventually, the TPTs used the public affairs guidance provided by the BN MPAD.

[130]Unfortunately, some may only remember Colonel Fontenot for remarks he made in December 1995 which irritated the FWF and thus did not support all objectives of the operational PSYOP campaign. Despite the FWF reaction to the suggestion that they may have killed people based upon race or ethnicity, Fontenot's ability to intimidate the FWF probably helped to enhance the safety and security of U.S. troops in the sector—a primary PSYOP, U.S., and IFOR objective. A more comprehensive discussion of PSYOP and force protection issues appears later in this chapter. See also Thomas Ricks, "U.S. Brings to Bosnia the Tactics that Tamed the Wild West," *The Wall Street Journal*, December 27, 1995.

[131] One of the intangibles that may have affected the ability of the key leaders to communicate effectively with the target audiences was the capability and the personality of the interpreters used by these individuals. It may be no coincidence then that Colonel Fontenot, the most effective communicator in the region, had one of the best interpreters in the region. The success of the TPTs was also determined to a large degree by the capability of its interpreters. An important lesson for the PSYOP campaign was that an engineered mix of local and DoD (U.S. national) linguists provided the best way to create products that could span the difficulties imposed by cross-cultural communication.

[132] Specifically, in October 1996 the COMCJIICTF ordered the DPSE commander to cease all radio contracting activities with local radio stations. This was ordered as a precaution against any pecuniary responsibilities falling upon the PSYOP chain. The COMCJIICTF also asserted at this time that the local radio broadcasts were COMCJIICTF's responsibility. Though he was correct, the matter was complicated by the fact that the TFE contracting office had set up these contracts with 1st A.D. funds.

[133] The force protection measures appear to have been largely a political decision in light of the U.S. experience in Somalia, where U.S. policy took a sharp turn after 18 American soldiers were killed in a single engagement in 1993. Indeed this decision was itself based on the larger belief that the U.S. public no longer expects its soldiers to die in battle. For an interesting take on the issue of "clean" conflicts, see Paddy Griffith, "The Politics of Getting Hurt," *Command*, summer 1994, pp. 8-13.

[134] Specifically, the PSYOP element in the RFCT/TF 1-18 AOR experienced a severe degradation in mission capability during the final 6 weeks of their deployment due to the replacement in late December 1996 of all but one of the BPSE/TPTs vehicles with unserviceable vehicles from the 7th PSYOP Group in MND(SW). Some of the vehicles suffered from what TF 1-18 mechanics cited as the "criminal neglect" of basic PMCS and damage due to improper engine maintenance. This was also exacerbated by a lack of repair parts for U.S. vehicles in the British sector. The vehicle swap, ordered by the CJIICTF, brought missions to a virtual standstill in one sector and limited capability throughout the TF 1-18 AOR. By the time the BPSE was replaced in February 1997 all the elements vehicles were still not mission capable.

[135] An additional point should be made that the first two rotations of PSYOP soldiers to the RFCT/TF1-18 AOR (from 4th POG and 2nd POG) both noted in their AARs that the weapons they carried were perhaps not always suitable for a STABOPS environment. They argued that rather than carrying only M-16A2s, soldiers on TPTs should also carry 9mm pistols so that M-16s would not have to be lugged through crowded markets and

brought into meetings with local political officials—indeed those situations where a pistol might be a better weapon in tactical terms. PSYOP soldiers in MND(SW) carried both M-16A2s and 9mm pistols and found this to be a satisfactory arrangement. See BPSE 940, 4th Psychological Operations Group AAR and BPSE 210 AAR.

[136]Although some in IFOR may have believed the U.S. approach to be "ham handed," this warfighting focus was understood and respected by the local faction military and thus reinforced their acceptance of the IFOR forces. In the words of one experienced peacekeeper, "...you want to make progress, you want belligerents to listen, obey, conform, then you got to carry the biggest stick; and every now and then, shake it at them, or pound one of them." Furthermore, the heavy, hard, and "armed to the teeth" approach convinced the local population that IFOR could indeed provide the people of the Posavina Corridor with one of Maslow's most base needs: security. The velvet touch really only proves useful in a more mature environment—not the type of environment during the initial IFOR mission. My thanks to LTC Anthony Cucolo for these insights.

[137]The particulars of the OPORD also meant that PSYOP would not "rate" a MSE or LAN line from the supported unit; therefore, even the availability of the necessary equipment would not have guaranteed operability of that system. The BN commanders determined priority for these lines unless otherwise dictated from above by division or COMIFOR.

[138]Ironically, in the last month of the deployment, handtalkies were delivered to the BPSE; however, they proved useless without instructions on how to program them to the correct frequencies and were subsequently returned to the CJIICTF.

[139]During the period June 1996-February 1997, the CPSE's role was somewhat ambiguous. In theory, the CPSE acted as the PSYOP Support Element to the ARRC, and as the link between the DPSEs and the CJIICTF. The CPSE, however, proved to be more of an appendage to the operation than a true conduit between the DPSEs and the CJIICTF. Per COMCJIICTF's instructions, guidance to the DPSE would sometimes come directly from the CJIICTF. Similarly, at times the CPSE did not evaluate information that came up from the DPSEs but merely passed it on to the CJIICTF. Finally, the COMCPSE did not, as a general rule, attend the supported unit's Information Coordination Group meetings held by COMARRC. Instead, representatives from the CJIICTF (either the DCOMCJIICTF or the CJ3 of the CJIICTF) would attend these meetings.

[140]During the follow-up rotation (February-September 1997) a Theater PSYOP Support Element (TPSE), as well as a DPSE, was based at MND(N). Thus, the COMTPSE could help deconflict the operational PSYOP cam-

paign as orchestrated by the CJIICTF with the needs of TFE. The DPSE commander could then truly provide tactical support to the MND without also having to engage in theater PSYOP planning.

[141]On the other hand, the vast majority of the PSYOP soldiers in theater were commended by various commands, to include COMEAGLE. These were not, by any means, gratuitous comments. MG Nash often commented on the quality of the tactical PSYOP soldiers (particularly the reservists) and their ability to contribute immensely to the success of the TFE mission. Indeed, the need to balance OPTEMPO with the recruitment, training, and retention and quality of personnel issues is one that must be addressed by both the RC and AC PSYOP forces.

[142]Commanders, to include both COMEAGLEs, expressed their displeasure not only in daily Battle Update Briefs but in their comments during debriefings and to various historical and assessment teams. For example see Chapter 3, "Psychological Operations Support to Peace Operations," *BHCAAT 9 Initial Impressions Report* (For Official Use Only).

[143]Indeed, during a variety of CTC exercises (CMTC, JRTC) to include those at Hohenfelz designed to train-up the 1st A.D. and the 1st I.D. for Bosnia, the PSYOP community had taught the maneuver elements to expect a much more responsive tactical PSYOP effort.

[144]In the absence of what Major General Meigs felt was adequate PSYOP support, the 1st I.D. turned to the Land Information Warfare Activities (LIWA) cell to help coordinate and conduct its Information Operations campaign. See Beavers and Shanahan, "Operationalizing IO in Bosnia-Herzegovina." MG Meigs also overcame what he believed to be a lack of support from the CJIICTF by taking a broad interpretation of the guidelines for Command Information in order to put out the information he felt would help his mission in the AOR.

[145]Interviews with TFE PSYOP personnel.

[146]A MIST team is a five-man PSYOP element with production, linguistic, and area specialties. It usually will support a U.S. ambassador and country team with expertise and advice, as well as print, audio, and A.V. information products. Though by doctrine it would have been based in Sarajevo, it could have been used to support U.S.-only objectives and thus might have been used for TFE in the PSYOP planning role as opposed to a DPSE purpose built tactical coordination element.

[147]Indeed, in June of 1996 the USACAPOC Commander stated to deploying troops that as the mission in Bosnia was a new one for the community the PSYOP troops would be "creating doctrine" as they went about their job.

[148]This statement is based on comments made by former Deputy Undersecretary

End Notes   465

of Defense (Policy) Craig Alderman to then Director for Psychological Operations, OSD, Col. Alfred H. Paddock, Jr. Conversation with Dr. Alfred H. Paddock, Jr., summer 1997.

[149]There were numerous after action reports, lessons learned reports, briefings, and interviews that served as the basis for this chapter. Those of particular importance were USAREUR Headquarters After Action Report, 5th Signal Command Lessons Learned Book for *Operation Joint Endeavor*, History of the 7th Signal Brigade's involvement in *Operation Joint Endeavor*, USEUCOM Lessons Learned, NACOSA briefing on *Operation Joint Endeavor* Communications and Lessons Learned, IFOR CJ6 Lessons Learned, ARRC Communications and Information Systems Lesson Learned, IFOR C-Support Lessons Learned, CJCCC Information Book, Air Mobility Command Lessons Learned, USAFE Lessons Learned, IFOR Joint Analysis Team report, CISA *Operation Joint Endeavor* Lessons Learned report, Army War College AAR, SOCOM SOF Mission Support Lessons Learned, JITC C4I Infrastructure Documentation Report for *Operation Joint Endeavor*, Center for Army Lessons Learned reports, and DISA-EUR Lessons Learned.

[150]The author would like to thank the many individuals who commented on this chapter in its various stages of development. In particular—from 5th Signal Command, BG Robert Nabors, USA, Col William Ritchie, USA, and Charles Smith; From NACOSA, GP CAPT Derek Ainge, RAF; The Air Force Historian office: Dr. Jay Smith; William Randall of DISA-EUR; Major Frederick Mooney, USAF; LTC David Perkins, USA; Col Fred Stein, USA (Ret.); and Patrick Deshazo and John Jannis, MITRE.

[151]There were a number of key interviews that set the stage for the NDU study and this chapter in particular: USEUCOM (J6): BG Randy Witt, USAF, and CAPT Tom Cooper, USN; BG Robert Nabors, Charles Riggs and 5th Signal Command staff; USAREUR: Col Fred Stein, USA; NACOSA: Gp Capt Ainge, RAF, and staff; SHAPE CISD: Kent Short; IFOR CJ6: CDRE Peter Swan, RN, and staff; AFSOUTH (CSG): Col Bob Hillmer, USAF, and in Zagreb Maj Flores, USAF; CJCCC: Col Rodawowski, USA, Col Dempsey, USA, and Lt Col Stan Howard, USAF; IFOR CJ6 (Sarajevo): Maj Fred Mooney, USAF; ARRC G6: LTC Lester, LTC Grey, and Maj Brand, UKA; MND(SE) G6: LTC DeMaillard, French Army; MND(SW) G6: Maj Pickersgill and Capt Allen, UKA; C-Support G6: LTC Rowe and Capt Bennett, USA; and the IFOR Joint Analysis Team: CAPT Peter Feist, GEN, Wg Cdr Nigel Reed, UKAFO, Cdr Magnussen, NON, Cdr Finseth, NON, Lt Cdr Jon Hill, USNR, and Lt Cdr Carol Clark, USNR.

[152]IFOR Fact Sheets.

[153]IFOR Fact Sheets and IDA report: *Operation Joint Endeavor-Description and Lessons Learned*, November 1996.

Appendix A: The Dayton Peace Agreement Summary[152]

The Dayton Proximity Talks culminated in the initialing of a General Framework Agreement for Peace in Bosnia and Herzegovina. It was initialed by the Republic of Bosnia and Herzegovina, the Republic of Croatia, and the Federal Republic of Yugoslavia (FRY). The Agreement was witnessed by representatives of the Contact Group nations—the United States, Britain, France, Germany, and Russia—and the European Union Special Negotiator. The Dayton Peace Agreement and its annexes are summarized below.

General Framework Agreement

Bosnia and Herzegovina, Croatia, and the Federal Republic of Yugoslavia agree to fully respect the sovereign equality of one another and to settle disputes by peaceful means.

The FRY and Bosnia and Herzegovina recognize each other, and agree to discuss further aspects of their mutual recognition.

The parties agree to fully respect and promote fulfillment of the commitments made in the various annexes, and they obligate themselves to respect human rights and the rights of refugees and displaced persons.

The parties agree to cooperate fully with all entities, including those authorized by the United Nations Security Council, in implementing the peace settlement and investigating and prosecuting war crimes and other violations of international humanitarian law.

Annex 1-A: Military Aspects

The cease-fire that began with the agreement of October 5, 1995, will continue.

Foreign combatant forces currently in Bosnia are to be withdrawn within 30 days.

The parties must complete withdrawal of forces behind a zone of separation of approximately 4 km within an agreed period. Special provisions relate to Sarajevo and Gorazde.

As a confidence-building measure, the parties agree to withdraw heavy weapons and forces to cantonment/barracks areas within an agreed period and to demobilize forces which cannot be accommodated in those areas.

The agreement invites into Bosnia and Herzegovina a multinational military Implementation Force, the IFOR, under the command of NATO, with a grant of authority from the UN.

The IFOR will have the right to monitor and help ensure compliance with the agreement on military aspects and fulfill certain supporting tasks. The IFOR will have the right to carry out its mission vigorously, including with the use of force as necessary. It will have unimpeded freedom of movement, control over airspace, and status of forces protection.

A Joint Military Commission will be established, to be chaired by the IFOR commander. Persons under indictment by the International War Crimes Tribunal cannot participate.

Information on mines, military personnel, weaponry, and other items must be provided to the Joint Military Commission within agreed periods.

All combatants and civilians must be released and transferred without delay in accordance with a plan to be developed by the International Committee of the Red Cross.

Annex 1-B: Regional Stabilization

The Republic of Bosnia and Herzegovina, the Federation, and the Bosnian Serb Republic must begin negotiations within 7 days, under Organization for Security and Cooperation in Europe (OSCE) auspices, with the objective of agreeing on confidence-building measures within 45 days. These could include, for example, restrictions on military deployments and exercises, notification of military activities, and exchange of data.

These three parties, as well as Croatia and the Federal Republic of Yugoslavia, agree not to import arms for 90 days and not to import any heavy weapons, heavy weapons ammunition, mines, military aircraft, and helicopters for 180 days or until an arms control agreement takes effect.

All five parties must begin negotiations within 30 days, under OSCE auspices, to agree on numerical limits on holdings of tanks, artillery, armored combat vehicles, combat aircraft, and attack helicopters.

If the parties fail to establish limits on these categories within 180 days, the agreement provides for specified limits to come into force for the parties.

The OSCE will organize and conduct negotiations to establish a regional balance in and around the former Yugoslavia.

Annex 2: Inter-Entity Boundary

An Inter-Entity Boundary Line between the Federation and the Bosnian Serb Republic is agreed.

Sarajevo will be reunified within the Federation and will be open to all people of the country.

Gorazde will remain secure and accessible, linked to the Federation by a land corridor.

The status of Brcko will be determined by arbitration within 1 year.

Annex 3: Elections

Free and fair, internationally supervised elections will be conducted within 6 to 9 months for the Presidency and House of Representatives of Bosnia and Herzegovina, for the House of Representatives of the Federation and the National Assembly and presidency of the Bosnian Serb Republic, and, if feasible, for local offices.

Refugees and persons displaced by the conflict will have the right to vote (including by absentee ballot) in their original place of residence if they choose to do so.

The parties must create conditions in which free and fair elections can be held by protecting the right to vote in secret and ensuring freedom of expression and the press.

The OSCE is requested to supervise the preparation and conduct of these elections.

All citizens of Bosnia and Herzegovina aged 18 or older listed on the 1991 Bosnian census are eligible to vote.

Annex 4: Constitution

A new constitution for the Republic of Bosnia and Herzegovina, which will be known as "Bosnia and Herzegovina," will be adopted upon signature at Paris.

Bosnia and Herzegovina will continue as a sovereign state within its present internationally recognized borders. It will consist of two entities: the Federation and the Bosnian Serb Republic.

The Constitution provides for the protection of human rights and the free movement of people, goods, capital, and services throughout Bosnia and Herzegovina.

The central government will have a Presidency, a two chamber legislature, and a constitutional court. Direct elections will be held for the Presidency and one of the legislative chambers.

There will be a central bank and monetary system, and the central government will also have responsibilities for foreign policy, law enforcement, air traffic control, communications, and other areas to be agreed.

Military coordination will take place through a committee including members of the Presidency.

No person who is serving a sentence imposed by the International Tribunal, and no person who is under indictment by the Tribunal and who has failed to comply with an order to appear before the Tribunal, may stand as a candidate or hold any appointive, elective, or other public office in the territory of Bosnia and Herzegovina.

Annex 5: Arbitration

The Federation and the Bosnian Serb Republic agree to enter into reciprocal commitments to engage in binding arbitration to resolve disputes between them, and they agree to design and implement a system of arbitration.

Annex 6: Human Rights

The agreement guarantees internationally recognized human rights and fundamental freedoms for all persons within Bosnia and Herzegovina.

A Commission on Human Rights, composed of a Human Rights Ombudsman and a Human Rights Chamber (court), is established.

The Ombudsman is authorized to investigate human rights violations, issue findings, and bring and participate in proceedings before the Human Rights Chamber.

The Human Rights Chamber is authorized to hear and decide human rights claims and to issue binding decisions.

The parties agree to grant UN human rights agencies, the OSCE, the International Tribunal, and other organizations full access to monitor the human rights situation.

Annex 7: Refugees and Displaced Persons

The agreement grants refugees and displaced persons the right to safely return home and regain lost property, or to obtain just compensation.

A Commission for Displaced Persons and Refugees will decide on return of real property or compensation, with the authority to issue final decisions.

All persons are granted the right to move freely throughout the country, without harassment or discrimination.

The parties commit to cooperate with the ICRC in finding all missing persons.

Annex 8: Commission to Preserve National Monuments

A Commission to Preserve National Monuments is established.

The Commission is authorized to receive and act upon petitions to designate as National Monuments movable or immovable property of great importance to a group of people with common cultural, historic, religious, or ethnic heritage.

When property is designated as a National Monument, the Entities will make every effort to take appropriate legal, technical, financial, and other measures to protect and conserve the National Monument and refrain from taking deliberate actions which might damage it.

Annex 9: Bosnia and Herzegovina Public Corporations

A Bosnia and Herzegovina Transportation Corporation is established to organize and operate transportation facilities, such as roads, railways, and ports.

A Commission on Public Corporations is created to examine establishing other Bosnia and Herzegovina Public Corporations to operate joint public facilities, such as utilities and postal service facilities.

Annex 10: Civilian Implementation

The parties request that a High Representative be designated, consistent with relevant UN Security Council resolutions, to coordinate and facilitate civilian aspects of the peace settlement, such as humanitarian aid, economic reconstruction, protection of human rights, and the holding of free elections.

The High Representative will chair a Joint Civilian Commission comprised of senior political representatives of the parties, the IFOR commander, and representatives of civilian organizations.

The High Representative has no authority over the IFOR.

Annex 11: International Police Task Force

The UN is requested to establish a UN International Police Task Force (IPTF) to carry out various tasks, including training and advising local law enforcement personnel, as well as monitoring and inspecting law enforcement activities and facilities.

The IPTF will be headed by a Commissioner appointed by the UN Secretary General.

IPTF personnel must report any credible information on human rights violations to the Human Rights Commission, the International Tribunal, or other appropriate organizations.

Appendix B: Chronology of IFOR Events[153]

In the light of the Peace Agreement initialed in Dayton on 21 November 1995, the North Atlantic Council (NAC) authorized on 1 December 1995 the Supreme Allied Commander Europe (SACEUR) to deploy Enabling Forces into Croatia and Bosnia-Herzegovina. This decision demonstrated NATO's preparedness to implement the military aspects of a Peace Agreement, and to help create the conditions for a lasting peace in the former Yugoslavia. The NAC also gave provisional approval to the overall military plan.

On 1 December 1995, SACEUR tasked the Commander-in-Chief Southern Europe to assume control of assigned NATO land, air, and maritime forces as the Commander IFOR, and to employ them as part of the enabling force. Movement of these forces began on 2 December 1995.

On 5 December 1995, NATO Foreign and Defense Ministers endorsed the military planning for the Implementation Force (IFOR). On the same day the Acting Secretary General announced that 14 non-NATO countries—which had expressed interest in participating—would be invited to contribute to the IFOR: Austria, Czech Republic, Estonia, Finland, Hungary, Latvia, Lithuania, Pakistan, Poland, Romania, Russia, Slovakia, Sweden, and Ukraine.

All the NATO nations with armed forces (Belgium, Canada, Denmark, France, Germany, Greece, Italy, Luxembourg, Netherlands, Norway, Portugal, Spain, Turkey, United Kingdom, and United States) pledged to contribute forces to IFOR. Iceland provided medical personnel to IFOR.

The Peace Agreement (General Framework Agreement for Peace in Bosnia and Herzegovina) was formally signed in Paris on 14 December 1995.

On 15 December 1995, the United Nations Security Council—acting under Chapter VII of the Charter of the United Nations—adopted the resolution 1031, which authorizes the Member States to establish a multinational military Implementation Force (IFOR), under unified command and control and composed of ground, air, and maritime units from NATO and non-NATO nations, to ensure compliance with the relevant provisions of the Peace Agreement. Member States are also authorized to take all necessary measures to carry out the tasks identified by the same resolution.

On 16 December 1995, the NAC approved the overall plan for the Implementation Force and directed that NATO commence *Operation Joint Endeavor* and begin deploying the main Implementation Force into Bosnia that same day. The Force had a unified command and was NATO-led, under the political direction and control of the NAC and under the overall military authority of NATO's Supreme Allied Commander Europe, General George Joulwan; the responsibility as Commander-in-Theater was assigned to Admiral Leighton W. Smith, Commander-in-Chief Allied Forces Southern Europe, who assumed command of IFOR. The IFOR operated under clear NATO Rules of Engagement, which provided for robust use of force if necessary.

The transfer of authority from the Commander of UN Peace Forces to the Commander of IFOR took place on 20 December, effective at 1100 hours local time. On that day, after all NATO and non-NATO forces participating in the operation came under the command and/or control of the IFOR commander, over 17,000 troops were available to IFOR.

On 21 December, the first meeting of the Joint Military Commission (JMC) took place in Sarajevo. The JMC was a consultative body for COMIFOR. Based on the terms of the Peace Agreement, the JMC was the central body to which the signatories brought any military complaints, questions, or problems. JMCs were formed at various levels, in order that problems could be solved at the lowest possible level.

On 19 January 1996 withdrawal of the forces of all parties behind the zones of separation, which included Sarajevo and Gorazde, was completed.

On 3 February 1996, the parties had fulfilled their obligations to withdraw from areas to be transferred. Some reported violations were attributed mainly to ignorance and lack of leadership rather than deliberate non-compliance. The parties were urged to fully comply with all aspects of the peace agreement.

On 18 February 1996, the parties reaffirmed in Rome their commitment to the Peace Agreement. In particular, specific statements were approved on the work of the Joint Civil Commission Sarajevo; on the status of the implementation of the Federation of Bosnia and Herzegovina; on the situation in Mostar; on the normalization of relations between the Republic of Croatia and the Federal Republic of Yugoslavia; and on agreed measures to strengthen and advance the peace process.

On 18 February 1996, SACEUR reported to the Secretary General of NATO the completion of the initial deployment of IFOR. Thirty-two nations had been part of the deployment, with some 50,000 troops provided by NATO nations and approximately 10,000 from non-NATO contributors. The movement of IFOR had involved more than 2,800 airlift missions, some 400 trains, and more than 50 cargo ships.

On 26 February 1996, the Secretary General of NATO transmitted to the UN Secretary General a progress report on the Implementation Force. The report included an assessment of the Commander of IFOR that Bosnian Serb forces had withdrawn from the zones of separation established in the Peace Agreement. The

UN Security Council announced on 27 February that the economic sanctions imposed on the Bosnian Serb party were suspended indefinitely.

On 14 March 1996, the Chairman of the UN Security Council Committee established pursuant to resolution 724 (1991) issued a statement confirming the termination of the embargo on delivery of weapons and military equipment to former Yugoslavia, except heavy weapons, whose delivery will continue to be prohibited until the fulfillment of terms established with UNSC resolution 1021 (1995).

On 18 March 1996, the parties to the GFAP met in Geneva and expressed their determination to provide the political leadership necessary to ensure the complete fulfillment of the spirit and the letter of the Agreement and of the commitments made in Rome on 18 February 1996.

On 20 March 1996—91 days after TOA—COMARRC completed his assessment of compliance with the military aspects of the GFAP. While assessment of overall compliance is in progress, IFOR expressed satisfaction for the military co-operation which had been provided, as an indicator of an intention to comply.

On 23 March 1996, the parties further reaffirmed in Moscow their commitment to the Peace Agreement.

On 30 March 1996, Muslim and Croat partners in the Bosnian Federation signed an agreement aimed at strengthening the new institution. The agreement marked progress on critical aspects necessary to establish a functioning Federation, including the merging of customs, a joint military command, and amendments to the constitutions.

April 28, 1996, was D+120, the last deadline in the military annex of the Peace Agreement. It was assessed that as of that date the parties were on their way toward compliance with the requirements for cantonment of heavy weapons and forces and their mobilization. Full compliance had not been achieved yet but that seemed to reflect practical difficulties, rather than an absence of intent. IFOR will continue actively to monitor progress towards full compliance.

On 29 April 1996, the NAC issued a declaration on IFOR's role in the transition to peace.

On 3 June 1996, the NAC—after a meeting in Berlin, at Foreign Ministers level—issued a statement indicating that, given the magnitude and complexity of the preparations for elections in Bosnia and Herzegovina, IFOR would be maintained at approximately its current force levels until after the elections and would retain its overall capability until December, when its mandate comes to an end.

The Peace Implementation Council met in Florence on 13-14 June 1996. All the parties reaffirmed their commitment to the GFAP.

On 18 June 1996, the UN Security Council lifted the heavy weapons embargo on the former Yugoslavia. As a consequence, the NATO/WEU embargo enforcement *Operation Sharp Guard* was suspended.

On 1 July 1996 Bosnia's first free elections since the end of the war were held in Mostar.

On 31 July 1996, Adm. T. Joseph Lopez relieved Adm. Leighton Smith as COMIFOR.

On 19 August to 24 August 1996, IFOR destroyed 252 tons of Bosnian Serb munitions under a operation code named *Volcano*.

On 27 August 1996, the Chairman of the Provisional Election Commission, OSCE Head of Mission to Bosnia and Herzegovina, Ambassador Robert Frowick, announced that the 14 September municipal elections in Bosnia would be postponed.

On 30 August 1996, the NATO Airbrone Early Warning E-3a Component flew its 50,000th flying hour in support of operations in the former Yugoslavia.

On 14 September 1996, nationwide elections, under the direction of OCSE, were held in Bosnia Herzegovina.

On 18 September 1996, the Secretary General of NATO announced that the NAC agreed to new command arrangements for IFOR, to allow for the phased withdrawal of Headquarters ARRC and Headquarters AFSOUTH from Bosnia and Herzegovina and their replacement by a Headquarters based on Allied Land Forces Central Europe (LANDCENT).

On 1 October 1996, the United Nation Security Council adopted the resolution 1074, which provided for the termination of sanctions against Federal Republic of Yugoslavia, following the occurrence of the elections provided for in the Dayton Peace Agreement. As a consequence, NATO and WEU terminated *Operation Sharp Guard*.

On 22 October 1996, the OSCE announced that the municipal elections in Bosnia and Herzegovina, which were to be held in November, would be further postponed.

The TOA from the Commander of the AFSOUTH/IFOR to the Commander of the LANDCENT/IFOR occurred on 7 November 1996 and from the Commander of the Allied Rapid Reaction CORPS (ARRC) to the Commander of the LANDCENT/IFOR on 20 November 1996.

On 10 December 1996, the North Atlantic Council, meeting in Ministerial Session, issued a statement on Bosnia and Herzegovina announcing that NATO was prepared to organize and lead a Stabilization Force (SFOR) to take place of IFOR, authorized by a UN Security Council Resolution under Chapter VII of the UN Charter.

On 12 December 1996, the UN Security Council adopted Resolution 1088 authorizing the establishment of SFOR as the legal successor to IFOR for a planned period of 18 months.

SFOR was activated on 20 December 1996. Its mission was to deter fresh hostilities and to stabilize peace.

Appendix C: References

[Abrams, 1996] LTG John Abrams, USA. *Operation Joint Endeavor Lessons Learned.* HQ V CORPS, May 1996.

[Ahlquist, 1996] Captain (N) Lief Ahlquist. *Co-operation, Command and Control in UN Peacekeeping Operations.* Swedish War College, 1996.

[Ainge, 1996] GP CAPT Derek Ainge, UK RAF. *Operation Joint Endeavor Communications Links.* NACOSA, Mons, Belgium, 1996.

[Allard, 1995] Kenneth Allard. *Somalia Operations: Lessons Learned.* National Defense University Press, Ft McNair, Washington, D.C., January 1995.

[Allard, 1996] Kenneth Allard. *Information Operations in Bosnia: A Preliminary Assessment.* National Defense University, Institute for Strategic Studies, Strategic Forum, Washington, D.C., November 1996.

[Asbery, 1997] Johnny Asbery and Arnie Rausch, DSA, and Michael Casey, CISA. *C4ISR Laydown.* CISA Architectures Directorate, Washington, D.C., 1997.

[Bell, 1996] Martin Bell. *In Harms Way.* Penguin Books, 1996.

[Berry, 1996] Col Thomas Berry, USAF. *Operation Joint Endeavor: Executive Lessons Learned.* HQ Air Mobility Command, Scott AFB, IL, April 1996.

[Boardman, 1997] Tony Boardman, UK. *Fellow Traveller.* HQ SFOR, Ilidza, BiH, 16 March 1997.

[Bonnart, 1996] Frederick Bonnart. *NATO'S SIXTEEN NATIONS: IFOR The Mission Continues...* Moench Publishing Group, Bonn, FRG, 1996.

[Brewin, 1996] Bob Brewin. *BOSNIA The Role of I.T. in Operation Joint Endeavor.* Federal Computer Week, Falls Church, VA, April 1996.

[Buchanan, 1996] William B. Buchanan. *Operation Joint Endeavor-Description and Lessons Learned (Planning and Deployment Phases).* IDA, Alexandria, VA, November 1996.

[Casey, 1997] Mike Casey, CISA, and Arnie Rausch and John Asbery, DSA. *IFOR C4ISR Laydown.* CD produced by CISA, 1997.

[CJCCC, 1996] Combined Joint Communications Control Centre. *CJCCC Information Book, CJCCC Information Book (D+180), and CJCCC Information Book (TOA LANDCENT).* HQ IFOR/AFSOUTH, Naples, Italy, 1996.

[Cook, 1996] Capt Rhonda Cook, USA. *AAR Operation Joint Endeavor 1st AD Intelligence Production.* HQ Task Force Eagle, Tuzla, BiH, 1996.

[Crouch, 1997] General William Crouch, USA. *USAREUR HEADQUARTERS AFTER ACTION REPORT (Volumes I and II).* HQ USAREUR, Heidelberg, Germany, May 1997.

[C-SUPPORT, 1996] C-SUPPORT Staff. *Excerpts from Lessons learned.* IFOR C-SUPPORT, Zagreb, Croatia, 1996.

[Davidson, 1996] Lisa Davidson, Margaret Daly Hayes, James Landon. *Humanitarian and Peace Operations: NGOs and the Military in the Interagency Process.* Advanced Concepts, Technologies, and Information Strategies, Institute for National Strategic Studies, National Defense University, Washington, D.C., December 1996.

[Davis, 1996] David Davis and Alexander Woodcock. *Analytic Approach to the Study of Future Conflict.* The Lester B. Pearson Canadian International Peacekeeping Training Centre, Clementsport, NS, Canada, 1996.

[Deutch, 1996] John Deutch. *Revision of Director of Central Intelligence Directive 1/7, "Security Controls on the Dissemination of Intelligence Information."* Director of Central Intelligence, Washington, D.C., April 1996.

[Dziedzic, 1996] Col Michael Dziedzic, USAF. *CIMIC and IPTF in Bosnia (Draft).* National Defense University, Institute for National Strategic Studies, Ft McNair, Washington, D.C., 1996.

[Feist, 1996] CAPT Peter Feist, GEN. *IFOR Joint Analysis Team Three Interim Reports and One Final Report.* JAT Press, Northwood, England, March/June/December 1996 and April 1997.

[Fields, 1997] Craig Fields. Report of the *1996 Defense Science Board Task Force on Improved Application of Intelligence to the Battlefield.* Office of the Secretary of Defense, Washington, D.C., March 1997.

[Forster, 1996] Col Larry Forster and Col Steve Riley, USA. *Bosnia-Herzegovina After Action Review I and II.* Army War College Peacekeeping Institute, Carlisle Barracks, PA, April 1996/1997.

[Gerald, 1997] LtCol Jeffrey Gerald, USAF, and John Christakos, Booz-Allen & Hamilton, Inc. *BC2A: Lessons Learned in Bosnia.* DARO, Washington, D.C., 1997.

[Gjelten, 1995] Tom Gjelten. *SARAJEVO DAILY.* Harper Perennial, 1995.

[GMU, 1997] George Mason University Center for National Security Law and The Lester B. Pearson Canadian International Peacekeeping Centre. *Strengthening the United Nations and Enhancing War Prevention.* GMU, Fairfax, VA, April 1997.

[Gow, 1996] Jams Gow, Richard Paterson, and Alison Preston. *BOSNIA BY TELEVISION.* British Film Institute, 1996.

[Grey, 1996] LTC A J Grey, UKA. *ARRC Communications and Information Systems Lessons learned.* HQ ARRC, Sarajevo, BiH, June 1996.

[Griffith, 1997] LtCol Laura Griffith, USAF. *BOSNIA Intelligence Lessons Learned Working Group.* DIA/J2, Washington, D.C., 1997.

[Hahm, 1996] William Hahm, Jennifer Chatfield, and Frank Franks, MITRE, Larry Wentz, NDU/CCRP and Anthony Simon, CISA. *Compendium of Operation JOINT ENDEAVOR Lessons Learned.* CISA Architectures Directorate, Washington, D.C., May 1997.

[Hairell, 1996] LtCol Oscar Hairell, USAF. *Operation Joint Endeavor Lessons Learned.* HQ USAFE, Ramstein AFB, 1996.

[Hartley, 1996] D.S. Hartley III. *Operations Other Than War: Requirements for Analysis Tools Research Report.* CINCPAC J53, Research and Analysis Division, Camp H. M. Smith, HI, December 1996.

[Hayes, 1996/1997] Richard Hayes, James Landon, and Richard Layton. *Draft Reports on IFOR C2 Structure, CIMIC, Information Operations and Other C4ISR Lessons Learned Activities.* Evidence Based Research, Inc., Vienna, VA, 1996/1997.

[JAT, 1996] IFOR Joint Analysis Team. *Observer Handbook.* JAT Press, Northwood, England, 1996.

[Johnston-Burt, 1997] CDR Tony Johnston-Burt, RN. *IFOR'S C4I and Information Operations: A Multinational Perspective.* Naval War College, Newport, Rhode Island, 1997.

[Joulwan, 1996] General George Joulwan, USA. *OPERATION JOINT ENDEAVOR: Joint After Action Review.* HQ USEUCOM (ECJ37-UCLL), December 1996.

[Keiler, 1997] CDR Doug Keiler, USN. *Bosnia Bandwidth Allocation Study (Draft).* National Defense University, Advanced Concepts, Technologies, and Information Strategies, Ft McNair, Washington, D.C., 1997.

[Kurspanhic, 1997] Kemal Kursphic. *AS LONG AS SARAJEVO EXISTS.* The Pamphleteer's Press, 1997.

[Last, 1997] David M. Last. *Theory, Doctrine and Practice of Conflict De-Escalation in Peacekeeping Operations.* The Lester B. Pearson Canadian International Peacekeeping Centre Press, Cornwallis Park, Clementsport, NS, 1997.

[Maass, 1997] Peter Maass. *LOVE THY NEIGHBOR.* Vintage Books, 1997.

[MacKenzie, 1993] Major General Lewis MacKenzie, Canadian Forces. *PEACEKEEPER.* Douglas and McIntyre, 1993.

[Mackinlay, 1996] John Mackinlay. *A Guide to Peace Support Operations.* Thomas J. Watson Jr. Institute for International Studies, Brown University, Providence, RI, 1996.

[Marks, 1996] Edward Marks. *Complex Emergencies: Bureaucratic Arrangements in the U.N. Secretariat.* Institute for National Strategic Studies, National Defense University, Washington, D.C., October 1996.

[Merrill, 1995] Christopher Merrill. *THE OLD BRIDGE.* Milkweed Editions, 1995.

[Mohr, 1996] Brad Mohr. *SOF Mission Support Lessons Learned.* HQ SOCOM, 1996.

[Nabors, 1997] BG Robert Nabors, USA. *Lessons Learned Book: Operation Joint Endeavor.* HQ 5th Signal Command, 1997.

[Nabors, 1997] BG Robert Nabors, USA. *AFCEA Briefing: Operation Joint Endeavor Communications.* HQ 5th Signal Command, 1997.

[NDU/CCRP, 1996] NDU/CCRP Bosnia Study Team. *Bosnia C4ISR Project Progress Reports (1st and 2nd).* National Defense University, Center for Advanced Concepts and Technology, Ft McNair, Washington, D.C., July/October 1996.

[Owen, 1995] David Owen. *Balkan Odyssey.* Harcourt Brace and Company, 1995.

Appendix C: References 485

[Palmer, 1996] Maj Rolf Palmer. *LOCE Lessons Learned.* HQ USEUCOM, 1996.

[Pfaltzgraff, 1997] Robert Pfaltzgraff, Jr. and Richard Shultz, Jr. *War in the Information Age: New Challenges for U.S. Security.* Brassey's, 1997.

[Phillips, 1996] LtCol Timothy Phillips, USMC. *JITC C4I Infrastructure Documentation Report for Operation Joint Endeavor.* JITC, Ft Huachuca, AZ, June 1996.

[Pistor, 1997] Charles Pistor. USEUCOM *Combined Communications Operations Manual.* Joint Interoperability Engineering Organization, Defense Information Systems Agency, Ft Monmouth, NJ, 1997.

[Rapaport, 1996] Richard Rapaport. *World War 3.1.* FORBES ASAP, October 1996.

[Roberts, 1996] Cdr T Roberts, USN. *IFOR Intelligence Sharing: Successes and Challenges Briefing.* DCI, 1996.

[Rogers, 1996/1997] LtCol Gary Rogers, USAF. *EUCOM JULLS.* HQ USEUCOM, 1996/1997.

[Seiple, 1996] Capt Chris Seiple, USMC. *The U.S. Military/NGO Relationship in Humanitarian Interventions.* Peacekeeping Institute, Center for Strategic Leadership, U.S. Army War College, Carlisle, PA, 1996.

[Siegel, 1996/1997] Pascale Combelles Siegel. *Information and Command and Control in Peace Operations: The Case of IFOR in Bosnia-Herzegovina.* Evidence Based Research, Inc., Vienna, VA, 1996/1997.

[Silber/Little, 1997] Laura Silber and Allan Little. *YUGOSLAVIA: DEATH OF A NATION.* Penguin Books, 1997.

[Smith, 1997] Dr. Jay Smith. *Bosnia Conflict.* Office of History, Air Force Command, Control, Communications and Computer Agency, Scott AFB, IL, 1997.

[Stewart, 1996] George Stewart. *CNA Involvement in Joint Endeavor.* Center for Naval Analysis, Alexandria, VA, October 1996.

[Strobel, 1997] Warren Strobel. *LATE-BREAKING FOREIGN POLICY: The News Media's Influence on Peace Operations.* United States Institute of Peace Press, 1997.

[Swan, 1996] Commodore P W H Swan, RN. *Operation Joint Endeavor-CJ6 Lessons Learned.* HQ IFOR/AFSOUTH, Naples, Italy, November 1996.

[Trewin, 1996] Wg Cdr I A Trewin, UK AF. *Operation Joint Endeavor Lessons*

Learned. SHAPE ACOS CISD, Mons, Belgium, October 1996.

[Walley, 1996/1997] Jim Walley. *Operation JOINT ENDEAVOR: Task Force Eagle Initial Observations; Title 10 Sustainment and Force Protection; and three Task Force Eagle Continuing Operations reports. Operation JOINT GUARD: Task Force Eagle Initial Impressions and Task Force Eagle Continuing Operation.* Center for Army Lessons Learned, Ft Leavenworth, KS, May/August/September 1996 and March/April 1997 and for Joint Guard report 1997.

[Wentz, 1991] Larry K. Wentz. *DCA Grey Beard Lessons Learned: Desert Shield/ Desert Storm.* MITRE, McLean, VA, August 1991.

[Wentz, 1992] Larry K. Wentz. *The First Information War: Communications Support for the High Technology Battlefield.* AFCEA International Press, Fairfax, VA, October 1992.

[Wentz, 1993/1994] Larry K. Wentz. *DISA Grey Beard Panel: Lessons Learned Operation Restore Hope (1993) and A U.S. Perspective of UN Operations (1994).* MITRE, McLean, VA, September 1993/1994.

[Wentz, 1996] Larry K. Wentz. *Managing The Peace Offensive: Coalition Operations Lessons Learned.* AFCEA Europe Brussels Symposium and Exposition, Brussels, Belgium, October 1996.

[Wentz, 1996] Larry K. Wentz. *C3I Observations: A View from the Theater.* National Defense University, Center for Advanced Concepts and Technology, Ft McNair, Washington, D.C., March 1996.

[Wentz, 1997] Larry K. Wentz. *C3I for Peace Operations: Lessons from Bosnia.* National Defense University, Center for Advanced Concepts and Technology, Ft McNair, Washington, D.C., May 1997.

[Wentz, 1996/1997] Larry K. Wentz. *Unifying the Analysis of Bosnia C3I Lessons Learned.* National Defense University, Center for Advanced Concepts and Technology, Ft McNair, Washington, D.C., 1996/1997.

World Wide Web URLs
(current as of 5 December 1997)

1. NATO official home page: http://www.nato.int/home.htm
2. NATO *Operation Joint Endeavor* (IFOR) information home page: http://www.nato.int/ifor/ifor.htm
3. Task Force Eagle: http://www.tfeagle.army.mil/.

Appendix C: References 487

4. TALON—Task Force Eagle's on-line magazine: http://www.tfeagle.army.mil/talon/index.html.

5. Center for Army Lessons Learned: http://call.army.mil/call.html

6. USAREUR: http://www.hqusareur.army.mil

7. USAFE: http://www.usafe.af.mil/index.html

8. US Navy News, Bosnia Operations: http://www.navy.mil/navpalib/bosnia/bosnia1.html

9. USEUCOM: http://www.eucom.mil

10. U.S. Department of Defense BosniaLink: http://www.dtic.mil/bosnia/

11. U.S. Department of State Policy on Bosnia home page: http://www.state.gov/www/regions/eur/bosnia/index.html.

12. USAID: http://www.info.usaid.gov/

13. NGO Sites: http://www.interaction.org/ia/sites.html

14. World Vision: http://www.worldvision.org/worldvision/master.nsf/stable/home

15. InterAction: http://www.interaction.org/ia/mission.html

16. Disaster Response Internet Directory: http://www.interaction.org/ia/disaster/director.html

IFOR Basic Documents

November 15, 1995, SHAPE OPLAN 40105
Joint Endeavor
AFSOUTH OPLAN 40105
ARRC OPLAN 60105

December 2, 1995, JCS EXORD for the U.S. Enabling Force
Joint Endeavor

December 2, 1995, USCINCEUR OPLAN 4243
Balkan Endeavor

December 6, 1995, SACEUR OPLAN 40105
Decisive Endeavor

December 14, 1995, Paris
The General Framework Agreement for Peace in Bosnia and
Herzegovina (a.k.a. The Dayton Peace Agreement).

December 16, 1995, JCS EXORD for the U.S. Main Body
Joint Endeavor

December 16, 1995, SACEUR OPLAN 10405
Joint Endeavor

January 26, 1996, Vienna
OSCE Agreement on Confidence- and Security-Building Measures in
Bosnia and Herzegovina.

February 18, 1996, Rome
The Rome Statement reflecting the work of the Joint Civilian
Commission Sarajevo Compliance Conference.

March 18, 1996, Geneva.
Agreed Measures.
Statement on the Federation of Bosnia and Herzegovina.

March 23, 1996, Moscow.
The Final Document of the Contact Group Ministerial Meeting.

June 13-14, 1996, Peace Implementation Council, Florence.
Chairman's Conclusions.
Chairman's Summary.

June 29, 1996, Lyon G7/G8 Summit.
Decisions concerning Bosnia and Herzegovina.

December 4-5, 1996, Peace Implementation Conference, London
Official Summary of Conclusions.
Conclusions: Bosnia and Herzegovina 1997: Making Peace Work.

Appendix D: Acronyms

A

ABCCC	Airborne Command and Control
ACC	Air Component Commander
ACE	Allied Command Europe
ACFL	Agreed Cease-Fire Line
AD	Architectures Directorate
ADAMS	Allied Deployment and Movement System
ADCI/MS	Associate Director of Central Intelligence for Military Support
ADSI	Air Defense System Integrator
AFMSS	Air Force Mission Support System
AFSOUTH	Armed Forces Southern Command
AIFS	Allied Information Flow System
AMC	Air Mobility Command
AMCC	Allied Movement Control Center
AMIB	Allied Military Intelligence Battalion
AMS	Automated Manifesting System
AOCG	Airlift Operations Coordination Group
AOR	Area of Responsibility
AOT	Area of Transfer
APOD	Aerial Port of Debarkation
ARL	Air Reconnaissance Low
ARRC	ACE Rapid Reaction Corps
ASAS	All Source Analysis System
ASD/C3I	Assistant Secretary of Defense for Command, Control, Communications, and Intelligence
ATM	Asynchronous Transfer Mode
ATO	Air Tasking Order

AUTODIN	Automatic Digital Network
AWACS	Airborne Warning and Control System
AWE	Advanced Warfighting Experiments

B

BC2A	Bosnia C2 Augmentation
BCT	Brigade Combat Team
BDA	Battle Damage Assessment
B-H	Bosnia-Herzegovina
BMC	Broadcast Management Center
BHAAR	Bosnia-Herzegovina After Action Report
BTIC	Bosnia Technology Integration Cell

C

C2	Command and Control
C2IPS	C2 Information Processing System
C3I	Command, Control, Communications, and Intelligence
C4I	Command, Control, Communications, Computers, and Intelligence
C4IFTW	Command, Control, Communications, Computers, and Intelligence for the Warfighter
C4ISR	Command, Control, Communications, Computers, Intelligence, Surveillance, and Reconnaissance
CAAT	Combined Arms Assessment Team
CALL	Center for Army Lessons Learned
CAOC	Combined Air Operations Center
CAP	Combat Air Patrol
CARS	Contingency Airborne Reconnaissance System
CCIRM	Collection Coordination Intelligence Requirements Management
CCITT	International Telephone and Telegraph Consultative Committee
CCRP	Command and Control Research Program
CEWI	Combat Electronic Warfare Intelligence
CHS	Combat Support Hospital
CI	Counterintelligence
CIA	Central Intelligence Agency
CIAP	Command Intelligence Architecture/Planning Program
CIC	Counterintelligence Corps
CICG	Commanders Information Coordination Group
CIMIC	Civil Military Cooperation

Appendix D: Acronyms 491

CINC	Commander-in-Chief
CINCAFSOUTH	Commander-in-Chief, Allied Forces Southern Europe
CINCIFOR	Commander-in-Chief, Implementation Force
CINCSOUTH	Commander-in-Chief, Southern Region
CINCUSNAVEUR	Commander-in-Chief, U.S. Navy Europe
CIS	Communications and Information Systems
CISA	C4I Integration Support Activity
CISCC	Communications Information Systems Control Center
CISD	Communications and Information Systems Division
CISD	Command Intelligence Strategy Document
CJCCC	Combined Joint Communications Control Center
CJCIMIC	Combined Joint Civil Military Cooperation
CJIICTF	Combined Joint IFOR Information Campaign Task Force
CJTF	Combined Joint Task Force
CNA	Center for Naval Analysis
COMAIRSOUTH	Commander, Air Forces Southern Europe
COMIFOR	Commander, Implementation Force
COMINT	Communications Intelligence
COMNAVSOUTH	Commander, Allied Naval Forces Southern Region
COMSEC	Communications Security
COP	Common Operation Picture
COTS	Commercial off-the-Shelf
CPIC	Combined Press Information Center
CRC	Control and Reporting Center
CRESP	Crisis Response Prototype
CRONOS	Crisis Response Operations in NATO Operating Systems
CSA	Chief of Staff of the Army
CSCE	Conference on Security and Cooperation in Europe
CSCI	Commercial Satellite Communications Initiative
CSS	Common User Data Network

D

DASH	Deployable Automation Support Host
DCI	Director of Central Intelligence
DCSINT	Deputy Chief of Staff for Intelligence
DDN	Defense Data Network
DDP	Detailed Deployment Plans
DHS	Defense HUMINT Service

DIA	Defense Intelligence Agency
DII	Defense Information Infrastructure
DISA	Defense Information Systems Agency
DISE	Deployable Intelligence Support Element (USAREUR)
DISN	Defense Information System Network
DITDS	Defense Intelligence Threat Data Base System
DoD	Department of Defense
DPA	Dayton Peace Accords
DSCS	Defense Satellite Communications System
DSN	Defense Switched Network

E

E1	European and CCITT Digital Standard (2.048 Mbps)
EAC	Echelons Above Corps
EBRD	European Bank for Reconstruction and Development
ECB	Echelons Corps and Below
ECHO	Evolutionary Capability for Headquarters Operation
EDP	Electronic Data Processing
ELS	Exportable Logistics System
E-mail	Electronic Mail
ENGCC	Engineer Coordination Center
ESC	Electronic Systems Center
EU	European Union
EUCOM	European Command
EW	Electronic Warfare

F

FAX	Facsimile
FDDI	Fiber Distributed Data Interface
FERN	Free Elections Radio Network
FMS	Foreign Military Sales
FOUO	For Official Use Only
FPB	Force Protection Branch
FPIR	Force Protection Information Report
FPT	Force Protection Team
FRAGO	Fragmentary Order
FTP	File Transfer Protocol
FWF	Former Warring Factions
FY	Former Yugoslavia

Appendix D: Acronyms 493

G

GCCS	Global Command and Control System
GFAP	General Framework Agreement for Peace
GMF	Ground Mobile Force
GOTS	Government off-the-shelf
GPS	Global Positioning System
GRCS	Guardrail Common Sensor
GSM	Ground Station Module
GSR	Ground Surveillance Radar

H

HF	High Frequency
HLWG	High Level Working Group
HCG	HUMINT Coordination Group
HAC	HUMINT Analysis Cell
HUMINT	Human Intelligence

I

IARRCIS	Interim ARRC Information System
ICARIS	Integrated C4I Architectures Requirements Information System
ICC	IFOR Coordination Center
ICRC	International Committee of the Red Cross
ICTY	International Criminal Tribunal for the former Yugoslavia
IDA	Institute for Defense Analyses
IDIP	Interim Digital Interface PTARMIGAN
IDNX	Integrated Digital Network Exchange
IEBL	Inter-Entity Boundary Line
IEC	Interstate Electronics Corporation
IEW	Intelligence Electronic Warfare
IFOR	Implementation Force
IIC	IFOR Information Campaign
IIR	Intelligence Information Report
IMARSAT	International Maritime Satellite
INFOSEC	Information Security
INSCOM	Intelligence and Security Command
INSS	Institute for National Strategic Studies
INTSUM	Intelligence Summaries
IO	International Organization
IP	Internet Protocol
IPB	Intelligence Preparation of the Battlefield

IPL	Intelligence Priority List
IPN	IFOR Private (Peace) Network
IPTF	International Police Task Force
ISARC	Intelligence, Surveillance, and Reconnaissance Cell
ISB	Intermediate Staging Base
ISR	Intelligence, Surveillance, and Reconnaissance
ISR	Intelligence, Surveillance, and Reconnaissance
ITV	Intransit Visibility
IVSN	Initial Voice Switched Network

J

JAC	Joint Analysis Center
JAT	Joint Analysis Team
JAWS	Joint Analytical Workstation
JBS	Joint Broadcast Service
JCC	Joint Civil Commission
JCO	Joint Commission Officer
JDISS	Joint Deployable Intelligence Support System
JIB	Joint Information Bureau
JIEO	Joint Interoperability Engineering Organization
JITC	Joint Interoperability Test Command
JLOC	Joint Logistics Operations Center
JMC	Joint Military Commission
JMCC	Joint Movement Control Center
JNA	Yugoslav Army
JOC	Joint Operational Cell
JOPES	Joint Operations, Planning and Execution System
JRC	Joint Reconnaissance Center
JSTARS	Joint Surveillance Target Attack Radar System
JTAV	Joint Total Asset Visibility
JTF	Joint Task Force
JTF-PP	Joint Task Force - Provide Promise
JULLS	Joint Universal Lessons Learned System
JWICS	Joint Worldwide Intelligence Communications System
JWID	Joint Warfare Interoperability Demonstration

K

KCC	Contracting Coordination Center

L

LAN	Local Area Network

Appendix D: Acronyms   495

LANDCENT	Land Forces Central Europe
LES	Large Extension Node
LIWA	Land Information Warfare Agency
LMDS	Local Multipoint Distribution Service
LNO	Liaison Officer
LOCE	Linked Operations-Intelligence Centers Europe
LOS	Line of Sight

M

MAE	Medium Altitude Endurance
MASH	Mobile Army Surgical Hospital
MASINT	Measurement and Signature Intelligence
MCS	Maneuver Control System
MDCI	Multi-Discipline Counterintelligence
MEDCC	Medical Coordination Center
MEDCOC	Medical Co-ordination Center
MI	Military Intelligence
MIDS/IDB	Military Integrated Data System/Intelligence Database
MIST	Mission Information Support Team
MITT	Mobile Integrated Tactical Terminal
MNC	Major NATO Command
MND	Multinational Division
MND(N)	Multinational Division-North (US-led, Tuzla-based)
MND(SE)	Multinational Division-Southeast (France-led, Mostar-based)
MND(SW)	Multinational Division-Southwest (UK-led, Banja Luka-based)
MNMF	Multinational Maritime Force
MORS	Military Operations Research Society
MPA	Maritime Patrol Aircraft
MPAD	Mobile Public Affairs Detachment
MRE	Meal Ready-to-Eat
MSE	Mobile Subscriber Equipment
MWR	Moral, Welfare, and Recreation

N

NABS	NATO Air Base
NAC	North Atlantic Council
NACCIS	North Atlantic Command Control Information System
NACISA	NATO CIS Agency

496 Lessons from Bosnia

NACOSA	NATO CIS Operating and Supporting Agency
NAEWF	NATO Airborne Early Warning Force
NAI	Named Area of Interest
NAI	NATO Analog Interface
NAMSA	NATO Maintenance and Supply Agency
NATO	North Atlantic Treaty Organization
NC3A	NATO Consultation, Command and Control Agency
NCCAP	NATO CIS Contingency Assets Pool
NCMC	National Collection Management Cell
N-D	Non-doctrine, Non-doctrinal
NDU	National Defense University
NES	Network Encryption System
NGO	Non-Governmental Organization
NIC	National Intelligence Cell
NICS	NATO Integrated Communications System
NIDS	NATO Integrated Data Service
NIPRNET	Non-classified Internet Protocol Router Network
NIST	National Intelligence Support Team
NMJIC	National Military Joint Intelligence Center
NRL	Naval Research Laboratory
NSA	National Security Agency
NSE	National Support Element

O

OAB	Operational Analysis Branch
OHR	Office of the High Representative
OJT	On-the-Job-Training
OOA	Out Of Area
OODA	Observation, Orientation, Decision, and Action
OOTW	Operations Other Than War
OPCOM	Operational Command
OPCON	Operational Control
OPLAN	Operation Plan
OPORD	Operations Order
OPSEC	Operational Security
ORBAT	Order of Battle
OSC	Objective Supply Capability
OSCE	Organization for Security and Cooperation in Europe
OSINT	Open source Intelligence
OSO	Operational Support Office
OSS	Office of Strategic Services
OTG	Operational Task Group

Appendix D: Acronyms   497

P

PABX	Private Access Branch Exchange
PAIS	Prototype ACE Intelligence System
PAT	Permanent Maritime Analysis Team
PBX	Private Branch Exchange
PfP	Partnership for Peace
PI	Public Information
PIC	Peace Implementation Council
PIO	Public Information Office
PIR	Priority Intelligence Requirements
PME	Professional Military Education
POC	Points of Contact
POP	Point of Presence
POTF	PSYOP Task Force
PSYOP	Psychological Operations
PTT	Post Telephone and Telegraph
PVO	Private Voluntary Organization

R

R&S	Reconnaissance and Surveillance
RAF	Royal Air Force
RAMCC	Regional Air Movement and Coordination Center
RAP	Recognized Air Picture
RCC	Regional Control Center
REL IFOR	Releasable to Implementation Force
REL NATO	Releasable to North Atlantic Treaty Organization
REL	Releasable to
REMBASS	Remotely Monitored Battlefield Sensor Systems
RF	Radio Frequency
RFCT	Ready First Combat Team
RFI	Requests For Information
RITA	Reseau Integre de Transmissions Automatique
RS	Republik Srbska
RSSC	Regional Space Support Center
RVT	Remote Vehicle Terminal

S

SACEUR	Supreme Allied Commander, Europe
SAR	Synthetic Aperture Radar
SAT	Satellite
SATCOM	Satellite Communication

SCI	Sensitive Compartmented Information
SCSG	Satellite Communication Sub-Group
SEAD	Suppression of Enemy Air Defense
SEN	Small Extension Node
SFOR	Stabilization Force
SGT	Satellite Ground Terminal
SHAPE	Supreme Headquarters Allied Powers Europe
SHF	Super High Frequency
SIPRNET	SECRET Internet Protocol Router Network
SITREP	Situation Report
SOCOM	Special Operations Command
SOF	Special Operations Forces
SOP	Standard Operating Procedure
SPIRIT	Special Purpose Integrated Remote Intelligence Terminal
SPOD	Sea Port of Debarkation
SSO	Stability and Sustainment Operation
STAGNAG 4206	NATO Standardization Agreement, Digital Telephony
STAGNAG 5040	NATO Standardization Agreement, Analog Telephony
STAGNAG	NATO Standardization Agreement
STAMIS	Standard Army Management Information Systems
STC	SHAPE Technical Center
STEP	Standard Tactical Entry Point
STONS	Short Ton
STU	Secure Telephone Unit
SWO	Staff Weather Office

T

T1	North American Digital Signal (1.544 Mbps)
TACOM	Tactical Command
TACON	Tactical Control
TACSAT	Tactical Satellite [Terminal]
TADIL	Tactical Data Information Link
TARE	Telegraph Automatic Relay Equipment
TAV	Total Asset Visibility
TCP	Transmission Control Protocol
TCP/IP	Transmission Control Protocol/Internet Protocol
TCS	Temporary Change of Station
TDDS	Tactical Data Dissemination System
TENCAP	Tactical Exploitation of National Capabilities Program
TFCICA	Task Force CI Coordinating Authority

Appendix D: Acronyms 499

TFE	Task Force Eagle
TFM	Theater Frequency Management
TFMC	Theater Frequency Management Cell
TIBS	Tactical Information Broadcast System
TNOC	Theater Network Operations Center
TOA	Transfer of Authority
TOC	Tactical Operations Center
TOE	Table of Equipment
TPN	Tactical Packet Network
TRI-TAC	Tri-service Tactical Communications
TROJAN SPIRIT	TROJAN Special Purpose Integrated Remote Intelligence Terminal
TRRIP	Theater Rapid Response Intelligence Package
TS	Top Secret
TSCM	Technical Surveillance Countermeasures
TSGT	Transportable Satellite Ground Terminal
TSGT	Transportable Satellite Ground Terminal
TSO	Telecommunications Service Order
TSSR	TROPO/SATELLITE Support Radio
TTA	Tactical Terminal Adapter

U

UAV	Unmanned Aerial Vehicle
UCIRF	USAREUR Combat Intelligence Readiness Facility
UHF	Ultra High Frequency
UN	United Nations
UNCRO	UN Confidence Restoration Organization
UNHCR	UN High Commissioner for Refugees
UNMIBH	United Nations Mission in Bosnia-Herzegovina
UNPREDEP	UN Preventive Deployment
UNPROFOR	United Nations Protection Force
UNSCR	UN Security Council Resolution
UNTAES	UN Transitional Administration for Eastern Slavonia
US	United States
USACAPOC	U.S. Army's Civil Affairs and Psychological Operations Command
USAFE	United States Air Forces Europe
USAID	United States Agency for International Development
USAREUR	United States Army Europe
USEUCOM	United States European Command
USG	U.S. Government

UWF Unified Weather Forecast

V
VHF Very High Frequency
VSAT Very Small Aperture Terminal
VTC Video Teleconference

W
WAN Wide Area Network
WEU Western European Union
WWMCCS World-Wide Military Command and Control System
WWW World Wide Web

X
X.25 Packet Switch Protocol

Z
ZOS Zone of Separation

About the Contributing Editor

Larry K. Wentz is on special assignment to the National Defense University (NDU) as the acting Director of the Command and Control Research Program. Prior to his assignment to NDU, he held the positions of Director of Joint Operations for the MITRE Washington C3 Center and Technical Director of MITRE's Joint and Defense-Wide Systems Division and led the U.S. National Expert support to the NATO Communications and Information System Agency (NACISA) for more than 18 years. He has extensive experience in NATO C3 and C4I support to Coalition Joint Task Force operations, including leading a number of Lessons Learned studies for operations such as *Desert Shield, Desert Storm,* and *Restore Hope.* He is currently leading an NDU study of the C2 Structure and supporting C4ISR for the Bosnia operation, *Joint Endeavor.* Mr. Wentz has a BSEE from Monmouth College and an MS in Systems Engineering and Operations Research from the University of Pennsylvania. He has completed the Executive Management Program at the University of Pennsylvania's Wharton Business School and the Harvard John F. Kennedy School of Government Program for Senior Executives in National and International Security. Mr. Wentz was awarded the AFCEA Meritorious Service Award for his contributions to international C3 and was a contributing author to the AFCEA Information Press book, *The First Information War.*

About the Authors

Richard L. Layton is the Director of the Military Studies Division at Evidence Based Research, Inc. He retired from the U.S. Army after over 20 years of service, during which time he served overseas in Vietnam as an Infantry Officer, in Korea as a counter-intelligence officer, in Japan as a Special Forces Platoon Leader, and in Hawaii as a theater-level intelligence analyst. His assignments in the United States included counter-intelligence officer, force structure/plans officer—U.S. Army Intelligence and Security Command, and plans officer and executive officer for the Deputy Chief of Staff for Intelligence, Headquarters, Department of the Army. Since retirement he has been analyzing the evaluation of command and control of military systems and processes. Currently he directs work in decision making, Bosnia operations, peace and coalition operations, information warfare, operations other than war, Joint Vision 2010, and Defense Advanced Research Projects Agency's functional architecture for the Command and Control Research Program at the National Defense University.

James J. Landon is an analyst at Evidence Based Research, Inc. His current projects focus on civil-military relations, multinational peacekeeping and humanitarian assistance operations, and coalition command and control. He is a member of the NATO Joint Analysis Team (JAT) supporting the IFOR/SFOR deployment to the former Yugoslavia where he is involved in analyzing multinational CIMIC doctrine and operations and the implementation of the civil aspects of the Dayton Peace Agreement.

Andrew Bair serves as Senior Advisor to the Special Representative of the President and Secretary of State for Implementation of the Dayton Peace Accords. Previously, he served two tours with the United Nations in the former Yugoslavia as a political officer, first during 1993 in the UN-protected areas in Croatia and, most recently, in Bosnia during 1995-1996 as the Special Assistant to the UN Chief of Mission there. Afterward, Mr. Bair served as the Political Advisor to the Commissioner of the UN's International Police Task Force. From 1988 to 1994 Mr. Bair was Senior National Security Analyst and Manager of the Center for National Security Negotiations of Science Applications International Corporation. Mr. Bair holds an M.A. from and is currently a doctoral student at The George Washington University, Washington, D.C.

Michael J. Dziedzic specializes in peace operations and security affairs in the Western Hemisphere at the Institute for National Strategic Studies, National Defense University. Previously, he was a member of the faculty at the National War College, served as Air Attache in El Salvador during the implementation of the peace accords, and was a professor in the Department of Political Science at the U.S. Air Force Academy. His writings include *Mexico: Converging Challenges* and articles on Mexican defense policies, the transnational drug trade, and hemispheric security matters.

Pascale Combelles Siegel is an independent researcher based in Arlington, Virginia, where she works on media and defense issues. She is currently completing her dissertation in political science on 'Ideological conflict and practical reliance: The U.S. military-media relationship in times of conflict since Grenada.' From January to June 1997, Mrs. Combelles Siegel participated in NATO's Joint Analysis Team final report on operations *Joint Endeavor* and *Joint Guard*. All data used in her chapter were collected prior to this assignment.

Mark R. Jacobson earned his M.A. at King's College, London, and is a doctoral candidate at Ohio State University, where he is completing his dissertation on U.S. psychological warfare during the Korean War. During his USAR career he has completed psychological operations courses in the United States and the United Kingdom and in 1996 deployed in support of *Operation Joint Endeavor*, where he served with the PSYOP elements supporting 1st Armored Division and 1st Infantry Division.

Lieutenant Colonel Perkins, USA, is currently detailed to the Office of the Vice President, National Security Affairs, as a Military Advisor to the Vice President. He is assigned to the CI and HUMINT Directorate, Office of the Deputy Chief of Staff for Intelligence, Department of the Army. He has participated in various contingency operations including deployment to Panama, *Operation Just Cause*, and Bosnia Herzegovina during *Operation Joint Endeavor*, where he was the G2X (CI/HUMINT Mission Manager) in support of Task Force Eagle. Lieutenant Colonel Perkins holds a Bachelor of Arts degree in Psychology from the University of Vermont and a Master's degree in Criminal Justice from George Washington University.

Colonel Kenneth Allard, U.S. Army (Ret.), retired in 1996 from his position as Senior Military Fellow at the Institute for National Strategic Studies after serving on a special assignment in Bosnia with the U.S. 1st Armored Division. Col. Allard is also the author of two NDU Press books, *Command, Control, and the Common Defense* and *Somalia Operations: Lessons Learned*. A consultant and media commentator on information assurance and national security issues, he serves as a Senior Associate at the Center for Strategic & International Studies and an Adjunct Professor at Georgetown University.

Order Form

We hope you enjoy your complimentary copy of this CCRP publication. The publications listed on the reverse side of this form are available at no cost through CCRP. Simply mark the publication(s) you would like to receive and return these sheets to the following address:

CCRP Publications Distribution Center
c/o Evidence Based Research, Inc.
1595 Spring Hill Road, Suite 250
Vienna, VA 22182

☐ Please send me the publications I have marked.
☐ Please remove my name from your mailing list.
☐ Please change my listing in your database.

Name _____
Title _____
Company _____
Address _____
City _____ State _____ Zip _____
Phone _____
E-mail _____
Area(s) of Expertise _____

I would like to see more publications on the following subject(s):

I use these publications primarily for the following reason(s):
☐ Personal reference   ☐ Course textbook
☐ Work reference   ☐ I don't read these books

For further information on CCRP, please visit our Website at
http://www.dodccrp.org.

CCRP Publications

Command and Control
☐ Coalition Command and Control (Maurer)
☐ Command, Control, and the Common Defense (Allard)
☐ Command and Control in Peace Operations Workshop
☐ Command Arrangements for Peace Operations (Alberts & Hayes)*
☐ Complexity, Global Politics, and National Security (Alberts & Czerwinski, eds.)

Information Technologies and Information Warfare
☐ Defending Cyberspace and Other Metaphors (Libicki)*
☐ Defensive Information Warfare (Alberts)*
☐ Dominant Battlespace Knowledge (Johnson & Libicki)*
☐ The Information Age: An Anthology on Its Impacts and Consequences (Papp & Alberts, eds.)*
☐ Information Warfare and International Law (Kuehl, ed.)
☐ The Mesh and the Net: Speculations on Armed Conflict in a Time of Free Silicon (Libicki)
☐ Second International C2 Research & Technology Symposium Proceedings Document
☐ Standards: The Rough Road to the Common Byte (Libicki)*
☐ Proceedings of the Third International Symposium on C2 Research & Technology
☐ The Unintended Consequences of Information Age Technologies (Alberts)*
☐ What is Information Warfare? (Libicki)*

Operations Other Than War
☐ Interagency and Political-Military Dimensions of Peace Operations: Haiti - a Case Study (Daly Hayes & Wheatley, eds.)
☐ Joint Training for Information Managers (Maxwell)*
☐ Lessons from Bosnia: The IFOR Experience (Wentz, ed.)
☐ NGOs and the Military in the Interagency Process (Davidson, Landon, & Daly Hayes)
☐ Operations Other Than War*
☐ Shock and Awe: Achieving Rapid Dominance (Ullman & Wade)*
☐ Target Bosnia: Integrating International Information Activities in Bosnia-Herzegovina

* Published in conjunction with the NDU Press.